America's Promise

America's Promise

A Concise History of the United States, Volume II

William J. Rorabaugh,
Donald T. Critchlow,
and Paula Baker

ROWMAN & LITTLEFIELD PUBLISHERS, INC.
Lanham • Boulder • New York • Toronto • Oxford

ROWMAN & LITTLEFIELD PUBLISHERS, INC.

Published in the United States of America
by Rowman & Littlefield Publishers, Inc.
A wholly owned subsidiary of The Rowman & Littlefield Publishing Group, Inc.
4501 Forbes Boulevard, Suite 200, Lanham, Maryland 20706
www.rowmanlittlefield.com

PO Box 317
Oxford
OX2 9RU, UK

Distributed by National Book Network

British Library Cataloguing in Publication Information Available

Library of Congress Cataloging-in-Publication Data

Rorabaugh, W. J.
  America's promise : a concise history of the United States / William
J. Rorabaugh, Donald T. Critchlow, and Paula Baker.
    p. cm.
Includes bibliographical references and index.
  ISBN 0-7425-1189-8 (v. 1 : alk. paper) — ISBN 0-7425-1191-X (v. 2 :
alk. paper)
  1. United States—History. I. Critchlow, Donald T., 1948– II. Baker,
Paula C. III. Title.
  E178.R79 2003
  973—dc22

                                2003016131

Printed in the United States of America

♾™ The paper used in this publication meets the minimum requirements of
American National Standard for Information Sciences—Permanence of Paper
for Printed Library Materials, ANSI/NISO Z39.48-1992.

Contents

MAPS

TABLES

Preface

American history consists of such a bewildering array of facts and events that students can easily become overwhelmed and disoriented. A major goal of this book, therefore, has been to *organize* history, that is, to keep students focused on the *ideas* that hold the facts together. We tried to accomplish that goal in several ways.

First, we confined each discussion to the minimum information necessary to understand what happened, why it happened, and why it matters. Second, we begin each major section within each chapter with a preview of the main ideas that will be developed in that section. Third, the section headings and subheadings both highlight main ideas and help carry along the narrative. In addition to providing a conceptual framework, these headings and subheadings offer a practical way to help review for exams.

We sought to integrate the latest scholarship in social, cultural, and political history in this brief textbook. In the process, we tried to capture the rich and often amusing character of the American people. The story of the United States is a tale not only of triumph and tragedy but also of foibles and unexpected consequences. We did not hesitate to bring out that side of the story.

We have also given special attention to the rich literature on the role of ethnic minorities, women, and other groups in shaping American history. In this way we seek to provide a synthetic account of American history that is useful to students, with the expectation that students will seek further details of American history in advanced courses and specialized studies.

We also made room for a glossary at the end of the book. We recognize that terms such as *impressment, free silver,* and *trust* can be confusing. So can the difference between *nationalism* and *nationalization.*

Also at the end of the book is a chronology (timeline) to help students keep track of events. At the end of each chapter is a list of recommended readings. Because we believe that students should read original historical documents whenever possible, we have included primary reading materials in these lists.

Maps have been included in generous numbers for a concise book because we believe that they portray, pinpoint, and illuminate key events.

Among the things we deliberately left out of the book are expensive color illustrations. Sharing students' concerns about high prices of textbooks, we wanted to keep costs, and therefore price, to a minimum. We wanted a book of high quality that every student could afford.

We, the authors, have collaborated on this venture at every point, arguing over nuances and details and debating how best to work often shapeless social and cultural history into a political framework. To satisfy the curious, we confess that Rorabaugh is primarily responsible for chapters 1–15; Baker, for chapters 16–25; and Critchlow, for chapters 26–31.

Acknowledgments

We thank the staff at Rowman & Littlefield who participated in this project, including Jonathan Sisk, Stephen Wrinn, Mary Carpenter, Laura Roberts, and Terry Fischer. We owe special thanks to April Wells-Hayes, the manuscript editor and production editor. We also want to thank Robin Sand for obtaining the photographs and Steve Thomas for the Instructor's Manual and the Web site.

America's Promise

15

❧

Reconstruction, 1863–1877

OVERVIEW Wartime chaos forced the adoption of Reconstruction policies even before the Civil War ended. In 1865–1866, President Andrew Johnson and the Radical Republican majority in Congress fought bitterly over policy. Congress won and in 1867–1868 imposed harsh Reconstruction policies on the South. Blacks gained political rights but lacked economic security, and southern whites responded with anger, intimidation, and violence. By the early 1870s Republican rule in the South began to fail, and the last Radical governments were sold out in the bargain over the presidential election of 1876.

WARTIME RECONSTRUCTION, 1863–1865

Reconstruction began in 1863 as a wartime experiment at Port Royal, South Carolina, when thousands of slaves came under Union army control. Late in that year President Abraham Lincoln proposed formal rules for readmitting the southern states to the Union, but Radicals in Congress found these rules too mild and in 1864 passed harsher requirements, which Lincoln pocket vetoed. At the end of the war, in 1865, thousands of ex-slaves embraced their new freedom, but without education, property, or consistent protection from mounting violence, their prospects were grim in the war-torn South.

EXPERIMENTING AT PORT ROYAL, 1863 Before the Civil War ended, Americans began to rebuild their war-ravaged country. As the war raged, President Abraham Lincoln, who understood the importance of symbols, ordered workers to finish the huge dome over the Capitol building. The Republicans also broke ground for a transcontinental railroad. With the exception of Senator Andrew Johnson, representatives and senators from the Confederate states had resigned, and the northern-dominated Congress easily designated a northerly route from Omaha to San Francisco. Northerners believed that this railroad would keep the West in the Union even if the South won independence.

The most strenuous efforts toward Reconstruction, however, involved parts of the South that the Union army had occupied. By 1862 Yankees controlled New Orleans, Louisiana's sugar plantations, and coastal South Carolina, where thousands of blacks, abandoned by their former masters, lived inside Union lines. Lincoln had to govern these areas, and he recognized that, if the North won the war, his policies would become models for postwar Reconstruction throughout the South.

Union commanders in coastal South Carolina tried a number of policies that became known as the Port Royal Experiment. Confederate landholders had fled. Black residents, who acted as if they were free even before the Emancipation Proclamation was announced, took over the plantations. They resisted planting rice or cotton, the normal cash crops, and refused to work in the usual gangs. Instead, they divided the land among themselves and, turning to family-based subsistence agriculture, primarily raised corn. Although blacks demanded ownership of the land they farmed, the army lacked the authority to grant it. The army could recognize only the right of black residents to use the land while the war continued. In some cases, white landowners did lose land for failure to pay property taxes, but most of these owners successfully reclaimed their property after the war.

The Port Royal Experiment captured the imagination of northern abolitionists. Experts from the U.S. Sanitary Commission traveled to Port Royal, offered technical advice about agriculture, and then brought in dozens of northern female schoolteachers, both black and white. These teachers, who included the black Charlotte Forten, found both children and adults eager to learn to read and write. The African-American community quickly chose its own black Christian preachers. The black church became the community's most important organization, performing social, economic, and political functions as well as religious ones. It continued to thrive after the end of Reconstruction.

Although residents prospered, supporters noted the lack of legal authority for the Port Royal Experiment. Technically, the blacks remained slaves, and absentee whites held legal title to the land. Many doubted that this new order in South Carolina would survive the end of the war. Few believed that such a change could be imposed across the entire South, due to massive white resistance and an inability to supply northern help on such a large scale. As feared, at the end of the war white landowners returned to Port Royal to demand that blacks either resume plantation-style agriculture or leave.

LINCOLN AND CONGRESS DEBATE RECONSTRUCTION, **1863–1864**   Louisiana, with a population about half white and half black and with a large number of free African Americans in New Orleans, proved more troublesome than coastal South Carolina to the occupying Union army. To free the army from controversy surrounding the occupation, Lincoln wanted to establish a new, pro-Union government as soon as possible.

In December 1863, he announced a plan for Reconstruction. Louisiana or any other Confederate state could rejoin the Union under simple terms. Residents who had participated in the rebellion could take a loyalty oath and then would be given amnesty. Lincoln would recognize a new state government after 10 percent of the number of men who had voted in the 1860 election had taken the oath, provided the state accepted slavery's end.

At first Lincoln did not propose political rights for blacks, but after some of Louisiana's numerous articulate free blacks protested during a visit to the White House, he privately asked the new state government to give literate African Americans the vote. However, the state's white Unionists, some of whom still defended slavery, declined. In 1864 Lincoln recognized governments in Arkansas and Louisiana under these terms, but Congress refused to seat their representatives.

Radical Republicans in Congress found Lincoln's plan too mild. They also resented the president's attempt to increase the power of the executive branch at their expense. In 1864 Congress passed its own plan for Reconstruction, the Wade-Davis Bill. This measure required a majority of the voters in each seceding state to take an oath pledging both past and future loyalty. Under this procedure some southern states were likely to remain out of the Union for a long time.

With the war ongoing, with the belief that former Whigs might lead new southern governments, and with the hope that mild terms might encourage Confederate states to capitulate, Lincoln determined that the harshness of the Congressional policy was unwise. He declined to sign the bill, which failed because it had been passed at the end of the session. (A bill becomes law without the president's signature if passed during a session, but an unsigned bill fails without the signature if Congress adjourns. This is called a pocket veto.) The Radicals attacked Lincoln, but he postponed further consideration of Reconstruction until after the 1864 election.

When the Civil War ended, African American soldiers in the Union Army were discharged with celebrations marking the end of slavery, like this one in Little Rock, Arkansas. (Library of Congress)

SLAVERY DIES, 1865   As the Confederacy collapsed in 1865, Union army officers and slaveholders throughout the region informed blacks that slavery was dead. Blacks hardly needed to be told. One said to his former master, a defeated Confederate soldier passing by, "Hello massa; bottom rail top dis time!"

Heralded as the Day of Jubilee, slavery's end brought joyous, even riotous, celebration. After the excitement of the moment waned, blacks often tested their newly won freedom by traveling—sometimes in search of lost relatives, but often just to prove to themselves that they had actually gained freedom. The ability to move unchallenged by slave patrols gave freedom vivid meaning.

Many African Americans, including previously loyal houseservants, deserted the plantations and farms where they had always lived to search for better opportunities or at least different whites with whom to deal. Freedmen, as the ex-slaves were called, shrewdly calculated that whites who remembered particular African Americans from slavery days would never treat them with respect. Better to trust a stranger.

The result was a kind of chaos. Searching for both opportunies and distance from white supervision, many blacks moved to southern towns and cities. Concentrated populations also discouraged the sporadic violence against blacks often found in rural areas. Used to slavery, slave patrols, and control over the black population, white city residents grew fearful.

Blacks also wandered through the countryside, seemingly uninterested in work. Confederate soldiers returned home and, finding their labor force gone, seethed when passing blacks declined their offers of work on the plantations. Blacks resented and resisted traditional modes of labor, and agriculture suffered. For example, production on Louisiana's sugar plantations dropped to 10 percent of its prewar level.

African Americans did not wish to work for whites on white-owned plantations. Rather, they wanted to acquire land for their own family farms. At the time, few blacks had either the capital or the valuable labor skills that would enable them to earn the capital to buy land. Indeed, the postwar South was a sorry place for anyone, white or black, to make money. Many years passed before the region regained its prewar number of farm animals and planted acres. As late as 1880 the per capita income in the South was only one-third of the national average.

Nor were blacks educated. In 1860 more than 90 percent could neither read nor write. Most southern states had prohibited teaching slaves to read. During Reconstruction blacks demanded that the South establish public schools. Eager for education, African Americans reluctantly accepted white insistence on segregated schools. Within a generation half of all blacks were literate.

JOHNSON AND CONGRESS QUARREL, 1865–1866

In 1865 President Andrew Johnson surprised the Radical Republicans in Congress by adopting conservative Reconstruction policies. The Constitution was amended to end slavery, but the southern states enacted Black Codes that all but reinstated slavery under another name. In 1866 Americans debated four distinct theories of Reconstruction, the harshest of which became congressional policy. Congress passed radical laws over Johnson's veto, as well as the Fourteenth Amendment to the Constitution. In 1866, northern voters backed the Radicals' program, and white southerners organized the Ku Klux Klan to intimidate blacks.

JOHNSON ADOPTS CONSERVATIVE RECONSTRUCTION POLICIES   After Lincoln's assassination, Andrew Johnson became president. An obscure former senator from Tennessee, he had been a lifelong Democrat. Born into poverty in North Carolina, he became an apprentice tailor and then ran away to the mountains of East Tennessee. There he married Eliza McCardle, who taught the ambitious but illiterate young man to read. A naturally good stump speaker with the common touch, Johnson successfully practiced law and politics.

In the prewar years he denounced slaveholding planters, even though he owned five slaves, and when Tennessee seceded, he became the only senator from a Confederate state who remained in office. He was a racist. "Damn the Negroes," he said during the war, "I am fighting these traitorous aristocrats, their masters." Hating both planters and slavery, this quarrelsome and eccentric man welcomed emancipation. He had been put on the Republican ticket in 1864 to help win Democratic votes. Most Republicans knew little about him except that he was a southern Unionist who had been drunk at his inauguration.

Johnson told Radical Republican leaders that he favored harsh measures against the South. Almost immediately, however, Johnson shocked the Radicals by adopting Lincoln's mild policies. The new president, with support from most of his cabinet, concluded that, to become a great president, he needed to heal the war's wounds by moving rapidly to restore power in the South to conservative whites.

Johnson believed, wrongly as it turned out, that the Confederacy's leaders had been discredited and lacked a constituency. Instead, he expected onetime Unionists to gain control, create stable governments, and generate the confidence that would produce postwar economic development. Though he was relieved by the way the war had destroyed slavery, he opposed extending any rights to blacks.

In mid-1865 Johnson issued a proclamation to recognize conservative, white-only governments in all eleven former Confederate states. He also granted amnesty to most Confederates who took an oath of allegiance. One important exception involved persons who held more than $20,000 worth of property. These wealthy planters had to apply to Johnson personally for a pardon. They did so and found the president generous. Johnson spent much of his time signing more than thirteen thousand pardons in two years.

Conservative state governments organized along these lines accepted the abolition of slavery by approving the Thirteenth Amendment to the Constitution, repudiated Confederate war debts, and made provisions for sending representatives to Congress. In December 1865, the Thirteenth Amendment was ratified.

THE SOUTH ENACTS BLACK CODES   These same state governments, often led by former Confederates, moved quickly to recreate the old order as closely as possible. They passed laws called Black Codes that regulated the conduct of blacks. Some states merely took old laws regulating slaves and changed the word *slave* to *freedman*. Under these laws blacks were treated as noncitizens without the rights to vote, serve on juries, or testify against whites. Furthermore, blacks had to sign annual labor contracts and could not change employment while under contract. In some states employers had the right to whip employees, who could be forced to work in gangs. In others blacks could not lease land independently. Blacks (but not whites) who lacked labor contracts or large sums of cash could be charged with vagrancy. The penalty for this crime was having the right to one's labor sold, with preference given to a former owner.

The Black Codes infuriated northern whites and southern blacks, including a good many Union army veterans. When Johnson accepted the southern white view that such laws were necessary to maintain order in the South, Radical Republicans in Congress became the president's bitter enemies. A new battle was about to be joined between the president and Congress over the direction of Reconstruction in the South.

CONGRESS BEGINS RADICAL RECONSTRUCTION, 1866   In Congress most Republicans, especially those from evangelical, moralistic New England, had become Radicals. Deeply offended by Johnson's behavior, they feared that the long, bloody war had changed little inside the South and that arrogant white southern planters would soon be running the federal government. In the North, Republicans faced a large and growing opposition from immigrant-oriented Democrats, and many Radicals worried that a coalition of white southerners and immigrant northerners might gain control of the national government. Indeed, southerners had dared to elect ex-Confederate officials to represent them in Congress. Georgia sent the former Confederate vice president, Alexander Stephens, to the Senate. The Radicals responded by refusing to seat representatives from any of the former Confederate states.

In early 1866 Congress passed a bill expanding the powers of the Freedmen's Bureau, which had been established a year earlier to distribute food and clothes to the former slaves in the South. The new bill placed nine hundred federal agents, most of them former Union soldiers, in those southern counties with large black populations to monitor race relations and negotiate disputes between whites and freedmen. Except for the post office, this was the first massive federal bureaucracy. Although the bureau could not stop white harassment, it did put such action under a watchful federal eye. Citing cost and states' rights, Johnson vetoed the bill. The angry Radicals quickly overrode the veto and showed that they had more than a two-thirds majority in Congress.

Congress then passed the Civil Rights Act. By granting citizenship to blacks and all other persons born in the United States, this law directly overturned the Black Codes and the 1857 Dred Scott ruling that denied citizenship to African Americans. The measure could also be interpreted to prohibit racial discrimination in public facilities, such as trains or restaurants. The bill, however, did not provide for voting rights. At this time most northern states had not granted the vote to blacks, and Radicals did not wish to irritate northern voters.

The Radicals passed this bill over Johnson's veto. The provisions concerning public accommodations were seldom enforced, and in 1883 the Supreme Court ruled the act unconstitutional.

PROPOSING THE FOURTEENTH AMENDMENT, 1866   Worried about a possible loss of power in the future, Radicals decided to use their overwhelming majority in Congress to guarantee black rights with the Fourteenth Amendment to the Constitution. The longest and vaguest of all amendments, this measure repealed the Dred Scott decision by granting citizenship to all persons born in the United States. Citizens were guaranteed "due process of law" and "equal protection of the laws." The federal government, in other words, would intervene if the southern states mistreated the freedmen. In the long term, the Supreme Court would apply these two clauses to all sorts of situations and greatly expand the power of the federal government.

To pressure the South to give blacks the vote, the amendment provided for reduced representation in Congress if the vote was denied. This provision was never enforced. The amendment also barred most former Confederates from federal office unless pardoned by *Congress,* and the southern states were prohibited from paying off Civil War debts.

To ensure the Fourteenth Amendment's adoption, Radicals indicated that representatives from each ex-Confederate state would be admitted to Congress only after that state had ratified the amendment. Congress was determined to take control of Reconstruction away from Johnson. Tennessee ratified and was readmitted, but the other ten ex-Confederate states rejected the amendment and waited for the fall 1866 congressional elections. The southerners, along with Johnson, believed that the Radicals had misjudged public opinion.

NORTHERN VOTERS BACK THE RADICALS, 1866   Taking his case for milder measures directly to the people, Johnson used the midterm congressional election of 1866 to make a campaign "swing around the circle" to the Northeast and across the Midwest and then south to St. Louis.

Although Johnson's trip went well at first, Radicals quickly organized an all-out attack. Radicals "waved the bloody shirt," a reference to wartime flags carried by the Union army in battle, by reminding northern voters how much the war had cost in treasure and lives and how the southern-born president now proposed yielding power to the former rebels.

By focusing on the war, by associating the Democrats with treason, and by linking the Republicans to the Union cause, the Radicals secured an overwhelming election victory. This success totally discredited Johnson's policies, and the already large Radical majorities in Congress actually increased.

CHAOS AND KU KLUX KLAN VIOLENCE ARISE IN THE SOUTH   Slavery had collapsed, but nothing had been put in its place. Blacks believed that the federal government would seize land owned by Confederate planters and give it to the freedmen, and some northerners encouraged this belief. "Forty acres and a mule!" cried some Radicals, including Thaddeus Stevens. African Americans quickly learned that this idea had little support. Northern property holders saw no advantage in endorsing a proposal that questioned the sanctity and permanence of private property. A government that confiscated land from planters today might take away someone else's property tomorrow.

Thomas Nast, America's greatest political cartoonist, portrayed the Democrats' White League as colluding with the Ku Klux Klan to oppress southern blacks during Reconstruction. (Library of Congress)

In addition, few northerners wanted to create a politically powerful, property-owning black society in the South, nor did most northerners want the planters to regain their prewar national political influence. The North's policy, then, was to keep the South poor, to maintain northern dominance of the country politically and economically, and to divide southern whites and blacks. Radicals accomplished this result by the paradoxical policy of giving blacks political rights while denying them the means to economic self-sufficiency.

Southern whites were self-confident, resourceful, educated, skilled, and well connected. They retained ownership of almost all the land, buildings, and tools but frequently lacked political rights. Insecure, illiterate, and ignorant blacks had political rights, granted through northern pressure, but lacked economic security. Blacks had no land, and whites had no labor. Both fell into dependency upon outside northern forces, especially Yankee-controlled railroad companies, which came to dominate the South's economy and politics.

Almost immediately, southern whites lashed out with violence. Infuriated by ex-slaves daring to assert their rights, frightened planters and ex-Confederate soldiers organized the Ku Klux Klan in 1866 in Pulaski, Tennessee, to force the freedmen to become docile, pliant tools. The Klan, which rapidly spread across the South, favored midnight visits to black homes, where they rousted blacks from bed, dragged them outside, and then took them into the woods to be beaten or killed. The Klan's whippings were designed, more than anything else, to remind freedmen of slavery.

The organization especially targeted African Americans perceived to be leaders in the campaign for rights, those who lacked proper humility in white eyes, and those known to be literate and therefore more capable of making trouble, such as writing complaining letters to federal officials. The Klan, even more than the Black Codes, led Radicals to seek federal intervention in the South.

At the same time, both races began to move toward a new relationship. Blacks insisted that they would not work as gang laborers on plantations. Instead, they rented land from planters and farmed in family units. Prewar slave housing, which had been built in dense blocks, gave way to freestanding family cabins in the middle of fields. Black tenant farmers adopted the white view that women should not work in the fields.

In desperate poverty, black tenants brought little except labor to this system and usually had to be financed by a planter or a merchant at a nearby general store. Many of these creditors were themselves in debt to railroad corporations. The planter or merchant usually got half the tenant's crop. Many tenants found that their living costs exceeded their earnings. Tenancy and the system of sharecropping quickly became ways of life in the rural South for poor whites as well as blacks.

RADICALS CONTINUE RECONSTRUCTION, 1867–1873

In 1867–1868 Radicals in Congress continued Reconstruction with stern new laws. Tiring of Johnson's opposition, they impeached the president but failed by one vote to convict him. Black votes in the South enabled the Radical Republican candidate, U. S. Grant, to win the 1868 presidential election narrowly. Blacks in the South gained some political power under Radical rule, but Radical power faded quickly. Conservative white southerners already were regaining control when Grant won a second term in 1872. The postwar years in the North brought immigration, factories, and the purchase of Alaska in 1867, but also labor strife and a depression that began in 1873.

CONGRESS PASSES STERN MEASURES, 1867–1868   In 1867 the Radicals moved to impose the kind of harsh military Reconstruction long advocated by Thaddeus Stevens. The Reconstruction Act, passed over Johnson's veto, established five military districts covering ten former Confederate states (Tennessee had been readmitted). Under this law and several supplementary measures, twenty thousand federal troops, including a number of black units, occupied the South. Military rule replaced the conservative state governments previously recognized by Johnson.

To be readmitted to the Union, the southern states had to adopt new state constitutions drafted by conventions elected by universal male suffrage. There was, however, a catch. Most ex-Confederates were barred from voting. This rule was consistent with the Fourteenth Amendment, which awaited ratification. Thus, in many southern states the freedmen's vote exceeded the white vote.

To guarantee fair elections, the United States army registered voters. In all ten southern states 703,000 blacks and 627,000 whites were registered. Blacks formed a majority of the registered voters in Alabama, Florida, Louisiana, Mississippi, and South Carolina. African Americans were more than half of the population in South Carolina and Mississippi. Congress also required that the new state governments guarantee blacks the right to vote and ratify the Fourteenth Amendment. The Radicals reserved to Congress all final decisions about what constituted compliance and when a state could regain its representation in Congress.

Throughout the South the Radicals used military rule, the Freedmen's Bureau, and the black vote organized through Union League Clubs to create a powerful Republican Party. In the upper South, including parts of Virginia and North Carolina, white Unionists formed an important Republican core to which were now added black voters from the former plantation districts.

This biracial Republican coalition proved inherently unstable. African Americans demanded protection for civil rights and massive increases in spending on public education, to be paid for with substantially higher property taxes on white landowners. On average, taxes rose to ten times the prewar level. Although poor white Republicans from the mountains disdained planters, they usually opposed black rights and resisted higher property taxes. Relatively quickly this unnatural Republican political alliance collapsed, and the planters regained their prewar political power.

In the Deep South the situation was different. These states had large black populations, and most whites had supported the Confederacy and could not vote. In South Carolina, Mississippi, and Louisiana the Republicans prevailed due to large black majorities among the electorate.

On the other hand, in these states most Republican Party leaders were white. Some were "scalawags," that is, southerners who had been Unionists or who now believed that personal advantage came from the Republicans. Others were "carpetbaggers," that is, northerners who had moved to the South, usually with initial hopes for economic gain, who had subsequently turned to politics.

In 1868 the Radicals in Congress approved the new state constitutions for seven states and readmitted them into the Union in time for the coming presidential election, in which they were expected to vote Republican.

Georgia's white Republicans, however, then proceeded to join with the few Democrats in the legislature to expel all twenty-eight black Republican members of the legislature. This action, which contradicted the pledges that Georgia had made to the Radicals concerning black rights, enraged the Radicals. They withdrew recognition, reinstated military rule, and demanded that the state reseat the black legislators and ratify the Fifteenth Amendment to the Constitution before being restored to the Union. Georgia was readmitted a second time in 1870.

CONGRESS IMPEACHES JOHNSON, 1868 Meanwhile, the Radicals had decided to impeach President Johnson and remove him from office. Thaddeus Stevens, leader of the Radicals in the House of Representatives, eagerly pushed the impeachment through the House. The Radicals charged Johnson with a number of violations, including the attempted removal of Secretary of War Edwin Stanton in defiance of a dubious prohibition passed by Congress, but in reality the issue was more political than legal.

Although the Radicals had a two-thirds majority in the Senate, seemingly enough votes to convict Johnson, public opinion began to question the proceedings. Business leaders disliked the impeachment because it made the government look unstable and upset the financial markets. In addition, the next person in line for the presidency was the president pro-tem of the Senate, Benjamin Wade of Ohio, a widely disliked, angry Radical. Johnson was acquitted, 35 to 19, one vote short of conviction. Seven Republicans joined the Democrats in opposing removal.

THE ELECTION OF 1868   For the 1868 presidential election the Republicans nominated General Ulysses S. Grant on a platform supporting Radical Reconstruction. The Democrats picked Horatio Seymour, a colorless New York governor. Public opinion had shifted away from the Radicals, and Grant won only a narrow victory. Due to an overwhelming vote among southern whites, Seymour won a majority among white voters, but Grant carried most of the electorally rich North. His margin was enhanced by Radical control in six southern states where there were many black voters. The Radical-dominated Congress barred three southern states suspected of Democratic tendencies from participation in the election.

The narrowness of this victory made the Radicals more determined to maintain control of the South. In 1869 Congress passed the Fifteenth Amendment to the Constitution, specifically guaranteeing the black vote. Congress brushed aside attempts by women's groups, led by Elizabeth Cady Stanton and supported by Senator Charles Sumner, to use the amendment to give women the vote too. Mississippi, Texas, and Virginia were finally readmitted to the Union in 1870, after they had banned ex-Confederate voters and ratified the Fifteenth Amendment.

BLACKS GAIN POWER BRIEFLY IN THE SOUTH   Mississippi became staunchly Radical and was the first and only state to elect two African Americans to the U.S. Senate, Hiram Revels and, later, Blanche K. Bruce. Of the fourteen blacks from the South who served in the House during Reconstruction, four were Union army veterans. The most flamboyant was Robert Smalls, a former South Carolina slave who, after the Emancipation Proclamation, had stolen a steamboat and sailed it through the Confederate navy to the federal fleet.

Although blacks provided about four-fifths of the Republican vote in the South, they accounted for less than one-fifth of the officeholders. Most blacks served in city and county offices or in state legislatures. South Carolina's legislature was the only one with a black majority. Black officials tended to be well educated and light-skinned. Many had been free before the war. Only a few held statewide office, and none was elected governor.

In 1872–1873, P. B. S. Pinchback, who had been elected lieutenant governor, served briefly as governor of Louisiana.

RECONSTRUCTION EBBS PRIOR TO THE ELECTION OF 1872   Radical Reconstruction, however, was already in decline. Georgia and Virginia slipped quickly under conservative control, and northerners resisted using federal troops to maintain Radical rule. At the same time, scandal had hurt the Grant administration. A number of officials had taken bribes, and in 1872 numerous prominent Republicans in Congress were revealed to have accepted stock from the Crédit Mobilier, a front for the Union Pacific Railroad, to which Congress had given huge land grants.

By 1872 many Republicans, including Horace Greeley, loathed both Radical Reconstruction and the era's sleazy, crooked politics. Organizing themselves as Liberal Republicans, they nominated Greeley for president. The Democrats endorsed Greeley, as did the German immigrant reformer and former Union general Carl Schurz, and two crusading journalists, E. L. Godkin of *The Nation* and Henry Adams. Grant, the regular Republican nominee, won by an increased majority, and a broken-hearted Greeley died suddenly. Grant, corruption, and Reconstruction lurched forward uneasily.

THE POSTWAR NORTH, 1867–1873   The immediate postwar years brought even more rapid change in the North than in the South. Fueled by the paper greenback currency issued during the war, the postwar northern economy boomed, along with considerable inflation, and industrialists converted factories from military to civilian production. Union army veterans returned home to resume farming, business, and handicrafts, but many soon made their way west along the newly built rail routes, including the transcontinental railroad to California, which opened in 1869. Largely stopped during the war, massive immigration from Europe resumed. Irish, Germans, and Britons were joined by Scandinavians, who settled on farms in the upper Midwest.

Dynamic growth even led to a renewed interest in territorial expansion. In 1867 Secretary of State Seward learned that the Russians, pressed for cash, wanted to sell Alaska. Partly to keep the territory out of the hands of the British, who controlled Canada, and partly in faith that a land as large as Alaska must contain valuable resources, Seward resolved to buy the frozen northland. The Russians demanded $7.2 million, generally considered an outrageous price, and the secretary had to cajole and bribe Congress to pay it. Popularly scorned as "Seward's Folly," the territory of Alaska more than paid for itself within a few years in timber and salmon alone.

Change was not always kind. Many workers had organized success-ful unions during the war, but returning soldiers and immigrants now en-larged the labor pool and made it possible for employers to break strikes. Workers also discovered that the Republican Party, which had rallied both business and labor to the antislavery cause, fell more and more under the control of business interests eager to pursue antilabor policies, including the outlawing of strikes. Labor newspapers that had started during the war collapsed, leaving only the probusiness partisan press.

By 1873, the year that brought the collapse of Jay Cooke's Philadel-phia bond firm and the beginnings of a depression, many northerners were bored by the Republicans, by Reconstruction, and by talk of north-ern wartime sacrifices.

CONSERVATIVES REGAIN POWER
IN THE SOUTH, 1868–1877

Conservative white southerners used both sophisticated political tactics and economic power to overthrow the Radicals and regain control of the political system. Violence and intimidation also played a role. In the dis-puted presidential election of 1876, a Republican–southern Democratic deal gave the Republicans the presidency and the Democrats the South. The last Reconstruction state governments were sold out.

WHITE REDEEMERS USE POLITICS AND ECONOMICS   White southerners, espe-cially ex-Confederates, had never accepted the legitimacy of Reconstruc-tion. Many resisted the end of slavery, and even those who accepted slav-ery's death found the freedmen's right to vote bizarre. Perhaps a few might have conceded the merit of universal suffrage as a theory, but al-lowing blacks to vote while depriving whites of the ballot enraged white southerners.

The enforcement of these rules by the military, by the Freedmen's Bu-reau, and by Radicals in Congress embittered white southerners. Deter-mined to restore what they considered to be the natural order of southern society—that is, white supremacy—they swore to use any and all means to achieve their goal.

Although most conservative white southerners were Democrats, some, like the opportunist Governor Joe E. Brown of Georgia, joined the Republi-cans. In addition to plotting the expulsion of black Republicans from the legislature, Brown sought to reduce black influence by moving the state capital from Milledgeville, in the heart of the black belt, to Atlanta, where railroad companies willingly paid legislators for votes. Brown, like many other white Republicans, emphasized economic development over civil rights. Southern Democrats soon realized that they, too, could make this same appeal to northern business interests.

Conservatives in South Carolina, where blacks had a legislative majority as late as 1876, felt they could regain control only by rallying virtually the entire white vote and winning a share of the large black vote. That state's Radical Republican regime self-destructed with weak leadership, internal bickering, and charges of corruption. The conservative Democrat Wade Hampton, an antebellum planter and ex-Confederate general, won election as governor in 1876. Hampton pledged to retain black voting rights and act honorably toward blacks. One wonders if he made the pledge with a wink.

Economics worked against black political power. Whites owned virtually everything and had a monopoly on the most valuable job skills. In 1876 only 5 percent of African Americans in the Deep South owned land. Economic intimidation, if not outright vote-buying, was used to produce a black electorate effectively controlled by whites. In those few areas where blacks had achieved a degree of landownership, such as parts of coastal South Carolina, economics tended to reinforce black political power, which remained potent for another generation. The last southern black congressman until modern times left office in 1901.

USING VIOLENCE TO INTIMIDATE BLACKS AND GAIN WHITE RULE   Conservative white southerners called themselves Redeemers because, they said, they were redeeming or saving the South from Radical Republican misrule. Most significant in the Redeemers' movement to reclaim the power of government for Democrats, however, was the use of intimidation and violence against blacks. Although southern whites learned that the high visibility of organizations such as the Ku Klux Klan generated unfavorable publicity in the North and threatened to bring a resumption of northern intervention, the Klan's mere existence intimidated blacks.

The Klan was not the only means to reclaim white rule. Other militant white supremacist political organizations, such as South Carolina's Red Shirts and Alabama's White League, countered the Republicans' Union League Clubs. Mississippi Democrats took the motto, "Carry the election peaceably if we can, forcibly if we must."

Most important were individual threats or acts of violence directed at politically active blacks and white Republicans. Campaigns of arson and assassination took place throughout the South. These were little publicized, since Democrats had no reason to advertise undemocratic methods, and Republicans knew that publicity only revealed their own weakness.

Blacks sometimes responded to the tension by deciding to move. Some talked about Africa, and a few actually went there, although most returned disillusioned. Others looked to homesteading on federal land in the West. A number, collectively known as the Exodusters, founded new black communities in Kansas. Others migrated to Texas or to western mining towns. Most blacks, however, remained in the South and increasingly under conservative white control.

By 1876 conservative white Democrats had, by one means or another, regained control of most southern states. When Democrats won state power, they routinely destroyed black power in predominantly African-American counties by requiring officials in those counties to be appointed by the governor rather than locally elected. In 1876 only South Carolina, Louisiana, and Florida remained under Republican rule, and Radical control in those states faced serious challenges, electoral and otherwise.

THE DISPUTED ELECTION OF 1876   Grant's second administration was dogged by more scandals, including the Whiskey Ring, where distillers bribed high officials to evade liquor taxes. Worse, the economy slipped into a depression following the Panic of 1873. In 1876 Democrats recog-

In 1877 it was announced that Rutherford B. Hayes had defeated Samuel J. Tilden for the presidency by a vote of 185 to 184 in the Electoral College. In a secret compromise, the Republicans won the White House, and Democrats got control of the southern states. Tilden became a great book collector and donated his collection to the New York Public Library. (Culver Pictures, Inc.)

nized that scandal and hard times gave them an excellent chance to win the presidential election.

The Republicans nominated Rutherford B. Hayes, an Ohio politician and the husband of a leading temperance reformer, and the Democrats picked Samuel J. Tilden, a wealthy Wall Street lawyer. Although Tilden won the popular vote, the Electoral College result was close and uncertain. Indeed, Republicans quickly realized that if South Carolina, Florida, and Louisiana were counted for Hayes, he could win, 185 to 184.

The actual vote in the three southern states will never be known. Black voters were intimidated into staying away from the polls, ballot boxes were stuffed or burned, and two sets of votes were collected in some communities. Incumbent Radical administrations in all three states declared both Hayes and new Republican state governments victorious. Democrats challenged those outcomes, organized their own vote counts, and announced victories for Tilden and themselves.

No one could say for sure who had won the southern "elections," but it was clear that southern white Democrats were prepared to seize power in the three states and could be stopped only by federal military authorities. Grant, Tilden, and Hayes opposed such a use of force, each for his own reason.

Controversy about the election continued into early 1877, as Congress deadlocked. Democrats controlled the House, Republicans the Senate. Finally, Congress arranged a grand compromise. Republicans got the presidency, Democrats control of the three southern states. Northern Republicans stood aside as the last Radical governments in the three southern states fell to conservative Democrats. Amid reassurances from Hayes that he would withdraw remaining federal troops from the South, Congress sent the presidential election to a special commission composed of five Democrats, five Republicans, and four specified Supreme Court justices. These four were to choose a fifth justice. David Davis, an independent expected to be tapped, suddenly resigned from the Court to take a Senate seat, and the justices were forced to pick from among the Court's remaining justices, all of whom were Republicans.

After a secret meeting between Republican and southern Democratic leaders at the Wormley House hotel in Washington in February 1877, the commission's eight Republicans and seven Democrats followed their leaders' orders and by a strict party vote awarded all the disputed electoral votes to Hayes, who won, 185 to 184. Tilden, fearing civil war, seemed relieved.

Reconstruction was over. Although slavery had ended, the right to vote and the other rights blacks had won and exercised during Reconstruction would be lost during the 1890s. Modest gains survived, including segregated schools and black colleges, such as Howard, Atlanta, and Fisk.

In part, white racism and the white southern desire for a political system based upon white supremacy were to blame. In part, the failure to provide the freedmen with land created economic dependency that made it difficult for African Americans to keep political rights. A measure of economic security, if not actual equality, is necessary to maintain democratic politics. In part, too, northern Republicans, having concluded that Reconstruction had brought their party few benefits, were prepared to sell out the southern Radical Republicans. In the new order, men of wealth from all sections had much in common.

CONCLUSION

Reconstruction cast a long shadow across the country and especially the South. Much more than the Civil War had, the era generated great bitterness among honor-driven southern whites, who looked upon northern-imposed black rights with seething anger. Maintaining white supremacy became a hallmark of southern politics for almost a hundred years. Blacks, too, grew bitter. Promised much by northern Radicals, they were handed modest amounts of power, only to be abandoned in the end for political convenience. Never again did blacks entirely trust Republicans. Reconstruction produced only losers and goes far toward explaining the tawdry politics of the generation that followed.

Recommended Readings

DOCUMENTS: Ira Berlin, et al., eds., *Freedom: A Documentary History of Emancipation* (5 vols., 1982–2001); W. E .B. DuBois, *The Souls of Black Folk* (1903); Whitelaw Reid, *After the War* (1866); Albion W. Tourgée, *A Fool's Errand* (1879).

READINGS: (GENERAL) David Donald, *Charles Sumner and the Rights of Man* (1970); Laura F. Edwards, *Gendered Strife and Confusion* (1997); Eric Foner, *Reconstruction* (1988); Leon F. Litwack, *Been in the Storm So Long* (1979); (WARTIME) Louis S. Gerteis, *From Contraband to Freedman* (1973); William C. Harris, *With Charity for All* (1997); James L. Roark, *Masters without Slaves* (1977); Willie L. Rose, *Rehearsal for Reconstruction* (1964); (BLACKS) Paul Cimbala, *Under the Guardianship of the Nation* (1997); Edmund L. Drago, *Black Politicians and Reconstruction in Georgia* (1983); Barbara J. Fields, *Slavery and Freedom on the Middle Ground* (1985); Jacqueline Jones, *Soldiers of Light and Love* (1980); Claude F. Oubré, *Forty Acres and a Mule* (1978); Nell I. Painter, *Exodusters* (1976); Julie Saville, *The Work of Reconstruction* (1994); Donald Spivey, *Schooling for the New Slavery* (1978); Clarence E. Walker, *A Rock in a Weary Land* (1982); (POLITICS) Richard H. Abbott, *The Republican Party and the South* (1986); Michael L. Benedict, *The Impeachment and Trial of Andrew Johnson* (1973); Dan T. Carter, *When the War Was Over*

(1985); Richard N. Current, *Those Terrible Carpetbaggers* (1988); Steven Hahn, *The Roots of Southern Populism* (1983); William C. Harris, *The Day of the Carpetbagger* (1979); Thomas Holt, *Black over White* (1977); Peggy Lamson, *The Glorious Failure* (1973); William E. Nelson, *The Fourteenth Amendment* (1988); Edward Royce, *The Origins of Southern Sharecropping* (1993); Jonathan M. Wiener, *Social Origins of the New South* (1978); (REDEEMERS) Michael Perman, *The Road to Redemption* (1984); George C. Rable, *But There Was No Peace* (1984); Terry L. Seip, *The South Returns to Congress* (1983); Allen W. Trelease, *White Terror* (1971).

16

❧

The Frontier and Westward Expansion

OVERVIEW   In the aftermath of the Civil War, some observers were shocked by what appeared to be an American mania for accumulating wealth. New industries developed in the North; railroads spanned the continent; silver and gold were mined throughout the West; cattle ranches sprang up in the Southwest, and land speculation was rife in the nation's fastest-growing cities. Some consequences of westward expansion proved unfortunate for the environment and for the defeated Indians. People moved West for various reasons, and the results of their choices varied too. Some, with the right mix of opportunity, hard work and good luck, even got rich.

THE WEST SETTLED: ILLUSION AND REALITY

After the Civil War thousands of Americans moved west across the Mississippi River to better their lives. They came for land and for the chance to settle—to own property and exploit its riches. Miners followed every lead, hoping to strike it rich. These westward settlers benefited from federal legislation that encouraged migration, even if they resented the power of the federal government in their lives.

THE ILLUSION OF FORTUNE IN A LAND OF CONTRASTS   In late 1872 two miners discovered diamonds in a remote corner of northwestern Colorado. Reports of diamonds immediately stirred the imaginations of Denver's citizens, who had also heard of diamonds being found in South

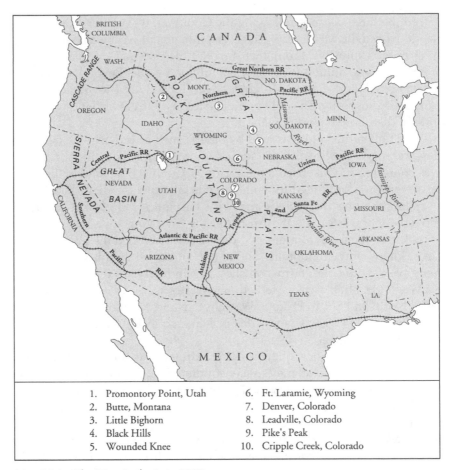

Map 16.1   The West in the Late 1800s

1. Promontory Point, Utah
2. Butte, Montana
3. Little Bighorn
4. Black Hills
5. Wounded Knee

6. Ft. Laramie, Wyoming
7. Denver, Colorado
8. Leadville, Colorado
9. Pike's Peak
10. Cripple Creek, Colorado

Africa: If in South Africa, why not in Colorado? After all, the mountains had yielded precious gold and silver. The gold and silver rushes were over, and the people of Colorado found themselves caught up in the new craze.

Within days twenty-five companies, capitalized at a total of $250 million, were formed. Trading in diamond stocks became rampant. At the same time, miners prepared to rush off to this remote section of the state with little concern for the approaching winter. Before long, though, a geologist exposed what became known as the "Great Diamond Hoax": The two miners who had first reported the discovery had salted the area with diamonds in hopes of selling stock to the unwary. The Diamond Hoax of 1872 revealed the acquisitive instinct and risk-taking temper of many who moved west.

In the three decades following the Civil War, wave after wave of pioneers crossed the Mississippi River. The movement west was part of a demographic explosion: From 1860 to 1900 the national population grew from thirty-one million to seventy-six million people. Beyond all else, the West offered land. Land held gold, silver, topsoil, and townsites, which promised prosperity. The only appropriate way to treat the land was to divide it, distribute it, and register it.

That often the land was held by others, such as Indians, Mexicans, or descendants of the Spanish conquest, did not hinder acquisition. The land was contested and taken from these groups. Conflict over land in the West, however, was not limited to whites against all others. Indians had fought over land among themselves and with Hispanics long before the mass movement of whites into the West after the Civil War.

Miners, ranchers, farmers, and the U.S. army battled the Indians of the Great Plains, of the mountains, and of the Southwest. In this way the frontier gave way to cities, farms, ranches, and industry. As the land between Kansas and California was settled, new states were created: Colorado in 1876; North and South Dakota, Washington, and Montana in 1889; Idaho and Wyoming in 1890; Utah in 1896; Oklahoma in 1907, and Arizona and New Mexico in 1912.

The West is a region of geographic extremes. As the settlers left their homes and moved west, they first encountered the vast rolling prairies of the Great Plains, which stretched from west Texas to Canada. Here approximately 300,000 Indians lived and hunted the thirteen million buffalo that roamed the region. Beyond the plains, the pioneers confronted the Rocky Mountains. On the other side of the Rockies lay the Great Basin, a vast desert lowland that included the Great Salt Lake. To the south, the hostile Sonoran desert, one of the world's major deserts, stretched across southern New Mexico, Arizona, and California and into northern Mexico. If the settlers pushed on still further, they faced the forbidding Sierra Nevada or the Cascade Mountains before they reached California or the northern Pacific coast.

INDIVIDUAL PURSUIT AND FEDERAL AID   Settlers arriving in the West generally distrusted the government in Washington. Nonetheless, through important legislation the federal government played an essential role in the West's development.

In 1862, with the passage of the Homestead Act, Congress opened western land for settlement. The intent of the bill was to distribute government-owned land to individuals for farming. The act offered 160 acres of public land to any person over twenty-one or to the head of a family if the person resided on the land for five continuous years. A homesteader also could purchase the land after six months for $1.25 an acre. Between 1862 and 1900 nearly 400,000 families received free plots of land through the Homestead Act. Although the vast majority of these purchases were honest, some land speculators took advantage of the law by sending in dummy entrymen to make claims. In any case, nearly two-thirds of the homesteads failed before 1890.

The Homestead Act was followed by the Timber Culture Act (1873), which allowed farmers to apply for additional land if they planted one-fourth of it with trees within four years. During the fifteen years this law remained on the books, people planted more than ten thousand acres with trees.

The Desert Land Act (1877) allowed a rancher to secure tentative title to 640 acres in the Great Plains or the Southwest for an initial payment of twenty-five cents an acre. If, after three years, it was proved that a portion of this land had been irrigated, the settler's title to the land became permanent upon payment of an additional dollar an acre. The price was a bargain and openly invited fraud. Many settlers simply dumped a bucket of water on the land, called it irrigation, and purchased the land. Under this single act, the federal government gave away over two and half million acres.

Timber interests took note of this act and lobbied for their own special legislation, the Timber and Stone Act (1878). This extraordinary statute allowed them to buy rich forests in California, Nevada, Oregon, and Washington for $2.50 an acre, about the price of one good log. By 1900 almost 3,600,000 acres of potentially valuable forests had been sold under this law.

The largest federal land program in the West subsidized railroad construction, in particular the transcontinental railroad. Through the Railroad Acts of 1862 and 1864, Congress awarded large tracts of land to railroad corporations to encourage construction of a transcontinental line. Individual states copied the federal policy. As a consequence, railroads became the largest private landowners in the West and remain so today.

The railroad system proved crucial to western development. The discovery of gold in California in 1849 had brought settlers into the Pacific coast region, but to reach the distant territory, a complex transportation and communications system needed to be built. Although many in the West distrusted eastern financial interests and the federal government, western interests joined with eastern capitalists to pressure Congress to grant subsidized stagecoach lines, telegraph corporations, and, most importantly, railroads to the West.

The secession of the South had allowed Republican congressmen to pass legislation to build a transcontinental railroad along a central route.

On July 1, 1862, Congress chartered the Central Pacific Railroad to begin construction from Sacramento through the Sierra Nevadas. At the same time, Congress chartered a second company, the Union Pacific Railroad, to build westward from Omaha, Nebraska. Each company was offered twenty odd-numbered sections of land for each mile of track they constructed. Congress also loaned the railroads from $16,000 to $48,000 per mile, depending on the nature of the terrain.

The first transcontinental railroad was one of the world's great engineering endeavors. To build a line through the Sierras had been the dream of a California engineer, Theodore D. Judah. On his own, he surveyed a path through the nation's largest mountains. Judah then persuaded four Sacramento promoters—Leland Stanford, Collis P. Huntington, Mark Hopkins, and Charles Crocker—to form the Central Pacific Railroad Company.

In 1864 construction of the line began in California and proceeded slowly eastward at a rate of about twenty miles per year. The company's difficulty finding labor was solved by importing Chinese workers, called coolies. The railroad appreciated their steady work in extremely dangerous conditions, and especially their sobriety in railroad camps that otherwise were little more than mobile saloons and brothels.

In the early 1880s the first transcontinental railroad was matched by a second line, the Atchison, Topeka and Santa Fe, crossing the southern route. In 1887 Henry Villard's Northern Pacific line linked Lake Superior and Puget Sound. The Southern Pacific connected Texas with Los Angeles, and James J. Hill's Great Northern provided another northern route along the Canadian border. Hill's was the only line constructed without federal land grants, and the only one that made money for the railroad companies. Dozens of other companies provided feeder lines, creating one of the best railroad systems in the world.

At the end of the Civil War, there were only 35,000 miles of track, mostly east of the Mississippi River and dominated by local lines that all used different track widths. By the end of the century, there were 240,000 miles of interconnected railroads. America's rail system impressed the world: The United States alone held one-third of the world's total railroad mileage.

By the 1890s the completion of five transcontinental railroads linked the Atlantic to the Pacific. In doing so, these lines enabled settlers to fill in the continent. The railroads also gave farmers access to midwestern and eastern markets.

The first continental line allowed the annihilation of the buffalo herds in a short period by affording hunters easy access to the land. The movement of settlers into the Great Plains and the elimination of the buffalo set

The frontier marshal Wild Bill Hickok helped tame the West until 1876, when Jack McCall shot Hickok in the back while the marshal was playing poker. Never sit with your back to the door. (Brown Brothers)

the conditions for confrontation with the Indians, who depended on buffalo for their livelihood. By providing an army to police the territory, the federal government once again played an essential role.

MINING FOR RICHES, STRIKING REALITY   Mining, too, drew people to the West. No other industry, with the possible exception of cattle ranching, had as great an impact on the region. The Gold Rush of 1849 had brought miners, merchants, speculators, and others to California; soon mines, camps, towns, mills, and smelters appeared across the countryside.

The California strike was followed in 1858 by discoveries of gold and silver in Colorado, Nevada, and British Columbia, Canada. The Colorado strike was particularly exciting. Hundreds of Indians and frontiersmen hunted for gold along the Arkansas River in Colorado. After months of searching, just as the expedition was beginning to give up and drift apart, pay dirt was struck near present-day Denver.

By the spring of 1859, the wildest rush in the nation's history was under way in Colorado, as nearly 100,000 gold miners rushed to Pike's Peak. During the 1860s other rich lodes of gold were discovered near Boulder. More discoveries were still to come. In the 1870s silver was discovered in Leadville, and a short while later gold was struck at Cripple Creek. These strikes accelerated the development of Colorado, which became a state in 1876.

The richest find was in Nevada. In 1859, two Irish miners discovered flake gold in the eastern foothills of the Sierra Nevada. They were joined by a third partner, Henry T. P. Comstock, who gave his name to the lode. In the next four years more than $15 million worth of pure gold and silver was taken from these mountains. In October 1864, Nevada became a state. In the next decade mine after mine opened, producing an aggregate $24 million annually. Paupers became millionaires overnight.

In 1880 rich copper ore was discovered in Butte, Montana. The industrial revolution in the East demanded copper, which Montana's mines readily provided. Thousands of miners, many of them immigrants, were employed in Butte's mines. The miners were vulnerable, for the copper barons of Anaconda (where the largest smelter was located) controlled the state, often battling one another for political control.

In 1898 the battle between William Clark and Marcus Daly for the U.S. Senate seat ended with Clark's bribe of members of the state legislature to elect him. When the Senate refused to seat him, Clark claimed in his defense, "I never bought a man who was not for sale."

Gold was found in the Black Hills of the Dakotas in the 1870s. Full exploitation of the area was retarded, however, by the fierce Sioux Indians, who were protected by federal troops intent on keeping all intruders from the lands. But in 1874, with rumors circulating of gold to be found in the hills, thousands of prospectors began to force their way into the forbidden territory. Under pressure, the military decided to send its own expedition into the territory to disprove the rumors. When this force of 1,200 soldiers and scientists, led by General George Armstrong Custer, instead discovered more gold in the Black Hills, a new rush began.

In October 1875 the military, without the agreement of the Sioux, opened the Black Hills to the gold seekers. That spring, prospectors flooded into the territory, establishing such "Wild West" towns as Deadwood Gulch. Among the miners were gunmen, gamblers, and camp followers, men and women such as Wild Bill Hickok, California Jack, Poker Alice, and Calamity Jane, who left their indelible marks on the mythic West.

Miners brought their own order to the mining towns of the West. Even before governments, miners established claim clubs, citizen courts, and vigilante committees. They were quite willing to use "stretched hemp" (a hanging rope) on desperadoes whose behavior was too unrestrained. One of the first acts of the Colorado territorial legislature in 1859 was to pass an act that gave legal status to decisions made by local miners' courts and meetings.

Following the Civil War, Nevada Senator William Stewart pushed the Mining Law of 1866 through Congress. This act, later revised in 1872, declared all mineral lands in the public domain free and open to prospectors; it also gave precedence to local customs and miners' rules. This law revealed the miners' preference for frontier law and minimal federal involvement. Miners called for law and order as long as it was on their own terms.

In the early days of prospector mining, the pickings were relatively easy. Men with a few tools and strong backs could extract minerals that lay close to the surface. Panning for gold also required little capital investment. Training in panning techniques in California came from experienced Mexican placer miners; the persistence of Chinese placers in Idaho allowed them to extract gold well after white prospectors had given up.

By the 1880s, however, most of the easy finds had been played out. Extracting minerals from deep underground required a large capital investment. Idaho and Montana mining was undertaken by commercial enterprises that employed permanent workforces. By the 1890s corporate mining dominated the industry. Often these corporations had absentee owners. In these circumstances, the miners had much in common with workers in the industrialized East, and tensions developed between employers and hired laborers.

Work in the underground mines became increasingly dangerous. Cave-ins and rock falls were common as hastily rigged timbers and shafts gave way. Premature or delayed blasts caused frequent dynamiting accidents.

The camaraderie of shared danger, separation from supervisors, and isolated communities helped to focus grievances about wages and working conditions. By the turn of the century, bitter labor struggles had erupted in western mining towns (and lumber camps). In 1893 the Western Federation of Miners was formed; this union quickly became a major force in the mining areas of Montana, Idaho, and Colorado.

AMERICAN INDIANS RESIST THE WESTWARD FLOOD

In the decades following the Civil War, white settlers flooded into Indian lands. Native Americans fought back, but they were outnumbered and overpowered. As European Americans broke one agreement after another, Indians tried negotiation, appeals to reason, war, and even escape into Canada, but nothing would stop the settlers' relentless drive for more land. Reservations were given to Indians, then taken back. Indians also suffered from the destruction of the buffalo herds on which they depended for livelihood, and from European Americans' diseases.

Eastern reformers took up the Native American cause, but their efforts did little to improve the condition of the Indian. The Dawes Act (1887) was meant to help Indians but resulted in even greater loss of land.

CONQUEST OF THE WEST AND AMERICAN INDIAN LIFE   As European Americans moved westward, older immigrant groups were joined by new arrivals. The Irish settled throughout the Great Plains states. Germans, already established in the upper Mississippi region, migrated to Kansas, Nebraska, and the Dakotas. Scandinavian immigration began in 1865, reaching a peak in 1882 when more than 105,000 arrived from Norway, Sweden, and Denmark. After Reconstruction thousands of freed slaves, known as Exodusters, left the South to establish settlements in Kansas.

The westward movement caused population booms in established states such as Kansas, Nebraska, and Texas. By 1880 Kansas boasted nearly a million inhabitants, while Nebraska had 450,000 people.

As whites and blacks moved westward, they confronted an Indian population remarkably diverse in language, culture, and economy. Tribes made contact with these migrants at different rates and in different circumstances; as a result, Indians drew different conclusions from these encounters. Even before the arrival of the westward migrants, Native American culture had been dominated by intertribal rivalry. Indian life included raids, counter raids, and alliances honored or broken. Often the arrival of whites appeared to play a peripheral role in this world, as whites were seen as either allies or enemies taking sides in intertribal warfare.

Nevertheless, contact with whites transformed Native American culture. The Indian population had been devastated by European diseases, including smallpox, cholera, typhus, influenza, malaria, measles, and yellow fever. By the middle of the 1800s, the Native American population had decreased to fewer than 500,000. In 1860 approximately 1.4 million Americans lived in the West; by 1890, more than 8.5 million did. The lands once dominated by Indians were now finally in the hands of the whites.

Whites transformed Indian culture in many ways. Western tribes acquired horses from the Spanish, while eastern Indians encountering whites gained metal knives, muskets, and rifles. Replacing the dog with the horse as the primary beast of burden increased mobility. As horse culture moved north from Mexico and rifle culture moved westward, they converged on the Great Plains, creating a buffalo-hunting culture.

Native peoples found themselves contesting the land, not only with white and black Americans moving west, but also with Hispanics moving north from Mexico after the Civil War. In some northern states of Mexico, governors in fact established scalp bounties on Apaches to discourage raids.

THE FAILURE OF FEDERAL INDIAN POLICY

After the Civil War the federal government sought to place Indians in one large reservation, called Indian Territory. Indians were to be confined to these reserved lands through negotiation if possible and through force as necessary. This policy became known as Grant's "peace policy." The failure of the policy and the horrid condition of Indians by the late 1880s led reformers to call for a new policy of assimilation, expressed in the Dawes Act (1887), which called for the division of tribal lands into private property. In implementing these policies, the federal government plunged the West into another period of brutal war. Defeated Indians would be left to rebuild their societies in a new and hostile environment.

In 1868 General George Armstrong Custer massacred the Cheyenne encamped along the Washita River in Oklahoma. Civil War veterans like Custer brought ruthlessness to Indian fighting. Custer died in battle at Little Big Horn, Montana, in 1876. He graduated last in his class at West Point. (Culver Pictures, Inc.)

AMERICAN INDIANS RESIST INTRUSION   Warfare against Indians was especially brutal in California, where miners and ranchers found peaceful, pastoral "Digger" Indians, who lacked even weapons of war. Whites launched a merciless war against these Indians, often spending their weekends in parties hunting down these unarmed people. Approximately 4,500 California Indians were killed this way. By the time the federal government moved to protect the California Indians, disease and violence had spared only a handful. Campaigns were carried out against the Snake and Bannock in Oregon and Idaho and against the Ute in Utah.

Southwestern and Plains Indians showed fiercer resistance. In the Southwest the Apache and Navajo battled the white settlers. Conflict reached a peak in New Mexico during the Civil War. Led by Kit Carson, the military launched an all-out attack against the Navajo. The Navajo fought more than 143 battles against Carson, but in the end they were forcibly removed to a reservation on the Pecos River in eastern New Mexico.

The Plains Indians, from the Sioux in the north to the Kiowa and Comanche in the Southwest, fought hard to resist white migration. Particularly fierce were the Sioux, who had continued to expand their hunting grounds at the expense of the Crow and the Pawnee. This caused intertribal warfare that continued even as whites entered Indian lands.

In 1851 at a meeting with federal officials at Fort Laramie, Wyoming, the chiefs of the Sioux, Crow, Cheyenne, and Arapaho were guaranteed land that stretched from the foothills of the Colorado to the Platte River in the Dakotas. Here, they were promised, they could live for all time. The federal government's Indian Office forcibly removed Indians from Kansas and Nebraska, which were organized as territories in 1854.

Trouble resumed in 1859 with the discovery of gold near Pike's Peak, Colorado. Fighting began in Colorado when more than 100,000 miners crossed the Plains and moved into Cheyenne and Arapaho lands. Federal agents only exacerbated troubles when they demanded that the two tribes abandon all claims to land, contrary to promises made at Fort Laramie, in exchange for a small reservation in eastern Colorado. In the summer of 1862, Indian hostilities intensified when the eastern Sioux in Minnesota went on the warpath after the district Indian agent refused to distribute food to the starving Indians. One white trader expressed the sentiment of many: "So far as I am concerned, if they are hungry let them eat grass or their own dung."

By 1864 Colorado was ablaze. Indians had murdered settlers, burned homes, destroyed mail stations, and attacked travelers. The countryside lay in ruins; Denver itself appeared threatened. Outraged settlers undertook a fierce military campaign against the Indians. When one Cheyenne chief—Black Kettle, a gentle, wise chief who embodied the Cheyenne peace spirit—tried to surrender, the local militia instructed him to take his 700 followers to Sand Creek. There, on November 28, 1864, the Colorado militia under Colonel J. M. Chivington surrounded the Indian camp and attacked. Black Kettle first raised an American flag, then a white flag, but the attack continued. The warriors were pushed to the river; women and children fled to the caves, only to be dragged out and slaughtered. Within a few hours, more than 450 Indians were killed. Black Kettle and a few young warriors escaped.

The Sand Creek Massacre was applauded in Denver; Indian scalps were put on display at the opera house. In the East the attack was widely condemned as a symbol of government mistreatment of Indians. A congressional report later condemned Chivington's militia for indulging "in acts of barbarity of the most revolting character." The Sand Creek Massacre inspired even greater resistance by the Cheyenne and Arapaho, who were joined by the Kiowa and Comanche rising up in the Southwest. Meanwhile, the northern Sioux in Montana went on the warpath. At issue was the federal government's attempt to link Montana with the east by building a road through the Powder River territory. The Bozeman Trail cut through the favorite hunting grounds of the Sioux, which extended to the rolling hills of the Big Horn. By 1866 federal troops were under constant attack, which culminated in the massacre of eighty-two troopers under William Fetterman.

THE FAILURE OF RESERVATION POLICY   Continued warfare with American Indians sharpened controversy over how to deal with the issue. The War Department, hardened by its experience in waging war against civilians during the Civil War, advocated a military campaign to bring the Indians to their knees. On the other side, the Interior Department, which housed the Indian Office, sought to negotiate peace treaties that would establish small reservations where Indians could be protected from white intrusion and could practice agriculture.

Those federal officials who advocated negotiations found support among certain tribal chiefs. These chiefs and their followers met with a federal peace commission at Medicine Lodge Creek in late 1867. In the end, almost every chief of importance on the southern plains was represented. The final treaty negotiated with the peace commission established new reservations south of the Arkansas River for the southern Cheyenne, Arapaho, and Sioux. In turn, the Kiowa and Comanche were forced to relinquish all claims to lands in central Texas, western Kansas, and eastern New Mexico.

A year later the treaty of Fort Laramie brought temporary peace with the Sioux. The treaty cost the Sioux as well as the Winnebago their traditional lands in Minnesota when they were forced to move west into a great reserve set aside for them in the Dakotas. The Navajo particularly welcomed the peace. They had suffered severely on their Pecos River reservation from Comanche raiders, drought, floods, and disease. Following the treaty of Fort Laramie, they were finally returned to their traditional lands in New Mexico, where they flourished.

The Medicine Lodge Creek treaty was shattered in October 1867, when a party of young Cheyenne warriors and a few Arapaho and Sioux went on a rampage in Kansas. A winter campaign headed by Generals William Tecumseh Sherman and Philip Sheridan crushed the uprising. In this campaign General George A. Custer attacked the sleeping Cheyenne village of Black Kettle, killing more than a hundred, including Black Kettle and his wife, who were shot in the back while fleeing to the river. In Texas the Kiowa and Comanche continued raids that lasted until 1875, when the last hostile Indians were transported to Florida as military prisoners.

The Sioux mounted the greatest challenge to peace. The treaty of Fort Laramie in 1868 established the Great Sioux Reserve west of the Missouri River in the Dakota Territory. Although many Sioux were lured to this reservation with promises of food and annuities, some warriors headed by Sitting Bull remained off the reservation.

In 1874 tensions were heightened when gold was discovered in the Black Hills and prospectors overran the area. Finally, in 1876 the secretary of the interior declared that all Indians not on the reservation, such as Sitting Bull, would be considered hostile. General Sheridan directed three military expeditions against the Sioux and their Cheyenne allies.

One of these columns, led by General Custer, launched a premature attack on the headquarters of Sitting Bull at the Little Bighorn on June 25, 1876. Some 2,500 warriors led by Crazy Horse slaughtered 300 cavalrymen in one of the most dramatic episodes in American history.

In response, the army sent heavily armed reinforcements to Montana to hunt down the hostile Sioux and Cheyenne. Finally, in early May 1877, Crazy Horse surrendered. Sitting Bull, who had fled into Canada with his followers, was finally forced back to the reservation in 1881.

Not all white assaults on Indians were so direct. For example, the building of the Union Pacific Railroad in 1867–1868 had divided the Plains buffalo into two herds. When commercial tanners in the East found a market for buffalo hides, hunters (including whites, blacks, and Indians) began slaughtering buffalo. Others shot buffalo for sport. Between 1867 and 1883, they killed three million annually, removing a major food source of the Indians. By 1878 the southern herd had been obliterated. By 1883, a scientific expedition could find only two hundred buffalo in the entire West. As a consequence, Native Americans were forced into a life of dependency on government handouts. Moreover, most Indian lands were unsuitable for subsistence agriculture. The Indians' attempts at self-sufficiency were further hampered by corrupt Indian agents, inefficient suppliers, and incompetent bureaucrats.

The struggles of the Indians during this period revealed the tragedy of reservation policy. The most dramatic example of resistance came in the mid-1870s, when Chief Joseph led his band of Nez Perce on a heroic attempt to escape into Canada from their reservation in Oregon. Joseph skillfully maneuvered his band east into Montana, down into the Yellowstone valley. The Nez Perce had almost reached Canada when they were trapped by General Nelson Miles, who promised them that they could return to Idaho but not to Oregon.

But higher army officials overruled the decision and instead moved Joseph and his followers to the unhealthful lowlands of the Missouri River. As he watched his people die slowly of disease and starvation, Chief Joseph went to Washington to plead the case for returning to Idaho. In 1879 he declared, "I see men of my race treated as outlaws and driven from country to country, or shot down like animals. I know that my race must change. . . . We only ask an even chance to live as other men live. We ask to be recognized as men." Under pressure from reformers who took up Chief Joseph's cause, thirty-three Nez Perce women and children were returned to Idaho in 1883, followed by another hundred two years later. Chief Joseph died before his wish to return to Oregon could be fulfilled.

The treatment of the Ponca, a small, peaceful Plains tribe, gave further witness to the shortcomings of reservation policy. In the treaty of Fort Laramie, the United States had ceded the entire reservation of the Ponca to the Sioux, the Ponca's traditional enemies. The plight of the Ponca became a rallying point for critics of federal reservation policy.

The crusade for Indian rights took a dramatic turn when Standing Bear, bearing the body of his son, who had died of malaria, returned to Nebraska from South Dakota with his band in 1879. The Ponca chiefs, Bright Eyes and Standing Bear, took their cause to the general public. Appearing in full tribal regalia, they spoke to assemblies of reformers throughout the country. When army officials arrested Standing Bear, who was appearing in Omaha, townspeople hired lawyers to defend the chief. In the celebrated case of *Standing Bear v. Crook,* the federal district court ruled in 1879 that "an Indian is a 'person' within the meaning of the laws of the United States." This important case guaranteed the right of habeas corpus to Indians.

REFORMING INDIAN POLICY   By 1880 the plight of the Indians on reservations had reached urgent, even apocalyptic, proportions. Fearful that Native

Americans were on the verge of extermination, eastern reformers began a campaign to overturn reservation policy and "detribalize" the Indian.

The key group in this campaign was the Indian Rights Association, founded in Philadelphia in 1882 and made up of evangelical Protestants who opposed federal subsidies and welfare for Indians as degrading. These reformers called for a new policy of individual land ownership and the protection of Indians through law and education. This prescription was based on the evangelical ethos of individual salvation. Reformers put great stock in the redemptive quality of private property: If Indians owned property as individuals rather than collectively as tribes, they would be on their way to becoming civilized and successful.

Just as military leaders drew from their Civil War experience, Indian reformers advocated a program similar to what they had demanded for freed blacks during Reconstruction: citizenship, equal protection under the law, and education aimed at adjustment to a democratic culture and a market economy. That the program remained unrealized for blacks in the South, or that it might be unsuitable for Indians, simply was not considered by most Indian reformers.

The reformers sought to promote "Americanism." As one reformer declared, the Indians needed to have "broader desires and ampler wants." This meant that federal policy should be aimed at getting the "Indian out of the blanket and into trousers, and trousers with pockets in them, and with a pocket that ache[d] to be filled with dollars."

Only the small and influential Indian Defense Association, headed by Dr. Thomas A. Bland, defended Indian ways. He warned that the dissolution of Indian tribes would be a disaster, but he was dismissed as a romantic and a reactionary.

Many Indian reformers were women. Mary L. Bonney, a Boston educator, organized the Women's National Indian Association, which became a key lobbying group in Washington. This organization brought others into the reform movement, including Alice C. Fletcher, an ethnologist who had spent much of her life among the Omaha, Winnebago, and other tribes. The woman who gained the greatest fame was Helen Hunt Jackson. In 1881 she published *A Century of Dishonor*, a sentimental overdramatization of the Indian problem that fitted perfectly the mood of eastern reformers. Three years later she wrote *Ramona*, a moving account of the plight of the California Mission Indians.

These reformers led the fight in Congress to "detribalize" Indians. They found a champion in Massachusetts Senator Henry L. Dawes. The Dawes Severalty Act (1887) divided tribal land. It provided 160 acres to each head of a family, 80 acres to every unmarried person over eighteen, and 40 acres to those under eighteen. Where farming was impossible, this allotment was doubled. Adult Indian males who received grants were given United States citizenship.

Senator Dawes worried that the transfer to private ownership was too rapid. His fears proved prophetic. Remaining Indian lands were quickly reduced. In 1881 Indians held approximately 155.5 million acres; by 1900 their lands had been halved to 77.8 million acres. Married Indian women were not protected under the law and could be turned out of the homesteads by their husbands. Only after 1890 would these women be offered any protection.

Many Indians lacked work animals or agricultural implements to work the land. During the disastrous droughts of the 1880s, many Indians slaughtered their work animals and cattle for food. In addition, attempts to educate Indians often failed. Efforts to educate Native American children suffered from sectarian fights between Catholic and Protestant missionaries. Richard Pratt's Indian Industrial School at Carlisle, Pennsylvania, won fame for playing football against Harvard, Cornell, and Pennsylvania but generally failed in its education program.

Year after year, thousands of Native Americans left the reservations permanently and became absorbed by the larger society. Still, a highly visible minority remained on reservations, dependent on government rations and subsidies. At the same time, government agents moved to suppress the nomadic life of the Indian, to replace native religions with Christianity, and to replace Indian languages and oral traditions with written and spoken English.

In the summer of 1890, the Sioux made a last effort to distance themselves from the hostile outside world. Their cattle and crops had been destroyed by drought, and epidemics of measles, influenza, and whooping cough swept through their reservation. In the midst of this devastation, a religious revival appeared among the Sioux. Introduced by a Paiute medicine man in Nevada who called himself the Messiah, the revival centered on a Ghost Dance that promised salvation. By the time the dance reached the Dakotas, the Sioux had turned it into a more militant demonstration. Concerned that Sitting Bull might join the demonstrations, the Indian agent at Pine Ridge sent tribal police to arrest him. When a crowd of angry Indians gathered to prevent the arrest, a melee broke out. Both sides fired their weapons. When the smoke and noise cleared, Sitting Bull and seven braves lay dead.

Major General Nelson A. Miles then sent the Seventh Calvary to round up 300 braves who had gathered at Wounded Knee. A confrontation occurred. Promised by their medicine men that their Ghost shirts would protect them from bullets, the young Sioux braves charged into army artillery and machine guns. In less than an hour, 150 braves had been killed and 50 wounded.

The end result of Indian reform was astutely summarized by one old Sioux warrior who sadly observed, "They [the whites] made us many promises, more than I can remember, but they never kept but one: they promised to take our land and they took it."

CREATING A COMMUNITY

Whites settled on the land once inhabited by the American Indian. Settlers came with their own dreams, grandiose and modest. All sought to impose new order. They erected new communities, established families, and cultivated "civilized" mores and tastes. In doing so, they often looked eastward toward the regions they had left.

CIVILIZING THE WEST   By the 1880s, the Native Americans having been swept from the plains, the new settlers had built a huge cattle empire that stretched from Texas through Colorado, Wyoming, Montana, the Dakotas, Kansas, and Nebraska. The profits from buying cattle in Texas for $6 to $7 a head and selling them in Kansas for $50 to $60 a head had led to widespread speculation in cattle ranching. Capital flowed in from the East and Europe. In 1883 in Wyoming alone, twenty cattle corporations, capitalized at a total of $12 million, were formed.

By 1885, however, it was clear that the bubble was ready to burst. Costs escalated and prices fell. In 1885–1886 the cold winter and hot dry summer killed off many herds. The severe winter of 1886–1887 brought final disaster to the industry. In one of the worst winters in the West, carcass piled upon carcass. Hungry animals stripped trees bare to feed themselves. Cattle froze standing upright. By 1895 the number of cattle in Wyoming had declined to three million, from nine million in 1885. Many cattle companies were forced into bankruptcy.

Yet sheep ranchers, farmers, and merchants continued to move west. They found life hard. Many early plains settlers lived in sod houses, which were dirty, cramped, and wet. Grass roots grew through the ceilings, bringing in mud and water during rains and snows. Women, in particular, found life difficult and lonely. As guardians of the home, the haven from the corrupt outside world, these pioneer women sought to maintain traditional values. However, the frontier had a way of breaking down family life. Wife beating, child abuse, and divorce were common. Combined with high mortality rates, this meant that many frontier children grew up in single-parent homes.

To counter the frontier's corrosive influence, pioneers sought to cultivate eastern values in the West through genteel learning, manners, and religion. Schools and churches were often the first public structures erected in a community. In Seattle, for example, Yankee pioneers created the University of Washington in 1861, when there were no buildings, no professors, no books, and no students. Pioneers knew that education was important.

TECHNOLOGY AND THE WEST   Westerners were aided in their efforts to bring civilization to the frontier by railroads, the telegraph, and an improved national mail service that brought letters, books, periodicals, and religious tracts from the East. In this way the settlement of the West was very much a part of the Industrial Revolution that transformed the entire nation after the Civil War.

The Industrial Revolution was of major importance in Western development. The use of fertilizers increased farm productivity significantly. At first the tough sod of the Great Plains seemed impervious to plows, but James Oliver's smooth-surfaced plow easily slipped through the rich soils of the Plains without clogging up. The seated plow followed. The flat expanse of the Plains invited further technological innovation, which soon included reapers, seed scatterers, grain drills, and mowing machines. A combine that harvested and tied wheat was developed in the 1880s by Cyrus McCormick. Such machinery freed farmers from much of the drudgery of manual labor and from the need to assemble large gangs of workers for the harvest. At the start of the Civil War, a farmer could plant and harvest no more than seven and half acres of wheat; by 1890 he could plant and harvest 135 acres.

Although most farms and ranches remained small and were operated by single families, huge "bonanza" farms emerged in the northern Plains states. Some of these farms occupied tens of thousand of acres, employed hundreds of migratory workers, and used heavy equipment to harvest vast amounts of wheat or corn. In 1881 one North Dakota farm produced some 600,000 bushels of wheat.

Similarly, wheat farmers in California's Central Valley harvested huge quantities of hard winter wheat. California farmers readily accepted technological advances, using steam-driven harvesting combines that could thresh and bag as much as 450 pounds of wheat a minute. In the early 1880s wheat prices remained high and farmers profited.

Farmers found a ready market for their wheat. In the 1880s they exported 153 million bushels of wheat to England each year. Railroads, grain elevators, and shipping companies prospered. Hard spring wheat thrived in Minnesota and the Dakotas, while Kansas and Nebraska proved to be ideally suited for hard kernel red wheat. Flour mills in Minneapolis, Kansas City, and St. Louis took advantage of new processing methods and marketing techniques.

To protect their lands from roaming cattle and trespassers, westerners strung barbed wire, the invention of Joseph F. Glidden of DeKalb, Illinois. Produced in mass quantities by a Massachusetts manufacturing firm, barbed wire transformed much of the western landscape. Similarly, mechanical refrigeration and assembly-line slaughtering transformed the meatpacking industry, allowing mass quantities of processed beef to be shipped to eastern cities, first from Chicago and later from cities farther west such as Omaha. Refrigeration also allowed California to ship fruits, nuts, and vegetables to eastern markets.

Anticipating that farmers, ranchers, and miners would need services, settlers often established towns in the West before the farms, ranches, and mines existed. Some towns that offered transportation and manufacturing services developed into sizable cities, bringing together a rich mix of peoples and religions. This diversity itself created social tensions. On the West Coast, and especially in San Francisco, these feelings were expressed in an anti-Chinese movement that spilled over to state politics when Dennis Kearny, leader of the Workingman's Party, forced the inclusion of a clause in the revised state constitution of 1879 that read, "No native of China, idiot, insane person, or person convicted of an infamous crime . . . shall ever exercise the privileges of this state."

CONCLUSION

Two years after Wounded Knee, a young historian from the University of Wisconsin named Frederick Jackson Turner appeared before the annual meeting of historians in Chicago to read his essay, "The Significance of the Frontier in American History." In this seminal paper he declared that the frontier had passed, replaced by civilized society. By the 1890s the plains and the mountains between the Mississippi River and the Pacific Ocean had been settled by people streaming westward from the Missouri River and eastward from the Pacific shore. They had come seeking wealth in gold and silver, timber and agriculture, commerce and politics. In doing so they displaced and nearly destroyed native peoples, united a continent, and prepared the nation for its destiny.

Recommended Readings

DOCUMENTS: Samuel Clemens (Mark Twain), *Roughing It,* (1871); Sallie Reynolds Matthews, *Interwoven: A Pioneer Chronicle* (1982); H. G. Merriam, ed., *Way Out West: Recollections and Tales* (1969); Mari Sandoz, *Old Jules* (1935); Wallace Stegner, *Wolf Willow: A History, a Story, and a Memory of the Last Plains Frontier* (1983).

READINGS: Ray Allen Billington, *Westward Expansion: A History of the American Frontier* (1967); Dee Brown, *Bury My Heart at Wounded Knee* (1970); Albert Camarillo, *Chicanos in a Changing Society* (1976); David Dary, *Cowboy Culture: A Saga of Five Centuries* (1981); Richard Griswold del Castillo, *La Familia: Chicano Families in the Urban Southwest* (1983); Arnoldo de Leon, *They Called Them Greasers: Anglo Attitudes Toward Mexicans in Texas* (1983); Robert K. Dykstra, *The Cattle Towns* (1968); Elizabeth Hampsten, *Read This Only to Yourself: The Private Writings of Midwest Women, 1880–1910* (1982); Howard Robert Lamar, *The Far Southwest* (1966); Patricia Nelson Limerick, *The Legacy of Conquest: The Unbroken Fast of the American West* (1987); Robert Mardock, *Reformers and the American Indian* (1971); Sandra L. Myres, *Westering Women and the Frontier Experience* (1982); Rodman Wilson Paul, *Mining Frontiers of the Far West* (1963); Francis Paul Prucha, *American Indian Policy in Crisis* (1976); Robert J. Rosenbaum, *Mexicano Resistance in the Southwest* (1981); Lillian Schlissel, *Women's Diaries of the Westward Journey* (1982); Richard Slotkin, *The Fatal Environment* (1985); Robert M. Utley, *The Indian Frontier of the American West* (1984) and *The Last Days of the Sioux Nation* (1963); Elliot West, *Growing Up with the Country: Childhood and the Far West Frontier* (1989); Richard White, *"It's Your Misfortune and None of My Own": A New History of the American West* (1991).

17

❧❧

Industry and Labor in the Gilded Age

OVERVIEW   The late nineteenth century was an age of enterprise. Huge industrial combines flourished, creating wealth previously unimaginable. The country was on its way to becoming the wealthiest economic power in history. This second industrial revolution brought mass-produced goods and new technology to the average American consumer, raising the nation's standard of living but also creating profound tensions between labor and capital. To many Americans of this period, the United States appeared to be a study in contrasts.

AN INDUSTRIAL GIANT IS BORN

By the late nineteenth century, the United States, although growing, was not yet the dominant force in the world economy. Great Britain led the world in industrial output, and both France and Germany produced more than the United States. But the United States was catching up; by 1900, U.S. production surpassed the combined output of the major European industrial powers. The gross national product, corrected for inflation, tripled between 1860 and 1900. This second industrial revolution, following the earlier Market Revolution, transformed industry, manufacturing, transportation, and work itself. In many industries, factories became more extensive operations, hiring larger workforces and employing more complex, more productive machinery. Railroad lines and telegraph systems transformed isolated communities into a single society. Railroad lines cooperated in setting standards, but their unscrupulous business practices prompted the government to begin to regulate private enterprise.

At the time, many people understood the country's economic growth as a tale of the deeds of heroic individuals: The inventors who by 1900 were jamming the U.S. patent office with more than a million new inventions a year, and men like Andrew Carnegie, John D. Rockefeller, James J. Hill, Philip Armour, and James B. Duke, who created huge corporations. Yet there were no research and development programs to speak of; American firms imported some of the most important technologies. And although the drive of individual men played a role in building businesses, so did less personal conditions. The nation possessed two-thirds of the world's known coal deposits, high-quality iron ore in abundance, and enough precious metals, gold, silver, and copper to arouse the envy of the ancient pharaohs. The next decades were to reveal immense reserves of petroleum. Between 1870 and 1900, the population of the United States grew from 39,905 to 96,094, creating a huge domestic market. Immigrants accounted for a good deal of the population increase, supplying skilled and unskilled labor and entrepreneurial energy. Lastly, the United States possessed a legal system friendly to private property, financial markets that organized investment, and governments at all levels that promoted business.

Economic expansion, however, did not follow a smooth upward curve. All Western industrialized nations felt the effects of a long trend of deflation. Prices fell as new machinery and methods increased the productivity of farms and factories and the industrial goods and staple crops of more and more nations competed for shares of the world market. This was a good trend for consumers and surviving businesses, but it was a persistent headache for farmers and businessmen poised on the edge of failure. Severe depressions from 1873 to 1877 and from 1893 to 1897, as well as a milder panic from 1883 to 1885, punctured economic growth. Overall, real wages rose during the late nineteenth century; but businesses' incessant drive for greater productivity spawned a remarkably high level of labor militancy. Businessmen despised competition and the instability of the business cycle, and they searched for ways to insulate themselves from the market's danger.

PRODUCING AN ECONOMIC REVOLUTION   During the economic expansion, new steel and petroleum industries were created. Manufacturing output soared from $1.8 billion in 1860 to $13 billion in 1900. Textile and iron production doubled.

Greater output meant larger factories. In many industries the average plant size doubled. Before the Civil War, a workforce of four hundred employees in a firm was rare. By 1900 there were more than one thousand factories that employed more than five hundred workers. In the steel industry fourteen foundries each employed six thousand or more workers. Many industries introduced techniques of mass production; by the 1870s and 1880s, continuous production methods were in use for oil, sugar, and whiskey. These techniques allowed raw materials to be refined into finished products in a single factory.

New machines also created breakthroughs. For example, the introduction of a cigarette-making machine in 1881 changed the tobacco industry forever. A single worker could make 3,000 cigarettes per day; by the mid-1880s one machine could make 120,000. New machinery also was introduced in the match, soap, and grain-milling industries.

RAILROADS TRANSPORT A REVOLUTION   As manufacturing concerns and production grew, the various parts of the United States were linked as a nation and a market by the extensive railroad and telegraph system. The railroads brought farm and factory, country and town closer together, while the telegraph, and later the telephone, increased knowledge, business efficiency, and public debate. In 1860 the nation had only thirty thousand miles of railroad track; by 1900 more track had been laid than in all of Europe, including Russia. In 1866 the three leading telegraph companies merged to form Western Union. By 1915 this company operated 1.6 million miles of wire. This transportation and communications system linked every state and major city, integrating regions and isolated communities into a single society.

Nothing short of the Civil War armies matched the complexity and scale of the railroads. The cost of track, buildings, maintenance, and equipment dwarfed that of even the largest pre–Civil War firms. To help the railroads raise money, the federal and state governments pitched in with land grants and loans. Government aid was especially important in the West, where the sparse population meant that return on investment was far in the future. Private investment, both domestic and foreign, provided the rest; organizing it made the New York Stock Exchange an important player among world stock markets. The vast territory and workforce, and the complex calculations needed to figure rates and costs, forced railroads to create new accounting methods and bureaucratic structures. Competition was a potentially ruinous hazard, so managers and owners groped for effective ways to bring order to the industry.

As early as the 1860s and 1870s, the railroads tried to find ways to coordinate both rates and operating systems. Managers made relatively quick work of setting uniform standards for track, equipment, and operating procedures. The railroads even defined time: In 1884 they divided the nation into four time zones, a scheduling convenience that soon set the watches of Kansas farmers, Cleveland factory workers, and railroad conductors alike. Curbing competition proved more difficult. Busy routes enticed competitors, who offered generous discounts to large customers or dropped prices. Given the steep fixed costs in the industry, the resulting rate wars, which aimed to drive out existing lines or manipulate stock prices, could ruin lines. In the 1870s some railroads entered into pooling agreements with their competitors, in which they agreed to charge certain rates and divided the territory they served. But, as one executive remarked, "the only bond which holds this government together is the intelligence and good faith of the parties." Inevitably, intelligence and good faith failed. When hard times struck in the 1870s, railroads desperate to meet debt payment cut prices to increase their market shares. Both farmers and merchants smelled unethical collusion in pooling agreements, but the temptation for railroad owners to break ranks trampled these agreements more thoroughly than any action by customers could have.

Jay Gould, the notorious speculator, kicked off the next round of efforts to control competition. Inspired by the number of lines that had not recovered from depression-induced financial distress in the late 1870s, Gould began to borrow and buy with an eye toward constructing his own transcontinental system. By 1882 Gould had put together a ragtag system consisting of 15,854 miles of track, or 15 percent of the nation's total. Gould made no real attempt to run it; not all of his empire connected. His system soon fell apart, although, as was typical, not without profit for Gould.

Gould's bold attempt chastened railroad executives. To prevent future disruptions from the likes of Gould and to minimize competition and costs, they set about building their own systems. The Sante Fe Railroad added links to the Pacific coast and to the East from its base in the Southwest; by 1888 it covered eighteen thousand miles. The Union Pacific Railroad expanded eastward; the New York Central Railroad bought railroads that served the Midwest. By 1893 thirty-three companies owned 69 percent of the nation's rails. Four major trunk lines served the Northeast, five the South, and five the regions west of the Mississippi. Much of the expansion came from buying existing lines, but the railroads also built new track: seventy-five thousand miles of it, more than in any other single decade. Railroad managers believed that expansion was the only route to long-term stability, even if expansion risked insolvency. Indeed, by the onset of the depression of the 1890s, more than half of the new mileage had fallen into receivership. By 1893, with discipline enforced by investment bankers, the era of railroad warfare and empire-building was over. Still, debt lingered: By 1900 the combined debt of the railroads stood at $5.1 billion, nearly five times the debt of the federal government.

The railroads were central to the process of American industrialization, but their legacy was mixed. They provided a national transportation system, with more than 193,300 miles of track laid by 1900 (almost four times the mileage that existed in 1870); their reliable and rapid service made nationwide operations affordable for other firms. They made travel safer and quicker for ordinary Americans. They created new towns and cities and gave farmers a national market. They bequeathed bureaucratic structure, management practices, and accounting procedures to other corporations. For example, in the 1850s the Pennsylvania Railroad restructured its organization to enable regional superintendents to provide elaborate accounting and traffic reports to a central headquarters so that rates could be set and profits accurately predicted and measured. In linking their regional offices to the central office, railroads organized a complex communications system that relied on the telegraph.

Corruption and shady deals also traveled the rails, and the railroads left a public suspicious of corporate practices. The scent of corruption always followed the aid the government extended to the railroads, even though the railroads repaid the loans with interest, and much of the land given to them was all but worthless to anyone else. Such aid ceased to be important to the railroads by the 1880s, but corruption continued. Pennsylvanians believed that the Pennsylvania Railroad owned their legislature; Californians suspected that the Union Pacific ran their state. Politicians received free passes for travel (which they doled out to their constituents) and campaign contributions. Far too common were sales of watered stock (offerings priced well beyond the suspected value of a company) and bonds cashed in for roads never built. A pricing system that made it cheaper to ship goods across the country than between cities a hundred miles apart made sense to managers but not to customers. Because so many people depended on them, the railroads' attempts to shield themselves from competition alarmed many Americans.

Public pressure resulting from such abuses pushed Congress to establish the five-member Interstate Commerce Commission (1887) to oversee the practices of railroads. The creation of the ICC marked an important turning point in government–business relations in America: The federal government now exercised its power to regulate private enterprise in the public interest. Railroads changed the law in other ways, one of the most significant being in bankruptcy law. In 1884 the federal district court of Missouri agreed to place Jay Gould's Wabash line into receivership before it actually defaulted on its loans; moreover, the court agreed to appoint receivers friendly to Jay Gould. Many interpreted the ruling as the result of Gould's insidious influence on the courts, but the importance of the case rested in the court's implicit acknowledgement that a system of transportation was more important than its parts.

THE REVOLUTION SPREADS   Most businesses in America were not big. Firms owned by a single individual or a partnership and employing only a handful of people accounted for most manufactured products. Yet the same circumstances that produced the massive railroad corporations also led to consolidation in important sectors of American manufacturing. The techniques of mass production—new technologies and machinery, division of labor, and continuous production—lowered prices. In some industries, larger firms enjoyed economies of scale: They could demand discounts on material and transportation and make the most efficient use of expensive machinery. Some corporations grew through vertical integration, gaining control of costs by handling every aspect of manufacture and distribution of a product, from raw materials to advertising. Others expanded through horizontal integration, buying out erstwhile competitors in the same business. Most giant corporations used both methods. Size, however, did not eliminate competition. Like the railroads, manufacturers formed pools and trusts to combat the effects of competition. Two examples, steel and oil, and the two celebrity figures who dominated them, illustrate the process of corporate expansion. A third figure, J. P. Morgan, illustrates how finance brought some order to industrial expansion.

Steel: Andrew Carnegie   The story of steel is the story of Andrew Carnegie. Of all of the great industrialists, his life comes closest to a rags-to-riches tale. Born in Scotland to a handloom weaver and his wife, young Carnegie immigrated to the United States with his parents in 1848. Starting out as a bobbin boy at the age of thirteen, he eventually landed a job as a telegraph operator with the Pennsylvania Railroad. Carnegie's hard work, charm, and talent caught the eye of Thomas Scott, then superintendent and later president of the railroad, who initiated Carnegie into the mysteries of modern management and stock market speculation. At the age of twenty-eight, Carnegie's success with the latter allowed him to pocket a millionaire's income on a salary of $2,400 a year, and in 1872 he moved on to a new interest: iron and steel.

At this point steelmaking was almost more a craft than a mass production industry. In 1857, however, a practical method for turning iron into harder, more durable steel was invented that involved forcing cold air through molten iron to fire out impurities. This required the judgment of skilled workers, who had both a union and the independence to hire their own men and set their schedules. New technologies—first the Bessemer

Andrew Carnegie (1835–1919), steel industrialist, devoted himself to social and educational advancement in the United States and Great Britain, funding the building of more than 2,500 public libraries. World War I shattered his dreams of international peace. (Brown Brothers)

converter, a British import, and later the open-hearth furnace and integrated production methods that linked the steps of the steelmaking process—reduced the need for skilled workers and opened the way to mass production. Carnegie adopted these new methods enthusiastically. Beginning with the first plant he opened, outside of Pittsburgh, he applied the management lessons he had learned from Scott, especially the idea that, if a manager watched costs, profits would take care of themselves. Carnegie was so fanatical about costs that he had a newly-installed Bessemer converter ripped out when the newer German-designed open-hearth furnace became available. To gain further control over costs, Carnegie bought ore fields in the Mesabi Range and ships, docks, warehouses, and railroad lines to transport the ore. Vertical integration was followed by horizontal integration; Carnegie's ability to produce steel far more cheaply than anyone else could enabled him to ride out depressions and induce rivals to sell out. By 1900 Carnegie dominated the entire industry except finishing, a field he chose not to enter. His plants produced 322,000 tons of steel in 1890 and 3,000,000 tons in 1900. His managers pored over accounts every month, searching for ways to "get it ten cents cheaper the next year or the next month," as one wrote. His giant Edgar Thompson works made steel for $36.52 a ton in 1878; twenty years later it turned out steel rails at $12.00 a ton. Profits did take care of themselves. Carnegie Steel posted profits of $40,000,000 in 1900 alone.

Carnegie eventually turned away from business toward writing about capitalism, democracy, the evils of war, and the responsibilities of wealth, and toward giving away as much of his fortune as possible before he died. He endowed libraries by the score, as well as museums, civic buildings, and schools, and set up a foundation dedicated to the advancement of peace. His was a household name in the United States and Europe.

Oil: John D. Rockefeller   As dour in public as Carnegie was voluble, and lacking Carnegie's knack for public relations, John D. Rockefeller became the reviled king of the oil trust. The tight-lipped, pious son of strict Baptist parents, Rockefeller grew up in upstate New York. Discipline came from his mother, who tied him to a post and beat him for transgressions; business skills came from his father, a peddler of quack patent medicines who cheated his sons in trades to "make 'em sharp." Upon moving to Cleveland with his parents, Rockefeller opened a grain business and advanced loans to farmers. Benefiting from government contracts during the Civil War, his business prospered. Rockefeller took the profits to invest in a new industry: oil.

Petroleum was hardly a new discovery, but the lack of an efficient method of extracting it from the earth limited its applications. In 1859 Edwin Drake figured out how to drill for oil in northwestern Pennsylvania, and the boom was on. Derricks soon pounded the landscape in western Pennsylvania, southwestern New York state, and Ohio, turning country villages and farms into a mess of boomtowns, mud, and grease, and causing spectacular fires that drew spectators from miles away. Rockefeller correctly determined that money was to be made in refining, not drilling; Drake died broke, and the thousands of small drilling operations did not make their owners wealthy. After touring northwestern Pennsylvania in 1863, Rockefeller decided to build his first refinery in Cleveland.

Like most young industries, the oil business suffered from competition generated by numerous inefficient producers and wildly fluctuating prices. Rockefeller hated what he saw as the waste of competitive capitalism and sought to bring the industry under his own control. His Standard Oil Company, founded in 1867, operated efficient refineries, but efficiency alone would not make Standard Oil dominant in the industry. First, Rockefeller raised the funds to secretly buy all of the refineries—more than one hundred—in Cleveland and Pittsburgh. But periodic spikes in prices still brought new drillers and refineries into the business, which then saturated the markets for petroleum products and forced prices ruinously low. So Rockefeller extracted secret agreements from the railroads to ship his products at a lower rate than his competitors paid, in exchange for large, regular shipments. He and the owners of other large refineries received rebates, a portion of the higher rates charged to those outside the charmed circle. Rockefeller also formed a cartel among eastern producers in the early 1870s. This experience taught him that "producers' and refiners' associations were ropes of sand": Like such arrangements among railroad companies, this one broke under the incentive to undersell the cartel. The experience generated bad press as well as a lesson about informal cartels; complaints from drillers and small refineries inspired an investigation by the Pennsylvania legislature and closer legislative scrutiny of his corporations.

Rockefeller turned to an ultimately more efficient method, the trust. He persuaded rivals to sell out to him for cash or stock or face the consequences of his command over efficient production and cheap shipping. These, too, were secret agreements; on paper, it appeared that the companies still existed independently. Secrecy aided arm twisting, since no one but Rockefeller knew which companies had decided to join Standard Oil, a fact that left the extent of the corporation's power to the imagination. These stock agreements raised legal problems because states prohibited the corporations they chartered from holding stock in other corporations. Standard Oil lawyers found a way around that limitation in 1881. A board of trustees headed by Rockefeller held the stock of both Standard Oil and subsidiary companies and exchanged it for certificates from a "trust" estate. Other industries, notably sugar and whiskey, soon copied Standard Oil's innovation. The public uproar that followed was enough to persuade Congress to pass the Sherman Antitrust Act in 1890, which aimed to curb combinations that monopolized or restrained trade. Rockefeller responded by reorganizing his firm into several companies, which he controlled through interlocking boards of directors.

New Jersey made controlling the industry even easier. In 1899 the state legislature passed a new incorporation law that permitted companies to hold stock in other firms. Numerous corporations, including Standard Oil, promptly moved to New Jersey, which, with Delaware, remained "the mother of trusts" even after other states passed similar laws. Rockefeller's empire continued to grow. By the 1890s Standard Oil refined over 90 percent of the nation's oil and recorded profits of about $8 million each year. Early in the twentieth century, profits rose to about $57 million; by 1913 Rockefeller had amassed a personal fortune of $325 million, even after giving millions to charity. According to Rockefeller, his consolidation of the oil industry merely represented progress: "The movement was the origin of the whole system of modern economic administration. It has revolutionized the way of doing business all over the world. The time was ripe for it. It had to come, although all we saw at the moment was to save ourselves from wasteful conditions. . . . The day of combination is here to stay. Individualism has gone, never to return."

Finance: J. P. Morgan   Carnegie and Rockefeller consolidated the steel and oil industries, respectively. They were innovators who introduced the modern business practices of cost accounting, expertise, and continuous production. In this way, they participated in the emergence of corporate capitalism; but it was their contemporary, financier J. P. Morgan, who brought a new vision of corporate capitalism.

John Pierpont Morgan's background and career differed radically from Carnegie's and Rockefeller's. Born to wealth in 1835, he was the son of a well-known American financier based in London. His grandfather, for whom he was named, had founded the Aetna Fire Insurance Company. Although J. P. grew into a hulk of a man who stood 6'2" and weighed 230 pounds, he suffered from a skin disease, which so disfigured his nose that some would turn away in disgust. Later, on Wall Street, his enemies called him "liver nose."

Morgan distrusted the old days of cutthroat competition. Early in his career as an operator on Wall Street, he had seen unscrupulous speculators bring disaster to business and financial markets alike. Morgan saw the market as a man-made institution. Because the market was a creation of society, not of nature, he believed that it could be organized and rationalized. Because he believed that the market was not a God-given and unchanging institution, he sought to consolidate and stabilize capitalism by eliminating unnecessary competition and creating cooperation among corporations.

In 1856 he joined his father's firm in London, but the two remained estranged. The following year Morgan returned to New York to work as a representative for both the prestigious George Peabody Company and his father's firm. During the Civil War he speculated in army supplies and gold. In 1871, with Anthony J. Drexel, he formed the investment company of Drexel, Morgan and Company. Through associates in Philadelphia, Paris, and London, Morgan's firm became one of the most powerful banking houses in the world. Following the collapse of Jay Cooke's company in 1873, the Morgan firm became the leading government financing agency.

One of his greatest triumphs came in 1895, when he formed an international syndicate that effectively halted a drain of gold from the federal treasury. Morgan's syndicate made approximately $300,000, but rumors placed profits in the millions. This incident only confirmed what many critics had claimed: Wall Street and the moneyed interests had a stranglehold on the federal government (see chapter 20).

Morgan also showed a talent for financing and reorganizing American railroads. He understood that European investors wanted stability. He sought, therefore, to eliminate ruthless competition in order to maintain European confidence in American securities. When William Vanderbilt's New York Central Railroad threatened war with J. Edgar Thompson's Pennsylvania Railroad, Morgan brought the two parties together on his yacht, the *Corsair*, to resolve their differences.

Morgan's greatest triumph came during the depression of 1893, when he refinanced many American corporations and railroads that were on the verge of collapse. During the 1880s the railroads had overexpanded, laying more than seventy-five thousand miles of track in that decade alone. Foreclosure sales during the depression closed forty thousand miles of track. Morgan stepped in to refinance the Santa Fe, Erie, Northern Pacific, and Reading lines. The entire southern system was reorganized. The price he extracted was modest: He insisted on consolidation and placed his men on the boards of many of these corporations. If his methods were seen as ruthless at the time, he nonetheless contributed to corporate stability in this new age of capitalism.

In 1900 he went head to head with Andrew Carnegie. Morgan had become interested in steel when he financed the Federal Steel Company and the National Tube Company. These firms challenged Carnegie in finished steel products. Carnegie threatened to build new furnaces and plants to take on his rivals, including Morgan. Knowing full well what a fight with Carnegie would mean, the other steelmakers urged Morgan to make peace. Morgan and Carnegie met, and Morgan asked Carnegie how much he wanted for his company. Carnegie wrote his price on a napkin: $500 million. Morgan agreed. With the purchase of Carnegie Steel, Morgan consolidated his other steel interests and organized U.S. Steel, the first billion-dollar corporation. In 1901 the massive U.S. Steel Corporation consolidated the steel industry, controlling about three-fifths of the business essential to building industrial America. It was the right size, Morgan believed, to compete successfully in world markets against German and British competitors, as well as in the American market. Others found its size and power frightening. Journalist Ray Stannard Baker wrote, "It receives and expends more every year than any but the very greatest of the world's national governments. Its debt is larger than that of many of the lesser nations of Europe; it absolutely controls the destinies of a population nearly as large as that of Maryland or Nebraska."

In the 1890s a coincidence brought industry and finance together, largely on the financiers' terms. In the 1870s and 1880s, corporations usually financed their empires though partnerships and money borrowed from local lenders, while financiers focused on trade in railroad securities, government bonds, currency, and precious metals. The great era of railroad building had passed by the 1890s and with it the lively market in railroad securities. At the same time, some businesses searched for reliable forms of combination. The state of Ohio voided the trust Standard Oil had constructed, and the courts of Louisiana, Nebraska, Illinois, and New York attacked trust agreements in the cotton oil, whiskey, and sugar industries. Thus the holding company was born, in which stock from a number of companies was transferred to the remaining firm. Achieving enhanced economies of scale mattered in some mergers, but evading competition mattered more. The depression of the 1890s had brought on a round of price cuts in many industries in the face of falling demand. Combination would eliminate "ruinous" competition.

As they had in the case of the railroads, financiers stepped in to reorganize the businesses and restore profits and peace. Men such as J. P. Morgan brought companies together, giving stock in the new company to the sellers, the remaining owners, and to their own firms. The rest went to the investing public, which funded the deal. By 1904, when the merger movement faded, 318 mergers had taken place, involving 5,300 plants and an investment of more than $7 billion. About 1,800 firms disappeared, and the new consolidated firms usually controlled half or more of their markets. Mergers gave a new boost to the stock market and appeared to quiet competitive pressures.

The merger movement sparked anxiety. Many Americans feared that monopolies had taken control of the economy and had the power to dictate to their workers, consumers, and government alike. Some firms did come out of the merger movement with near-monopolistic control. The American Sugar Company held 98 percent of the nation's cane sugar refining capacity in 1892; International Harvester made more than 90 percent of the grain binders, 80 percent of the mowers, and 60 percent of the rakes. But the American Sugar Company's market share dropped to 42 percent in 1910 as beet sugar provided an alternative to cane sugar. International Harvester's share also dropped as competitors entered the field. Even Standard Oil failed to stave off competition for long. Rockefeller could not control the discovery of new oil deposits, such as the tremendous Texas and Oklahoma fields discovered in the early twentieth century. And Standard Oil did not anticipate that fuel oil would be an important market. The firm stuck with kerosene, even as electric lights replaced kerosene lamps, and by 1911 other companies controlled 70 percent of the fuel oil market. In industries where fashion, innovation, and ease of entry made consolidation unlikely—bicycles, wallpaper, buttons, and glue, for example—combinations failed. But the monopoly question roiled the nation's politics and courtrooms in the late nineteenth and early twentieth centuries, driven by the common perception that big business was driving out small business.

TRANSFORMING THE MIDDLE CLASS   The greatest transformation brought about by the corporate revolution was the rise of the middle class. The corporation created new occupations for middle managers, accountants, service employees, and office workers. In 1870 less than 2 percent of the workforce was employed in clerical operations; by 1900 more than 35 percent was white collar. Women were all but absent from this workforce in 1870, but by 1900 they held a quarter of all clerical jobs.

New white-collar occupations provided upward mobility. Prerequisites for working in the new corporate office were a solid foundation in English grammar and a proficiency in writing. Many managers came up through the ranks of labor. Others were drawn from the 8 percent of the population that graduated from high school. Although they gave up some individuality to work in new bureaucratic structures, workers gained new opportunities and a sense of challenge through participating in the creation of new forms of business.

The middle class and, increasingly, the working class became the market for new products and cheaper versions of standard items. Canned food, for example, had existed for many years, but people used it mostly in emergencies: It was expensive (a tinsmith might make 1,500 cans per day) and sometimes lethal (mistakes were made in processing). In 1883 Edwin and O. W. Norton put their "automatic line" canning system into production; it soldered 50 cans a minute and closed 4,400 an hour. H. J. Heinz, a producer of pickles and relishes in the Pittsburgh region, offered such exotic items as canned pineapples as well as pickles, relishes, pears, tuna, and ketchup to a national market. Gail Borden, who dreamed up no end of goofy inventions, learned that, although a ship that could sail the prairies had no takers, canned condensed milk did. In all of these cases and more—crackers, matches, biscuits, soap, and soft drinks—companies used advertising and trademarks to build national markets and national name recognition for inexpensive, mass-produced consumer goods.

New products tempted middle-class consumers. George Eastman, a maker of photographic paper and glass plates in Rochester, New York, found a way to mass-produce a paper-based film attached to gelatin emulsion that recorded negative images. A new market, amateur photographers, took to the product, and soon middle-class vacationers produced their own records of landscapes and family gatherings. The telephone proved its importance to both businesses and consumers. Alexander Graham Bell had emigrated from Scotland to Canada and then to Boston in his twenties. After a series of experiments, he devised a working telephone in 1876; he publicly demonstrated it in a conversation linking New York and Boston a year later. His Bell Telephone Company, formed in 1877, fought off a series of lawsuits from Western Union over patents and became the core of American Telephone and Telegraph in 1900.

Men like Thomas Edison made new technology fit traditional values. Edison's was a story of the virtues of hard work, of self-confidence cloaked in appealing modesty, and of native intelligence triumphing over formal training. Edison, whose teachers found him unpromising and dull, left school at the age of seven but retained a fascination with chemistry and physics. He was selling newspapers and candy on a railroad when his lucky day came: The child of a stationmaster was about to killed by a train when Edison rescued him. To reward Edison, the stationmaster taught him telegraphy. Edison also tinkered, developing a stock ticker to keep track of the growing volume of trades on Wall Street and a telegraph wire that could simultaneously send and receive as many as four messages at a time.

With the proceeds from the sales of these items, Edison opened an "invention factory" in Menlo Park, New Jersey, complete with time schedule: "a minor invention every ten days and a big thing every six months or so." Edison and his assistants (who had the formal training Edison lacked) perfected a movie camera and developed the electrified railroad, the fluorescent lamp, and the storage battery. The phonograph, one of Edison's few solo inventions, recorded sound on wax cylinders, the wonder of which drew paying customers to see the machine that talked. Edison gained fame as the inventor of the electric light bulb, and his dream of "lights so cheap that only the wealthy can afford to burn candles" came to pass.

The greatly increased quantity and variety of consumer goods changed retail sales. Urban residents shopped in palatial department stores, a retail trend that developed in the late 1850s. Selling all manner of goods at fixed prices and offering amenities such as large sales staffs, lunchrooms, rest areas, and soda fountains, these stores made shopping entertainment for middle-class women. In small towns, dry-goods stores replaced generic barrels of flour and crackers with a variety of packaged and branded goods, most made hundreds of miles away. Rural merchants ignored the new, lower-priced products at their peril, for mail-order companies such as Sears, Roebuck and Montgomery Ward sold everything from houses to underwear through their catalogues. Businesses quickly adopted inventions that improved the quality of information their operations required; armies of white-collar workers kept tabs on production and costs with adding machines (1888), produced neat correspondence on typewriters, and accelerated communication with the telephone.

One innovation led to the next. Flat phonograph records replaced Edison's cylinders, which opened the way to a use for the invention that Edison never imagined: recorded music. Railroad work and travel were made safer by George Westinghouse's inventions: the air brake, which replaced hand cranks that stopped each car individually, and a signal system that regulated traffic. He also improved on Edison's electrical system. Edison's electrical devices were powered by direct current, which was safe but unable to generate power practically over long distances. Westinghouse used alternating current, trickier to handle but able to travel further without degradation. Edison did his best to win the battle of the currents, even illustrating the dangers of alternating current by having his assistants connect stray dogs and cats to an alternating current generator. The electrocuted animals failed to win the argument for Edison. Alternating current became the standard, and distant generating stations passed current through transformers to power cities, villages, and even scattered farms. The New York state legislature, however, alerted by Edison to the deadly possibilities of alternating current, inquired about its effects on people. Satisfied, the state had Westinghouse design an electric chair that waited at the end of death row in New York.

Americans argued about what all of this technological change meant for them. The price of basic items and even small luxuries dropped to within the reach of nearly anyone, and amazing new products promised to make life easier and more pleasant. Yet, fouled water, soil, and air followed massive industrial production everywhere. Mass production spewed out goods inexpensively but put increasing pressure on workers, who watched their working conditions deteriorate and control over the pace of their labor diminish. No clear answer emerged to the question of how to square a fast-paced commercial culture with traditional ideas about neighborliness and respect for skill.

JUSTIFYING WEALTH   The appearance of consumer goods and industrial wealth was rapid enough to demand explanation. Charles Darwin's *Origin of Species* inadvertently provided one theory. Species best suited to their environments survived, said Darwin, and the strongest within each species reproduced. Herbert Spencer, a British intellectual, applied to human society the idea that blind forces weed out the weak and reward the strong. Unlike Darwin, he argued that evolution was progress: Society improved, but only if humans, like animals, would simply allow nature to take its ultimately benevolent, if immediately messy, course. Philosophers had no trouble picking apart the wishful thinking and hazy assumptions in Spencer's work, but social Darwinism, as the theory was labeled, found a large audience in the United States.

Spencer's books sold well. Protestant ministers cited his ideas approvingly; businessmen feted Spencer during his tour of the United States. Yet few people swallowed his ideas whole. The Reverend Henry Ward Beecher and his well-heeled Brooklyn congregation might like the part about success demonstrating fitness, but most were unwilling to concede that charity impeded the progress of the race or that public schools encouraged the unfit to reproduce. Andrew Carnegie tirelessly promoted Spencer's work, but the two disagreed about charity and even progress: Where Carnegie saw progress in the smoke pouring from Pittsburgh steel mills, Spencer, with the steel magnate as his tour guide, saw a soot-covered vision of hell. William Graham Sumner, the Yale sociologist considered Spencer's most devoted American disciple, argued that, in the interest of progress, government should do no more than protect the property of men and the honor of women. But Sumner's heroes were not the captains of industry who, given half the chance, used government to gain monopolies. Sumner sang the praises of the Forgotten Man who, lacking a great fortune, got by without help and minded his own business.

Even if the particulars of social Darwinism were open to interpretation, the general idea had two immediate uses. First, it provided a justification for the great fortunes, as well as the gap between rich and poor, of the late nineteenth century. If lavish displays of wealth stank of corruption in the early years of the republic, they were featured newspaper articles in the Gilded Age. The second use of Spenserian sociology was to justify a limited role for government in the economy. While few were willing to see government stripped down to a police force and court system that protected private property, the nation's economics professors and legal theorists argued for the tiniest possible amount of interference in the economy. Judges in the nation's appellate courts had the opportunity to put these ideas into practice. Where weak-minded legislatures sometimes attempted to regulate railroads and corporate practices, the courts often stepped in to restore the rights of property. "There are so many jackasses about nowadays who think property has no rights that the filling of Supreme Court vacancies is the most important function of the Presidential office," said one railroad executive.

The courts' impact was especially felt in labor law. In the 1880s and 1890s, the appellate court of New York defended property rights in throwing out a law aimed at closing sweatshops in the cigarmaking industry. Courts in Pennsylvania and Missouri defended "freedom of contract" in voiding laws that prohibited payment in script rather than legal tender. Courts in several states limited picketing and striking for unionized workplaces. In the 1880s the United States Supreme Court shielded the property rights of corporations by finding that corporations were "persons" under the Fourteenth Amendment, having substantive rights to do business as they saw fit without government interference. The courts were not always reliable; lower courts, in particular, rendered decisions that broke with laissez faire orthodoxy. Still, workers who tried to protect themselves met severe legal barriers.

THE CHANGING WORLD OF INDUSTRIAL WORK

The advent of mass production changed the world workers faced, but not completely or in any single direction. Mechanization and assembly-line organization created unskilled and semi-skilled jobs and eliminated the need for workers with certain skills. The diminished need for skilled workers in steelmaking, meatpacking, and other industries allowed employers to reassert their authority on the shop floor. They ousted skilled workers who had functioned as subcontractors, who had hired and paid workers and set the tempo of work. Foremen appointed by management now coordinated the work of employees paid weekly by management. Some foremen sided with workers, but most did management's bidding, at times with an abusive flair.

Overall, wages rose from $1 to $1.50 per day between 1860 and 1890, or from less than $300 to more than $425 per year. Falling prices, too, improved the standard of living of American workers. While all workers enjoyed cheaper necessities and luxuries, skilled workers accounted for a good deal of the increase in wages. Making up 10 to 20 percent of the working class, they earned more than than three times the wages of unskilled workers. These workers could aspire to respectability: a home or comfortable apartment with carpets and perhaps a piano, a wife at home and children in school. All was not well, however; depression years saw unemployment rates of 7 to 10 percent, with 30 percent out of work at some point during a bad year. Even in "normal" years, twenty percent of industrial workers were laid off at some point; in seasonally affected industries such as construction, food processing, and clothing, workers could be laid off for as long as four months.

The creation of new unskilled and semi-skilled jobs pulled in new industrial workers. Outside the South, immigrants filled a good deal of the demand. For male immigrants, unskilled labor in factories or construction was the typical first step, and for most there was no second. Immigrants were joined by native-born migrants from rural areas. Between 1860 and 1900, perhaps as many as eight million men and women left the countryside to take jobs in cities, drawn away by the fading prospect of owning a farm, hard times, the decreasing need for farm labor that came with the mechanization of agriculture, low wages, or simple boredom. A growing but still small number of African Americans and women of all races entered the industrial workforce. African Americans who looked for industrial work had trouble finding it. Southern industries hired African-American men for only the nastiest, lowest-paying jobs, and even then fixed the wage so that it would not compete with agricultural labor. In the North, African-American men also suffered discrimination. Some held the lowest-level, most onerous jobs in industry, but most found work in the ill-paid service sector as porters, waiters, servants, and bootblacks. The majority of women of all races who worked for wages still found jobs as domestics. Most preferred factory work, which paid better and did not entail the personal demands and insulting, round-the-clock supervision domestics endured. By 1900, women made up 17 percent of the industrial labor force, four times the number in 1870. Still, most industries did not hire women, and those that did—light industries such as makers of garments, artificial flowers, boxes, hats, canned food—paid them far less than they paid male workers, even less than survival wage for a single person. Commercial laundries also employed women, as did the more respectable department stores, offices, and schools. The female industrial labor force was largely young and single, made up of immigrants and the daughters of immigrants. Married black women were more likely than white women to remain in the paid labor force, because most African-American men earned so little and they preferred to keep their children in school. Children labored on farms and in shops as they always had, but also in factories. Adding as much as $250 to their families' budgets, children as young as twelve as well as their older siblings worked alongside their mothers in canneries and textile mills.

Industrial workers labored under dangerous conditions. Steel mills had never been safe places, but mass production made them worse. Expensive machinery only paid when it ran, so steelmakers ran their furnaces constantly. Workers put in twelve-hour days and seven-day weeks, with one twenty-four-hour shift and one day off every two weeks. The surfaces in some areas were so hot that workers wore wooden shoes; molten metal showered workers, burning and blinding some. In lumber mills, workers lost fingers, hands, and arms to saws. Railroad safety improved somewhat over the days of expansion, when Chinese workers who died laying track were buried without markers, but even in the early twentieth century twelve railroad workers died on the job every week. Mining remained the most dangerous industry; men died in explosions, cave-ins, and fires. As the western quartz mines went deeper into the ground, miners worked in temperatures as high as 150 degrees. Cages that lowered and raised workers into and out of the mines often lacked sides, so a slip could send a man plunging to his death. The platforms crushed some workers; and men snagged between platforms and walls lost arms or legs. In eastern anthracite coal mines, "breaker boys" perched along steep, lengthy chutes picked out slate and rock from the coal passing to the breaker. Bleeding hands (they were forbidden to wear gloves) were expected on a job that often began a boy's career in the mines. For some boys it was the last job, as coal and rock crushed their hands or they fell to their deaths. Long-term illnesses such as lead poisoning and silicosis (caused by the dust of mines, bakeries, and textile mills) were as serious as and even more common than dramatic accidents.

Injured workers and the families of those who died on the job had little recourse. With no system of workers' compensation, workers and their families could try their luck in the courts, but their chances of winning were slim. Employers argued that workers who took dangerous jobs knew the risks going in, which absolved employers of responsibility. Failing that, employers' lawyers invoked the "fellow servant" rule: If another worker, even a foreman, knew about malfunctioning equipment or other dangerous conditions, that man, not the employer, was responsible. If neither of those defenses applied, "contributory negligence" remained. The plaintiff had to demonstrate that he or she had in no way contributed to an injury. With few incentives to incur the expense, few employers bothered to provide guards on saws, gloves for breaker boys, equipment (even open doors) to keep down dust in textile mills, fire escapes, fans to expel volatile gases in mines, or enclosures on elevators.

CHALLENGING EMPLOYERS' POWER

Changes that mechanization brought to the workplace inspired worker activism. Skilled workers whose jobs were threatened by mechanization fought to keep their positions and to maintain customary shop floor privileges. Skilled workers knew their hard-earned respectability, including the pride they took in their skills and the independence those skills bestowed, was at stake. Both skilled and unskilled workers protested the wage cuts that often accompanied price wars, especially the cuts that were businesses' response to depressions. Arbitrary foremen also generated grievances. In the late nineteenth century, workers took part in a level of labor militancy matched only by the upheavals of 1919 and the 1930s. In 1886 alone, the Federal Bureau of Labor Statistics counted 1,432 strikes and 140 lockouts, affecting 610,024 workers. During the two decades between 1876 and 1896, there were more strikes in America than in any other industrial nation. These strikes were particularly violent; more people were injured and killed in these labor protests than in any other nation. Often, strikes involved mobs, property damage, and looting. Workers were no more willing than their employers to accept the dictates of the market.

Unions were one way of fighting back, but workers were undecided about the proper direction for their unions. In a certain sense, the late nineteenth century was an age of experimentation and choice for workers just as it was for industry and business. Some unions embraced political action, while others saw it as a distraction. If Carnegie, Rockefeller, and Morgan symbolized business in the late nineteenth century, three men represented labor and its various organizational forms. Terence Powderly, head of the Knights of Labor, preferred arbitration to strikes. Samuel Gompers, founder of the American Federation of Labor, focused on immediate labor issues and established the basis of modern unionism. Eugene Debs, founder of the American Railway Union and, later, the Socialist Party of America, rejected capitalism altogether.

TERENCE POWDERLY OVERSEES THE RISE AND FALL OF THE KNIGHTS OF LABOR   By the end of the Civil War, American labor had a well-developed union tradition, although only about 5 percent of workers were unionized. Workers in many cities organized to demand an eight-hour workday. In Boston, Ira Steward organized the Eight-Hour League, which drew national attention.

In 1866 labor activity culminated in the organizing of America's first national union, the National Labor Union (NLU), under the leadership of William Sylvis. The NLU also encouraged black workers to organize. Led by Isaac Meyers, a black shipcaulker, black workers formed the National Colored Labor Union. The NLU became increasingly involved with political reform through the Greenback movement. Greenbackism attracted reformers with its call for the federal government to issue inflationary paper money (greenbacks) not backed by gold. Sylvis's death in 1869 and the turn to political reform weakened the NLU. The depression of 1873 brought its demise.

The depression also temporarily killed the union movement in general. By 1877 only nine national unions remained. The breaking of a strike

The year 1877 brought many strikes, which were often violent. In Pittsburgh a railroad strike led to a worker's funeral being held among the smoldering ruins of a company building. (Library of Congress)

in the anthracite coal fields of Pennsylvania led to violence. Following the strike, a kind of guerrilla war broke out, with a series of assaults and murders of strikebreakers and company officials. Finally, the company placed an agent named James McParland under cover to spy on the Irish miners. He collected dubious evidence against an alleged secret society, the "Molly Maguires," which led to the arrest, conviction, and execution of thirteen men.

Class tensions worsened. There was a general strike by workers in the summer of 1877. Only the calling out of federal troops by President Hayes quelled the rioting, which left $10 million in damage.

While the strikes of 1877 ran their brutally violent course, a young labor organization planned its first national convention. The Holy and Noble Order of the Knights of Labor was the most successful of a number of attempts in the 1860s and 1870s to build a national labor organization. Founded in 1869 by Uriah S. Stephens, a Philadelphia garment cutter, the Knights began as both a union and a secret society. Fraternal organizations were extremely popular in nineteenth-century America, and the Knights supplied the rituals, fellowship, and sickness and death benefits typical of such groups. At its peak the Order counted 750,000 members and a chapter in virtually every county in America; at some point between 1870 and the early 1890s, two to three million people had joined the organization. Offering both a focus for discontented workers and a critique of the structure and values of industrial America, the Knights were the most important labor organization of the Gilded Age.

Terence V. Powderly, who became Grand Master Workman of the Knights in 1879, provided both organizational skill and support for the Knights' broader vision. A humorless, prim, genteel teetotaler, Powderly left school when he was thirteen years old to work on the railroads and rose to become a machinist and mayor of Scranton, Pennsylvania. His vision of the labor movement fit firmly within the republican equal rights tradition that dated back to the Revolution. A just industrial society, the Knights claimed, would value cooperation over competition, the dignity of labor over money, and the contributions of the producing classes over the parasitic speculators. Powderly abhorred strikes and favored arbitration ("I curse the word *class*," he once declared), believing that conflict between labor and capital was not inevitable. Industrial monopolies and their politician and financier allies stood in the way of the cooperative commonwealth. "The recent alarming development and aggression of aggregate wealth, unless checked, will inevitably lead to the pauperization and hopeless degradation of the toiling masses," stated the Knights' Declaration of Principles. "[I]f we desire to enjoy the blessings of life . . . a check should be placed upon its power and upon unjust accumulation." Producers, that is, the laborers, craftsmen, farmers, and businessmen who actually made things, created wealth; the lawyers, speculators, financiers, and industrialists who sought monopoly power did not. In their drive for profits, big business and its minions cut wages to the point that independence and a full life, with leisure for self improvement and time for family, were impossible for many workers.

The effort to see that "industrial moral worth, not wealth" became the "true standard of industrial and national greatness" drew a diverse membership. The Knights departed from the trade union model, in which unions tried to organize the men of the individual skilled trades; anyone who was not a liquor dealer, speculator, lawyer, or banker could become a member. African Americans contributed about 10 percent of the Knights' membership at its peak; another 10 percent were women, who worked as shoe stitchers, carpet weavers, domestics, and housewives. The Knights created a woman's department and made its director a general officer of the union. Leonora Marie Barry, who had become a millhand after the death of her husband, joined the Knights in 1881 and became the first general investigator of the woman's department. Through her efforts Pennsylvania passed the Factory Inspection Act (1899). Although the Knights were willing to include blacks and women, they stopped at the Chinese contract labor imported by companies. The Knights argued in favor of the exclusion of Chinese contract labor rather than the exclusion of Chinese immigration, but they were counted among the supporters of the Chinese Exclusion Act (1882), which placed a ten-year moratorium on Chinese immigration. Some Knights in the West did not see the distinction; three years later, Knights in Wyoming massacred twenty-eight Chinese workers.

The Order was the most inclusive union in the United States until the Congress of Industrial Organizations in the 1930s. The breadth of its goals matched its membership. The Order favored an end to child and convict labor, equal application of the laws, equal pay for equal work, temperance, a graduated income tax, the establishment of cooperative factories, government ownership of the telegraph, telephone, and railroad systems, and the eight-hour day.

The Knights were a confederation of local assemblies, not a centralized organization, and local chapters usually defined their own goals and strategies. The Order officially declared its independence from political parties, but numerous assemblies from New York City to small towns supported candidates for office and even won some municipal elections. Although Powderly and the national leadership sanctioned arbitration instead of strikes, local assemblies walked out on their employers nonetheless. Indeed, new members poured into the Order after a successful strike against Jay Gould's Southwestern Railroad system in 1885. Building on the suggestion of a trade union, many Knights enthusiastically planned a strike for May 1, 1886, that would demonstrate labor's power and desire for the eight-hour workday. But the Order's success in attracting new members opened internal disagreements. Trade unionists distrusted reformers, evangelical Protestants distrusted atheists, and socialists distrusted the tactics and goals of the trade unionists. Those disagreements hardened into recriminations in 1886 after a series of defeats, including a rematch against Jay Gould. The Knights would not recover from the worst defeat in Chicago.

HAYMARKET AND THE END OF THE KNIGHTS OF LABOR

In Chicago, the Knights, along with various trade union and radical organizations, planned a rally for workers who had participated in the May 1 nationwide strike for the eight-hour day. A strike at the McCormick Harvesting Machinery Company, the nation's major producer of farm machinery, set off a tragic chain of events. On May 2, 1886, a group of

Chicago unionists and radicals marched to the massive McCormick works to show their support for striking workers. Fights broke out between protesters and strikebreakers leaving the plant, while an anarchist speaker denounced the capitalist system. Police fired into the crowd, killing four people. Chicago anarchists called a protest meeting for the next evening at Haymarket Square. The crowd of two thousand fell below organizers' expectations, and it thinned further as rain began. Just as the last anarchist speaker was wrapping up, a police captain came to the podium to order the crowd to disperse. Then a bomb exploded in front of a line of police, killing one policeman instantly and fatally wounding seven others. Angry and frightened police then fired randomly into the tumult, wounding sixty more officers and killing seven or eight people in the crowd.

"The city went insane," said a union activist. Hundreds of people were arrested in connection with the bombing. Although no one saw who threw the bomb (to this day no one knows who was responsible), eight anarchists were arrested, tried, and sentenced to die. Four were hanged; one committed suicide in prison; and the others were pardoned by the governor of Illinois in 1893. Meanwhile, the taint of violence and anarchism hung over all radical and union activity following Haymarket. With public opinion now apparently on their side, many employers took the opportunity to break unions, including those affiliated with the Knights. In the South, union busting took a violent turn; a mob killed dozens of African-American sugar plantation workers affiliated with the Knights in Louisiana. The Order's leadership did not help matters. Powderly reiterated the no-strike policy and even revoked the charters of some local assemblies unwilling to abide by the rule. Membership plummeted. By 1890 only 100,000 members remained, chiefly in small towns.

SAMUEL GOMPERS STICKS TO THE BASICS   Samuel Gompers was saddened by the aftermath of Haymarket. "A single bomb has destroyed the eight-hour movement," he said. But he was not surprised. The former cigar maker, who had emigrated to the United States at the age of thirteen, had never been convinced that the reform agenda and broad membership base of the Knights were the solution to the problems of American workers. In contrast to Powderly, Gompers fit the stereotype of a labor leader: gruff, cigar-chomping, and unlikely to turn down a drink with his mates. He became the most recognizable and powerful union leader in the nation, heading the American Federation of Labor (AFL) for all but one year from its organization in 1886 to his death in 1924. Gompers's leadership combined his early education in Marxism with what

In 1866 Samuel Gompers, a cigar maker and a Jewish immigrant from London, founded the American Federation of Labor, which became a powerful organization for skilled workers. Gompers believed that unskilled workers could not be unionized. (Library of Congress)

he believed was a grim but realistic assessment of the anti-union climate in the United States.

Two facts were clear to Gompers: A permanent working class had developed in the United States, and big business commanded a great deal of economic and political power. A number of conclusions flowed from those observations. First, the workers' best chance was with unionization. State or federal labor laws were likely to be weak, and even those might not survive the scrutiny of conservative courts. The AFL did not flirt with minor political parties or form a labor party; it dealt with Democratic and Republican politicians, and then with the hope that government would leave labor alone. Second, unions had to organize skilled workers, or at the very least unskilled workers, into tight "craft" unions. Such organization gave workers a relatively stronger bargaining position. The relevant division in industrial America was between capital and labor, not "producers" and "parasites." Third, the AFL encouraged its members' loyalty by providing concrete benefits. It gave wide latitude to its local affiliates but built a formidable organization with dues high enough to endow a strike fund and generously compensate its officers. Finally, the AFL focused on wages, hours, and work rules.

Most members of the AFL were white, fairly well-established males. In trying to protect its members by becoming the monopoly provider of certain skills, the AFL sometimes saw outsiders—recent immigrants, African Americans, and women workers—as potential strikebreakers and threats to wages. A small number of African-American workers, chiefly longshoremen, teamsters, and coal miners, joined AFL unions. In 1892 AFL unions joined others in New Orleans in a general strike in support of black teamsters. That was an exception, however, and the AFL's record on race would grow worse by the early twentieth century. The AFL was not convinced that women made good unionists, because many left factory work after marriage. The AFL supported the family wage, where a husband "should receive enough to give his family a respectable living." In the early twentieth century, the AFL gave its blessing to state laws that regulated the wages and hours of women workers, but it rejected similar laws for men: Legislation might help women, but men should take care of themselves with the aid of their unions.

Gompers led a union that was narrower but far more durable than the Knights of Labor. The AFL's approach, however, did not lack critics. The militant Western Federation of Miners broke from the AFL in 1897, demanding "revolution of present social and economic conditions to the end that justice may be meted out to all people of the earth." Inside the AFL, socialists worked for a more ambitious political agenda. Yet in the context of the often violent repression of unions, the AFL's prudent course was perhaps the most that could be done. Despite its fiery rhetoric, even the Western Federation of Miners focused on providing benefits to its members and fighting for higher wages and improved working conditions. The AFL weathered the storm of the 1890s that saw many more defeats than victories for striking workers. Not so the steelworkers.

A UNION SETBACK IN STEEL

Events in Pittsburgh in 1892 convinced Gompers that, if anything, he had been too optimistic about the state of labor relations in America. Andrew Carnegie had prided himself on being an uncommon industrialist, one who cared about his employees; he had written favorably of unions as one source of self-improvement. The Amalgamated Association of Iron and Steel Workers was a different matter. Comprised of the remnants of skilled workers in the industry, the Amalgamated's 1889 contract pegged pay rates to the price of steel, with a floor under wages but no ceiling, and described a detailed list of work rules. In 1892 Carnegie and his new partner and com-

In the economically depressed 1890s, both rural and urban Americans were in a frenzy. In 1892 workers and private detectives from the Pinkerton agency fought violently during a strike at the Homestead steel works near Pittsburgh. (Library of Congress)

pany chairman, Henry Clay Frick, determined to eliminate this last barrier to the total control of production.

While Carnegie was conveniently out of reach on an extended vacation in Scotland, Frick prepared for a siege at the Homestead works, a few miles southwest of Pittsburgh. After going through the motions of negotiating a new contract with the Amalgamated, Frick abruptly announced that talks were over and that the steelworkers would have to take a 20 percent wage cut or the mills would run with nonunion workers. With a twelve-foot-high fence topped with barbed wire protecting the plant, Frick locked out the workers on July 1. Homestead workers had also prepared. The Amalgamated, joined by 2,400 unskilled workers not included in the union, organized a militia to picket the plant, keep order in town, and watch for the strikebreakers Frick was sure to import. On July 6 lookouts spotted two Carnegie tugboats pulling two Carnegie barges down the

Monongahela River, packed with a motley collection of laid-off workers, college students on break, ex-convicts, and veteran strikebreakers provided by the Pinkerton Detective Agency. The union's communication system worked as planned, and soon armed men, women, and children ran to the riverfront to greet the Pinkertons.

They began firing even before the barges churned into range. Trapped inside the hot and stuffy barges, the Pinkertons hoped to dash inside the plant's fortified gates. Townspeople, however, had overrun the fences, and when a contingent of Pinkertons announced their intention to take the plant and tried to walk ashore, gunfire broke out between the leader of the Pinkertons and the crowd. Soon two strikers were dead and dozens wounded; townspeople tried everything from dynamite to setting fire to the barge by lighting an oil slick to roust the stranded Pinkertons. After a twelve-hour battle, the Pinkertons surrendered. Their ordeal was not over: They had to run a gauntlet of furious men and women who kicked and beat them, some to the point of unconsciousness, before they were shipped out of Homestead. The battle left nine workers and seven Pinkertons dead and hundreds wounded.

On July 12, eight thousand federal troops arrived to take control of the plant and the city. Strikers were arrested and charged with everything from treason and murder to incitement to riot. None was convicted, but no union leader found work in a steel mill again. Under the protection of troops, the mill reopened with nonunion workers. To talk about a union thereafter was to court dismissal: "If a man wants to talk in Homestead, he talks to himself," a worker claimed. Frick wrote Carnegie, "I never want to go through another such fight." There was no choice, he believed; "We had to teach our employees a lesson, and we have taught them one that they will never forget."

Gompers would not forget. "Sometimes my heart almost sinks at the thought of what we . . . may yet witness as the result of the overweening greed of the corporate and capitalist class," he wrote. An even more cautious approach seemed to be in order for unions. Even unionized skilled workers could not stand against large corporations with the resources to shift production to other plants, the advanced technology that made skilled workers superfluous, and the ear of the state and federal governments. The AFL could only watch as Carnegie Steel busted a constituent union. More militant unions fared no better. In 1892 in Idaho's Coeur d'Alene River region, miners struck after the Mine Owners' Association (MOA) instituted a wage cut. MOA made double use of Pinkertons. Along with bringing in nonunion workers, Pinkertons infiltrated the unions; one even served as secretary. As the strike wore on, frustrated miners attacked mine property and destroyed expensive machinery. MOA had martial law declared; soldiers arrested strikers and, for good measure, businessmen and lawyers sympathetic to the union. Thereafter, townspeople would think twice before siding with a striking union. With an economic depression settling in, the remainder of the decade did not seem to promise better times for unions.

EUGENE DEBS RADICALIZES   Within the AFL a large socialist faction continued to challenge Gompers for power. Socialists called for greater political involvement through the establishment of a labor party. Socialists also called for municipal ownership of public utilities and government ownership of railroads, telegraphs, and the telephone. They found an articulate spokesman for their cause in Eugene Debs, a native-born Midwesterner of French ancestry.

In many ways Debs cut a figure completely opposite to that of Gompers. Raised in the railroad-dominated center of Terre Haute, Indiana, Debs grew up in the security of small-town America. He had worked for a railroad, moving up to fireman. He married the local physician's daughter, built a splendid home in the good section of town with his wife's money, and for a while dabbled in local Democratic Party politics, winning a seat in the state assembly. He also became an active unionist. In 1893 he helped organize the American Railway Union (ARU), of which he became president. The union quickly gained a membership of 150,000.

The growth of the ARU frightened railroad owners. Through their General Managers Association, a half-secret combination of twenty-four railway companies, they decided to confront the ARU. One spokesman declared, "We can handle the railway brotherhoods, but we cannot handle the ARU. We cannot handle Debs. We have got to wipe him out." Their opportunity came quickly.

Among those who joined the American Railway Union were the Pullman Palace Car workers. These workers lived in a town built by George Pullman, the company's owner. Pullman spoke with pride about this model town and the care he took of his employees. Even fellow businessmen dismissed Pullman's rhetoric. Mark Hanna, a Cleveland industrialist, declared, "Model—go and live in Pullman and find out how much Pullman gets selling city water and gas ten percent higher to those poor fools."

Pullman responded to the depression of 1893 by cutting wages 25 percent. A year later a delegation of workers went to the company to ask for relief. Rents had increased, as had company profits, but wages had not been restored. When Pullman discharged three leaders of the delegation, the employees went on strike. Against the warnings of Debs, the rank and file of the ARU railway unions decided to strike in support of the Pullman workers. By the summer of 1894, the entire railroad system of the United States had been effectively shut down.

The General Managers Association demanded action. They found a spokesman in Richard C. Olney, attorney general in the Grover Cleveland administration. A member of several railroad boards, Olney urged Cleveland to take action. He reported that the nation was on the verge of anarchy. Finally, he went to federal court to get an injunction based on the Sherman Antitrust Act, stating that the strike was restraint of trade and was preventing the transportation of federal mail. Olney sent in 2,600 deputies to enforce this injunction and others later passed against picketing and boycotts. Three days of rioting followed. The strike was completely broken. Debs was arrested for disobeying the injunction and sentenced to prison.

In prison Debs was converted to socialism. Although he voted for the Democratic presidential nominee, William Jennings Bryan, in 1896, this would be the last time he would support the mainstream party system. Shortly after leaving prison in 1895, Debs joined Victor Berger, a Milwaukee socialist devoted to labor, and the handsome and eloquent Morris Hillquit, a Russian-born Jew and garment worker organizer, in organizing the Socialist Party of America.

CONCLUSION

The second Industrial Revolution created new industry and new organizations for businesses and labor. After the Civil War, manufacturing was transformed in the iron, steel, oil, and consumer goods industries. Men such as Carnegie, Rockefeller, and Morgan transformed the way business was conducted in America. At the same time, labor experimented with new forms of organization: Terence Powderly led the Knights of Labor; Samuel Gompers established modern unionism with the American Federation of Labor; and Eugene Debs proposed a socialist program.

The emergence of the new corporate order coincided with the creation of the largest middle class in history. And this middle class came to characterize and inform American politics and society in the twentieth century as much as did the new corporate order and labor.

Recommended Readings

DOCUMENTS: Andrew Carnegie, *Autobiography* (1920); Eugene V. Debs, *Writings and Speeches of Eugene V. Debs* (1948); Thorstein Veblen, *The Theory of the Leisure Class* (1899).

READINGS: (LABOR) David Brody, *Steelworkers in America: The Nonunion Era* (1960); Melvyn Dubofsky, *Industrialization and the American Worker* (1975); Leon Fink, *Workingmen's Democracy: The Knights of Labor and American Politics* (1983); Herbert G. Gutman, *Work, Culture, and Society in Industrializing America* (1976); Gerald D. Jaynes, *Branches without Roots: Genesis of the Black Working Class in the American South* (1986); Jacqueline Jones, *Labor of Love, Labor of Sorrow: Black Women, Work, and the Family from Slavery to the Present* (1986); Susan E. Kennedy, *If All We Did Was to Weep at Home: A History of White Working-Class Women in America* (1979); Alice Kessler-Harris, *Out to Work: A History of Wage-Earning Women in the United States* (1982); Alexander Keyssar, *Out of Work: The First Century of Unemployment in Massachusetts* (1986); David Montgomery, *The Fall of the House of Labor* (1987); Daniel Nelson, *Managers and Workers: Origins of the New Factory System in the United States* (1975); Daniel T. Rodgers, *The Work Ethic in Industrial America* (1974); Stephen J. Ross, *Workers on the Edge: Work, Leisure and Politics in Industrializing Cincinnati* (1982); Nick Salvatore, *Eugene V. Debs* (1982); John L. Thomas, *Alternative America: Henry George, Edward Bellamy, Henry Demarest Lloyd, and the Adversary Tradition* (1983). (INDUSTRY) Robert W. Bruce, *Alexander Graham Bell and the Conquest of Solitude* (1973); Alfred D. Chandler, Jr., *The Visible Hand: The Managerial Revolution in American Business* (1977); Carl Degler, *The Age of Economic Revolution* (1977); Samuel P. Hayes, *The Response to Industrialism* (1957); Thomas P. Hughes, *Networks of Power: Electrification in Western Society* (1983); Maury Klein, *The Life and Legend of Jay Gould* (1986); Naomi R. Lamoreaux, *The Great Merger Movement in American Business* (1985); Harold C. Livesay, *Andrew Carnegie and the Rise of Big Business* (1977); Alan Trachtenberg, *The Incorporation of America: Culture and Society in the Gilded Age* (1982); David O. Whitten, *The Emergence of Giant Enterprise* (1983); Olivier Zunz, *Making America, 1870–1920* (1990).

18

❦

The Structure of Gilded Age Politics

OVERVIEW   Sandwiched between the crisis of the Civil War and the reforming sprit of the early twentieth century, the late nineteenth century seemed to some both dull and embarrassingly corrupt. Instead of strong national leadership, the period seemed to produce nothing but bewhiskered, interchangeable presidents, memorable only for their quirks. Yet voters enthusiastically turned out for elections at percentages not equaled since. Until the 1890s, national elections were very close; competition shaped party platforms, issues, and nominations, produced tight organization, and encouraged voters' interest. For all of the hoopla attached to presidential elections, the presidency was not yet the central institution it would become in the twentieth century. State and local governments handled tasks of immediate importance to most citizens. Some citizens registered their dislike of corruption, the patronage system, and lack of federal response to some issues by supporting seemingly purer third parties.

PARTY POLITICS STALEMATED

Politicians of the late nineteenth century reckoned with three central political facts. Firstly, the balance of power between Democrats and Republicans was almost even. Between 1876 and 1896, the largest margin of victory was 4.4 percent in 1896, a relative landslide. The margin over the previous five presidential elections averaged 1.4 percent. Democrats held the White House twice between 1876 and 1896, although the party's candidates won the popular vote, but not the electoral vote, in two other elections. Control of Congress was just as uncertain: In the ten sessions between the 1875 and 1895, Republicans had majorities in the Senate for seven sessions, while Democrats controlled the House for eight. For only the two years 1889 to 1891 did Republicans capture both the presidency and a majority in the House and Senate; the Democrats repeated the feat between 1893 and 1895. Close national elections and divided government were the rule in the late nineteenth century.

The second central fact was the different regional strengths of the major parties. When Reconstruction ended and federal troops left, the South gradually became a Democratic stronghold as white rule prevented more and more African Americans from voting. The Democratic Party uneasily combined its southern base with support in many of the nation's large northern cities. The Republicans counted on substantial majorities in New England and the upper Midwest. Some of the new western states remained competitive and, more importantly from the point of view of party leaders, so did a band of half a dozen states between New England and the South. New York, Ohio, and Indiana, with sizable populations and therefore large numbers of votes in the Electoral College, determined the outcomes of national elections.

Those regional strengths rested on the third fact: the partisan loyalties of voters. Most men voted for the candidates of the same party year after year. For some men, party loyalty dated to the Civil War; northern Union veterans, and to an even greater extent southern former Confederates, tended to "vote as they shot." African Americans in the North and those able to vote in the South overwhelmingly supported the party of Lincoln. Other voters, especially in parts of the Midwest and Northeast, broke along religious lines. Irish Catholics in many northern cities voted Democratic, as did many Episcopalians and German Lutherans. Evangelical Protestants—Baptists, Methodists, Congregationalists, Presbyterians, and Swedish and Norwegian Lutherans—tended to support Republican candidates. However, these differences were not hard and fast even in the Northeast and Midwest, and they hardly carried at all into the West. Mexican Catholics in California, for example, divided about evenly between the parties. The parties, however, counted on the regular support of blocs of voters.

The parties' positions on issues reinforced party loyalty. Broadly speaking, Republicans proposed using the power of a relatively active government to protect the nation's economy and morality, whereas Democrats believed that limited, economical government allowed greater personal freedom and prosperity. Republicans touted the benefits of high tariffs (taxes on imports) as an important protection for American industries, farms, and wages. The party was also against Mormon polygamy, public funding of Catholic schools, teaching in languages other than English, and, gingerly, alcohol and saloons. Evangelical Protestants appreciated the party's efforts on behalf of their moral vision and often pushed the party to take more decisive stands. Union veterans voted Republican, against the party of slavery and disunion. Different groups found the Democrats' plea for limited government congenial. Irish Catholics, often depicted as boorish, drunken minions of the pope, wanted protection from what they saw as the meddling of evangelical Protestants in their religious beliefs and personal behavior. White southerners were extremely touchy about a meddling government as well, recalling what they saw as degrading Republican federal control during Reconstruction. They voted for a Democratic Party that promised to maintain white supremacy in the South. White supremacy carried over into the Democrat's championing of the exclusion of Chinese immigration in the 1870s and 1880s. Although tolerant of the cultural differences of European immigrants, Democrats were less likely than Republicans to tolerate either the "heathen" Chinese or African Americans.

Campaign hoopla further encouraged partisanship. Voting was not an occasion for weighing the virtues of candidates and issues but an opportunity to celebrate partisanship. Election days were civic carnivals. Men milled about in polling places, which included saloons, barber shops, and stores, and secured their ballots from the party workers who greeted them. Which party a man supported was often known to the crowd, and voters often deposited their tickets in the ballot boxes to the cheers or catcalls of onlookers. Voters sometimes returned in the evening to await returns and perhaps a celebration.

COMPETITION SHAPES CANDIDATES AND POLICY   Close elections, steady support from certain regions and groups, and strong party loyalty explained the parties' circumspect choices of candidates and their caution on certain policies. Since the populous competitive states determined the outcome of national elections, party leaders chose candidates from those states. Of the twenty nominees for president and vice president between 1876 and 1892, eight were New Yorkers and five were from Indiana. Most voters held established party preferences, so party leaders usually steered clear of presidential candidates with strong personalities because such men had earned enemies as well as friends. They would be likely to reduce the regular party vote (disaffected voters would simply stay home on election day) without attracting staunch partisans from the other side. The parties usually sought out "available" men, candidates able to unite all factions within the party because they were relatively unknown, held unexceptional views on major issues, and had not picked fights within their own parties. In 1880 the Republicans passed over the flamboyant New York senator Roscoe Conkling and the charismatic James G. Blaine of Maine, the party's controversial stars, in favor of James Garfield. At the state and local levels, the parties tried to concoct "balanced" tickets, slates of candidates that mixed military service, ethnicity, and occupation in the right proportions for the local electorate. The parties were also careful not to push issues too far. Republicans moved cautiously on the temperance question because it divided the party's constituency. While many evangelical Protestants favored laws limiting or banning completely the availability of alcohol, German voters, whose support Republicans needed in Indiana and New York, opposed restrictions on their freedom to drink beer. To keep their fragile coalitions together, the major parties chose safety over foolhardy tilting at principle.

The political parties were largely unregulated private organizations unmentioned in the federal or state constitutions, yet they performed many tasks later left to governments, citizens, or individual candidates. They staged elections with little government interference. The parties, not the voters in primary elections, nominated candidates. They held a series of conventions that began with small election district meetings and culminated in national conventions held every four years. The parties, not the candidates, ran campaigns. They organized speakers and rallies, distributed pamphlets, and designed slogans and themes. Although independent newspapers were growing more popular in the nation's largest cities, most newspapers were affiliated with one of the parties and repeated that party's claims. Party organizations polled voters in competitive states by asking virtually all of them how they planned to vote. The states did not supply ballots; the parties printed their own. In some states each cluster of offices (presidential, state, judicial, and local) required a separate ticket; in others, long, narrow strips of paper covered with tiny print served as ballots. On election day, party workers "bunched" the tickets, which were printed using different colors and designs so that the illiterate too could identify the parties, and ticket peddlers hawked them to voters at polling places. Especially in competitive states, party workers fanned out to help voters get to the polls and might pay as much as $5 to those who needed encouragement. After the election, party leaders filled the government jobs available with loyal supporters.

Raising money, coordinating workers, and managing campaigns required a high level of organization. Party leaders or city and state "bosses" struggled to perfect their organizations and mute factional quarrels. Late-nineteenth-century bosses saw themselves as managers rather than political entrepreneurs. They included the father-and-son team of Simon and Don Cameron, who ran the Republican Party in Pennsylvania;

Matthew Quay, who held Philadelphia; Russell Alger of Michigan; J. S. Clarkson of Iowa; Joseph Foraker of Ohio; and Arthur Gorman of Maryland. Various men, including the infamous William Marcy Tweed, headed New York City's famous Tammany Hall machine and did battle with both reformers and rival organizations. Collis Huntington shaped California politics through his railroad fortune. Thomas Collier Platt gained control of the New York State Republican Party by the late 1880s, having learned from Conkling's mistakes. Like other successful party bosses, the "Easy Boss" followed more than he led. Most Sundays Platt convened a group of party notables, "Platt's Sunday School," at New York City's Fifth Avenue Hotel, where he gleaned suggestions rather than barked orders. David Bennett Hill, Platt's Democratic counterpart, survived by adeptly using patronage to maintain peace among the party's major local powers. Some of the bosses were governors or senators, but even bosses without elected office were more powerful than elected officials, in some cases even the president. They believed in their party's principles—Hill summarized his political views with the slogan "I am a Democrat"—but believed even more in their parties' success.

PATRONAGE BUILDS THE PARTIES   Patronage provided the means to build state and city machines and to maintain discipline in the ranks. Parties, Conkling once noted, "are not built up by deportment, or by ladies' magazines, or gush." George Washington Plunkitt, the shoeshine-stand philosopher of New York City's Tammany Hall machine, put it bluntly: "I acknowledge that you can't keep an organization together without patronage. Men ain't in politics for nothin'. They want to get somethin' out of it." Some wanted jobs out of it, and the growing size of government meant more of them. At the end of the Civil War, the federal government had 53,000 positions to fill; by 1885 the number stood at 130,000. Wisconsin Senator John C. Spooner received more than seven thousand letters, the great majority of them about government positions, in the four months after a new Republican administration took office in 1897. State and local governments provided yet more government posts, everything from laborers and janitors to powerful administrators. The entire Philadelphia police force turned over with the change of administration. Most positions did not pay handsomely, but the most valuable party workers collected paychecks for jobs that let them dedicate their full attention to politics. Plum jobs gave officials the opportunity to hire others and collect fees in addition to a salary. (As Collector of the Port of New York in the 1870s, Chester Arthur netted $50,000 in perfectly legal fees, equal to the salary of the president, in addition to his regular salary of $12,000.) Finally, at all levels of government there were commodities other than jobs to give away: printing contracts to newspapers, franchises for public utilities and transportation, tariff protection, reductions in tax assessments, and contracts for buildings and roads.

Filling government positions was victory's reward but also its burden. When Secretary of the Interior Lucius Lamar commented, "I eat my breakfast and dinner and supper always in the company of some two or three eager and hungry applicants for office," he echoed the complaints of officials throughout the nineteenth century. The hopeful job-seekers did not see themselves as nuisances or beggars but as men who had earned their positions through their work for the party. They were "friends" of the candidates who believed that politicians had a reciprocal relationship with voters.

PATRONAGE COMES UNDER FIRE   Critics of the patronage system saw it as the soul of incompetence and corruption. Reformers, drawn largely from the college-educated, urban elite, disdained partisanship and hoped to replace patronage with a civil service system. Government positions should be permanent, not vulnerable to change with every election, and subject to appointment through competitive examinations, not friendship or payback. Government employees should be allowed to do their jobs without political interference and demands to return portions of their salaries for campaigns. These reformers, with their cold, elitist style and distaste for the masses, hardly attracted a mass following. They hoped to see "the best men," ones closely resembling themselves, replace crude politicians and their immigrant allies in government service. Many politicians who believed that political parties would die without patronage ridiculed the reformers. "Snivel service," Conkling sneered, while Plunkitt imagined deserving, patriotic party workers denied their just rewards because they could not "answer a list of questions about Egyptian mummies and how many years it will take for a bird to wear out a mass of iron as big as the earth by steppin' on it once in a century."

Yet the reformers had a point. The patronage system produced its share of incompetence and corruption. A story circulated about an Indiana party loyalist appointed to the Navy Department who, when inspecting a warship, rapped its hull with his cane and exclaimed in amazement, "Why, the durn thing's hollow!" While it was not essential for the head of the New York City Health Department to know much about Egyptian mummies, it was useful to know the meaning of the word *hygiene*, which stumped one patronage appointee. Men assigned to oversee Indian reservations might have looked less at the money to be made and more to the laws they were charged to enforce.

Reformers began to make headway in 1881 with the passage of the Pendleton Civil Service Act. The law removed some federal jobs from the patronage rolls by placing them on the "classified" list, to be filled by competitive examinations. They had pressed for such a law for decades, but it took the assassination of a president to give them their opening. On July 2, 1881, President James A. Garfield waited at the gate with his Secretary of State, James G. Blaine, for the train that would take Garfield away for his summer vacation. Milling about was a slightly-built, forty-eight-year-old man, Charles Jules Guiteau. He moved nervously toward the president, reached into his pocket for a revolver, and fired. One shot grazed Garfield's arm; another lodged near his spine. "I am a Stalwart," Guiteau explained to the detectives who quickly apprehended him, "and Arthur will be President." Guiteau was plainly mad. He believed he was carrying out a coup that some in the government would be sure to support. By shooting Garfield and thereby placing Arthur's faction, the Stalwarts, in power, he would "save the Republican Party," a recent interest of his. Previously, Guiteau had tried to make a living as a preacher to whom God had given a special message about the Second Coming. But the idea stuck that a "disappointed office seeker," not a madman, had shot President Garfield, providing the necessary momentum to gain the votes in Congress and the signature of President Arthur, and the act passed. At first, just 15 percent of federal jobs landed on the classified list, but that percentage grew over time. It did so in part because administrations leaving the White House sought to give their employees permanent positions by assigning more jobs to the classified list, but even more because those who depended more than ever on the federal government for specific services, from mail delivery to engineering projects, demanded competent help.

PARTY WORKERS AND PARTY FUNDS   With or without the patronage system, political machines were never all-powerful as their critics charged. The workforce and the money that turned out the massive proportions of voters on election days also produced chronic problems. Local party workers realized that their extensive responsibilities enabled them to wreck the plans of party leaders. They prepared and distributed the ballots to voters, arranged the rallies, polled voters, and dispensed favors; they informed state leaders how voters were responding to campaigns. When unhappy with a convention's choice of candidates, they "knifed" the offending names, replacing them with others. Local workers' irregular tickets forced newspapers repeatedly to remind voters who the regular nominees were and to admonish voters to avoid odd ballots. Most often, knifings allowed voters to split their tickets for local races, which otherwise was difficult to do since ballots listed the candidates of only one party. Occasionally, however, knifings had broader consequences: Widespread knifing in New York contributed to Grover Cleveland's defeat in the presidential race of 1888.

Not only were party workers unruly, but they were among the largest campaign expenses parties incurred. In 1888 the Republican Party spent $73,465 in a hopeless attempt to organize Irish voters in New York City. The parties paid workers (Pennsylvania Republicans counted about twenty thousand), covered the expenses of speakers, rented headquarters, printed and distributed campaign books, and purchased advertising. On election days they provided the ballots, transportation for some voters, and payment for still others. Raising money was a persistent problem. "Voluntary" contributions from government workers brought in funds. So did candidates, whom the parties charged for the honor of running for office. Candidates who failed to pay local workers risked knifing. Local party organizations were also enriched by owners of brothels and gambling establishments and illegal liquor dealers who paid police and politicians for protection from harassment.

The parties also counted on contributions from large business interests, although politicians differed as to how to tap corporate money. Some, such as Conkling, wanted contributions but also independence from specific corporations. They periodically shook down corporations by threatening to pass regulations that affected a corporation or industry (a "strike bill") or by receiving contributions in exchange for moving imported items through customs smoothly and quickly. By the 1880s and 1890s, steadier relationships with businesses replaced these haphazard methods. Party leaders established solid connections with transportation, utility, construction, and insurance firms, which paid far more for party operations than assessments of government workers had, reduced buccaneering by individual legislators, and actually saved money for the corporations. Important politicians of both parties increasingly made tidy side incomes by serving as corporate officers.

Controversy, however, followed regular corporate support. Reformers of various stripes and the opposition party inevitably claimed that some politicians were merely the puppets of some industry or another. Some no doubt were. But Republican congressmen who believed high tariffs were the key to prosperity hardly needed lobbyists to persuade them with contributions to support bills protecting American industries and agriculture. Not surprisingly, congressmen and senators supported the interests of the businesses in their districts and states; yet business interests often disagreed with each other about what they wanted from government. Sheep farmers wanted high tariffs on wool; owners of woolen mills, the lowest possible tax. Finally, politicians and businessmen often distrusted each other. James G. Blaine blamed stingy businessmen for his narrow loss in the presidential election of 1884: "With all the immense interests of the tariff at stake, I don't think a single manufacturer gave $20,000. I doubt one gave $10,000." Politicians explained to industry lobbyists that the masses of ordinary citizens, not corporate bigwigs, "furnish the votes that will decide this election." For their part, businessmen expressed a weary disdain for politics and politicians. Joseph Wharton, the nation's largest nickel manufacturer, claimed, "I have supported and aided the government more than it has supported and aided me. I am not a pauper nor a lawyer. . . . I am one of the men who create and maintain the prosperity of the nation and who enable it to survive even the affliction of wrong-headed or cranky legislators." The structure of late-nineteenth-century politics and divisions among businessmen did not allow single business interests to control politics.

GOVERNMENT RESPONDS TO INDUSTRIAL AMERICA

Political facts also shaped the policies parties advanced. At the national level, divided government meant that neither party maintained majorities in Congress long enough to pursue their favored policies. Riding any single issue too hard also potentially threatened to unsettle the fragile coalitions that put politicians in office. Yet politicians did not simply sit back and watch industrial expansion transform the nation. Large national corporations, violent labor conflicts, the development of communication and transportation systems, and the rapid growth of cities created demands for government action. Most of all, politicians sought to push industrial and agricultural prosperity forward across the nation, especially in their own states or districts. The federal government promoted business and farming, but the complexities and size of the American economy required government to do more for industry than encourage it. Tariff policy, the currency question, and the regulation of business occupied Congress and divided the parties. Finally, the federal government provided a host of new services to constituents, from pensions to scientific research, prefiguring the expanded role of the federal government in the twentieth century.

GOVERNMENT PROMOTES BUSINESS   The promotion of economic enterprise was a mainstay of government policy throughout the nineteenth century. From the states' support of canal building to the writing of uniform incorporation laws to the rapid opening of land for white settlement, the federal and state governments encouraged economic activity. State and federal governments gave the railroads land grants and loans to speed the construction of a nationwide railroad network. The federal government made land, usually territory earlier reserved for the use of Indians, available to white farmers, ranchers, and miners. Congress supported industry and agriculture with high tariffs designed to allow American enterprise the time to develop free from foreign competition. Federal troops and state militias that battled strikers to protect the property of private industries might be considered another form of promotion.

The federal and state governments distributed the resources at their disposal to promote private enterprise. Distributive policies were inexpensive, well adapted to the strengths of the political parties, and generally popular. Because benefits flowed to particular states and regions, distribution perfectly matched the organization of the political parties. Politicians were happy to pass out favors because distribution inspired little grumbling; giving benefits to one industry did not preclude giving something else to another. Tariff protection, however, did divide Democrats and Republicans. It was the most important, if confusing, political issue of the late nineteenth century.

THE TARIFF QUESTION   To listen to Republican and Democratic politicians, it seemed the fate of the republic rested on tariff rates. High tariffs, Republicans argued, were "essential to the life of the nation, for the protection upon which depend vitality and strength, and for the wages and comforts and elevation of the citizens, upon which rest national sanity and growth, and the conditions of greatness and splendor." Democrats claimed in equally soaring language that only lower tariffs could guarantee individual freedom against a grasping government. Free trade fit the Democrats' preference for small government, low taxes, and the largest practical measure of personal freedom.

What tariff rates meant in practice was less clear. The tariff was the major source of revenue for the federal government. Tariffs had little impact on the nation's economy, as imports and exports accounted for less than 7 percent of the gross national product (by contrast, imports and exports accounted for 20 to 40 percent of Great Britain's gross national product in the late nineteenth century). Still, tariff rates mattered greatly to some economic interests. Sugar beet growers in Louisiana wanted protection from sugar imported from the Caribbean; iron and steel manufacturers, sheep farmers, and other industries possibly threatened by foreign competition fought hard for high tariff rates for their products. Industries that had large foreign markets, such as meatpacking, grain growing, and cattle raising, sought low rates, fearing that high tariffs would encourage foreign governments to retaliate by raising rates against American products. As a practical matter, Democrats representing the home areas of protection-seeking industries voted for high rates, while Republicans from districts where imports were important argued for low rates. In the end, the tariff policy was a crazy quilt of rates that reflected the many discrete adjustments demanded by various special interests. One remark about the 1883 tariff bill was true of those that followed: "Its general character cannot be easily described; in truth, it can hardly be said to have any general character."

Pressure for tariff reform mounted through the 1880s. The tariff had generated so much income that the federal government sat on an embarrassingly large surplus. Something had to be done to reduce the surplus; adjusting rates was one answer. Some reformers hoped for a "scientific" tariff, with rates arrived at through a careful examination of trade statistics. Free-trade Democrats sought tariff reductions because the surplus invited Republican spending and larger government. President Grover Cleveland devoted his entire December 1887 message to Congress to the need for tariff reform. "Our present tariff laws, the vicious, inequitable, and illogical source of unnecessary taxation, ought to be at once revised and amended," he wrote. High rates were "a burden upon those with moderate means and the poor, the employed and unemployed, the sick and well, and the young and old . . . a tax which with relentless grasp is fastened upon the clothing of every man, woman, and child in the land." The message was a sensation; it inspired 151 speeches in the House as representatives considered tariff revision. While the resulting 1888 tariff, like the Wilson-Gorman tariff of 1894, claimed to follow free-trade principles, it did so no more than had the Republican, protectionist McKinley tariff of 1890 and the Dingley tariff of 1897.

THE MONEY QUESTION   The currency question produced divisions within the parties rather than between them. If anything, it was even more confused and freighted with symbolic importance than the tariff question. The Constitution gave the federal government the power to coin money, and by the mid-nineteenth century, it exercised that authority. The reigning orthodoxy was that the paper money issued had to be backed by precious metal. In theory, holders of bank notes could cash in their paper for precious metal coins. Backing paper with metal smoothed foreign trade because precious metals had internationally recognized value. Paper backed by metal was "real" money.

Basing money on metal, however, presented difficulties. Precious metals, unlike paper money, had uses other than as currency. Their values rose and fell with demand and supply. New discoveries of precious metals stepped up supply and the volume of money in circulation; demand for money (which often occurred during periods of economic expansion) could lead to a tight money supply. Finally, there was the vexing question of which precious metal should be the basis for the currency. Gold and silver were the traditional standards in industrialized nations, although there was no internationally fixed ratio of the relative value of the two metals. By the 1870s gold was increasingly the lone international standard. Great Britain, the world's leading economy, adopted gold as the simple, modern, and scientific standard, and other nations felt pressure to follow.

Before the Civil War, the United States had officially declared a gold and silver standard but in practice had coined only gold. The price of silver was high relative to gold's, and no one sold it to the Treasury. During the Civil War, strapped for cash, both the Union government and the Confederate states issued paper money backed only by the good name of the government. These "greenbacks" were not redeemable in specie, or gold coin. By the end of the war, the half-billion dollars worth of greenbacks traded at half their face value. The Union government also had issued a variety of short-term bonds, about $2 billion worth, which investors expected would be redeemable in gold. By the end of the war, respectable opinion—bankers, businessmen, Treasury Department officials, members of Congress, and economists—concurred that the United States should return to the gold standard as soon as possible. In 1866 the Treasury Department authorized the return to specie payment. When resumption proved too deflationary, taking too much currency out of circulation and disrupting business, Congress repealed the order to return the nation to specie payments.

The money issue combined financial interest, morality, and partisan wrangling. Bondholders waited impatiently for resumption in the hope of turning a profit on their investment. Debtors, especially farmers, feared deflation. Those who had borrowed "cheap" dollars dreaded the prospect of having to repay their loans with scarcer and more expensive gold-backed currency. Advocates of resumption considered the debtors' dilemma to be an unfortunate but necessary bump on the road to fiscal stability. Both sides argued that true morality was with their side. Those in favor of the gold standard talked as if money had character: Gold-backed currency embodied the traits of gentlemen. It was "solid," "honest," and "sound." Unlike sly, deceptive paper money, it had "intrinsic value" that allowed men to place their trust and confidence in it. Opponents of resumption argued that money was simply a device that eased the process of trade. Gold was no better suited than paper to the task; whether backed by gold, silver, or sheer faith, there should be enough money in circulation to meet the demands of trade. The United States, they said, should not allow Great Britain, greedy bondholders, or bankers to dictate how much currency circulated in the United States. In the 1870s both parties were divided internally on the issue, but the Republicans did a better job of muting their divisions. Republican moderates took control of the issue and presented themselves as the sane managers who could smoothly lead the transition to the gold standard. Democrats were openly divided, allowing Republicans to paint them as unreliable and perhaps even radical on the issue.

As long as the economy functioned smoothly, the currency issue interested few Americans. In early 1873, Congress passed a coinage bill designed to stabilize the currency. No one noticed that the bill dropped the silver dollar, although three years of wrangling went into the bill's other details. The depression that began in 1873, however, inspired southern and western Congressmen of both parties to press for an expansion of the money supply. Eastern Republicans, who had promised that "[i]f we finally take the road to specie payment, justice, prosperity, integrity, safety, and honor will result to our whole country," beat back the effort to enlarge the volume of unsecured greenbacks in circulation. They struck a compromise: The federal government would increase the number of national bank charters, which would indirectly raise the amount of bank notes in circulation. In exchange they extracted an agreement to return to specie payments by 1879. Before that happened, southern and western Congressmen worked to return silver to the coinage list. The "Crime of '73," the decision to drop the silver dollar, had plunged the nation into depression, they argued. Here, too, eastern Republicans compromised. The Bland-Allison Act of 1878 remonetized silver but limited the amount the Treasury could coin. There things stood until the 1890s: The United States returned to specie payments, coined a limited amount of silver along with gold, and moved toward retiring the Civil War debt. The depression lifted by 1878. Yet sectional divisions, along with the theories, interests, and moral certainties that underpinned them, lay in wait for an even more bruising battle in the 1890s.

REGULATING THE ECONOMY   The idea that government ought to regulate as well as promote industry and commerce went back as far as the colonial period, when laws mandated such things as the proper weight of a loaf of bread and the size and weight of nails. Late-nineteenth-century economic expansion, especially the rise of big business and the creation of the trusts, created demand for new regulations to control business. To many Americans, railroad corporations served a public purpose. Because people depended upon them for their livelihoods, railroads were more

This cartoon depicts a Grange farmer warning a sleeping public that democracy will be crushed by railroad interests. The Grange, organized in 1867, helped push through state laws regarding railroads. (Culver Pictures, Inc.)

than just private businesses to be operated as their owners saw fit. Big businesses that formed trust agreements ran against cherished values, seeming to defy the principle of competition that many believed necessary to both economic growth and freedom itself. If a single firm or a small group of firms controlled an important industry, many Americans feared that such monopolists would simply pad their profits and stamp out potential competitors, limiting others' opportunities and stifling economic progress.

Traditionally, economic regulation had been a function of state governments. By the 1870s, states moved to regulate railroads as well as promote them. Pressure to do so came from many quarters: from farmers who complained about high rates to store and ship their produce, from businessmen who objected that other communities enjoyed cheaper rates, and from merchants who were annoyed about the rebates large shippers received. A number of Midwestern states enacted so-called "Granger" laws, named after the Grange, a farmers' organization active in the campaign for regulation, although the laws reflected the efforts of merchants and shippers as well as farmers and spread beyond the Midwest to the Northeast. They typically set maximum rates for freight and storage of grain at the depots, outlawed rebates to large shippers, and created commissions to enforce the rules. The laws delivered a good deal less than their supporters hoped. Due less to the power of the railroads than to the divergent agendas of those who used the railroads, state courts and legislatures trimmed the statutes and reduced the commissions' control. Some farmers wanted low rates, but others wanted to make sure that their competitors paid higher rates; some merchants wanted an end to rebates, while others who had been bypassed by the railroads wanted no regulations, to improve their chances of getting a line. In 1877 the Supreme Court upheld the constitutionality of state railroad regulation in *Munn v. Illinois*, but by the 1880s the Court had limited the ability of states to dictate rates: Railroads were interstate operations, which made state efforts to control railroad rates unconstitutional.

In 1887 the federal government stepped in with its own effort to regulate the railroads. It had the authority to oversee interstate operations and the potential to resolve the problems of groups across the nation: the New York merchants and farmers who complained about the advantages enjoyed by other eastern ports and western farmers; the oil producers angered by the low shipping rates Standard Oil commanded; the Midwestern shippers and farmers convinced that their rates were too high; and the railroads concerned about "ruinous" competition. The Interstate Commerce Act banned differential rates for short and long hauls and railroad pooling agreements that divided traffic and fixed rates, published rates, and outlawed rebates. It created the Interstate Commerce Commission (ICC) to hear complaints. The ICC also compelled the railroads to install safety devices such as the automatic coupler and Westinghouse air brakes. Aggrieved parties still had the option of going to court, and the ICC did not solve the problems of the railroads; early in the twentieth century, major legislation would revisit the problems of railroads, shippers, and the public. The act was nonetheless a landmark: For the first time, the federal government instituted regulations and set up a quasi-judicial commission to address some of the problems of industrial expansion.

REGULATION AND THE STATES   States, however, continued to shoulder most of the regulatory load. By 1900 states had created twenty fish commissions, twenty-five railroad commissions, twenty-five bureaus of labor, and thirty boards of health. Over time, new demands expanded the power of these boards. New York created its Department of Insurance in 1859; by 1905 twenty-two states had followed its lead. The largest insurance companies had little quarrel with these commissions, as they focused on driving out unsound companies, which helped the industry in the public's estimation. Only at the turn of the century did some states examine the investments of insurance companies. In response to demands of workers' organizations and the period's labor strife, states passed laws that governed the hours and conditions of factory labor and limited the hours of female and child laborers. In the 1880s alone, states passed 1,600 laws that affected labor. A number of states appointed factory inspectors to ensure that factory safety laws were being obeyed. States collected statistics on the workforce, working conditions, and strikes. Poor administration, small staffs, and loopholes made the laws more like suggestions for employers than rules; still, states exercised their power to protect public health and safety to the extent that their administrative abilities and pressure from opposing interests allowed.

Local governments also stepped up regulatory activity. Sanitation drew the most attention. Both cities and states passed laws that mandated the inspection of tenement houses. Cities improved the quantity of water for their growing populations, even if the quality of the water remained fouled by the waste of factories and sewers. City health inspectors assigned to guard the milk supply inspected creameries and tested the products sold to urban consumers. They closed "creameries" attached to breweries that milked diseased cows fed with the waste from beermaking and outlawed the sale of "swill" milk thinned with water and fattened with oil. The courts gave the cities wide latitude in regulating in the interest of public health. Louisiana had chartered the Crescent City Live Stock Handling and Slaughterhouse Company as New Orleans' sole slaughterhouse in order to bring hygiene and standards to the industry as well as to reward the political friends who owned the company. Butchers outside the charmed circle sued, claiming the state had no right to deprive them of their rights as citizens. In 1873 the Supreme Court ruled that public health concerns outweighed the rights of the excluded butchers. Cities had wide power to regulate, although scandalous conditions remained that would inspire further attempts at reform in the early twentieth century. If American cities were not paradises of cleanliness and order, their governments had made the first steps toward lessening the chaotic consequences of rapid growth.

Education was the concern of state and local governments. Even more than in other areas of state administration, education gained an expanded bureaucracy and a good deal of freedom from partisan politics. By 1900 most states had established boards of education to set and oversee policy, which were rare in the 1870s. They also created county boards of supervisors to oversee local school districts. By the turn of the century, most states had teacher's colleges to produce trained instructors and ongoing teachers' institutes for further training. States mandated curriculum, graded schools, and made attendance compulsory. Spending on education increased fourfold between 1860 and 1880. Professional educators, rather than political appointees, increasingly filled positions on state boards and in local schools, since many Americans believed that education, unlike the tariff, belonged "out of politics." By the 1890s many states allowed women to vote for school officials and even to run for the positions; presumably concerned solely with children's welfare and untainted by partisanship, women could have a say in education denied them in other areas of public policy.

States might have exercised their regulatory powers more vigorously but for financial constraints. In the 1870s and 1880s, both state and local governments relied almost solely on property taxes to pay for their operations. In the North and especially the South, state governments staggered under the load of Civil War–era debts in addition to expenses generated by a growing stack of new programs. Owners of real property—farmers, city homeowners, and businesses—complained loudly about their tax burden. Politicians responded by promising economical government and sometimes cutting back programs they had just enacted. Local governments tried to duck the tax problem by borrowing money, floating bonds that became difficult to cover in depression years to pay for railroad subsidies, water and sewer systems, and roads. State governments tried to find new tax sources. In the 1890s, New Jersey's and Delaware's corporate franchise fees, part of their relaxed incorporation laws, attracted enough new corporations to go a long way toward paying for state government. Other states enacted new corporate taxes, inheritance taxes, and liquor taxes. By the turn of the century, most states no longer relied on property taxes to meet their obligations, freeing up the funds to administer programs and launch new ones and leaving property taxes for local use.

The courts also limited state regulatory powers. By the 1880s and 1890s, the federal and state courts had developed a not undeserved reputation as the most reliably conservative branch of government. Federal judges issued injunctions against striking workers, while state courts invalidated laws intended to protect workers' safety, such as a New York ban on cigar making in tenement apartments. Appeals judges championed the rights of property against what they saw as legislative assault: Corporations had the same rights as persons to equal protection and due process under the Fourteenth Amendment. They also held that laws aimed at improving working conditions and limiting the length of the workday violated workers' "freedom of contract." This line of reasoning culminated in a series of Supreme Court decisions at the turn of the century, including *In re Debs*, which upheld an injunction against striking railroad workers, and *Lochner v. New York*, which invalidated a New York law limiting the working hours of bakery employees. But while most of the era's most prominent jurists may have believed passionately in the rights of property and the obtuseness of politicians, there were more laws than appeals. The courts let stand numerous laws that limited the hours women and children worked and the working conditions of men. Cases such as *Lochner* did not check the states' willingness to regulate.

Widespread fear of the power of big business also drew legislative attention. Although holding companies had quickly replaced trusts as the preferred form of business combination (Standard Oil had pioneered both in the 1880s), trusts, understood as large, grasping, monopolistic firms, were the target of state legislatures in the 1880s. Ten states deemed trusts illegal; courts in six states determined trusts constituted an unlawful restraint of trade. A campaign for federal legislation followed state action, which produced the Sherman Antitrust Act of 1890. It prohibited "every contract, combination in the form of trust or otherwise, or conspiracy, in restraint of trade or commerce." Passed by an overwhelming margin, the law was purposefully vague: By not trying to specify the proper size of businesses, it might survive judicial scrutiny. It left enforcement to the courts rather than a regulatory agency, which meant that prosecutions were handled by a Justice Department not always up to the task. In *United States v. E. C. Knight* (1895), the less than vigorous argument on the part of the Attorney General led to the Supreme Court's finding that, although the American Sugar Company refined more than 90 percent of the nation's sugar, it did not violate the Sherman Antitrust Act. The Court found, however, that union-led strikes and boycotts constituted an unlawful restraint of trade. The Sherman Antitrust Act was not useless as a tool against monopolistic practices; private parties, rather than the federal government, successfully brought cases against illegal price and trade practices. The Sherman Antitrust Act showed both the government's willingness to act against monopolistic business behavior and the difficulties of doing so.

GOVERNMENTS EXPAND SERVICES   Within their limitations, state and federal governments responded to the novel problems of industrial America by providing new services and extending older ones. Here, too, the states took the lead. In the 1880s many industrial states established Bureaus of Labor, which collected statistics on working conditions and labor unrest. In 1884 the national Bureau of Labor did the same and investigated how the industrial economy affected workers' lives. To further agricultural productivity, the United States Department of Agriculture, together with state departments, hired scientists to conduct research and communicate the findings to farmers. State colleges of agriculture and state experiment stations trained scientists and organized research projects. In the western territories, the federal government extinguished Indian land claims, organized land for settlement, and ineffectively tried to prevent fraudulent claims. It also dealt with complex claims concerning timber, mineral, and water rights that made some western lawyers rich. The federal government's often corrupt or incompetent agents administered the nation's shifting policy toward Indians.

The federal government provided for veterans of the Union Army, an obligation that soaked up about one third of the federal budget. In 1862 Congress rewrote the Revolutionary War–era laws that provided for veterans. Those who had suffered war-related injuries or disabilities and the widows and children of soldiers who died as a result of their service received pensions. As the federal surplus ballooned and as the Grand Army of the Republic, a Union veteran's organization, honed its lobbying skills, pensions expanded in generosity and reach. Those who slipped through the cracks asked their congressmen to push special bills through, clogging the congressional calendar. (In the 1880s Friday evening was "pension night" for Congress.) After 1890 it was enough to have served ninety days and to show some disability, whatever its source; the widows and children of veterans could collect benefits whether their husbands or fathers had died of wartime injuries or streetcar accidents. It was, according to the GAR, "the most liberal pension measure ever funded by any legislative body in the world, and will place upon the rolls all of the survivors of the war whose conditions of health are not practically perfect." Veteran's pensions, driven up by large numbers of Union veterans in the North, amounted to an old-age relief program for northern men, further supplemented by hospitals, old-age homes, and pensions granted by state governments. Southern states provided their own pensions and homes for aged and infirm Confederate veterans.

For all the talk about small government, the federal government grew substantially by the turn of the century. In 1871 roughly 53,000 people worked for the federal government; by 1901 the number had increased nearly fivefold to 256,000. Some worked for the new cabinet-level agencies, the Justice Department and the Department of Agriculture. Others worked for the new Interstate Commerce Commission, the Civil Service Commission, or one of the numerous new bureaus. The size of the government workforce reflected the federal government's expanded tasks. The work was not always accomplished efficiently. Honesty was also a problem: The pension office and the Interior Department had more than their share of scandals. But even as the states handled many of the immediately important tasks of government, the federal government began to expand its reach into people's lives.

THIRD PARTIES CHALLENGE THE MAJOR PARTIES

Some innovations resulted from pressure applied by third parties. Although most men identified strongly with the Democrats or Republicans, the close competition between them magnified the importance of third parties. With presidential elections at times decided by as little as 0.4 percent of the vote, the defection of even a small number of voters in an important state could determine the results. Men's attachment to the parties was not mindless. Voters usually signaled their dissatisfaction by staying home on election day. But sometimes disgust with patronage, scandals, compromised principles, or economic conditions moved voters to protest by voting for a third party. A series of third parties attracted votes in the late nineteenth century and forced responses from the major parties.

Late-nineteenth-century third parties typically tried to appeal as widely as possible, hoping to attract not only those who believed in their cause but also those dissatisfied with the parties for other reasons. The Greenback Party, which reached its peak strength in the late 1870s, focused on the currency issue. Greenbackers blamed the depression on the contraction of the money supply after the Civil War and argued that the Treasury should increase the money supply in order to right the economy. They favored fiat money and currency based on the trust people had in it rather than metal, and claimed that resumption of specie payments drove down wages and prices and hurt debtors in particular. Defying economic orthodoxy in a way that especially attracted farmers, Greenbackers also made a play for the votes of discontented industrial workers. Formed in the midst of a depression, the Greenback Party decried monopolies and the dominance of capital over labor, and endorsed an eight-hour workday, health and safety regulations protecting workers, a graduated income tax, the end of convict labor and the importation of Chinese workers, and public control of railroads. It also opposed the disfranchisement of African Americans in the South and nominated African Americans for state offices and congressional seats.

In 1884 some Republicans were so disgusted with their presidential nominee, James G. Blaine, that they campaigned for the Democrat, Grover Cleveland. They were called Mugwumps, an Algonquin word, because they were said to have gone "off the reservation." Cleveland won. (© Bettmann/CORBIS)

The currency issue dominated Greenback campaigns in the West and Midwest, where the party attracted farmers taken with the "cheap money" idea, while in the East labor issues topped the party's agenda. In the off-year election of 1878, the party won several congressional seats and more than a million votes. But in the presidential campaign of 1880, Greenbacker James B. Weaver won only slightly more than 3 percent of the vote; by 1884 Benjamin Butler gained only 2 percent of the vote. It did not help the Greenback cause that the depression began to lift. They suffered as well from the typical pains of new parties. Internal dissension that pitted currency reformers against labor reformers made deciding on platforms and candidates difficult. The party never built effective state-wide organizations; Greenbackers, like members of many nineteenth-century third parties, believed their party was above mere politics, the trimming of principles, patronage, and petty organizational concerns. The party's voters drifted back to their major party moorings or joined new third parties.

Some found homes in labor parties organized at city and state levels. Labor parties dated back to the early nineteenth century, but in the mid-1880s a new round of party building efforts coincided with the growing strength of the Knights of Labor. In a number of small industrial cities, variously-named labor parties backed by the Knights gained control of local governments. They mounted serious challenges in large cities as well. A labor-backed independent party elected a mayor in Milwaukee. In New York City, Henry George, proponent of tax reform and candidate of the United Labor Party, came in second in the 1886 mayoral election, with the Republican candidate, young Theodore Roosevelt, a distant third. These labor parties did not generally offer a coherent, positive vision for city government. They promised, however, to curb the use of local government against organized workers by refusing to use police against strikers and opposing the use of injunctions against strikes. The placards workers carried in parades to support George's campaign tell the story: "Down with Bribable Judges, Corrupt Legislators, and Vile Police Despotism!" "Boycott the Enemies of Labor!" and "No Charity: We Want Fair and Square Justice."

The Prohibition Party drew from a constituency different from the Greenback or labor parties', although it shared some of those parties' goals and their hostility toward partisan politics. Coming together out of various organizations working for temperance in the late 1860s, the Prohibition Party's main issue was the elimination of the sale of alcohol, or at the very least, the abolition of the saloon. Drink, Prohibitionists claimed, was at the root of social problems ranging from crime to poverty to family violence. Its base was in the North among evangelical Protestants, ministers, and the middle class. It also gained the support of many women who had joined the Woman's Christian Temperance Union. Although they could not vote, members of the WCTU worked for prohibition candidates and for local campaigns to ban saloons in their communities. That their work often came to nothing persuaded many of these women, previously indifferent to woman suffrage, that they needed the vote. They would become a force in the campaign for woman suffrage.

Like other third parties, the Prohibition Party reached for a wide range of issues. It stood not only against alcohol but also against monopolies and political corruption; it was in favor of woman suffrage, reform in policies toward Indians, and English-only instruction in the schools. Widening the party's platform went for nothing, if election returns were any guide. In the party's best years (in the mid-1880s to early 1890s), it never gained more than 2 percent of the vote nationwide. But by siphoning off Republican votes in important competitive states, the Prohibition Party turned state elections, lost the 1884 presidential election for the Republicans, and prevented them from gaining a majority in 1888.

Other groups found ways to register their displeasure with Gilded Age politics. The Grange tinkered with third-party politics but mostly hoped that lobbying both major parties would prove more effective. Oliver Hudson Kelley, a clerk in the federal Department of Agriculture, conceived the idea of the Grange after his trip to the South in 1866. The Grange adapted the rituals, secrecy, and ceremonial offices of the Masons to rural life, in an effort to relieve isolation, celebrate the farm family, and promote fellowship. In the mid-1870s the depression turned the Grange into a political and economic organization as well as a social one. It grew especially strong in the Midwest, where Grangers supported railroad regulation. Grangers sought to avoid entanglement in party politics, but this did not rule out plans for government policies. Grangers sought state regulation of the railroads and the rigorous collection of taxes on personal property. The Grange equally involved men and women; reflecting the interests of some of the female leadership, it supported prohibition and woman suffrage. To reduce the farmers' traditional problem of buying at retail and selling at wholesale, it organized cooperatives for purchasing supplies and providing inexpensive fire insurance. The collapse of most of the cooperatives led to the organization's steep decline in the late 1870s; thereafter it carried on largely as a social group in the East.

Some upper-class Republicans, eventually joined by some Democrats, hoped to make their mark in politics through independence. The Liberal Republican movement in the 1870s failed as both a third party and a faction able to control the Republican Party. Fashioning themselves as independent of the major parties, the Mugwumps, as they were derisively named, aimed to shape policy and determine elections through their willingness to vote for candidates of either party who came closest to their preferences, especially regarding civil service reform and lower tariffs. It was a small group without a great deal of popular appeal, but using their prominent positions as editors of leading magazines and writers, the Mugwumps had advantages that other movements lacked.

The attacks on the major parties by third parties and independent voters left their mark on policy in the Gilded Age. Close elections forced the major parties to respond to voters who threatened to withhold their usual support. Democrats answered the Greenback threat by championing Chinese exclusion and, in industrial states, proposing labor legislation. To stave off the Prohibitionist challenge, Republicans supported high license fees for saloons in some states and outright prohibition in a few others. Both parties combined to pass the Sherman Antitrust Act to demonstrate their opposition to monopolies. Both parties joined to offer civil service reform and railroad regulation. Offering even a small measure of what third parties wanted was usually enough to lure back regular party voters.

CONCLUSION

In popular memory, men interchangeable in their lack of distinction, achievement, and personality presided over a corrupt and dormant government in the Gilded Age. Although the period's presidents were not strong chief executives by twentieth-century standards, they worked within the political realities of strong parties, close elections, partisan voters, and dangerous third parties. Within these constraints, Congress passed and presidents signed landmark legislation, while state governments regulated and supported industry and provided services to citizens.

Recommended Readings

DOCUMENTS: Henry Adams, *Chapters of Erie, and Other Essays* (1871) and *The Education of Henry Adams: An Autobiography* (1907).

READINGS: John Garraty, *The New Commonwealth, 1877–1890* (1968); Richard J. Jensen, *The Winning of the Midwest: Social and Political Conflict, 1888–1896* (1971); Morton Keller, *Affairs of State: Public Life in Late Nineteenth Century America* (1977); Paul Kleppner, *The Cross of Culture* (1970); Gerald W. McFarland, *Mugwumps, Morals and Politics* (1975); Michael E. McGerr, *The Decline of Popular Politics* (1986); H. Wayne Morgan, *From Hayes to McKinley* (1969) and *Unity and Culture: The United States* (1971); Walter Nugent, *Money and American Society* (1968); David J. Rothman, *Politics and Power: The United States Senate* (1966); Mary P. Ryan, *Women in Public: Between Banners and Ballots* (1990); John Sproat, *"The Best Men": Liberal Reformers in the Gilded Age* (1968); Mark Wahlgren Summers, *Rum, Romanism, and Rebellion: The Making of a President, 1884* (2000); Richard E. Welch, Jr., *George Frisbie Hoar and the Half-Breed Republicans* (1971).

19

❧

Immigrants and the City Transform American Society

OVERVIEW   In the late nineteenth century, Americans saw their society transformed as millions of immigrants poured into the United States. Immigrants made up more than 14 percent of America's population by 1910. Most of these late arrivals ("new immigrants") were from eastern and southern Europe. They did not speak English and brought with them customs viewed as strange in their new homeland. Many Americans found these changes disturbing. One minister warned that the new industrial metropolis created by this influx of settlers was a "serious menace to our civilization." By 1890 Americans had begun using the phrase "the modern city" to denote this social transformation. Rapid urbanization created immense problems with transportation, housing, sanitation, crime, and poverty. City officials and reformers all sought solutions to these ills, with varying degrees of success.

IMMIGRANT EXPERIENCES

Immigrants came to the United States (and elsewhere in the Americas) to better their lives. "Better" could include a Russian escaping the draft, an Eastern European Jew avoiding persecution, or an Italian hoping to earn enough money to return to Italy and buy a farm. Immigrants after 1880 were more likely than earlier immigrants to be poor, single, and non-Protestant. Traveling to America was arduous, even with improvements in transportation. New arrivals often faced difficulties, and ethnic groups stuck together for comfort and protection.

DECIDING TO LEAVE HOME   The most noticeable change in late nineteenth-century America was the rich diversity created by the influx of immigrants. In the four decades between 1880 and 1920, more than twenty-three million immigrants came to America, 80 percent of them from eastern and southern Europe. By 1890 adult immigrants outnumbered native adults in eighteen of the twenty largest cities.

This massive migration was part of a global pattern. People left their native lands to settle in South America, Canada, and Australia. Brazil and Argentina aggressively recruited immigrants by offering subsidized travel, duty-free entry of personal belongings, and full resident status upon arrival. These policies drew significant numbers of Germans, Italians, and Jews from Europe to South America.

The United States government did not offer travel subsidies or other direct inducements, although immigrants were recruited by private companies seeking employees, steamships needing passengers, and states anxious for settlers.

To promote expansion of the rail system, railroads actively sought immigrants to settle new western lands. The Kansas Pacific, Missouri Pacific, Santa Fe, and Wisconsin Central Railroads deluged Europe with pamphlets and brochures telling of the splendors of the Midwest and Great Plains states. Railroads offered reduced fares, provided low-interest loans for purchasing farmland, and sometimes even built churches and schools. Promotional literature claimed that the Midwest and Great Plains states were ideal places to live. Stories were told of invalids miraculously getting well. Jay Cooke of the Northern Pacific went so far as to print fraudulent weather maps showing a deceptively mild climate in the Great Plains. These bogus maps, which were circulated throughout Europe, inspired some wits to rename the Northern Pacific Railroad the Banana Belt.

A free or cheap ride would not alone have induced many people to pack what belongings they could, leave family and friends behind, and travel thousands of miles to a land where they did not know the language or customs. Even the prospect of miracle climate might not be a sufficient lure. People left in large numbers because they saw few other good choices. America was an appealing option for Russian and Eastern European Christians and Greeks, Italians, and residents of the Balkan region: Growing populations simply could not be supported on small peasant holdings. The military draft was a further inducement for Russians; service was for a term of twenty-five years, and families would hold funeral services for drafted young men because they would not expect to see them again. In the Austro-Hungarian empire, the term was twelve years. At home eastern European Jews had only religious repression and bursts of government-tolerated (if not encouraged) violence against them to count on. Mexican peasants pushed north across the border, displaced by large sugar and coffee plantations.

Although immigrants represented a wide range of religious, cultural, and social backgrounds, most shared a strong belief in the primary importance of family and kinship. Leaving home was a well-considered family decision and a practical act for most.

These late immigrants came to the United States with differing aspirations. Some sought fortunes, many simply wanted jobs, and others dreamed of earning money and returning home. More than half of the Hungarians and southern Italians, forty percent of the Germans and Greeks, and nearly a third of the Poles returned, often as planned, to their native lands. Many shuttled back and forth.

The newcomers brought widely divergent social, political, and religious views. Some were socialists, others Catholics. Among the German immigrants alone there were Catholics, Lutherans, Jews, and free-thinkers. Immigrants arriving after the Civil War joined the 4 million who had settled in America in the 1840s and 1850s. Before the 1880s most newcomers were northern Europeans. From 1860 to 1890, more than 7 million Germans came to the United States. They were joined by 2 million English, Scottish, and Welsh settlers, 1.5 million Irish, 1 million Scandinavians, and 800,000 French Canadians.

Beginning in the 1880s, however, increasing numbers of eastern and southern Europeans—Slavs, Jews, Italians, and Greeks—crossed the Atlantic. More than 18 million "new immigrants" came to this country before 1920. These new immigrants differed from the "old" immigrants. They had unfamiliar names, such as Stanislawski and Alioto, that ended in vowels and tripped up old-stock English speakers. Many were Roman Catholics, Eastern Orthodox, or Orthodox Jews. They tended to be poorer than earlier settlers. After 1880 even many German and British immigrants were unskilled workers or displaced peasants. Furthermore, increasing numbers of young single men arrived, while before 1880 most immigrants came with their families.

SAILING TO AMERICA   Improved land and sea transportation made the journey to America easier than it had been earlier in the century, but travel was still arduous. For example, many Russians and easterns Europeans had to hike for days or weeks with their belongings on their backs or in handcarts just to reach railroad terminals, then faced long rail trips to major European seaports to board a steamship.

Immigrants favored certain ports. The busiest were Liverpool, England; Hamburg, Germany; Fiume, Austria-Hungary; and Palermo, Italy. Steamship companies vied with each other for passengers. By 1880, forty-eight steamship companies were competing for Atlantic traffic. This competition led steamship lines to make the transfer from the train to the ship as smooth as possible. Company employees met each train to ensure that emigrants were protected from thieves and confidence men. The Cunard Steamship Line built a huge complex that housed more than two thousand people in ten dormitories.

At the port of departure, company representatives who spoke a variety of eastern European languages were on hand. Conditions were comfortable and sanitary. Kosher food was available for Jewish travelers, and fish was offered on Fridays for Catholics. Later, in Germany, the Hamburg-Amerika line constructed an entire immigrant village with its own railway station, churches, and synagogue. In 1891 American immigration law required that steamship companies vaccinate, disinfect, and give health exams to passengers before voyages. Often American physicians were assigned to European ports to help in this process.

Improvements in shipbuilding and steam engines made travel across the Atlantic faster and easier. The voyage usually took eight to fourteen days. In the 1870s and 1880s most immigrants traveled in steerage, below-deck compartments without portholes that had been used as cargo holds. In these steerage compartments, passengers were crammed into two or more tiers of narrow metal bunks. Travelers brought their own straw mattresses, which they threw overboard on the last day of the trip. Men and women were segregated, sometimes only by a flimsy curtain of blankets.

Emigrants brought their own food, which they cooked on ranges and in boilers and vegetable cookers in the ship's galley. Ships usually provided herring because it was inexpensive and helped combat seasickness. Toilet facilities were generally poor on pre-1890 ships. Some vessels provided only twenty-one toilets per thousand passengers.

Steamships continued to make marked improvements in accommodations throughout this period. By the 1890s steerage had been replaced by third-class cabins that accommodated two to six passengers. Outside promenades were constructed to allow exercise. Lounges and smoking rooms were provided. Meals were served in small dining areas, while concession stands sold beer, drinks, and tobacco. Many steamship lines employed nurses, physicians, and chaplains for the benefit of passengers.

ARRIVING IN AMERICA   Upon arrival in an American port, travel-worn immigrants were full of expectation and anxiety. Typical advice came from one immigrant who warned, "When you land in America, you will find many who will offer their services, but beware of them because there are so many rascals who make it their business to cheat immigrants." American immigration officials sought to protect newcomers as much as possible from those who might prey on them, but their primary concern remained protecting America from potentially dangerous immigrants.

The busiest immigration port was New York. From 1855 to 1892, Castle Garden at the tip of Manhattan served as the major entry facility. In 1893 Congress abandoned this facility for a new depot on nearby Ellis Island, close to the New Jersey shore. After the original wooden structure on the island burned in 1897, Congress began construction of an enormous red brick complex.

At its peak Ellis Island processed hundreds of immigrants per day. The first floor housed the reception facilities, a railroad ticket office, food counters, and a waiting room. Other floors were used for administrative offices. An adjacent building offered new arrivals a restaurant, a laundry, and shower facilities. Here immigrants got their first taste of the New World. Sometimes the experience was humorous. One immigrant later recalled, "I never saw a banana in my life and they served a banana. I was just looking at it." Others, she said, tried to eat their bananas with the skins on before they learned bananas should be peeled.

Under mandate from Congress, American immigration officials sought to keep out people they considered dangerous. During the late nineteenth century, Congress imposed more restrictive immigration policies. In 1882 Congress excluded "lunatics," convicted criminals, and people likely to become public charges. Later restrictions barred prostitutes, "idiots," polygamists, and those suffering from contagious or "loathsome" diseases. Still, 80 percent of all entering immigrants were admitted without difficulty. Of those initially detained for further examination or questioning, more than half were later admitted.

SETTLING IN AMERICA   An extensive network of private charities and benevolent societies were located at Ellis Island to aid the new arrivals. Immigrants were introduced to American life by Jewish, Irish, German, and other mutual aid societies, by the Salvation Army, the Women's Home Missionary Society, the New York Bible Society, and myriad other groups. Immigration officials instructed these groups to remain sensitive to the needs of the immigrant. One official cautioned Christian missionary groups to imagine themselves in the shoes of Jewish immigrants: "When they have Christian tracts printed in Hebrew put in their hands, apparently with the approval of the United States government, they wonder what is going to happen to them there."

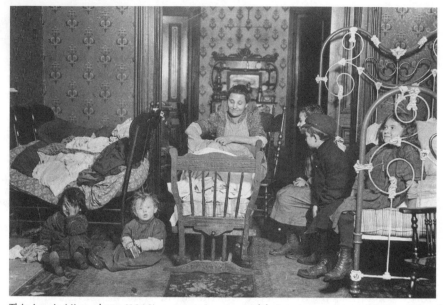

This Lewis Hine photo (1910) captures immigrant life in a tenement on the East Side of New York City. (Culver Pictures, Inc.)

From these ports of entry, immigrants spread throughout the nation. Many of the Irish and Jews remained in large cities, particularly in the Northeast. Many Poles, hoping to earn enough money to return home, opted to work for high wages (by eastern European standards) in the coal fields of Pennsylvania, the stockyards of Chicago, and the steel mills of Buffalo.

Italians and Greeks also preferred the city, and many took jobs as menial laborers. Those with sufficient money opened restaurants, fruit stores, or shoe repair shops. Certain regions attracted specific immigrants; the Genoese Italians in Chicago and San Francisco often became saloon keepers, restaurant owners, or fruit vendors. Major enterprises, such as the Del Monte Corporation and the Bank of America, were launched by Genoese Italians. Many Germans and Scandinavians traveled to the Midwest to settle on farms or work in cities such as Racine, Wisconsin, and Minneapolis and Duluth, Minnesota.

Immigrants usually emphasized close family bonds and ties of friendship within their own ethnic groups. Kinship provided protection, and immigrant families tended to reinforce older traditions even as they encountered the New World. At the center of most families was the mother. As one Irish immigrant recalled, "Mother always handled the money; my father never even opened his pay envelope." With large families to tend, many mothers helped bring money into the household by taking in borders, doing seasonal work (such harvesting and canning in upstate New

York factories), and performing "home" work, where, for example, a woman and perhaps many of her children worked on bundles of sewing in the garment trade. Many immigrant families (especially southern Europeans and eastern European Christians) expected their children to contribute to the family income. The youngest might shine shoes or hawk newspapers, while older children began factory work. Children were asked to contribute their wages to the family and to help aging parents.

Immigrants who settled in cities tended to congregate. Although most large cities had Italian, Polish, German, or Chinese districts, usually no single neighborhood was composed exclusively of one ethnic group. Most ethnic neighborhoods contained a diverse population. Also, sharp regional, occupational, religious, and class differences often divided ethnic groups. In New York there was not just one "Little Italy"; one could find Neapolitans and Calabrians on Mulberry Street, Genoese on Baxter Street, Tyrolese on 69th Street. Genoese Italians fought the newly arrived Sicilians. Poles divided along Prussian and Galician lines. Middle-class "lace-curtain" Irish looked down on the "shanty" Irish. In St. Louis factionalism divided the German population. German Jews who had immigrated in the early nineteenth century seemed embarrassed by Jews from eastern Europe and Russia.

Leads from contacts in the United States and ethnic stereotyping led members of different ethnic groups into particular industries. The Irish could be found in construction; Italians in bricklaying, quarrying, mining, and construction; Slavs (a catchall term for people from the Balkans and eastern Europe) in mining and steel; Germans in brewing, furniture making, and cigar making; and Jews in the garment trades.

Divisions also occurred between ethnic groups. Germans and eastern Europeans deeply resented Irish domination of the Catholic Church hierarchy. In Buffalo, German Catholics joined forces with anti-Catholic legislators to oppose legal ownership and inheritance of church property by an Irish Catholic hierarchy. In Detroit, Poles became so upset when a Polish priest was dismissed by the local Irish Catholic bishop that parish women actually blocked the newly appointed pastor from entering their church.

EXCLUSION AND ASSIMILATION

To many Americans, the new immigrants were unwelcome. Discrimination was sometimes overt, sometimes subtle. The immigrants themselves were torn between adopting American ways and preserving their old ways. They formed organizations to help their own people succeed in America. Public schools helped immigrant children assimilate into American society.

IMMIGRANTS ORGANIZE TO HELP EACH OTHER   Tensions within ethnic communities were tempered by deep loyalties to the family, neighborhood, and Old World traditions. Immigrants also formed mutual aid societies, physical culture clubs, patriotic societies, foreign language newspapers, and churches and synagogues. Greeks and Turks opened coffee houses. German beer halls were found in every large city, catering not just to men but to entire families. To maintain ethnic values and pride, immigrants created such associations as the Polish National Alliance (1880), the (Irish) Ancient Order of Hibernians (1836), the (Greek) Pan-Hellenic Union (1907), and the Order of the Sons of Italy (1905).

Mutual aid societies offered low-interest loans to their members to start small businesses and buy homes. The New York Hebrew Free Loan Society, for example, enabled Jewish businessmen to become a dominant force in Harlem. Jews also established an array of other institutions, including the Hebrew Immigrant Aid Society, the Educational Alliance, and the Hebrew Sheltering Society.

In some cities, such as Detroit, home ownership was a higher priority among the immigrant working class than among the native white middle class. In Cleveland, by 1910 more than 70 percent of Italian and Slovak immigrants owned homes.

Associations such as the Polish National Alliance and the Polish Women's Alliance invested well over 80 percent of their assets in home mortgages. Italians formed their own life insurance companies, while certain banks, most notably A. P. Giannini's Banca d'Italia (later Bank of America) served San Francisco's Italians. Japanese-American credit associations (Tanomashi) enabled members to pool money to buy and operate garden farms whose crops found a ready market in Los Angeles.

The church and the synagogue were major sources of social stability within immigrant communities. As early as 1860, there were twenty-seven synagogues in New York City. As German Jews became Americanized, however, their attitudes toward religious life changed. A reform movement led by Isaac M. Wise made Cincinnati the center of Reform Judaism. Wise was joined by other German Reform rabbis who immigrated to the United States. By 1890 there were more members of Reform synagogues than Orthodox synagogues in the United States. Emphasis on religious education was evidenced by the establishment of three hundred schools to teach Hebrew.

The majority of new immigrants were Roman Catholics. At the end of the Civil War, there were three thousand Catholic churches in the United States; by 1900 there were ten thousand. Tensions between the Irish and other ethnic groups, especially Germans and eastern Europeans, troubled the Catholic Church in the late nineteenth century. Tensions became so strained that in 1891 German Catholics asked the Vatican to allow each ethnic group to have its own priests and parishes. Officially the church denied the request, but tacitly it pursued a policy of appointing ethnic clergy. These churches played a key role in preserving ethnic family values. For example, the St. Stanislaus Kostka church in Chicago formed a mutual benefit association, women's groups, youth clubs and even a parish bank. Catholic immigrants also played an active role in creating an extensive parochial school system that included elementary schools, high schools, and colleges. Non-Catholics also supported education. The Missouri Synod of the Lutheran Church established an extensive elementary and secondary school system throughout Illinois, Indiana, Missouri, Minnesota, and Ohio.

Still, many immigrant children dropped out of school to go to work. In 1910 fewer than 10 percent of Italian, Polish, and Slovak children in Chicago and Cleveland stayed in school beyond the sixth grade. Despite traditional Jewish educational values, only one-third of Jewish children completed high school in these cities.

LEARNING NEW WAYS AND PRESERVING OLD   Educational reformers encouraged immigrant children to attend public school in order to assimilate quickly into American culture. Most educators believed that learning English was the key to success in America. Schools also sought to further assimilation by offering personal health and grooming instruction. A key leader in education reform for immigrant children was William Wirt, who developed the Gary, Indiana, public school plan. His plan stressed basic reading and writing skills and provided for vocational training and moral instruction. Time for religious instruction was built into the curriculum. In 1914 Wirt arranged with Protestant churches to set up a program of Bible study. Understanding the importance of the immigrant family, Wirt's plan encouraged children to take their Bibles home for study. Wirt also established night schools to reach immigrant steel workers. The Gary plan became the model for schools in New York, Philadelphia, and El Paso.

Many religious leaders encouraged assimilation. Liberal Catholic clergymen like Cardinal James Gibbons and Bishop John Ireland actively opposed the "Cahensly Movement," which sought to appoint American bishops based in part on how well they represented various immigrant groups. Catholic leaders in Cincinnati and Louisville tried to discourage their parishioners from speaking German. In Chicago, Archbishop George Mundelein sought to undermine ethnic separateness and supported standardized education in Chicago parochial schools.

In daily life even those who did not attend school learned at least a smattering of English, along with unfamiliar dialects of their native language and bits of other languages common in their neighborhoods. They adapted to American foods and the absence of many native products. They also changed the daily lives of the native born, as Yiddish expressions worked their way into English, Italian restaurants became stops for adventurous diners, and songs written by immigrants became popular parlor music. Immigrants contributed to the American economy as workers. They also changed its culture.

NATIVES OPPOSE THE NEWCOMERS   Cultural change was an unsettling prospect to some native-born Americans. Ethnic jokes appeared regularly in newspapers and magazines. *Harpers, Atlantic Monthly, Puck,* and *Life* all published jokes about the "frugal Scottish," the "lazy Irish," the "cheap Jews," and the "ignorant Italians." Ethnic slurs could also take more malevolent forms. Italians, often considered "nonwhite," were frequent targets, sometimes maligned as criminals. One leading sociologist observed that Italians were prone to violence. He wrote that an Italian is "quite familiar with the sight of human blood as with the sight of the food he eats."

In 1890 anti-Italian sentiment took a particularly nasty turn in New Orleans. The popular police superintendent, David Hennessy, was assassinated shortly after announcing he had proof that a Sicilian mob was operating in the city. Public outcry over his murder led to the indictment of nineteen Sicilians, but eight managed to flee and avoid prosecution. When the trial of the remaining eleven ended in a hung jury, an outraged mob stormed the jail, shot nine prisoners on the spot, and hanged two others from lampposts.

Discrimination against ethnic groups took more subtle forms as well. Social ostracism was common. As the number of Jews increased, hotels, clubs, and colleges began to exclude them. Many universities and colleges refused to accept Jews as either students or faculty members. Some German Jews tried to counter this bigotry by arguing that Jews should not be judged by "the ignorant . . . bigoted, and vicious [Jewish] Poles and Russians arriving on the scene." Such strategies failed to overcome the ingrained prejudice of many native-born Americans.

PEOPLING THE MODERN CITY

The massive influx of immigrants transformed American cities physically and culturally. At the same time, internal migration of people from rural to urban centers accelerated the growth of urban America. In this transformation, cities competed to become significant regional economic and cultural centers. The emergence of the industrial city also altered the social landscape as new urban spaces were created for living, working, and playing.

Rapid urbanization, however, created immense problems with housing, sanitation, and poverty. American cities were not prepared for the influx of millions of people. Cable cars and, later, electric streetcars improved transportation within cities and made suburbs possible. Residential buildings overflowed with people, and cities experimented with alternative housing approaches. Architects developed new ways of building and created skyscrapers, made possible by the invention of the elevator.

CITIES GROW AND COMPETE   The growth of the urban population was startling. From 1860 to 1910, American cities absorbed nearly seven times their population in 1860. The population of Buffalo tripled; Chicago's quadrupled. In 1870 New York City comprised only Manhattan and the small islands in the East River. In 1898 the city incorporated the five surrounding boroughs—including Brooklyn, the nation's third-largest city in its own right—so that within a decade New York City's population reached five million.

The growth of the modern city transformed the cultural landscape. The fast pace of the city placed a premium on youthful energy. The latest fashions and fads took precedence over tradition and respect for elders. The diversity of people living in the new city challenged old patterns while creating new expectations and anxieties.

The modern American city resulted from fierce competition by civic leaders to attract people, industry, and wealth. Most major American cities were founded before 1890. Notable exceptions were Miami, Florida, established in 1896 on a new railroad line linking the west and east coasts of the state, and Tulsa, Oklahoma, which emerged as a major city with the discovery of oil in 1901. New York remained the most populous city; by the turn of the century, older cities like Philadelphia, Baltimore, Boston, and New Orleans had fallen in the rankings as newer western and southern cities expanded.

Midwestern cities grew rapidly. By 1890 Chicago, despite a disastrous fire in 1871, had outdistanced its regional rival, St. Louis, to become the nation's second-largest city. The rivalry with St. Louis for regional dominance was fierce and left its mark on both cities. The English poet Rudyard Kipling described Chicago as a place of barbarism, boasting, and violence. "Having seen it," he said, "I urgently desire never to see it again."

Other cities in the Midwest vied to become regional centers, where ordinary commerce, banking, and services would attract patronage from the surrounding countryside and small towns. For example, in the 1870s many thought Leavenworth, not Kansas City, would dominate that region. Many thought Duluth, Minnesota, would become more important than Minneapolis. Similar competition occurred between Abilene, Texas, and Wichita, Kansas.

By 1900 the Midwest had emerged as a leading manufacturing region due to its natural resources and transportation facilities. Three-fourths of American manufacturing was concentrated there. More than three-fourths of American manufacturing workers lived in the belt east of the Mississippi River and north of the Ohio River. St. Louis, Cleveland, and Detroit ranked nationally as fourth, sixth, and ninth in population, respectively. These cities were joined as major regional centers by Omaha, Nebraska; Kansas City, Missouri; and Minneapolis, Minnesota.

Western cities also grew quickly as shipping, finance, agriculture, mining, and tourism became major industries in the region. San Francisco remained the West's most prominent city, with its fine port and splendid vista overlooking the bay. By 1880 it had become the nation's ninth most populous city. Suburban communities across the bay, such as Oakland and Berkeley, enjoyed continued growth into the twentieth century.

Los Angeles was second to San Francisco in the West. The "City of Angels" grew when a rate war between competing railroads in the late 1880s brought an influx of people. Real estate speculators saw this boom as an opportunity to profit from rising land prices. Within a three-month period in 1887, as the railroads battled for passenger traffic, more than twenty town sites were laid out along the rail lines. That year Los Angeles ranked below only Chicago and New York in total real estate sales.

In this land frenzy, unscrupulous entrepreneurs inevitably entered the picture. Some developers deceived "greenhorns" from the East by hanging oranges on Joshua trees in the desert to make the land appear suitable for farming. Sidney Homberg sold four thousand lots in the Mojave Desert, which he claimed were in the cities of "Manchester" and "Border City." Manchester and Border City proved to be nonexistent. One wit observed that the desolate, roadless wasteland of the alleged Border City was most easily accessible by means of a balloon and as secure from attack as the home of the Cliff Dwellers. In this real estate boom fewer than 40 percent of the one hundred towns mapped out for Los Angeles County between 1884 and 1888 were ever built. Still, some boomtowns became permanent, including Burbank, Monrovia, and Azusa.

Seattle, located on the beautiful Puget Sound, had a port second only to San Francisco in the West. Its emergence as a major city, however, came largely as a result of the promotion tactics and business acumen of New England-born business leaders. In 1860 Seattle persuaded the territorial legislature to locate the planned territorial university in the city. The community then built a hall and started classes. Despite this Yankee enterprise, Seattle languished until business leaders lured a major railroad terminus to the city. Regional competition marked the development of the West. Salt Lake City competed with Ogden for economic dominance, while Denver struggled with a number of towns, including Cheyenne, Wyoming, for economic control of the mountain states.

The South did not show strong urban development. Although a number of interior cities did emerge, including Atlanta, Nashville, Louisville, Memphis, Dallas, and Birmingham, the South's population remained primarily rural. Even by the turn of the century, only 15 percent of southerners lived in urban areas.

SOLVING CITY TRANSPORTATION PROBLEMS   Adequate public transportation quickly became a major problem, and many cities suffered daily traffic gridlock. In the 1850s horse-drawn street railways were introduced, so that by the 1880s most cities with populations over fifty thousand had streetcars. But the main means of transportation, the horse, was slow and

Suburban streetcar systems gave women the freedom to travel to work or to shop at downtown department stores. Care had to be taken when boarding, however; to show the ankle was considered obscene. (Brown Brothers)

messy. In 1880 an estimated fifteen thousand horses died in New York City. Horses fouled the city streets, and their droppings endangered public health. The city of Rochester figured that the daily excrement produced by horses there would be enough to fill an acre-sized hole 175 feet deep.

City officials and private investors sought innovative solutions. By the 1870s city officials had begun experimenting with the steam engine to run cable cars. Chicago developed the first cable car. By 1887 it operated more than eighty-six miles of track. The cable car was perfectly suited to the hills of San Francisco and Seattle.

In the 1890s many cities turned to electric trolley cars. The first electric streetcar system was installed in Richmond, Virginia, by Frank J. Sprague, an engineer who had worked for Thomas Edison. Electric car systems quickly spread to other cities. By the turn of the century, ownership of electric streetcar and utility companies had become increasingly concentrated, as holding companies were formed to extend their control regionally and in some cases nationally.

CRAMMING THE CITIES AND SPREADING INTO SUBURBS   The development of efficient transportation systems encouraged the growth of suburbs. American electric streetcar companies, unlike their European counterparts, charged a flat fee of a nickel for short or long trips, allowing commuters to live farther from the city without paying more for transportation. In fact, many streetcar companies purchased land on the city's periphery in hopes of cashing in on suburbanization. Companies made more profits from land sales than from fares.

Other new transportation systems also encouraged the growth of suburbs. In 1864 Hugh B. Wilson, after studying the London underground railroad, proposed building a subway in New York City, but the state legislature defeated his proposal. He turned instead to building an elevated rail line for New York. Within a decade New York "Els" were carrying 175,000 passengers a day. New York became the model for other cities, including Kansas City, Brooklyn, and Chicago.

Although some suburbs had emerged as early as the 1820s, suburban sprawl came only in the late nineteenth century. The growth of suburbs allowed both the upper classes and the prosperous middle classes to move out to a safe, sanitary haven from city life. In this period the wealthy began to move to fashionable suburbs, such as Bryn Mawr on the Pennsylvania Railroad "Main Line" west of Philadelphia, Brookline near Boston, and Shaker Heights near Cleveland. Suburbs also attracted the prosperous middle class, including both white-collar and skilled workers with family incomes of $600 to $1,000 per year. Developers offered affordable homes for $1,000 to $4,000. In the 1890s a Chicago developer, Samuel E. Gross, built a subdivision outside the city that advertised houses for as little as $10 a month.

Those who remained in the city, however, faced a housing shortage. Builders failed to keep up with the demand. In most cities with populations over 100,000, urban dwellers usually rented. At first, older houses were divided into rooms for rent, or rooms were added. As early as the 1850s, five-story tenement buildings arose in New York. These buildings, which offered small rooms for rent, housed up to 500 people, as did the Gotham Court building. In New York in 1864, more than 15,000 tenements housed 500,000 of New York's 800,000 people. Thousands of others lived in basements or damp, dirt-floored cellars within these buildings.

In 1877 James E. Ware won a magazine contest for a better-designed tenement. Ware proposed a multiple-floor building with a ten-foot-by-four-foot air shaft to allow more light and ventilation. This type of building soon became known as the "dumbbell" tenement because of its unusual shape. Stairs, hall, and common bathrooms filled the central parts of the building.

Tenements allowed cities to squeeze thousands of people into confined spaces. Some blocks housed as many as ten thousand people. This congestion was unhealthful because of inadequate sanitation and the increased exposure to contagious diseases like tuberculosis. In one Chicago district only 24 percent of the residents had access to bathrooms with running water. The rest relied on outhouses, called privy vaults, located in backyards or underneath porches.

If the poor faced housing problems, so did the middle class. The shortage of living space led to the creation of the city apartment, or flat. This new form of housing became socially acceptable only in 1869 in New York, when Rutherford Stuyvesant built the first luxury apartment house, modeled on Paris structures. Soon "French flats," as middle- and upper-class apartments were called, became fashionable in a few large cities.

BUILDING THE CITY   The confined space of the city restricted business as well. Strongly desiring central locations near services, banks, and railroad stations, companies were forced to build upward. Architects experimented with cast iron and, later, steel. Fireproof terra-cotta tiles were used for façades. As early as the 1840s, James Bogardus, a New York watchmaker and ingenious inventor, developed an erector-set-like technique using cast-iron columns to construct an entire building. Others followed. In 1874 Richard Morris Hunt designed the New York Tribune Building with a cast-iron interior structure, and in 1884 William Le Baron Jenney pioneered the steel skeleton structure in his ten-story Home Insurance Building in Chicago.

The greatest contribution to the modern skyscraper came from Louis Sullivan, a Chicago architect. Sullivan gave form and substance to the skyscraper with his Wainwright Building (1891) in St. Louis. His designs, often associated with the Chicago School, set the style for American skyscrapers for the next half century. Sullivan's belief that a building should express its cultural purpose attracted other Chicago architects, including John W. Root, Daniel Burnham, Dankmar Adler, and Frank Lloyd Wright (who had once worked as Sullivan's draftsman).

Skyscrapers became feasible only with the development of the elevator, another American contribution to engineering. The elevator evolved through a series of innovations that began in 1853, when Elisha G. Otis's safety device was installed to protect passengers in case of a cable break. By the 1870s hydraulic power, gearing techniques, and electricity had brought elevators into common use.

REFORMING THE CITY

In the late 1800s filthy, overcrowded American cities were ravaged by disease, crime, fire, and poverty. Sanitation, health, police, fire, and social services emerged only slowly, and the police were often corrupt. In these conditions reformers sought to transform the city morally, socially, and politically. They set up public institutions to help the disadvantaged, fought vice, and worked to reclaim power from corrupt politicians. Women, finding new opportunities for education and employment, asserted independence and led many reform efforts. Despite its problems, city life gave diverse people something in common.

CLEANING THE CITY   Rapid population growth created problems, but the very density of the population aggravated conditions. A survey conducted in 1901 showed that one Polish section in Chicago had an average of 340 people per acre of land. One three-block area was home to 7,300 children. Trash, garbage, and manure littered the streets. Throughout the late nineteenth century, outbreaks of cholera, typhus, and yellow fever plagued the cities. Tuberculosis, pneumonia, and dysentery killed many children. Indeed, Pittsburgh had one of the world's highest mortality rates from typhoid.

Many cities had grown along rivers, which were the obvious places to dump garbage, sewage, and waste. Rivers were, however, the water supplies for cities downstream. The use of cesspools (holes for disposing of waste) only worsened conditions. Washington, D.C., had 56,000 vaults (small private sewage pits), while Philadelphia had 82,000 vaults and cesspools. The census of 1880 reported that New Orleans was literally saturated with the "oozings of foul private vaults." Baltimore had 80,000 cesspools that were absorbed by the city's porous soil and threatened to pollute water wells.

Despite the overwhelming problems of pollution, city officials throughout the nation responded slowly, although on occasion ingeniously. In 1889 the city engineer of Chicago, Ellis S. Chesbrough, persuaded the state legislature to create a 185-square-mile sanitary district to provide uniform, modern services for the city. In 1900 the Chicago Sanitary and Ship Canal helped reverse the flow of the Chicago River so that the city would be rid of the "menace of a contaminated water supply."

Water treatment and sewage treatment plants came slowly to most cities. A key figure in introducing new sanitation methods to the city was George Waring, Jr., a scientific farmer and engineer. In 1878 when a yellow fever epidemic killed nearly five thousand people in Memphis, the city hired Waring to build a new sewage system. Ironically, Waring rejected the latest scientific theory that germs caused disease but instead asserted that filth was the cause. Nonetheless, Waring's work in Memphis earned him national acclaim. Later he served as New York City's first commissioner of street cleaning from 1895 to 1898, where he introduced regular garbage pickup and sweeping.

By the turn of the century, sewage and water treatment systems had been created in most large cities. By 1910 more than ten million residents in metropolitan areas drank filtered water. Such actions reduced mortality rates by a fifth in major cities. Even more dramatically, deaths from typhoid fever fell 65 percent for the nation.

PROTECTING THE CITY   The modern city also suffered from high crime rates. In Philadelphia the homicide rate tripled in the three decades following the Civil War. Gangs patrolled their turf. Gambling, prostitution, and public drunkenness were common sights in most cities. Cities had tried to cope with these problems by establishing volunteer or paid night watches, but these proved inadequate. The first modern police force in the United States was established in New York in 1845. New York provided the model for other cities, including Philadelphia, Baltimore, and Boston. These police departments, staffed by local political bosses, usually performed additional city functions, including street cleaning, operating lodging houses for the indigent, and inspecting boilers and produce markets.

Some police forces proved vulnerable to corruption. An investigation of the New York City force by state senator Clarence Lexow in 1894 revealed that police were involved with gambling, prostitution, and liquor interests. Lexow's scathing report prompted New York to appoint

Theodore Roosevelt as police commissioner. Between 1895 and 1897, Roosevelt introduced a number of reform measures, but the situation gradually eroded after he left office, and corruption reappeared.

Fire continually threatened the modern city due to overcrowding, poor fire control service, and wooden buildings. Death by fire was as common statistically as death from typhoid fever. In the 1870s fire took enormous tolls on life and property in New York, Boston, Pittsburgh, and Chicago. After the great Chicago fire of 1871, sixty-four insurance companies went bankrupt. The older volunteer fire companies had proven inadequate to meet the needs of the modern city. Cincinnati is credited with the first municipal fire department, and the development of new steam fire engines with automatic water pumps brought new technology to firefighting. By the turn of the century, American cities had some of the world's best fire departments.

CARING FOR THE CITY   While cities established and improved their public police and fire departments, addressing the needs of the urban poor was even more daunting. The lines between private and public charity were often blurred. Many workers for private charities were distrustful of public relief and political influence. The development of specialized public institutions to deal with poverty, mental illness, and other social ills coincided with the emergence of experts with specialized knowledge in the care and management of their clients.

Throughout the late nineteenth century, these experts sought to improve the institutional care of the poor and the mentally and physically afflicted. One of the first relief efforts for the poor was Robert M. Hanley's organization of volunteers to visit the poor in their homes. Operating through the New York Association for Improving the Condition of the Poor, founded in 1843, volunteers went into the inner city to instruct the poor about sanitation, food preparation, and child care. Following the Civil War, Hanley's association was a strong advocate for pure milk laws, public baths, and better housing.

There were similar efforts at reform on behalf of children. In 1853, Charles Loring Brace founded the New York Children's Aid Society. Brace's organization established dormitories, reading rooms, and workshops where young boys could learn work skills. Brace was also involved in a controversial foster care program that eventually transferred more than ninety thousand boys from the city to foster homes and farms in Illinois, Michigan, and Wisconsin. Since many of these young boys were Roman Catholic, the Catholic Church was particularly wary of Brace's efforts, which often sent children to Protestant foster homes. Moreover, the fostering families seemed more interested in a farm labor force than in child welfare.

The late nineteenth century was a period of experimentation in addressing the needs of the poor and the indigent. The Salvation Army was one of the most interesting attempts to address social problems. Established in England in 1865 by a Methodist minister, "General" William Booth, the Salvation Army was a religious denomination organized along quasi-military lines to convert the poor to evangelical Christianity. Introduced to America in 1880, the Salvation Army provided food, temporary shelter and employment, and child care. The Salvation Army's lively street bands became a frequent sight in many large cities.

The Young Men's Christian Association (YMCA) also provided shelter to those coming to the city. The YMCA, which had strong support from the Methodist Church, then the leading Protestant denomination in the United States, was brought from England in 1851. By 1900 more than 1,500 YMCAs and YWCAs (Young Women's Christian Associations) provided housing for many young people seeking a better life in the city.

After the Civil War, the creation of Boards of State Charities was a key effort to coordinate public relief on the local level. Still, the care of the poor and the afflicted largely remained local and voluntary. A Chicago directory in 1895 listed fifty-seven asylums and hospitals, twenty-eight infirmaries and dispensaries, forty-one missions, sixty temperance societies, and hundreds of benevolent associations, camps, and lodges.

Leading the movement to make charity work more efficient was the Charity Organization Society (COS) founded in 1882 by Josephine Shaw Lowell. Always dressed in mourning black for her husband, who had died in the Civil War, Shaw brought scientific management to private charity in New York City. COS representatives compiled files on all who sought or received aid. They also visited the homes of the poor to encourage and advise them. Shaw was proud that her organization avoiding giving direct relief—money or food—to the poor. Such aid would only sap the initiative of the "worthy" poor and reward the unworthy for their sloth.

Other reformers attacked what they considered the foundations of poverty: liquor, gambling, and prostitution. Anthony Comstock and his New York Society for the Suppression of Vice (1872) undertook a vigorous campaign urging municipal authorities to close gambling houses and to censor obscene publications. Although his attacks against what he viewed as "obscene" literature and art led to controversy (the Comstock law is still federal law), his earlier activities against gambling made Comstock a powerful force in municipal reform.

While Comstock focused his attention on moral corruption in government and society, others probed the underlying values that contributed to poverty in America. In the 1870s Washington Gladden, minister of a Congregational church in Columbus, Ohio, launched the Social Gospel movement. Applying Christian principles to society, he argued that the poor were victims of a society that created an environment that enabled poverty to exist. His call to bring Christianity to the streets was taken up by Walter Rauschenbusch, a Baptist minister in New York's notorious "Hell's Kitchen" district. He later described Hell's Kitchen as a place where "one could hear human virtues cracking and crumbling all around." In a series of articles and books that included *Christianity and Social Crisis* (1907), Rauschenbusch influenced a generation of ministers and reformers to reject older nineteenth-century views that blamed the poor for their misery.

WOMEN REFORMERS GET INVOLVED   Middle-class women, some of whom took advantage of new opportunities for education, became involved in a wide range of reform efforts. Working-class women displayed a sharp sense of independence by joining trade unions, often ducking the aid of charity workers. By the first decade of the twentieth century, nearly sixty-five thousand working women had joined more than five hundred trade unions. With the development of the typewriter and telephone, whole new fields of employment opened to women. Still, by 1900 almost 40 percent of working women were servants in private homes.

Middle-class women enjoyed new educational opportunities. Before the Civil War only a few colleges, such as Oberlin College and Elmira College, admitted women. In the 1860s and 1870s, however, new women's colleges were founded, including Vassar, Smith, and Wellesley. Beginning with those in Iowa in 1856, state colleges and universities opened their doors to women.

Educated, middle-class women became active in a number of reform groups. The Woman's Christian Temperance Union (WCTU), under the leadership of Frances E. Willard, claimed a membership of 500,000 women. Although its primary focus was on banning liquor sales, Willard championed a "do-everything" approach that encouraged local chapters to get involved in many causes. Local branches, including segregated southern groups, campaigned for woman suffrage, labor legislation for women, reform of policies toward Indians, and kindergartens in public schools. The General Federation of Women's Clubs, chartered by Congress in 1901, was a coalition of local societies of middle-class women who helped create better parks, recreational centers, and public schools in many cities. African-American women's clubs worked for both racial uplift and urban reform.

Jane Addams of Chicago epitomized this concern with the social ills of the city. During a stay in England, Addams studied the settlement house movement, in which reformers sought to introduce community centers—so-

In 1874 Frances E. Willard helped found the Women's Christian Temperance Union, which became the largest voluntary organization in the United States. Willard, a former college dean, was devoted to education and woman suffrage as well as to Prohibition. Friends called her Frank. (Culver Pictures, Inc.)

cial settlement houses—to working-class neighborhoods to ease the harsh social conditions of the industrial inner city. Upon her return to Chicago, Addams joined her friend Ellen Gates Starr to open Hull House in Chicago in 1889. Hull House provided recreational, educational, child care, and health facilities to recent Italian and Greek immigrants. The daughter of a wealthy Illinois state senator, Addams sought not only to help the poor but also to provide a role for educated women in society. She also became involved in the nonpartisan community reform movement in Chicago. In her *Hull House Papers* (1895), she surveyed housing and sanitation conditions in the city,

Jane Addams typified the reform spirit of many women involved in the settlement house movement. In 1889 Addams founded Hull House in a poor section of Chicago. A pacifist, she won the Nobel Peace Prize at the age of seventy-four. (AP/Wide World Photos)

providing an objective assessment of the need for reform in Chicago. Hull House became a model for other reformers, and by 1895 there were more than fifty settlement houses in other cities. The settlement houses flourished from 1895 to 1935, after which their functions were largely absorbed by government relief agencies.

REFORMING CITY POLITICS   Addams's involvement in nonpartisan reform politics occurred at a time when many middle-class activists were calling for an end to politics as usual. In the late 1890s city bosses and machine politicians were blamed for the growing social problems of the modern city. As the costs of running cities skyrocketed, reformers called for efficiency and economy in government. With burgeoning populations, many cities had gone into debt to meet normal services. Fifteen of the nation's largest cities saw their populations rise on average by 70 percent and their debts increase by 271 percent. At the same time, city bosses had links to utility and trolley interests that received lucrative franchises. Some cities, such as St. Louis, were profoundly corrupted by these utility interests.

As a consequence, middle-class nonpartisans called for a series of reforms. One was "home rule," a plan to take power from state legislatures and give it to city government. Reformers also advocated strong mayors to take power away from corrupt city councils. In the first decade of the twentieth century, reformers extended this concept further and advocated a powerful city manager working under a weak mayor to handle the city's business affairs. Reformers also demanded that nonpartisan regulatory agencies and boards be created to further weaken political control by city political bosses. One reformer quipped, "Whoever heard of a Republican park or playground, a Democratic swimming bath, a Prohibitionist street clearing department, or a Populist mortuary?"

For many reformers, William Marcy Tweed's political machine, which dominated New York politics in the 1870s, symbolized "boss" government. Although the corrupt Tweed died in prison, there were other bosses like him: James McManes dominated Philadelphia politics from 1860 to 1880; "Blind" Alexander Sheppard ran Washington, D.C., from 1860 to 1873; "Boss" George B. Cox dominated Cincinnati from 1888 to 1910; and "Big Jim" Pendergast controlled Kansas City, Missouri, from 1910 to 1939. Political machines also ran Baltimore, Atlanta, San Francisco, and other large cities.

In the 1880s reform movements took control of a number of cities. Reform mayors such as Grover Cleveland in Buffalo, Seth Low in Brooklyn, and James D. Phelan in San Francisco called for low taxes and a more economical and efficient city government. The appeal of economy to city voters who needed services tended to wear thin fast, and reform mayors did not last long in office. The economic depression that marked the 1890s prompted many reformers to turn to social issues. In city after city, reform-minded mayors were swept into office: Samuel M. Jones, the "Golden Rule" mayor of Toledo; Tom Johnson of Cleveland; Hazen S. Pingree in Detroit. Reform was in the air and would set the stage for the Progressive movement of the next decade.

SHARING CITY LIFE

Despite the social and political problems of the modern city, a rich, vibrant urban life emerged. Although the rich and the poor were divided into clearly defined neighborhoods, they shared the common experience of urban life. Cities were now tied together by better transportation systems. Communication was easier because by 1900 there were nearly 800,000 telephones in the nation. New printing and production techniques allowed publishers like Joseph Pulitzer and William Randolph

Hearst to sell "penny" papers to a mass audience. As a result, dailies doubled in readership as newspapers developed well-defined editorial, news, sports, entertainment, and women's sections. The new metropolitan press introduced a distinct urban mentality to America.

Urban dwellers shared a common, democratic experience. Spectator sports like baseball brought together people from all walks of life; fandom knew no social boundary. By the late 1870s there was a clear distinction between professional and amateur baseball players, which only seemed to increase fans' interest. Cities vied for major league teams. Even organized baseball, however, still excluded blacks. In 1867 the National Association of Baseball Players barred blacks from membership.

Downtowns were made more attractive to bring women shoppers to the new department stores. Across the nation, department stores displaced the old dry-goods stores. John Wanamaker's first success with his department store in Philadelphia became the model for Morris Rich in Atlanta, Adam Gimbel and Rowland H. Macy in New York, Marshall Field in Chicago, and Joseph L. Hudson in Detroit. Advertising developed by these stores urged urban people of all ranks to dress in the latest fashion. The development of the modern department store opened new job opportunities for women. Increasingly, stores hired women for their sales staffs and provided some of the few opportunities for women to attain managerial positions. Still, consumption itself offered a shared, seemingly democratic experience.

CONCLUSION

The emerging modern city could be a disturbing and frightening place. The mass migration of immigrants from southern and eastern Europe transformed America socially and culturally. In America these immigrants created new communities around mutual aid societies, churches and synagogues, and social clubs. The diverse population and new manner of life threatened the old order and brought new dangers. With its social ills and divisions, the city appeared to embody the worst aspects of American capitalism. Yet for most Americans, especially immigrants and those who left rural farms to come to the city, urban life offered opportunities, excitement, challenge, and a radically new way of ordering their world.

Recommended Readings

DOCUMENTS: Jane Addams, *Twenty Years at Hull House* (1910); William L. Riordon, *Plunkitt of Tammany Hall* (1905); Lincoln Steffens, *The Shame of the Cities* (1904); Josiah Strong, *Our Country* (1885).

READINGS: (THE CITY) Gunther Barth, *City People: The Rise of Modern City Culture in the Nineteenth Century* (1980); Susan P. Benson, *Counter Cultures: Saleswomen, Managers, and Customers in American Department Stores* (1986); Howard Chudacoff, *Evolution of American Urban Society* (1975); Clifford E. Clark, Jr., *The American Family Home, 1800–1960* (1986); Ruth S. Cowan, *More Work for Mother: The Ironies of Household Technology from the Open Hearth to the Microwave* (1980); Charles N. Glaab and A. Theodore Brown, *A History of Urban America* (1967); Dolores Hayden, *The Grand Domestic Revolution: A History of Feminist Designs for American Homes, Neighborhoods, and Cities* (1981); Daniel Horowitz, *The Morality of Spending* (1985); John F. Kasson, *Amusing the Millions: Coney Island at the Turn of the Century* (1978); Lawrence H. Larsen, *The Urban South* (1990); Terrence McDonald, *The Parameters of Urban Fiscal Policy* (1986); Blake McKelvey, *The Urbanization of America* (1962); Zane Miller, *Urbanization of America* (1975); Eric H. Monkkonen, *America Becomes Urban* (1988); Howard H. Rabinowitz, *Race Relations in the Urban South 1865–1890* (1978); Roy Rosenzweig, *"Eight Hours for What We Will": Workers and Leisure in an Industrial City* (1983); Stephan Thernstrom, *Poverty and Progress: Social Mobility in the Nineteenth-Century City* (1964); Sam Bass Warner, *Streetcar Suburbs: The Process of Growth in Boston* (1962) and *The Urban Wilderness* (1972). (IMMIGRANTS) Thomas J. Archdeacon, *Becoming American* (1983); Josef Barton, *Peasants and Strangers: Italians, Rumanians, and Slovaks in an American City* (1975); John Bodnar, *The Transplanted: A History of Immigrants in Urban America* (1985); Jack Chen, *The Chinese of America* (1980); Leonard Dinnerstein and David M. Reimer, *Ethnic Americans: A History of Immigration and Assimilation* (2nd ed., 1982); Mario Garcia, *Desert Immigrants: The Mexicans of El Paso, 1880–1920* (1981); John Higham, *Strangers in the Land* (1955) and *Send These to Me: Jews and Other Immigrants in Urban America* (1970); Yuji Ichioka, *The Issei: The World of the First-Generation Japanese Americans* (1988); Frederic C. Jaher, *The Aliens: A History of Ethnic Minorities in America* (1970); Edward Kantowicz, *Polish-American Politics in Chicago* (1975); Alan M. Kraut, *The Huddled Masses: The Immigrant in American Society* (1982); Moses Rischin, *The Promised City: New York's Jews* (1962); William V. Shannon, *The American Irish* (1963); Barbara Solomon, *Ancestors and Immigrants* (1956).

20

❧

Depression, Protest, and Politics

OVERVIEW   The stalemate that had characterized late-nineteenth-century politics began to break down in the 1890s, at first in favor of the Democrats. Elements of the Republican base in the Midwest and East defected, resulting in large Democratic victories in 1890 and 1892. In 1893, however, an economic depression reversed the Democrats' fortunes. Meanwhile, farmers in the South and the Midwest broke ranks with the two-party system, forming the Populist Party. The Populists hoped to win the White House in 1896, but these dreams were shattered when the Populist Party fused with the Democratic Party to support William Jennings Bryan, who called for a new monetary standard based on both silver and gold. The Republican candidate, William McKinley, overwhelmed Bryan at the polls. Republicans would enjoy almost uninterrupted control of national politics until the 1930s.

THE DEPRESSION OF 1893:
LABOR RADICALIZES, CLEVELAND REACTS

When Grover Cleveland took office in 1892, the future seemed bright for him, for the Democrats, and for the nation. As he left office in December 1892, President Benjamin Harrison declared, "There has never been a time in our history when work was so abundant, or when wages were so high." But Cleveland was soon faced with a serious industrial depression, which came on top of existing distress in the agricultural South and Midwest.

Some citizens marched on Washington. Cleveland pursued a conservative strategy, trying to put the financial system back on a single gold standard. His efforts to increase the government's gold reserves convinced critics that moneyed interests were running the government. When the first income tax was passed, Cleveland lost even more support. The tax was quickly declared unconstitutional.

CLEVELAND'S LUCK RUNS OUT   Good fortune followed most of Grover Cleveland's political career. Born in Caldwell, New Jersey, in 1837, his father, a Presbyterian minister, died when Cleveland was young, and he grew up amid hard times in upstate New York. While working to help support his family, Cleveland studied law, specializing in the decidedly unflamboyant area of corporate law. It suited both his goal of financial security and his personality, which tended toward the dull and stolid. Cleveland approached life with a grim conviction of human unworthiness coupled with a sense of his own righteousness. "It is no credit to me to do right. I am never under any temptation to do wrong," he once told a friend. His personal outlook—his belief in human incapacity to create a better world and his belief that individuals made their own fate, good or bad—made him a Democrat who was suspicious of reform and in favor of a small government that did not interfere with the natural law of competition.

Normally, Cleveland's personality and political views would have been political liabilities, but good timing turned them into assets. Cleveland became sheriff of Erie County, New York, in 1870; by performing his tasks efficiently (he himself hanged two men sentenced to death), he earned a reputation for honesty. In 1881, to reverse its local reputation for corruption, the Democrats of Buffalo ran Cleveland for mayor. By doing little besides vetoing others' plans, he furthered his reputation as a reformer. With the (unacknowledged) help of the New York state Democratic machine, Cleveland's obscurity and clean image made him palatable to all factions, and he won the Democratic nomination for governor in 1882. As luck would have it, deep divisions among the Republicans handed him victory.

Cleveland moved on to even higher office in 1884. No clear favorite had emerged among those who angled for the presidential nomination. Cleveland became the ideal candidate through subtraction and careful work by his handlers. As an unknown on the national scene, he, unlike the other hopefuls, had few enemies; factions he had antagonized in New York, chiefly Tammany Hall, only burnished his image of honesty. Cleveland's managers kept him quiet (easy enough as he had no settled views on currency, the tariff, or other major issues at this point) while they lined up delegates. He won the nomination, and even the revelation that, years earlier, the bachelor had fathered an illegitimate child did not derail his good fortune. Cleveland's Republican opponent, James G. Blaine, had his own problems with old scandals, and Cleveland squeaked to victory.

In office Cleveland saw no reason to depart from the style that he believed had brought him success. He governed with the conviction that he should handle the tiniest details himself and that his dismal but necessary job was to forestall the foolish plans of others ("Of all the defective and shabby legislation which has been presented to me, this is the worst and the most inexcusable," he scolded in a gubernatorial veto message). He vetoed countless special requests for pensions, along with the Dependent Pension Bill of 1887, which would have made anyone with military service in the Union Army and their dependents eligible for pensions. Reformers cheered Cleveland's willingness to turn down dubious claims, to trounce where spineless legislators feared to tread. For critics, these actions captured Cleveland at his narrow, self-righteous worst. He "delighted in the little," one observed. "It was the bent of the infinitesimal that led him to put in hours darkly arranging a reason to shatter some old woman's pension with the bludgeon of his veto." He signed into law the bill that created the Interstate Commerce Commission, and he vaguely stood for hard money against inflation, while he racked up enemies with his maddening personal style and inept use of patronage. Reasoning that he needed an issue to win a second term, he banked everything on tariff reform. His party renominated him. The tariff proved a better issue for the Republicans than for the Democrats, and he was defeated by Benjamin Harrison in 1888.

In 1892 the Democrats remained a contentious mass of conflicting local interests, although the demographics of the electorate seemed to be on their side. Democratic support among Northern urban immigrants and Catholics, a growing population, might sooner rather than later make competitive states like New York reliably Democratic. Democrats turned to Cleveland in 1892 as a candidate who could pull the party together. This time, the Republicans were in greater disarray. Benjamin Harrison had not enjoyed being President (he referred to the White House as "my jail"), and many in his own party found him personally cold and uncooperative. But he would run again. Especially unpopular west of Pennsylvania, Harrison's candidacy stirred little enthusiasm. Cleveland won a substantial victory, with the solid Republican states of Illinois, Wisconsin, and California shifting to the Democratic Party. Voters gave the Democrats majorities in both houses for the first time since the Civil War.

Cleveland's good fortune ended in the spring of 1893, when a major industrial depression hit. The first signs of it in the United States were the Philadelphia and Reading Railroad's declaration of bankruptcy. Other railroads, including the Erie and the Northern Pacific and Santa Fe, entered bankruptcy. In May, weeks of wild fluctuations ended with the crash of the New York stock market. Banks tumbled from there, 128 closing across the country in June alone, followed by factory closings and layoffs. European investors dumped American securities, and the supply of gold in the United States Treasury dipped dangerously low. Economic distress grew. In 1894 more than 15,000 businesses failed. The rural banking system broke down, causing further strain on New York banks. Of 158 bank failures that year, 153 were in the West and the South. The number of unemployed soared, with estimates ranging from 2.5 to 4 million: one worker in five. The crisis overwhelmed city authorities everywhere. Chicago reported 100,000 homeless people. Across the nation, city officials opened jails and government buildings each night to shelter the unemployed who wandered the cities' streets. Although private charities and city government were overextended, few believed that the state or federal governments should aid the unemployed in a systematic fashion. The governor of New York rejected such aid with the explanation, "In America the people support the government; it is not the province of government to support the people."

The depression was caused by a long-term glut of worldwide productive capacity in the United States and Europe, not by specific policies of American politicians, but it would become Cleveland's and the Democrats' depression.

DISCONTENT IN THE SOUTH AND WEST   Well before the depression began, there were clear rumblings of political discontent in the South and West. Times had been hard on Midwestern farms since shortly after the end of the Civil War. Railroads had opened markets for farmers, and new machinery had increased productivity, but this had also greatly expanded the number of farms and the amount of staple-crop produce, principally wheat and corn. By the mid-1880s farmers found the traditional European market for their wheat crops restricted by tariff barriers and new competition from Argentina and Russia. The price of American wheat fell from $1.05 a bushel in 1875 to 67 cents in 1895. Farmers raised more crops but earned less money; the consequence was a surplus of crops selling for less money in a buyer's market. It was cheaper for farmers to burn their corn as fuel than to sell it to buy coal. Farmers who had gone into deb for land and equipment grew as much as they could, but their efforts brought steadily declining returns. Some gave up. From 1888 to 1892, thirty thousand people in South Dakota vacated their homes, and in western Kansas nearly half the population abandoned their farms. Some left in wagons carrying signs that read, "In God We trusted, in Kansas we busted." For

In 1887 running a sheep ranch on the Great Plains might mean living in a sod house. In particular, women on the frontier found life dreary and hard. (Culver Pictures, Inc.)

those who remained, by the late 1880s dashed economic expectations had turned to bitterness and anger.

The increasing number of Southerners dependent on cotton faced even harsher realities. Cotton prices were high during the war and stayed high for a few years afterward. However, although war had driven up the price of cotton by taking southern cotton off world markets, growers in India, Brazil, and Egypt rushed in to break the near-monopoly once held by the American South. Prices plummeted through the 1880s. Farmers, more and more of whom were tenants and sharecroppers who did not own the land they worked, planted more cotton anyway. Nothing else they could grow (corn, for instance) paid any better. Landowners often demanded that their tenants or sharecroppers grow cotton, as did the storekeepers who lent money and supplies: In most of the South, no other crop promised a return on investment. Farmers lost their land to their creditors; tenants and sharecroppers, black and white, found themselves in an unending cycle of debt. Nor was life easy for many of the shopkeepers who extended credit. Some cheated their borrowers out of even meager profits, but most had trouble just making ends meet. Many men got the idea that shopkeeping beat farming as a way to make a living; the ballooning number of stores created competition for capital and customers, further shriveling profits.

Farmers in the South and Midwest searched for explanations of their plight and ways to reverse it. Their list of culprits included the railroads, which charged farmers ruinous rates to store and ship produce; the makers of farm machinery, whose essential equipment cost more than farmers should pay; bankers, especially eastern bankers, who charged higher rates of interest in the Midwest than in the East; and the major party politicians, who did the bidding of the rich and mighty. Individuals did not stand a chance against such powerful opponents, they reasoned. Farmers as an organized force might be able to improve conditions; after all, they believed, farmers were the bedrock upon which the prosperity of the whole nation rested.

Southern and Midwestern farmers joined the Farmers' Alliance in large numbers in the 1880s. In the mid-1880s black farmers mobilized into a parallel organization, the Colored Farmers' Alliance. Although the Colored Alliance remained predominately black, a number of its key leaders were white. In 1888 and 1889, black and white recruiters of the Colored Alliance undertook an extensive drive throughout the South. By 1890 one key leader, the Reverend Richard Manny Humphrey, a white Baptist, claimed that the Colored Alliance had a membership of 1.2 million. The actual membership was probably a third of this figure, but little doubt remained within the white Southern Alliance that this black organization was a force to be reckoned with.

The Alliance borrowed a good deal from the Grange (see chapter 18). Like the older organization, it encouraged the membership and participation of entire families. Women were important to the success of the Alliance. Not only did they prepare and serve the food that assured good turnout for meetings, but they wrote for Alliance newspapers and traveled the countryside as speakers for the cause. Women's efforts laid the groundwork for the alternative culture the Alliance sought to build against the competitive ethic and partisan politics-as-usual. Also like the Grange, the Alliance turned to cooperative purchasing to solve some immediate problems. If railroads charged individual farmers too much to store and ship their crops, would a group of farmers be able to extract better rates? If they purchased all supplies in bulk, from the jute used for bags to farm machinery, could they receive discounts?

Alliance cooperatives scored a number of successes. Most famously, the Texas Alliance battled the "Jute Trust" and won. But Alliance cooperatives ran into the same problem as those the Grange operated: Banks, large and small, did not see them as good bets and turned down their requests for loans. Without sufficient capital, these cooperatives could never operate as nonprofit middlemen for farmers. Yet the lure of cooperatives brought new members in; once there, they heard a great deal of talk about their problems that might produce grander things than cooperatives ever could.

The Alliance program owed much to the analyses of conditions by third parties and labor organizations (see chapter 18). The nation's moral compass has gone terribly askew, Alliance speakers claimed. The ethic of competition and the celebration of wealth had trounced traditional Christian and republican values. Working people who created wealth grew poorer, while parasitic bondholders, bankers, speculators, and politicians cleaned up. "Wealth belongs to him who creates it," they argued. "Every dollar taken from industry without an equivalent is robbing." Government had fallen under the control of the "money power." Their goal, they said in their 1892 Omaha Platform, was to "restore the Government of the Republic to the hands of the plain people with whose class it originated. We assert our purpose to be identical with the purposes of the national constitution, to form a more perfect union and establish justice. We declare that the Republic can only endure as a free government while built upon the love of the whole people for each other and the nation."

For this to occur, the political system had to be reformed so that "the people," not the moneyed interests, wielded power. Toward that end, the Alliance proposed the direct election of senators; secret, state-printed ballots; the referendum (allowing citizens to make policy directly); and the recall (so that corrupt or unresponsive officials could be removed from office). In a polity so purified, policies that benefited the "whole people" might stand a chance. Such policies included a graduated income tax (to replace the tariff, plausibly a detriment to farmers who sold products on world markets), government ownership of railroad and telegraph lines, and an expanded money supply accomplished by either the free coinage of silver or greenback currency. The subtreasury plan aimed to further loosen money and credit. Farmers could store their crops in government-built warehouses, which would allow farmers to delay selling their produce until prices rose. The plan also proposed to free farmers from the clutches of the banks and merchants by having the federal government advance farmers low-interest loans, using their harvest as collateral.

THE ALLIANCE TURNS TO POLITICS   By 1890 farmers' organizations had enough strength at the state level to conduct their own political campaigns. In the midterm election of 1890, militant Southern farmers gained significant influence in eight legislatures and won four governorships. In Kansas a newly organized local Peoples' or Populist Party elected five congressmen and one senator. They also gained control of the lower house in the state legislature. In Nebraska a Populist named Omar Kerny was elected to Congress.

Alliance leaders began to speak of launching a national third party, the Populist Party, to challenge the Republican and Democratic Parties in the 1892 presidential election. Many who favored third-party political action felt that economic schemes promoted by the Alliance movement, such as cooperative exchanges and the subtreasury plan, could be achieved only by electing their own people to office. For many in the South, the drawback was that a third party meant breaking with the Democrats; this brought up the race question. If whites abandoned the Democratic Party, the Republican Party and their black allies would gain a chance to resume control of state governments, which was reminiscent of Reconstruction. Also, when an individual farmer bolted the Democratic Party, it was more than a political decision. It often meant breaking with one's neighbors, losing friends at the local church, or betraying party "tradition." Northern Alliancemen remained suspicious of the Southern Alliance and displayed little enthusiasm for the subtreasury plan.

Finally, in July 1892 Alliance leaders met to form a national Populist Party. The Populists' 1892 platform comprised all the Alliance programs plus a few others aimed at urban workers: the eight-hour day, immigration restrictions, and an end to the use of Pinkerton armies against strikers. For president they nominated the old Greenback candidate, General James Baird Weaver. On a campaign trip to the West, Weaver did exceptionally well; however, his tour of the South was less successful. Egg-hurling crowds made Weaver "a regular walking omelet," Populist leader Mary Lease observed. Still, the results of the election gave the Populists hope for the future. Weaver received more than one million votes, 8.5 percent of the vote. He also received an absolute majority in three silver producing-states and carried Kansas.

For the first time since the end of the Civil War, a third party had broken into the Electoral College. Moreover, Populists elected governors in Kansas, North Dakota, Colorado, and Washington. Washington's Populist governor, John Rogers, refused to take the train to his inauguration and instead traveled on a series of independent interurban streetcar lines, thus ensuring his popularity. During the campaign Populist leaders with such colorful names as Mary "Raise Less Corn and More Hell" Lease, "Sockless Jerry" Simpson, "Whiskers" Peffer, and the "One-Eyed Ploughboy" Ignatius Donnelly became national celebrities.

The election also revealed some of the serious problems of running a third-party campaign. In Alabama and Georgia, whites waged a campaign of terror against blacks to keep blacks from voting Populist. In Tom Watson's congressional race in Georgia, Democrats indulged in bribery, stuffed ballot boxes, and counted votes fraudulently; the final vote showed twice as many votes as there voters in the district. Those

Populists who were elected found new difficulties once they took office. Davis H. Waite, the Populist governor of Colorado, faced a Republican-controlled lower assembly that systematically defeated his proposals for reform.

The Populist Party continued its complex strategies in opposing or fusing with the major parties. The Democratic Party had diminished to insignificance in parts of the Midwest, where the Populists competed head to head with the Republicans; in some silver mining states the Populists combined with the Republicans; in the South, some Populist leaders looked to build a coalition with African-American voters to defeat the Democrats. At this stage, the confusing set of alliances worked in the Populists' favor and added to the troubles of the major parties.

CLEVELAND RESPONDS TO THE DEPRESSION   Cleveland hoped to ride out what might prove to be a brief panic. His response reflected his negative view of government and sense of duty; federal relief was not a consideration. But as the depression lengthened, Cleveland thought he had discovered the cause of the economic problems and determined to bend his considerable stubborn energy to fixing it. Blaming the panic on the Sherman Silver Purchase Act of 1890, which provided for the coinage of silver as well as gold, Cleveland resolved to return the nation to prosperity through sane "hard money," the gold standard. Silver, he reasoned, had destroyed business confidence, spooked investors, and hindered foreign investment (see chapter 18).

Opponents bitterly assailed Cleveland. A young congressman from Nebraska, William Jennings Bryan, spoke extemporaneously from the House floor to declare that the silver issue represented the clash between "corporate interests" and the ordinary people of America. Actually, not all capitalists supported the repeal of the silver act. Businessmen in debt and those who relied on foreign imports, for example, supported an inflationary monetary policy. Still, no other issue since the debate over race in 1866–1868 divided the nation as did the silver question.

The Cleveland administration was intent on maintaining a $100 million gold reserve. Cleveland feared that a drain on gold reserves could create havoc in the international financial markets. Even before Harrison left office in 1893, this reserve had started to decline. By the time the Senate repealed the Sherman Silver Purchase Act in 1893, the reserve had sunk to $84 million. By the start of 1894, it had fallen even further to $62 million.

When the government offered $50 million in bonds at 4 percent interest, sales were slow. When purchasers redeemed Treasury notes for gold to pay for the bonds, a further drain was placed on the Treasury. The bond sale further hurt the Cleveland administration politically. To Cleveland's critics it appeared, as one senator declared, that the president was "now fastened by golden cords to a combination of the worst men in the world."

Still intent on raising the gold reserve, the government issued more bonds, which increased gold reserves past the magic mark of $100 million by December 1894; but by February 1895 the reserve had dropped again, this time to $42 million. Desperately, Cleveland turned to bankers J. P. Morgan and August Belmont to arrange for outside buyers to purchase $62 million worth of bonds. It was agreed that over half of the money used to purchase the bonds was to come from abroad. This arrangement only furthered talk of Cleveland's capitulation to the "moneyed interests." In 1896 the Treasury issued another $100 million in bonds through public subscription. This loan finally stopped the gold drain, but the public attitude toward the Cleveland administration had soured.

Cleveland's handling of the tariff question did little to improve his standing. Pressing forward the plan of his first term, to lower tariff rates, in December 1893 Cleveland prevailed upon House Democrats to pass a bill that reduced overall rates by 20 percent and placed wool, coal, iron, hemp, and flax on the duty-free list. The Senate gutted the bill, however, and the new bill became law without Cleveland's signature.

To make up the difference in revenue and to appeal to agrarian and labor sentiment, that tariff bill also included an income tax of 2 percent on incomes over $4,000. This aroused the opposition of manufacturing executives across the country. It was also unconstitutional. In *Pollock v. Farmers Loan and Trust* (1895), the Supreme Court ruled that a national income tax violated the constitutional provision against direct taxation: While state and local governments could directly tax their citizens (through, for example, property taxes), the federal government had to rely upon indirect taxes such as tariffs. For Justice Stephen Field the income tax also violated the Constitution's stricture that taxes be levied uniformly. "The legislation," he noted in his concurring opinion, "is class legislation. Whenever a distinction is made in the burdens a law imposes or in the benefits it confers on any citizens by reason of their birth, or wealth, or religion, it is class legislation, and leads inevitably to oppression and abuses, and to general unrest and disturbance in society. . . . Under wise and constitutional legislation, every citizen should contribute his proportion, however small the sum, to the support of the government, and it is no kindness to urge any of our citizens to escape from that obligation. If he contributes the smallest mite of his earnings to that purpose, he will have a greater regard for the government and more self-respect for himself, feeling that, though he is poor in fact, he is not a pauper of his government."

In the 1894 elections Cleveland lost the Democratic majority that had emerged in 1892, as well as the support of many of the remaining Democrats. By 1895 he described himself as "a man depressed and disappointed." Cut off from his Cabinet, Congress, and party leaders, Cleveland wrote, "Think of it! Not a man in the Senate with whom I can be on terms of absolute confidence."

DEPRESSION AND TENSION CONTINUE   In the hope of ending the depression, some tried to convince the federal government to do more than Cleveland would allow. In 1893 Jacob Coxey, a wealthy Ohio quarry owner, met Carl Browne, a former patent medicine salesman who was touring the country speaking on free silver and reincarnation. Coxey, who had a restless interest in philosophical matters, converted to both doctrines and concluded that he was the reincarnation of Andrew Jackson. (Browne thought he was the partial reincarnation of Jesus Christ). Coxey's plan to help the nation came to him in a dream. The nation's roads were horrible: clouds of dust in the summer, rutted swaths of mud after rains. If the federal government were to spend $500 million on roads and other public works, unemployment would end. The money would come from no-interest bonds, although the dream did not reveal who would buy such bonds and why. Coxey formed the Good Roads Association and planned a march to Washington, a "petition in boots," to present the plan in 1894.

On Easter Sunday, 1894, only 122 enlistees in Coxey's Army, including reporters and a Pittsburgh detective assigned to look for trouble as they neared his city, arrived in Ohio to begin the journey. More men tried to make it. Groups from as far away as the Pacific Northwest even hijacked trains when they were denied free travel, but mishaps, misadventures, and arrests frustrated their plans. Townspeople of the Great Plains tended to support the jailed would-be marchers, feeling a mix of sympathy for Coxey's idea, hatred for the railroads, and unease about knots of unemployed men marooned in their communities. As Coxey and his growing band of followers slogged across the Allegheny Mountains toward Washington, they received aid from local residents as well as instruction on the currency issue, astrology, and reincarnation.

On April 31, Coxey's Army prepared to march to the Capitol, where Coxey planned to speak from the steps. Fearing radical upheaval, Cleveland placed federal troops on alert. The District police denied Coxey a permit to march or rally. Coxey's Army, now numbering around four hundred, paraded toward the Capitol, headed by Coxey, his wife, and his son, Legal Tender. As Coxey climbed the steps to speak, he was stopped by the police. The next day, he and Browne were arrested for parading on the grass; they spent the next twenty days in jail. So it ended, with weeks of press coverage but without public works spending or the hoped-for revolt.

Coxey's march turned into a circus, but it was one in which the performers made the audience anxious. Open class warfare seemed possible. The summer following Coxey's march on Washington, even worse violence erupted when Eugene V. Debs's American Railway Union shut down the nation's railroads over a lockout of workers at the Pullman Palace Car Company. By the end of June 1894, more than twenty thousand railroad men were on strike in and around Chicago. This strike was felt in twenty-seven states. The use of the Sherman Antitrust Act to issue an injunction against Debs led to three days of rioting in Chicago. In the end more than twenty people were killed (see chapter 17).

Republicans, not reformers or radicals, were the big winners in the 1894 elections. Democrats lost seats they had won in 1892 and seats that had been theirs traditionally, even in the border and a few southern states. The Populists slipped too, particularly where they had made their largest gains. In power, Populists had been disappointing, especially in Kansas. A party in control that preached the evils of party found that experienced major party politicians knew a good deal more about how legislatures worked than they did. Elections stolen through violence, intimidation, and fraud in the South also hurt the Populist cause. Republicans were able to argue that the Populists were incompetent legislators with dangerous ideas and that Democrats had pushed the country into depression. They eagerly anticipated the election of 1896.

1896: REPUBLICANS TRIUMPH, POPULISTS FADE

Populist hopes ran high as the presidential election of 1896 approached. But Democrats stole the Populists' thunder by nominating William Jennings Bryan on a pro-silver platform. After bitter debate, the Populist Party endorsed Bryan. The Republicans turned to William McKinley, who used his well-financed, well-organized campaign to overwhelm Bryan on election day. The election was a turning point that marked the beginning of Republican domination of the White House, the return of prosperity, and the end of Populism.

THE PARTIES FIND THEIR NOMINEES Many of the party's most important figures hoped for the Republican presidential nomination in 1896. With careful management, however, William McKinley came into the June

In the 1896 presidential campaign, William Jennings Bryan (1860–1925) traveled more than eighteen thousand miles, making six hundred speeches in twenty-seven states, an unprecedented record. Although resoundingly defeated by William McKinley, Bryan set new standards for campaigning. (Brown Brothers)

convention with enough delegates to make his nomination certain. McKinley, a former Union Army captain, had gained the respect of his colleagues as a congressman and then as governor of Ohio. His tireless support of high tariffs gave him a national reputation; his genial personality and a partisanship tempered with flexibility won him friends inside the Republican Party. One of them was Marcus Alonzo Hanna, a wealthy Ohio industrialist with moneyed connections, a strong interest in politics, and fine managerial skills. His lack of tact precluded a political career, but he deeply admired McKinley and made the promotion of McKinley's career his project. "I love McKinley! He is the best man I ever knew," Hanna exclaimed, as the man whose campaign he managed won the Republican nomination on the first ballot. Although a leading spokesman for high tariffs, McKinley had waffled on the silver question, and indeed he had not opposed free silver. The Republican Party platform, however, revealed no ambivalence and strongly endorsed the gold standard. The platform also called for a high tariff, the annexation of Hawaii, the construction of a canal through Nicaragua, a larger navy, and the establishment of a labor arbitration board.

Dispirited and divided, the Democrats met in July. Custom dictated that Cleveland could not run again, which was just as well, since there was no chance that his party would nominate him. For months, southerners and westerners had worked to ensure that a Democrat who supported free silver would win the nomination. Initially, the leading candidate was Richard Bland, but at the age of sixty-one, "Silver Dick," as many called him, was considered too old and too dull. Convention speakers in turn denounced gold and Cleveland (which reflected the depth of the party's divisions) and warned of the dangers of backing silver and inflation. Then William Jennings Bryan rose to speak. Born in Illinois, Bryan had moved to Nebraska in 1887 to revive a failing law practice. Not yet old enough to run for president (although he would be by election day), Bryan had served two terms in Congress, where he made low tariffs his issue. He had been out of office since 1894, and after determining that currency, not the tariff, was the issue of the future, he spent the next two years touring the country on behalf of free silver.

The public speaking practice paid off in his speech to the convention. Opening modestly with apologies for his youth, he electrified the convention with his case for silver. Since wealth was created by its producers, not its manipulators, "their prosperity will find its way up through every class which rests upon them." Farmers sat at the head of the table of the producing classes. "Burn down your cities and leave our farms, and your cities will spring up again as if by magic. But destroy our farms, and the grass will grow in the streets of every city in the country!" Waiting for the whoops and applause to subside, he closed with his arms outstretched as if he had been nailed to the cross: "If they dare to come out into the open field and defend the gold standard as a good thing, we will fight them to the uttermost. Having behind us the producing masses of this nation and the world, supported by the commercial interests, the laboring interests and the toilers everywhere, we will answer their demand for a gold standard by saying to them, 'You shall not press down upon the brow of labor this crown of thorns! You shall not crucify mankind upon a cross of gold!'" If a vote could have been taken immediately, Bryan would have been nominated by acclamation. Silverites stood on their chairs, hollered, paraded, and threw their hats in the air in a "scene of perfect bedlam." Gold Democrats could only look on sadly and hope that a procedural delay in balloting would cool emotions. Bryan won the nomination on the fifth ballot. To appease the goldbugs, the convention selected as his running mate Arthur Sewall, a wealthy railroad owner from Maine. It did little good. Eastern "Gold Democrats" broke ranks to form their own National Democratic Party and nominated Senator John M. Palmer of Illinois. New York governor David B. Hill expressed the sentiments of many anti-Bryan Democrats who remained in the party when he explained, "I am still a Democrat—very still."

Populists had hoped that both major parties would defend the gold standard, which would leave the inflationary side of the currency issue entirely to them. Now they faced an impossible choice. If they fused with the Democrats and nominated Bryan as a Populist as many westerners and midwesterners suggested, southern Populists would be in trouble. For them it would mean joining forces with their enemies, who had stolen elections and did not support the full Populist program. If the Populists nominated their own candidate, one who stood for greenback currency and the subtreasury, one untainted by what some Populists thought was the silver fallacy, the election returns of 1894 hinted that the party would slip into irrelevance. Both choices pointed to the death of the party, but through different means. It would either die of failing support or be swallowed by the Democrats and silver. The Populist convention chose death by the latter means but, as a compromise, nominated their own vice-presidential candidate. Bryan never recognized the nomination.

THE BATTLE OF THE STANDARDS   Thanks as much to Cleveland as to Bryan or McKinley, the currency issue dominated the campaign. At first McKinley hoped that he could straddle the issue and focus on the tariff, but he and his party moved decisively in the direction of gold. Some western Republicans left the party (when a western Senator, a member of the party from its inception, tearfully announced that he had to leave because of the party's stand, Hanna shouted, "Go! Go!"). Yet the party was otherwise united around McKinley, and Hanna put corporate America's most advanced organizational practices to work for his friend. Businessmen, even Democrats, who feared silver, Bryan's support of the income tax, and what they saw as Bryan's wild radicalism, answered Hanna's requests by pouring an unprecedented $4 million into McKinley's campaign. Republican coffers were so full that many donors received refunds. Hanna spent it on mountains of literature printed in dozens of languages, speakers (especially in the crucial Midwestern states), and a centralized organization. While McKinley sat in Ohio and greeted the trainloads of visitors who trampled his lawn, Bryan, with far less money, traveled the country. Two contributions to McKinley's campaign, $500,000 each from J. P. Morgan and Standard Oil, alone totaled more than Bryan's entire campaign fund. His trek, covering 18,000 miles, 27 states, and more than 250 cities, broke tradition at a time when presidential candidates were still expected to maintain their dignity by not appearing to run too hard. Bryan had little choice, since many Democratic newspapers withheld their support, but he also believed that, by speaking directly to the people, he could persuade them. He spoke, always about silver, at every stop.

Republicans targeted urban voters in the Northeast and Midwest. Realizing that Bryan would probably win the Deep South and certain Plains states, Republicans saw that the Midwestern states of Ohio, Indiana, Illinois, Michigan, and Wisconsin were critical. Workers were told to vote their economic interests. More than 120 campaign documents and 275 pamphlets were sent to local and regional party leaders to distribute to voters. With titles such as "Advance Agent of Prosperity" and "Fill the Dinner Pail," this literature played on the fears of the average worker. Campaign manager Hanna cultivated the Catholic hierarchy to gain Catholic workers' support for McKinley. The case of John Ireland, the archbishop of St. Paul, is notable. He had been saved from bankruptcy by a loan from railroad financier James J. Hill. With Hill's assistance, Hanna won the archbishop's explicit endorsement of McKinley.

By October the enthusiasm of the crowds had convinced Bryan that he had a chance. He did not expect much support in the East, but a combination of organized labor (which endorsed his candidacy), farmers, western voters, and the party's traditional core in the South could bring him victory. His calculations were off. On election day the exciting contest brought turnout as high as 95 percent in the most competitive Midwestern states and victory for McKinley that was a landslide by late-nineteenth-century standards. He won 51 percent of the popular vote and 231 electoral votes, over Bryan's 47 percent and 176 electoral votes. Bryan had won the South and most of the West, but his defeat in the East was total (he carried but one rural county in all of New York and New England); he lost the Midwest and all of the nation's large cities except New Orleans. Urban workers and businessmen alike did not believe that free silver meant anything but higher prices, while McKinley demonstrated to normally Democratic, ethnic, working-class voters that he did not share the prohibitionism and anti-Catholicism of some other Republicans. His party also won impressive majorities in the House and Senate.

THE DUST SETTLES   The election of 1896 ended the deadlock that had shaped late-nineteenth-century politics and began an era of Republican domination that lasted until the 1930s. No large competitive states remained: The Republicans controlled the North and Midwest; the Democratic Party was left with a base in the South and in a few large cities. With command of the White House and Congress, Republicans maintained high tariffs and removed the issue from partisan politics. They wrote the gold standard into law, removing it, too, from future campaigns. Higher government spending took care of the surplus, while a federal law recognizing railway unions and providing for mediation forestalled conflicts such as the one at Pullman. Most important, the depression lifted. Discoveries of gold in the Alaska Territory, Australia, and South Africa, made the silver issue irrelevant and, with a business cycle recovery, allowed McKinley to preside over a prosperous economy. Democrats could still count on solid support in the South and in some Northern cities. Bryan retained a following; after the election, he became a professional lecturer, still drawing large crowds who came to see the "Great Commoner." He would run and lose twice more.

The election of 1896 was also the end of the Populist Party. Some Populists wandered back to their major-party homes; others latched onto the Socialist Party or ignored politics entirely. The Populists never figured out how to appeal to urban, working-class, Catholic voters and never found support among farmers not involved in raising staple-crop commodities for the world market; that is, farmers who grew diversified crops and perishable produce for local markets in the Northeast and on the Pacific Coast. In devoting their efforts to building a political party, Populists had also largely abandoned the Alliances and (despite a few famous exceptions) the regular participation of women that had grounded the party.

The Populists had also failed to solve the problem of race in the South. African Americans had created separate Alliances, and for a time it seemed possible that downtrodden blacks and whites in the South might make common cause. White Populists did bemoan how race-bating had poisoned southern politics, and some spoke idealistically about the need to throw off the weight of the past to solve shared problems. Yet African-American voters noticed that the actions of white Populists did not always match their rhetoric: It was not beneath white Populists to intimidate black voters, although they did not do so with the Democrats' brutal regularity. Even when white Populists sought black votes, they usually made it clear that they did not support "social" equality between blacks and whites: integrated schools and public accommodations. Perhaps because they remained suspicious of white Populists, African Americans stuck with the Republican Party when they had the choice. Once the Populist storm had subsided, Democrats, including some former Populists, made certain that not even a threat of an interracial coalition would disturb the South's economic and racial order. Those Southern states that had not already done so amended their constitutions to include devices to prevent African Americans from voting. In the South and elsewhere in the nation, new ballot laws made impossible "fusion" tickets, on which a third party combined with a major one. In the interest of reform, many states also supplied printed ballots, and in order to get a place on a state-provided ballot, a party had to meet certain criteria. These changes made it harder for third parties even to appear on ballots.

The Republican Party finally gave up its increasingly feeble efforts to help southern blacks exercise their right to vote. In the 1880s and well into the 1890s, blacks continued to hold minor political offices and elected black congressmen from southern states, including North Carolina, Mississippi, and South Carolina. Attempts to pass a civil rights act in Congress in the 1895 were overshadowed by the issue of free silver. Having gained a solid national majority without the South, Republicans had no remaining political interest in African-American voting rights.

In 1896 a Supreme Court decision (which had nothing to do with the election) completed the North's acquiescence to southern segregation. Building on the Court's ruling in the *Civil Rights Cases* (1883), *Plessy v. Ferguson* decreed that social equality was not the business of the federal government. Homer Plessy, a light-skinned black, brought the case against a Louisiana law requiring streetcar companies to provide separate cars for blacks and whites. His lawyers' arguments, that the Thirteenth and Fourteenth Amendments and the 1875 Civil Rights Act barred state-sanctioned segregation of public facilities, persuaded only Justice John Marshall Harlan. "Our Constitution," he wrote, "is color-blind and neither knows nor tolerates classes among citizens." He warned that the majority decision would "perpetuate a feeling of distrust" between the races. If blacks assumed "that the enforced separation of the two races stamps the colored race with a badge of inferiority," the majority wrote, "it is not by reason of anything found in the act, but solely because the colored race chooses to put that construction on it." *Plessy* did not cause segregation; it existed informally in the North and both informally and legally in the South well before the decision, even as African Americans protested its imposition. But the "separate but equal" doctrine would remain the law of the land until 1954.

CONCLUSION

The depression of 1893 created a brief outburst of radicalism among farmers in the Midwest and the South. The rise of populism promised radical change, but the issue of silver dominated political debate. The Democrats attempted to capitalize on this radicalism by endorsing a silver platform and nominating Bryan in 1896. McKinley's triumph over Bryan ensured Republican control of the White House for the next decade. With the prosperity that followed came a revived interest in world affairs and in America's place among the nations of the world.

Recommended Readings

DOCUMENTS: Henry Demarest Lloyd, *Wealth against Commonwealth* (1894); William Allen White, *The Autobiography of William Allen White* (1946).

READINGS: (DEPRESSION) H. W. Brands, *The Reckless Decade: America in the 1890s* (1995); Stuart Bruchey, *Growth of the Modern Economy* (1975); Ray Ginger, *The Age of Excess* (1965); Harold U. Faulkner, *Politics, Reform, and Expansion, 1890–1900* (1959); Charles Hoffman, *The Depression of the Nineties* (1970); Edward C. Kirkland, *Industry Comes of Age: Business, Labor, Public Policy* (1961). (POPULISM) Peter Argersinger, *Populism and Politics: William Alfred Peffer and the People's Party* (1974); Edward Ayers, *The Promise of the New South: Life after Reconstruction* (1992); Chester M. Destler, *American Radicalism* (1946); Lawrence Goodwyn, *Democratic Promise: The Populist Moment in America* (1976); James R. Green, *Grass-Roots Socialism* (1978); Sheldon Hackney, *Populism to Progressivism in Alabama* (1969); Steven Hahn, *The Roots of Southern Populism* (1983); John Hicks, *The Populist Revolt* (1931); Robert C. McMath, *American Populism: A Social History* (1992) and *Populist Vanguard* (1975); Bruce Palmer, *Man over Money: The Southern Populist Critique of American Capitalism*; C. Vann Woodward, *Tom Watson: Agrarian Rebel* (1938) and *Origins of the New South* (1972). (ELECTION OF 1896) Robert F. Durden, *The Climax of Populism: The Election of 1896* (1965); Ray Ginger, *Altgeld's America* (1958); Paul W. Glad, *McKinley, Bryan, and the People* (1964); J. Rogers Hollingsworth, *The Whirligig of Politics: The Democracy of Cleveland and Bryan* (1963); Samuel McSeveney, *The Politics of Depression* (1972).

21

❧

America Acquires an Empire

OVERVIEW   In his inaugural address to the nation on March 4, 1897, William McKinley focused primarily on domestic policy, much as he had done throughout the campaign. Yet foreign relations dominated his first term. Within three years of McKinley's election, the United States gained an empire that extended into the Caribbean and across the Pacific to Asia.

America's three-month-long war with Spain began in 1898 and gave the United States control of strategic islands in the Caribbean (Puerto Rico, Cuba, and the Dominican Republic) and in the Pacific (the Hawaiian Islands, the Philippines, and Guam). Shortly afterward, the United States waged a bitter war of suppression against Filipino insurgents. Anti-imperialists denounced American actions, but in the end the United States stumbled toward empire, emerging as a world power in the 1900s.

AMERICAN FOREIGN POLICY
BETWEEN TWO WARS, 1868–1897

Throughout the late 1800s, American foreign policy lacked a grand strategy. Presidents tended to move from crisis to crisis without a coherent vision. America got involved in disputes in Haiti, Chile, Venezuela, and Nicaragua, and Benjamin Harrison (1889–1892) made an abortive attempt to annex the Hawaiian Islands. A crisis in Venezuela revitalized the Monroe Doctrine's declaration of opposition to European interference in Latin America. Grover Cleveland (1893–1897) barely managed to maintain a policy of neutrality regarding Cuba's rebellion against Spain. Spain's brutal suppression of the rebellion and its mistreatment of American sailors strained relations with the United States.

FOREIGN POLICY BEFORE MCKINLEY: BETWEEN BELLICOSITY AND NEGLECT   Although McKinley spoke endlessly about the tariff and the international gold standard during the campaign of 1896, he entered office with little experience in foreign relations. In this way he was typical of most presidents of the late nineteenth century. American involvement in foreign policy was neither systematic nor well informed. Indeed, American presidents seemed to fluctuate between bellicose involvement in foreign relations and neglect of day-to-day diplomacy.

During Ulysses S. Grant's presidency (1869–1877), the administration constructed a magnificent new home for the State, War, and Navy departments. Begun in 1871 and completed in the mid-1880s, the building had a profusion of Italian-style granite pillars, carved balconies, and ornate windows. Standing next to the White House (it is now the Eisenhower Executive Office Building), it covered more than ten acres but housed only fifty clerks.

Grant showed a willingness to expand American influence abroad when he attempted to buy Santo Domingo, today known as the Dominican Republic. The Dominicans, in the midst of a debt crisis, tried to sell their nation. Grant offered $1.5 million, but the deal fell apart when Senator Charles Sumner of Massachusetts rallied fellow senators to oppose the bill.

Republican administrations after Grant pursued an activist role in international relations, but foreign policy in general remained a jumble of uncoordinated policies formulated to meet crisis situations. James G. Blaine, secretary of state under both James Garfield and Benjamin Harrison, sought to expand American commercial ties with Latin America through a pan-American alliance, but little came of his attempt. Indeed, the United States' aggressive tendencies in Latin America continued to undercut cordial relations. In 1889 America tried to gain a foothold in Haiti when Harrison aided rebel Florvil Hyppolite, but once in power, the rebel leader rebuffed the United States. Shortly afterward, Harrison threatened war with Chile when two American sailors on shore leave in the port of Valparaiso were killed in a drunken brawl with locals. War between the two nations was prevented only at the last moment, when the Chilean government sent $75,000 and an apology.

Benjamin Harrison's most important diplomatic effort was his attempt to annex the Hawaiian Islands in 1893, after a group of American sugar planters overthrew Queen Liliuokalani's government. The United

States minister to Hawaii openly aided the rebels by sending 150 marines to guard key locations in Honolulu, preventing the suppression of the rebellion. Only thirty days after the rebellion, Harrison sent a treaty to the Senate that would annex the islands. The sugar planters were not keen on annexation, as United States law would prevent them from continuing to import cheap foreign contract labor. Nor did Harrison consider himself an imperialist; as he told Blaine, "You know I am not much of an annexationist, though I do feel that in some directions, as to naval stations and points of influence, we must look forward to a departure from the too-conservative opinions which have been held heretofore."

Harrison's treaty annexing Hawaii bogged down in the Senate. Many members viewed American actions in the islands as a betrayal of American principles. They also feared bringing the islands—with far more Chinese, Japanese, and Portuguese (as well as native Hawaiians) than Americans—into the republic. This treaty languished in the Senate until Grover Cleveland, a foe of annexation, regained the White House. Although Cleveland refused to restore Queen Liliuokalani, he withdrew the treaty, explaining, "The mission of our nation is to build up and make a greater country of what we have instead of annexing islands." Cleveland took pains, however, to warn would-be European colonizers away from Hawaii.

CLEVELAND ARGUES FOR NATIONALISM AND AGAINST IMPERIALISM   Grover Cleveland knew that the late nineteenth century had become the age of imperialism. Like many Americans, he was dismayed as he watched European powers carve up the world in pursuit of prestige, power, and profit. In Africa, Italy sought control of Ethiopia; Belgium, the Congo; Germany, Cameroon. In West Africa, France seized Guinea, the Ivory Coast, and Dahomey. England took Uganda and South Africa. Throughout Latin America, the influence of France, Britain, and Germany was growing. In Southeast Asia, France took Indo-China (what is now Vietnam, Laos, and Cambodia). Most of the European nations looked hungrily at China. Cleveland wanted America to be a world power too, but not by betraying republican principles; thus he was fiercely opposed to European-style colonialism. In foreign relations he was a nationalist taking a defensive position, rather than an imperialist pursuing a calculated, aggressive strategy.

The depression that started in 1893, however, increased Cleveland's aggressiveness in the Western Hemisphere, principally for political reasons. In 1894 he sent American warships to Brazil, then in the throes of a revolution, to ensure that American goods were allowed to enter the harbor at Rio de Janeiro. A short time later, Cleveland protested when Great

A SET-BACK FOR IINGOISM.

In 1896 arbitration settled a boundary dispute between Venezuela, represented by the United States, and British Guiana (now Guyana), owned by Britain. Many applauded the trend toward negotiation, but two years later the United States declared war against Spain. (© Bettmann/CORBIS)

Britain sent soldiers to protect the Mosquito Indians, who claimed territory also claimed by Nicaragua. Cleveland's promise to protect these Indians' rights persuaded the British to withdraw and Nicaragua to incorporate the territory.

The stage was now set for Cleveland's boldest action in Latin America, his involvement in Venezuela during 1895–1896. Venezuela and Britain disputed the boundaries between Venezuela and the British colony of Guiana. At issue was control of the mouth of the Orinoco River, which many hoped was rich in gold. When Britain refused to accept arbitration of this dispute, in late 1895 Cleveland sought to weaken Britain's influence in Latin America by asking Congress to appropriate money for an American commission to examine the dispute. When aired by the press, the issue unleashed an outburst of Anglophobia (hatred of the British) and patriotism among the American people. A few talked of going to war. Britain, deeply involved in fighting the Boer War in South Africa, finally agreed to American arbitration. Ironically, the commission ruled in favor of Britain. Nonetheless, the crisis allowed the much-neglected Monroe Doctrine, America's declaration of opposition to European involvement in Latin America, to become standard policy.

CLEVELAND AVOIDS WAR IN CUBA   Cleveland's strong stance regarding the Venezuelan crisis made it easier for him to be flexible when the colony of Cuba rebelled against Spanish rule in early 1895. He pursued a policy of neutrality without fear of a strong political backlash. Thus, even as Congress and the general public showed increasing sympathy with the rebellion, Cleveland refused to recognize the belligerents, seeking instead to pressure the Spanish to institute reforms in Cuba. At the same time, Cleveland placed a strict embargo on shipments of arms and supplies to the rebels.

This policy differed markedly from the one followed twenty-seven years earlier by Grant during a similar Cuban rebellion in 1868. Then, Grant actively encouraged the rebels; American intervention was prevented only by a cautious secretary of state. As a consequence, the Spanish government finally crushed the rebellion, but only after ten years of brutal warfare. Still, many Americans felt deeply about the plight of Cuba, and calls to "free Cuba" ("*Cuba Libre!*") increasingly found their way into American politics. Nevertheless, Cleveland stubbornly refused to become actively involved in what he feared might become a long, devastating war in Cuba. Customs officials were told to prevent arms shipments to the rebels. As a result, of the seventy-one known shipments from New York to Cuba, only a third made it to the rebels. Cleveland's policy of neutrality struck many as overly cautious and inflexible.

Cleveland's call for reform found little sympathy in official Spanish circles. Instead, the Spanish government decided to crush the rebellion. By 1896 Spain had sent more than 150,000 soldiers to Cuba. As savage fighting continued, the Spanish intensified their campaign. Intent upon isolating guerilla rebels from their base of support among the civilian population, the Spanish undertook a campaign of terror against Cuba's peasants. In February 1896 the commander of the Spanish forces, General Valeriano Weyler, proclaimed a policy of reconcentration, whereby peasants were forced to abandon their homes and were herded into "protected" towns and cities. In pursuing this policy, Weyler's troops laid waste to the land, destroying cane fields, butchering livestock, and razing sugar mills. One New York newspaper declared, "Weyler has turned the island into a prison."

Spain's hard-line policy created a crisis between Spain and the United States. Between 1890 and 1896, American trade with Cuba fell to nearly a third of what it had been before the rebellion. Relations were further strained by Spain's policies of stopping and seizing ships on the high seas and of ignoring the rights of Cubans who had become naturalized American citizens. Shortly before he left office, Cleveland warned Spain of America's growing impatience with Spain's conduct of the war and its arrogant treatment of American citizens.

MCKINLEY FINDS HIMSELF ENTANGLED IN CUBA

In 1897 McKinley entered the White House intending to focus on domestic policy. However, foreign policy, especially the Cuban problem, quickly dominated his attention. Spanish atrocities in Cuba outraged Americans, who demanded intervention. At the same time, imperialists, worried that America was declining, pressed for new export markets and colonies, and some saw military expansion as one way to get them. McKinley continued to pursue diplomatic alternatives, but to no avail. When an American battleship, the *Maine*, blew up in a Cuban harbor, Americans accused Spain of sabotage and demanded war.

The Spanish-American War was fought on the Caribbean islands of Cuba and Puerto Rico and on the Spanish-controlled Philippines in the Pacific. Neither side's military was prepared for war, and many troops died from disease. Spain's ineptitude made it an easy fight for the Americans. As a result of the war, the United States acquired an empire, gaining authority over Cuba, Puerto Rico, Guam, and the Philippines. Theodore Roosevelt emerged from the war a national hero and a leading political figure.

WASHINGTON FOCUSES ON DOMESTIC AFFAIRS   Throughout his campaign against William Jennings Bryan, McKinley generally focused on domestic policy, often linking the tariff and currency issues to prosperity at home. Nevertheless, at one point during the campaign he vowed, "We want to avoid wars of conquest. We must avoid the temptation of territorial aggression." McKinley's initial lack of concern for military and foreign affairs was revealed in his appointments of the cranky (and, some said, senile) John Sherman as secretary of state and of an incompetent secretary of war. Still, McKinley learned diplomacy quickly, showing a flexibility and a sensitivity his predecessors had lacked.

McKinley entered the White House as the most popular president since Lincoln during a time of enthusiastic patriotism. Tensions between the North and South had drifted into sentimental reconciliation, as veterans' organizations of the opposing armies met to reminisce. Throughout the 1890s, more patriotic societies, such as Patriots of America and the Daughters of the American Revolution, were founded than in any other decade. In the nation's classrooms children now began the ritual of saluting the flag. A heady confidence in America as God's chosen nation was evidenced in public ceremonies and public displays. Immigrants and non-Protestants, however, were a grudging part of the national celebration. Nativists, those who sought to exclude immigrants from American political and social life, pressured a number of city governments not to hire Catholics. Others insisted that immigrants Americanize if they planned to remain.

Rather than close borders, other Americans looked to open them, at least in trade. Many businessmen agreed that the nation needed to expand into foreign markets. Europe remained the major overseas outlet for America's farms and factories, but Asia and Latin America also beckoned. New markets offered a means for addressing the economic ills brought by the depression that had begun in 1893. In 1895 a group of American businessmen founded the National Association of Manufacturers to open markets in Latin America. Many companies involved in overseas trade shunned governmental assistance, as they did not want to mix business with politics and the intrigue of foreign diplomacy. They thought that commercial growth could be accomplished without territorial expansion or European-style imperialism. Most American business leaders believed that colonies were expensive, unnecessary, and a betrayal of American democratic principles.

The national government focused on domestic affairs. The White House staff itself remained small; McKinley increased the number to eighty, but security was inadequate despite President Garfield's assassination. The White House ignored the international terrorism that had emerged in Europe with the anarchist movement. Threats against the president were handled by the city police.

If Washington initially seemed isolated from the rest of the world, McKinley nevertheless brought new dignity to the White House. He saw himself as a model for the nation and its people. A lover of good cigars, he refused to smoke in public because he believed that he should not "let the young men of this country see their president smoking."

A Civil War veteran, McKinley brought an understated firmness to the office that was not apparent to many upon first meeting him. His even temper led some to think that he lacked backbone, yet his fourteen years' experience as a leading congressman had taught him the arts of self-control and compromise. He carefully cultivated relations with the cabinet and Congress. As one congressman noted, Harrison froze people out, Cleveland kicked them out, and McKinley kissed them out. Thus, McKinley gave the appearance of being wishy-washy, a man without firm ideas, but beneath this exterior was a shrewd politician with sound judgment and an accurate understanding of people. He brought these strengths to the nation's growing involvement in international relations.

MCKINLEY HEARS THE VOICES OF IMPERIALISM   On the way to his inaugura-tion, the president-elect told Cleveland, "Mr. President, you are a happier man today than I am." Cleveland replied, "I am sure of that, Major." McKinley did not realize the full implications of the departing president's reply. He soon found himself confronting the seemingly insoluble Cuban problem.

As soon as he entered the White House, McKinley faced considerable pressure to intervene in Cuba, from within his own party as well as from growing public sentiment that America could not stand by idly as witness to Spanish atrocities. Within the Republican Party, McKinley faced an ac-tive group of imperialists who called for America to take its "rightful" place as a world power. Although differing over specifics, these imperial-ists presented an active voice in policy circles. They criticized McKinley's policies and laid the groundwork for American intervention in Cuba.

The imperialists proved particularly influential because of their abil-ity to articulate—sometimes quite eloquently—their vision of America as a world power. They drew upon the work of Captain Alfred T. Mahan, who taught at the recently established Naval War College. His widely read *The Influence of Sea Power upon History* (1890) argued that all great empires were great powers on the seas. Among those who heeded Ma-han's message were Theodore Roosevelt, assistant secretary of the navy in the McKinley administration; Senator Henry Cabot Lodge of Massachu-setts; and John Hay, ambassador to England and later secretary of state. These men advocated a naval modernization program that would replace the antiquated Civil War–era fleet with fast, well-armored, and effectively armed ships staffed by an officer corps schooled in new tactics that made the most of the fleet's mobility and power. Extending American naval power also required refueling stations and bases far from the nation's shores.

This expansionist message found a receptive audience in political circles, especially among congressmen from the Atlantic states. Certain newspapers and magazines advocated imperialist sentiment. Especially prominent were Whitelaw Reid's *New York Tribune*, Albert Shaw's *Review of Reviews,* and Walter Hines Page's *Atlantic Monthly.* The rhetoric of expansionism created growing support for American military intervention in Cuba.

The emergence of sensationalist newspapers—the "yellow press"—in New York City played upon public sympathy for the Cubans. Newspapers such as William Randolph Hearst's *New York Journal* and Joseph Pulitzer's *New York World* raised the specter of a cruel, oppressive, and decadent Catholic monarchy in Spain suppressing the democratic aspirations of the Cuban people. (It was rarely mentioned that Hearst and most Cubans were Catholic).

The influence of the yellow press reached beyond New York as other newspapers picked up these atrocity stories. The nation's press demanded intervention and alarmed Congress. As an associate of McKinley observed, "Every Congressman has two or three newspapers in his district, most of them printed in red ink, shouting for blood."

Such journalistic reports nurtured growing public support for intervention in Cuba. Here was a moral justification for war, one that fit well with the Protestant missionary impulse. American churches had been sending missionaries abroad for decades. These men and women reported back to the flocks that supported them about life in exotic foreign lands and the progress they had made in their work among the "heathens." Cuba, and the Spanish empire as a whole, provided another opportunity to improve the condition of the unchurched (including Catholics) and the backward. For some, war was also a chance to revitalize morals and virtues at home, which had grown flabby since the end of the Civil War. Theodore Roosevelt wrote a friend in 1897, "In strict confidence . . . I should welcome almost any war, for I think this country needs one."

Neither morals nor markets persuaded many in the upper class and financial circles to pick up the imperialist banner. As one member of the New York elite recorded, he had not found one friend "who considers that we have any justifiable cause for war. Below that crust . . . the wish for war is almost universal." Many American businessmen were naturally conservative and feared that a war would disrupt trade; an empire would drain the nation's finances. To Mark Hanna, now a senator from Ohio who fiercely opposed military intervention in Cuba, Theodore Roosevelt replied, "We will have this war for the freedom of Cuba, Senator Hanna, in spite of the timidity of commercial interests." Other attacks on business's opposition to military intervention were less polite. Some newspapers used anti-Semitic language in attacking Wall Street and its anti-interventionist position. The *New York Journal* and the *Sacramento Bee* published a poem that read, "Shall half a gross of merchants the Shylocks of the trade / Barter your heart, and conscience, too / While freedom is betrayed." This kind of language, although not pervasive, suited a time when nativism had reemerged in American politics with renewed vigor.

MCKINLEY PURSUES QUIET DIPLOMACY, 1897–1898   McKinley tried to prevent war with Spain through diplomacy while working to end the rebellion in Cuba. To help with both, he selected Stewart Woodford, a straightforward, honest man, to represent the United States to the Madrid court. In Cuba he retained the Cleveland appointee, Fitzhugh Lee, a jingoistic southerner who openly supported the Cuban rebels. McKinley hoped to pressure the Spanish government to accommodate the demands of the rebels through reforms that would lead to Cuban autonomy or independence. McKinley was distressed by Spanish policy. He openly denounced the policy of reconcentration and Weyler's strategy of waging war against civilians: "It was not civilized warfare. It was extermination."

McKinley's policy was aimed at liberalizing a reactionary, albeit democratic, Spanish government ruled by a weak queen regent. McKinley's policy seemed to be succeeding when, in the fall of 1897, liberals won control of the Spanish government following the assassination of the conservative prime minister. Hopes for a diplomatic solution to the Cuban problem were furthered when the new government recalled General Weyler. Shortly afterward, the queen regent proclaimed a new Cuban policy. Decrees, however, do not implement themselves, and the situation on the ground changed little. Meanwhile, Cuban rebels refused to negotiate.

AMERICA DECLARES WAR, APRIL 1898   Although McKinley continued to press for a diplomatic solution, he became convinced that the Spanish military would never accept compromise. A greater shock came when Hearst's *New York Journal* published a letter stolen from the Spanish ambassador to the United States, Enrique Depuy de Lôme, which revealed deep cynicism within the Spanish government toward reform in Cuba. Dupuy de Lôme had written the confidential letter to a Spanish official in Havana, reassuring him not to worry about the United States. "McKinley," he wrote, "is weak and a bidder for the admiration of the crowd, besides being a would-be politician who tries to leave a door open behind himself while keeping on good terms with the jingoists of his party." Captured by guerrillas, the letter was turned over to Hearst, who published it in full under the headline, "Worst Insult to the United States in Its History." As one "Cuban Junta" member remarked, "The Dupuy de Lôme letter is a great thing for us."

Indeed it was. War fever swept the country. Further trouble came on February 15, 1898. McKinley had sent the battleship *Maine* to Havana to demonstrate America's interest, while also inviting a Spanish battleship to visit New York to assuage Spanish feeling. As the *Maine* rode at anchor in Havana harbor that night, an explosion on board killed 260 sailors. Most Americans believed that the Spanish had sabotaged the ship, although evidence later suggested an engine explosion.

Americans demanded war. Only the Catholic and German-language presses remained neutral. On the other hand, the Hearst papers declared, "Remember the *Maine* and to hell with Spain." Theodore Roosevelt accused Spain of "an act of dirty treachery." William Jennings Bryan, the Democratic leader, announced, "The time for intervention has arrived." Yet McKinley hesitated. He continued to press for arbitration, even though the new Spanish ambassador to the United States seemed unaware of the growing war fever in the United States. Irate mobs in Virginia and Colorado burned effigies of McKinley.

Finally, the Spanish replied in late March 1898. They promised arbitration of the *Maine* incident, the end of reconcentration, and Cuban autonomy. The reply, in fact, differed little from what had been offered in previous messages. A few weeks later, the queen offered to suspend hostilities, to implement autonomy, and to accept arbitration from the pope. McKinley's cabinet rejected the offer in the belief that the Spanish government was unable or unwilling to fulfill its promises.

McKinley asked Congress to pass a resolution allowing him to intervene at his discretion. Both houses accepted an amendment offered by Senator Henry M. Teller of Colorado that ensured that the United States was "to leave the government and control of the Island [Cuba] to its people." On April 25 Congress declared war. Senator John Spooner of Wisconsin wrote, "Possibly the President could have worked the business without a war, but the current was too strong, the demagogues too numerous, and the fall elections too near." McKinley believed he had little alternative. He sought a complete end to Spanish rule in Cuba and viewed anything short of this as a betrayal of humanitarian impulses, economic interests, and geopolitical considerations. Spanish promises of autonomy had come too late.

A "SPLENDID LITTLE WAR" AGAINST SPAIN   The Spanish-American War lasted only a hundred days. Americans celebrated the war as a great victory, but it was won both because of Spanish ineptitude and plain good luck on the part of the Americans. As one journalist concluded at the war's end, "God takes care of drunken men, sailors, and the United States."

The declaration of war sparked an outburst of patriotism throughout the nation. Black regiments came from the West, rediscovering Jim Crow on their way to the port at Tampa, Florida. Even the wealthy rallied to the

This 1898 photograph of Theodore Roosevelt shows the colonel with his first voluntary cavalry regiment (the Rough Riders) during the Spanish-American War. Roosevelt chronicled the unit's exploits in *The Rough Riders* (1899). (AP/Wide World Photos)

cause. Wall Street brokers and clerks organized a regiment, and Helen Gould, the wife of financier Jay Gould, gave her yacht and $100,000 to outfit another regiment. Theodore Roosevelt resigned as assistant secretary of the navy to become a lieutenant colonel in the Rough Riders, an elite regiment he helped found.

Patriotic outbursts aside, America was unprepared. The regular army was small and lacked the logistical expertise to quickly arm, train, and transport the rush of volunteers. At the outset, McKinley ordered Cuba blockaded and called for 125,000 volunteers. By the end of the war, the army had mustered some 270,000 men. Moving 17,000 men to Cuba took seven weeks; all the army had to outfit them were wool uniforms badly suited to Cuba's summer heat. Tainted "embalmed beef" fed the troops.

Command of the army fell to General William R. Shafter, a comic, overweight figure. McKinley, wishing to integrate former Confederates,

Map 21.1   The Spanish-American War, 1898

appointed Senator "Fighting Joe" Wheeler to a field command. The ex-Confederate general had trouble breaking old habits. In Cuba he reportedly once became so excited in battle that he shouted, "We've got the damn Yankees on the run."

The navy was more ably commanded and generally in better shape. In 1883 Congress had appropriated funds for rebuilding an obsolete navy left over from the Civil War, but the new fleet of lightly armored cruisers could not match most European battleships, except Spain's. In terms of size, the American navy ranked thirteenth but was in better condition than Spain's.

Although Americans initially feared a naval attack, Spanish ships were antiquated and ill kept. Their gunners even lacked ammunition for target practice. Their army was in pitiful shape. Poorly trained recruits fought without shoes, medicine, rations, and tents; ambulances to remove the wounded were "as pitiful food for powder as was ever seen."

America's first victory came when Commodore George Dewey won a naval victory in the Spanish-held Philippine Islands on May 1, 1898, only six days after the declaration of war. Steaming into Manila Bay and easily destroying or capturing all ten of the Spanish ships anchored there, Dewey's fleet suffered one wounded; the Spanish had 371 casualties, including 161 killed in action. A month later Dewey was joined by army units sent to oust the Spanish troops already under attack from the Philippine leader, Emilio Aguinaldo. McKinley's fateful decision to send troops to the Philippines ensured further American entanglement in the islands.

Meanwhile, American troops who were supposed to invade Cuba remained in the staging area at Tampa. Lacking facilities and proper supplies, many soldiers fell ill. Transportation in and out of the port of Tampa proved inadequate. The single-track railroad was used by tourists who wanted to see the ships, which often prevented military supplies from being transported to the loading docks. After weeks of delay, the troops were finally loaded onto transport ships, but reports of a Spanish cruiser sighted off the Florida coast further delayed the invasion. For five days the troops waited in hot, steamy holds. Finally, when the convoy did set off, the thirty-five transport ships became so separated that they spread out across a distance of thirty miles. Fortunately, the Spanish did not attack.

The Cuba expedition proved decisive. The Spanish made a crucial mistake in not stopping the Americans before they landed in Cuba at Daiquiri. Although it took nearly a full day to unload six thousand American troops in this chaotic, ill-organized landing, within a month the troops had advanced to the outskirts of Santiago, the capital of Cuba.

At Santiago, American troops engaged in their bloodiest fight. The key to Santiago was control of San Juan Hill and Kettle Hill, overlooking the city. From this battle a new military hero emerged: Theodore Roosevelt. With his troops pinned down under fierce fire from seasoned Spanish soldiers, Roosevelt led a gallant charge up Kettle Hill. In the confusion, his Rough Riders and a regiment of black troops became mixed. In the midst of the battle, black and white troops secured the hill together. As one Rough Rider later described the fight, "I joined a troop of the Tenth Cavalry, colored, and for a time fought with them shoulder to shoulder, and in justice to the colored race I must say that I never saw braver men anywhere."

Following this battle, American and Spanish troops became deadlocked in a trench war. Conditions were appalling. Plagued by flies and mosquitoes, rain and mud, soldiers on both sides fell to disease. Each day's rain washed up the buried corpses of soldiers and mules.

While the campaign for Santiago had stalled to a gruesome impasse, on July 3 the American navy under Commodore Winfield Scott Schley and Admiral William T. Sampson defeated the Spanish fleet anchored in the city's harbor. The Spaniards made a desperate daylight run to escape the American fleet, losing four ships and 323 sailors. The Americans lost 21 sailors. Once again, the Spanish ships proved ill prepared for battle. More than 85 percent of their ammunition was defective.

On July 17 Santiago surrendered. Cuba had been liberated. The surrender of Santiago came just in time, for yellow fever, malaria, and dysentery had begun to sweep through the American camps. Within three days after the surrender, more than four thousand American troops were on sick call. By the time the main American forces began to withdraw from Cuba, more than five hundred soldiers had died of disease. More died in transport on the way home.

Taking the Spanish-held island of Puerto Rico proved easier than winning Cuba. There was only one significant battle, in which six Americans were wounded and six Spaniards killed. On Friday, August 3, 1898, Spain and the United States signed a peace protocol. The agreement gave Cuba its freedom, ceded Puerto Rico to the United States, and permitted the United States to occupy the former Spanish colony, the Philippines.

In December Spain and the United States agreed to a final settlement. Cuba became an American protectorate. In addition to Puerto Rico, the United States also acquired the former Spanish colony of Guam in the Pacific. Spain received a face-saving $20 million for ceding the Philippine Islands, seven thousand islands with seven million inhabitants.

The United States had gained an empire. Even before the war's end, McKinley had signed a joint congressional resolution annexing the Hawaiian Islands, important as a naval base, to the United States. With the acquisition of the former Spanish colonies of Cuba, Puerto Rico, and the Philippines, the empire of the United States stretched from the Caribbean to the far Pacific.

Americans celebrated their victory in parades and demonstrations throughout the nation. Theodore Roosevelt returned home a military hero and immediately won the governorship of New York. Roosevelt's success was rivaled only by Commodore Dewey's. The ticker-tape parade up Fifth Avenue in New York welcoming him drew thousands; his name endorsed soap, chewing gum, and a laxative. In the midst of these celebrations, Theodore Roosevelt's close friend, John Hay, wrote, "It has been a splendid little war, carried on with magnificent intelligence and spirit, favored by the Fortune which loves the brave." Perhaps the spirit was better captured, however, by the wit of newspaper humorist Finley Peter Dunne, who, speaking through his Irish character Mr. Dooley, declared, "We're a gr-reat people." Replied Dooley's friend Mr. Hennessey, "We arre that. An th' best iv it is, we know we ar-re."

The spirit of victory that united Americans proved short lived. Its heroes, with the single exception of Roosevelt, were quickly forgotten. The magnificent arch commemorating Dewey's victory—initially made out of plaster and intended to be replaced with a marble monument—soon fell into such disrepair that it had to be torn down.

AMERICA BECOMES AN EMPIRE

Having fought the Spanish-American War to free an oppressed people from a colonial empire, America now had a foreign empire of its own. Contrary to the wishes of an anti-imperialistic bloc in Congress, McKinley was just as reluctant as the Spanish to grant independence to Spain's former colonies in the Caribbean and the Pacific. Believing the Filipinos unable to govern themselves, and fearful that other nations might step in, America annexed the Philippines. Filipinos revolted, and America crushed the revolt. McKinley won reelection in a landslide and worked to keep China open as a market. He was soon assassinated, but his four years in office had transformed the United States into a world power.

AMERICANS DEBATE THE ANNEXATION OF THE PHILIPPINES   Americans now turned their attention to the consequences of empire. The signing of a formal peace treaty by the United States and Spain shortly before Christmas, 1898, brought into sharp relief the problems of ruling an empire that reached from the Caribbean into the western Pacific. Specifically at issue was McKinley's proposal to annex the Philippines.

Following Commodore Dewey's victory in the Philippines, McKinley could have simply withdrawn American naval forces and left the land war to the Philippine resistance leader, Emilio Aguinaldo. However, the president feared German and Japanese intervention if American troops withdrew. He also doubted the capacity of the Philippine people for self-rule.

McKinley proceeded cautiously. He sent eleven thousand American troops, double Dewey's initial request, although Dewey's view from his stateroom was optimistic and far below what commanders actually responsible for control thought was needed. On August 13, one day after the peace protocol had been signed, the Spanish garrison in Manila surrendered. American troops were instructed not to allow Filipino rebels to participate in the surrender of Manila.

Even with the large number of American troops occupying Manila, McKinley hesitated to take the next logical step, annexation. His own cabinet was divided on the issue, and the politically astute McKinley realized that annexation would cause a political fight. Nonetheless, he found himself in a predicament. Some, including those in his cabinet, had suggested annexing only the principal island of Luzon and its capital, Manila. McKinley's military advisers warned him, however, that Luzon could not be defended without the other islands. On the other hand, McKinley believed the Filipinos were unprepared for independence. He considered Aguinaldo childlike in his infatuation with uniforms and courtly etiquette, even though both Dewey and the commanding army officer in the Philippines had reported favorably about him. Relations between the American military and Aguinaldo began to sour with the first arrival of American troops. McKinley was not alone in his reservations about Philippine autonomy. Only a few radical anti-imperialists in America believed that the Filipinos could maintain their independence. Most Americans felt that an independent Philippine republic would lead to civil war or invite intervention by other foreign powers.

Specifically, McKinley worried that the British or the Germans would seize the islands. The British had already expressed an interest, and the Germans had deployed naval forces to observe the American actions in the Philippines. Distraught over what course to take, the devout president got on his knees and prayed for divine guidance. He prayed so long his knees hurt. In the end, McKinley concluded, as he later told a meeting of religious businessmen, the United States must "uplift and civilize and Christianize them, and by God's grace do the very best we could for them, as our fellow-men for whom Christ also died."

ANTI-IMPERIALISTS DECLARE BETRAYAL   Certain now as to which course to follow, McKinley sent a resolution to Congress calling for the annexation of the Philippines. His proposal unleashed a national debate. Many American businessmen who had long been acquainted with the islands believed that American interests in China could be sustained only through annexation of the Philippines. Although this view had wide support from the public and the press, an active group had organized against annexation under the auspices of the Anti-Imperialist League. As a result, the proposed annexation produced a full-blown fight in the Senate.

Roosevelt acerbically denounced the anti-imperialists as "little better than traitors." This barb, however, misconstrued the firm conviction that unified the anti-imperialists' movement: that annexation was alien to republican ideals and the American Constitution. Andrew Carnegie, a leading anti-imperialist who financed the lobbying efforts against annexation, wrote to McKinley: "Our young men volunteered to fight the oppressor. I shall be surprised if they relish the work of shooting down the oppressed." He closed, "Your Bitterest Opponent."

Many members of the Anti-Imperialist League were liberal Republicans, or mugwumps (an Indian term meaning "Big Man"), who had broken with Grant and had supported Cleveland in 1884. They included such New England intellectuals as William James, the Harvard University psychologist and philosopher; E. L. Godkin, editor of the influential *Nation*; and the novelist William Dean Howells. Mark Twain, born a southerner but living in Connecticut, joined the anti-imperialist crusade. Former

presidents Grover Cleveland and Benjamin Harrison also opposed annexation. Some labor leaders and southern politicians opposed imperialism because of their own vested interests; for example, Samuel Gompers,
president of the American Federation of Labor, opposed annexation because he feared the admission of Filipino workers into the American
workforce. Deep divisions were thus apparent among the anti-imperialist
coalition when it came to specific reasons for opposing imperialism. Some
opposed imperialism on humanitarian grounds; others, however, displayed racial animosity toward accepting Filipinos into the United States.
Many thought that Filipinos would never be prepared for democracy.

ANNEXATION OF THE PHILIPPINES SPARKS A NASTY LITTLE WAR   The fight in the
Senate over the annexation treaty opened in earnest in December 1899.
Throughout the fight, McKinley refused to compromise. He remained
confident that he had the support of the American people and the necessary votes in the Senate to carry the treaty. In early February 1900, pro-
annexation forces found their cause aided when Aguinaldo attacked
American troops in the Philippines.

The president understood immediately that Aguinaldo had made a
serious mistake. He observed, "How foolish these people are. This means
the ratification of the treaty; the [American] people will insist on ratification." With American troops under fire, doubtful Republicans swung to
ratification. McKinley used pork-barrel politics, patronage, and federal
judgeships to win over those who wavered. The Democratic Party's
efforts to oppose the annexation treaty were hurt when their leader,
William Jennings Bryan, decided to support the treaty. He hoped to make
imperialism—along with free silver—an issue in the election of 1900. The
treaty passed the Senate by a vote of 57 to 27, one vote more than the necessary two-thirds required to ratify a treaty.

The war proved to be difficult and complex, a fact ignored by historians who have portrayed a racist American force torturing and killing almost at random, pitted against a brave but sadly overmatched Filipino independence movement. Some of the complexity arose from the dual focus
of the American forces: to subdue the insurgency and, in keeping with
McKinley's views, to bring order and the guarantee of individual rights
and security of property to Filipinos. In addition, there was not one war
but many. Some parts of the archipelago saw no fighting at all; in others,
Americans fought both a conventional and a guerrilla war. Finally, there
were wars among the Filipinos themselves. This made pacification easier,
since there was no united independence movement, but also more complicated, since the United States command did not immediately understand the scope and nature of the discontent.

McKinley felt that the insurgents had struck the first blow, so he declined to negotiate with Aguinaldo until the rebellion was quelled. Initially, Aguinaldo's troops fought a conventional war, inexplicably delaying attack until the United States had had time to build up its forces. They were routed. Only slowly did Aguinaldo turn to guerrilla tactics, and that delay cost men, scarce weapons and ammunition, and morale. His tenuous command was diminished further as local and regional commanders made their own decisions without coordination. Filipino units proved incapable of supporting each other in a fight. American forces discovered that near-suicidal behavior, such as charging well-armed defenses, could succeed against even a brave enemy often so poorly led. Aguinaldo himself had little choice but to focus on evading capture, which he would do until 1901.

Under General Elwell S. Otis, United States commanders were directed to carry out civil action projects, such as installing native civil governments, opening schools, and improving sanitation, while subduing insurgents. Particularly in places where the Americans gained the support of local elites, operations went relatively smoothly. Some commands even trained and armed Filipino police forces that worked with the Americans. Otis's peacetime habits of underestimating the number of men needed and the costs involved, together with difficult terrain and disease, meant that his mission progressed more slowly and at greater cost than expected. In May 1900 a new general arrived, General Arthur MacArthur (the father of famed World War II commander Douglas MacArthur). He asked for an additional appropriation of $100 million to conduct the war. He also brought a new intensity to the war. Civic action was a lower priority than it had been under Otis. General Order 100, issued during the Civil War, sought to balance repression and conciliation in pacifying a population; MacArthur bore down harder than Otis had on repression. Soldiers should separate combatants from noncombatants; continued resistance could result in the destruction of crops and property, imprisonment, expulsion, or even death. At one point MacArthur ordered several Philippine prisoners of war executed in retaliation for the "murder" of American prisoners. This request led to inclusion of the Spooner amendment, proposed by Wisconsin Senator John C. Spooner, which directed the president to implement a system of self-government once the Philippines were subdued.

Some of the nastiest (and most atypical) fighting occurred during the last campaign of the war, on the island of Samar. Ignored through much of the war, Samar became important when rebels there threatened to undermine the pacification of nearby Leyte. MacArthur ordered the American command to "make this an emergency measure and clean up [Samar] as soon as possible." Navy gunships blasted formerly quiet villages, set fire to houses, and blockaded the ports, shutting down all commercial traffic. On the ground, troops followed orders to "Clear the country of all insurgents, capture the necessary guides . . . and generally speaking make the region untenable by the insurgents." The native population, rounded up into camps, suffered from disease and lack of food. As the insurgents lost cover and support, they drew closer to the camps and attacked American supplies. They also attacked the often poorly designed American patrols. An insurgent ambush took the lives of fifty members of one company; the mutilated bodies of the American soldiers were later discovered with their stomachs slit and stuffed with flour, jam, coffee, and molasses. One officer, Jacob "Hell Roaring Jake" Smith, a veteran of the battle of Wounded Knee, ordered his troops to take no prisoners. "I wish you to kill and burn, and the more you kill and burn the better it will please me." Although legendary in Marine Corps circles (for decades to come, when an American veteran of the Samar campaign entered a room, marines of all ranks would stand and salute), the campaign was neither successful nor more difficult than what soldiers had encountered elsewhere in the Philippines. And it brought dishonor to all those who served in the Philippines. Smith was relieved of his command; he and two other officers were court-martialed.

When American forces captured Aguinaldo in late March of 1901, the insurgency had already been largely broken. Upon capture, Aguinaldo signed an oath of allegiance and retired to private life, living to the age of ninety-six. The same month Aguinaldo was captured, the American military government in the Philippines was replaced by a civilian commission headed by William H. Taft, a former circuit judge and future president of the United States.

The suppression of the Philippine rebellion required four times as many American soldiers as the invasion of Cuba and cost three times as many American lives as the entire Spanish-American War. Reports of war atrocities in Samar finally led to a Senate investigation. While the committee was in session, reports arrived in Washington that American soldiers had executed 1,300 Filipino prisoners of war on the main island, Luzon. The American military claimed that 16,000 Filipino insurgents died in the war. Anti-imperialists, guessing from worthless Spanish census data and unreliable counts by Americans, claimed it was more like a million. While there is no doubt that some American troops tortured and killed prisoners and abused civilians, the civilians largely acquiesced to American military control. Rebels, after all, also abused civilians and tortured and killed those they believed had cooperated with the Americans. In return, the rebels had offered only taxes and the forced conscription of young men. Many Filipino civilians opted for security.

Shortly before the defeat of the insurrection, American courts had ruled that the United States Constitution did not extend to the Philippines or Puerto Rico. These islands, the Court declared, were dependencies subject to congressional authority. As a result, the inhabitants of the Philippines and Puerto Rico were endowed with a curious mixture of civil rights and noncitizenship. However, Congress's promise to grant independence to the Philippines in the Jones Act (1916) was not fulfilled for thirty years.

Although critics accused the United States of betraying its anticolonial and republican principles by taking control of Spain's former colonies, American rule turned out to be humane. For example, American occupation forces in Cuba and the Philippines constructed roads, sanitation facilities, and schools. A commission of army surgeons working under Dr. Walter Reed identified the mosquito as the source of malaria (as first suggested by a Cuban physician, Dr. Carlos Finlay). In March 1901, Congress passed the Platt Amendment to a military appropriations bill, which allowed the president to end the military occupation of Cuba provided that Cuba consent to American future intervention if necessary to preserve its independence. The United States was also promised a naval base in Cuba at Guantanamo. Meanwhile, when the Japanese invaded the Philippines during World War II, Filipinos joined Americans in resistance.

1900: MCKINLEY WINS AGAIN; BRYAN LOSES AGAIN   In 1900, William Jennings Bryan, again received the Democratic nomination, as expected. McKinley's nomination by the Republicans, too, was a foregone conclusion. The great surprise at the convention came when party bosses, led by New York's Tom Platt, selected Theodore Roosevelt to run as McKinley's vice president. Fearing that Governor Roosevelt might gain control of the New York party, the bosses "kicked him upstairs." Neither McKinley nor Senator Mark Hanna favored Roosevelt, but the party bosses were too strong to be circumvented.

Bryan hoped to rally voters against imperialism, but in the end prosperity decided the vote. McKinley won in a landslide. He was the first president since Grant to win a second consecutive term. The following years were a golden age for the Republican Party; the GOP controlled the White House for the next three terms. In his second term, McKinley displayed a confidence lacking in most administrations since the Civil War.

AMERICA TURNS EAST   In foreign affairs, Secretary of State John Hay forged a new Anglo-American alliance in keeping with America's new position as a world power. Under Hay's guidance, the United States also attempted to exert its modest influence in Asia by preventing China from being carved up by the European powers to the detriment of American business interests. The United States announced the Open Door policy, which demanded that China's market be open to all trading partners. Although American trade with China was relatively small, many saw the potential for a lucrative market. After all, exports to China had doubled from 1896 to 1899. This export trade was particularly significant for the American textile industry, which made nearly half of its foreign sales in China.

By the end of the 1890s, Germany, Britain, France, and Russia had gained spheres of influence, areas in China where they received key trading and commercial rights. In a series of diplomatic notes, Secretary of State Hay called upon these nations to maintain an open door policy in Chinese ports.

In 1900 the Boxer Rebellion, an uprising against foreigners and western missionaries, placed Peking's foreign population under siege. An international force, to which America contributed five thousand troops, quelled the rebellion but once again threatened Chinese sovereignty. On July 3, 1900, Hay sent a second Open Door note, which promised to uphold China's territorial integrity. Although America was not willing to enforce this policy militarily, the new policy expressed America's new self-image as a first-class power.

MCKINLEY ASSASSINATED   In 1901 McKinley was at his height of popularity. In early September he traveled to Buffalo, New York, to address an industrial exposition. There, at a public reception, an anarchist named Leon Czolgosz shot McKinley. Czolgosz was seized immediately. McKinley, bleeding, was led to a chair. He told his aids, "My wife—be careful . . . how you tell her—oh, be careful." He then looked at his assassin and said, "Don't let them hurt him." Seven days later McKinley died.

CONCLUSION

William McKinley's presidency marked a transition for the American political order and for the nation. McKinley entered the White House primarily concerned with domestic economic problems; nevertheless, his administration directed most of its attention to international affairs. There was no turning back. America had emerged as a world power. McKinley set the stage for more dynamic leadership in the presidency, as his successor, Theodore Roosevelt, turned to the problems created by the corporate order.

Recommended Readings

DOCUMENTS: Theodore Roosevelt, *The Rough Riders* (1899).

READINGS: (GENERAL DIPLOMATIC) Robert Beisner, *From the Old Diplomacy to the New* (1975); Charles S. Campbell, *The Transformation of American Foreign Relations* (1976); Foster Rhea Dulles, *Prelude to World Power* (1965); David Healy, *United States Expansionism: The Imperialist Urge in the 1890s* (1970); Walter LaFeber, *The New Empire: American Expansionism* (1963); Ernest R. May, *American Imperialism* (1968); H. Wayne Morgan, *America's Road to Empire* (1965); Thomas J. Osborn, *"Empire Can Wait": American Opposition to Hawaiian Annexation* (1981); Emily S. Rosenberg, *Spreading the "American Dream": American Economic and Cultural Expansion* (1982); William A. Williams, *The Roots of the American Empire* (1969). (THE SPANISH-AMERICAN WAR) Robert L. Beisner, *Twelve against Empire: The Anti-Imperialists* (1968); Frank Freidel, *The Splendid Little War* (1958); W. B. Gatewood, Jr., *Black Americans and the White Man's Burden* (1975); Walter LaFeber, *Inevitable Revolutions: The United States in Central America* (1983); Gerald F. Linderman, *The Mirror of War: American Society and the Spanish-American War* (1974); Stuart Creighton Miller, *"Benevolent Assimilation": The American Conquest of the Philippines* (1982); David R. Trask, *The War with Spain* (1981); Richard E. Welch, *Response to Imperialism* (1979). (LATIN AMERICA / ASIA) Michael Hunt, *The Making of a Special Relationship: The United States and China* (1983); Akira Iriye, *Across the Pacific: An Inner History of American East-Asian Relations* (1967); Walter LaFeber, *The Panama Canal* (1979); Thomas J. McCormick, *China Market: America's Quest for Informal Empire* (1967); David McCullough, *The Path between the Seas: The Creation of the Panama Canal* (1977); Marilyn B. Young, *The Rhetoric of Empire: American China Policy* (1968).

22

&

The Progressive Years

OVERVIEW   Between 1900 and America's entry into World War I in 1917, the nation experienced an outburst of reform that extended to nearly all of its institutions and included local, state, and national government. Differing in vision, method, and goals, Progressive reformers included wealthy industrialists, the middle class, and working people. Many were Republicans, but others were Democrats, Socialists, or independents. Progressivism took different forms in the Northeast, the South, and the West.

Whatever their differences, Progressives shared a general belief that government had a new role to play in society. Nineteenth-century governments had never kept out of the economy and social life. But Progressives imagined new and more vigorous purposes for government. They differed among themselves over the government's specific role, but by World War I government had significantly larger responsibilities in regulating both the economy and American life in general.

AMERICAN CULTURE AND SOCIAL LIFE TRANSFORMED

Technological innovations introduced new products and devices that made life easier. Shorter workweeks gave people time to enjoy sports, music, and movies. New ideas in science and culture gave Americans a new view of the world as continually changing in no specific direction; therefore they themselves could force and direct change. The new corporate economy flourished. Giant corporations accumulated more wealth and economic power than ever, and their mass-production techniques transformed the nature of work while lowering the prices of goods. Nonetheless, many Americans lived in abject poverty.

TECHNOLOGY REVOLUTIONIZES AMERICAN LIFE   "Never in the history of the world was society in so terrific a flux as it is right now," declared the popular writer Jack London in 1907. "An unseen and fearful revolution is taking place in the fiber and structure of society."

While London expressed concern, most people welcomed the new age. Americans sensed the high drama of new businesses being organized, of new technologies being introduced, and of social life breaking with the past. American history is a record of changes, but never had change been so rapid or so profound.

Most dramatic were technological changes that influenced people's daily lives. Technology empowered the generation that came of age at the turn of the century. Ordinary Americans began to use electric lights, telephones, and aspirin. Chemistry provided new medicines to doctors, nitrogen fertilizers to farmers, and new products to consumers, from saccharin to the first plastics, including fashionable brush, comb, and mirror sets. Inexpensive red dyes allowed average people to wear brighter colors and decorate even modest homes in splendid colors.

One English visitor exclaimed, "Life in the States is one of a perpetual whirl of telephone, telegrams, phonographs, electric bells, motors, lifts [elevators], and automatic instruments." By the turn of the century, Thomas Edison's inventions (and other inventors' improvements upon them) could be found in most American homes. Electric lights and lighting systems, phonographs and movies, sewing machines and stoves, electric fans and flatirons became common household conveniences. Telephones linked millions of homes. Electric streetcars tied the city together. And movies brought a shared popular culture that cut across class lines and regional divisions.

The American economy boomed. From 1896 to 1901, per capita income rose from $188 to $467 (in 2002 dollars, from $4,004.97 to $9,850.97). Manufacturing became the nation's pride, and exported goods made their way throughout the world. The Singer Sewing Machine Company had sales offices in a half dozen countries; Ford made cars in England and France; the American Tobacco Company produced cigarettes in China.

This was a golden age for American agriculture as well. From 1897 to 1920, American farmers enjoyed unprecedented prosperity. They raised more cotton, tobacco, wheat, and corn than ever before. The introduction of irrigation opened western deserts to specialty crops, including citrus. Refrigerated cars allowed perishables to be sent east, and oranges, grapefruit, and lemons found their way into middle-class diets. Consuming more coffee, sugar, and cigarettes, the average American also dined on more red meat, fats, processed foods, and fewer cereals than in the past.

Although their diets might not be considered healthy by today's standards, Americans were living longer. Better sanitation accounted for most of the gain. Small changes had a big impact. Providing clean water to cities and towns instead of foul river or well water; inspecting milk to ensure that it did not spread tuberculosis; introducing sewer systems that removed and treated waste before it sickened or killed; and strengthening housing regulations—all these improvements prevented diseases that had killed Americans, especially the young. In the first two decades of the century, life expectancy of white males alone grew from forty-six years to fifty-five years. That increase resulted from declining child mortality (the greater chance that a one-year-old would see adulthood) rather than from adults living longer. The birth rate declined as well, and so older people became a larger portion of the population during the century's first two decades.

Medicine itself experienced revolutionary changes brought about by new technologies, although medical science had a long way to go before cure, not prevention, would improve health. American doctors began to use x-rays, better anesthetics, and blood transfusions. Medical research blossomed through private foundations such as the Rockefeller Institute for Medical Research and the Carnegie Foundation for the Advancement of Teachers. The Carnegie Foundation's study of medical education, issued as the Flexner Commission Report (1910), changed the way doctors were trained, by prompting the upgrading of educational standards.

AMERICANS RELAX   In these years American social life changed as well. The average workweek had shortened from sixty-six hours in 1850 to fifty-six hours in 1900, and by 1920 it had fallen to forty-one hours. Increased leisure time led to new forms of recreation. In larger cities, people went to municipal zoos, playgrounds, or parks; they could walk, ride bicycles, rent canoes, or picnic. Commercial amusement parks like New York's Coney Island drew thousands. Dance halls attracted young men and women. Baseball attracted spectators from both the working and middle classes. In 1903 the World Series was initiated. Football, popular in colleges, remained at first an upper-class sport but soon spread to industrial towns in the Midwest.

Pianos could now be found in many homes, as mass production lowered prices. Songs like "Take Me Out to the Ball Game" and "Daisy" thrilled the country. Phonographs enabled average Americans to hear recordings of professional singers in the privacy of their homes. The record industry helped change musical tastes. Songs like "You Can Go as Far as You Like with Me in My Merry Oldsmobile" ridiculed older popular tastes.

The movie industry became a major force in American popular culture. Thomas Edison had launched the movie industry with his invention of the kinetoscope, a machine that enabled viewers to look to through a peephole to watch a moving film. Other entrepreneurs, mostly immigrants, began to project films on walls or large screens. They charged five cents' admission and called their theaters "nickelodeons." Primarily aimed at urban working-class audiences, these silent films attracted hundreds for shows that lasted only ten or fifteen minutes. Movies became increasingly daring in their approach and material; *The Great Train Robbery* (1903), for example, introduced audiences to the first movie murder. People of all classes loved it. Largely to escape Edison's cartel of movie production and distribution, the movie industry moved from New York to Hollywood, California. There, film executives, often Jewish immigrants, produced more sophisticated fare. D. W. Griffith's *The Birth of a Nation* (1915) introduced such new techniques as the close-up, crosscutting, and shadows, even as its racist message provoked riots and stimulated the rebirth of the Ku Klux Klan.

Actors now became stars both on and off screen. Fans followed the careers and personal lives of comedians like Harold Lloyd and Charlie Chaplin, cowboys Tom Mix and William S. Hart, and leading men like Douglas Fairbanks. Gloria Swanson and Mary Pickford enchanted the public. For the first time, America had an aristocracy, even if it was only made of tinsel.

Movies introduced the public to new ways of talking, dressing, and behaving. Many reacted negatively to the morality (or lack of it) projected on the silent screen. Critics complained that movies glorified criminals, ridiculed public authorities, and degraded women. Most large cities, such as Chicago and New York, appointed censors who cut scenes from hundreds of movies.

New styles in fashion and clothes were also evident. Cosmetics gained wider acceptance. Women began wearing their hair piled high on their heads. They discarded tight-fitting corsets, wore their skirts shorter, and, to the shock of their elders, revealed their ankles. Popular culture introduced exotic dances, beginning with the fox-trot, which soon gave way to the ragtime rhythms of the bunny hug, the grizzly bear, and the turkey trot.

INTELLECTUAL LIFE TRANSFORMED   New theories in the natural sciences, the social sciences, art, and literature changed the way many Americans viewed the world. The general acceptance of Darwin's theory of evolution, followed by revolutionary theories in mathematics and physics, challenged world views based on an absolute, unchanging, and knowable Newtonian universe. Now the universe was seen as continually changing.

The emergence of the modern social sciences—economics, sociology, anthropology, history, and political science—also brought a new critical sensibility to Americans. Academics in these fields often cut their scholarly teeth on criticism of the nineteenth-century applications of Darwin to social change, which emphasized the creation of winners and losers through seemingly cruel and senseless competition. According to its critics, social Darwinism overlooked the benefits of cooperation in the human and natural worlds. It was also dead wrong about how society changed: Men and women could change it for the better.

During this period, young professors, many of whom had been trained in German universities, launched an attack on "formalism," rejecting truths based on a single absolute. For example, they considered the natural rights that had been so important to the Founders a sentimental fiction, useful once for overthrowing monarchy but not as a current guide to action. Scholars such as William James, the Harvard psychologist and brother of the novelist Henry James, and the philosopher John Dewey, believed that truth followed a shifting standard, not an absolute one, and could only be discovered in one's experience of the world. Historian Charles Beard attacked traditional assumptions about the United States Constitution in *An Economic Interpretation of the Constitution* (1913). Harvard law professor Roscoe Pound argued that law must take into account the nature of a changing society.

The shift from absolutes to relatives became most apparent in the visual art of the day. The New York Armory Show (1913) introduced such modern European painters as Picasso, Matisse, and Cézanne to America. Although to traditionalists like Theodore Roosevelt they were the "lunatic fringe," European avant-garde artists influenced American artists, including Georgia O'Keeffe. Other American artists, such as George Luks, John Sloan, and George Bellows, became known as the Ash Can School for their realistic portrayals of drab, violent city life. They shared with some novelists, such as William Dean Howells and Theodore Dreiser, a critical sensibility and the conviction that the gritty "reality" of American life was a fit subject for literature. Frank Norris and Jack London described a deterministic world in which men and women lacked control over their fates.

Eager to break with tradition, younger writers and artists consciously defined themselves as radicals. These "New Bohemians" formed loose-knit artistic communities in Chicago and in New York's Greenwich Village. They prided themselves in shocking middle-class society and the older, more genteel, Victorian generation. Small magazines such as Max and Crystal Eastman's *The Masses* published John Reed, Edna St. Vincent Millay, and Eugene O'Neill. In rebelling against the past, these intellectuals emphasized youth and its virtues. One young writer declared, "It is the young people who have all the really valuable experience. . . . Very few people get any really new experience after they are twenty-five. . . ."

AMERICA INCORPORATES   By the turn of the century, a growing number of Americans had become uneasy about the expansion of corporations. While they welcomed prosperity, they also disliked the growing concentration of economic power in the hands of large corporations. A wave of mergers transformed the economy and resulted in more than three hundred highly concentrated companies. These companies, which often held monopoly power over entire industries, controlled more wealth than many nations did.

Certain industries appeared especially concentrated. For example, just seven railroad groups controlled more than 85 percent of the nation's railroad mileage. John D. Rockefeller's Standard Oil dominated the oil industry. (Today its descendants include Exxon, Chevron, Mobil, and Amoco.) J. P. Morgan dominated national banking through his control of the First National Bank of New York, the National Bank of Commerce, the Chase National Bank, and many others. He also held a controlling interest in the nation's three largest insurance corporations, New York Life, Mutual of New York, and the Equitable Life Assurance Society. United States Steel, cleverly created by Morgan, was a holding company that owned eleven other steel companies, operating nearly eight hundred mills and controlling more than 60 percent of all steel production.

Major corporations created in these years included General Electric, National Biscuit Company (Nabisco), American Can, Eastman Kodak, United States Rubber, and American Telephone and Telegraph (AT&T). The legal framework of these enterprises had been created under liberal state laws in New Jersey and Delaware that allowed industrialists to form vast corporate holding companies.

These new corporate entities changed the nature of work in America by forcing the development of new, more complex administrative and managerial structures. DuPont, General Electric, and International Harvester became models for other corporations. Heading these organizations were not owners but new top managers, such as Theodore Vail of AT&T, Elbert Gary of U.S. Steel, and George Perkins of International Harvester. Beneath them were arrays of lesser managers, salaried employees from division heads to supervisors.

Large corporations employed an increasing percentage of the nation's workforce. By 1910 just 5 percent of manufacturing firms employed more than 60 percent of all workers in the United States. At the bottom rung of the employment ladder were new immigrants from southern and eastern Europe. Moreover, new techniques of mass production transformed the nature of work by upgrading highly skilled work while downgrading semiskilled and unskilled labor.

The automobile industry presents a classic example. Henry Ford and his associates introduced continuous line production. By assigning workers to a moving assembly line and giving them only limited, specific tasks, Ford cut the time to assemble an automobile from 12½ hours to 1½ hours. This allowed Ford to produce 500,000 Model T Fords a year. As a result, he was able to lower the price of this automobile from $950 to $290. With mass production came mass consumption, but lost in the process were large numbers of older craft workers.

The emergence of vast, powerful corporations also threatened many farmers, small businessmen, and socially concerned citizens. The new corporate order appeared to subvert older democratic and individualistic values. Concentration at the expense of small business enterprise appeared to be the wave of the future. Few noted the failure of a number of monopolies, including American Bicycle, U.S. Leather, and National Salt, and other mergers that did not enjoy complete success. For example, because of its failure to adjust to new technology, U.S. Steel lost 20 percent of its market share from 1901 to 1920. Standard Oil's control of petroleum refining fell from 90 percent in 1900 to 50 percent by 1920. Management did not anticipate that gasoline would become an important oil product and could not control the vast new finds in Texas and Oklahoma. Standard Oil lost market share to rivals Texaco, Gulf, and Union.

Although this new corporate economy brought cheaper goods into the marketplace, not everyone could afford them, even at lower prices. In his study *Poverty* (1904), sociologist Robert Hunter estimated that 20 percent of the population in industrial states lived in abject poverty. Other sociologists, such as Thorstein Veblen, contrasted the plight of the poor with the "conspicuous consumption" and extravagant lifestyles of the rich. Fewer than 2 percent of the population owned 60 percent of the nation's wealth. Andrew Carnegie, for example, made a tax-free $23 million a year while he paid the average steelworker $450 a year.

REFORM SWEEPS THE NATION

Willingness to break with the past reflected a general mood and set a context in which Americans could rethink the political and social order.

This Lewis Hine photograph from 1911 shows a boy working in a factory in Alexandria, Virgina. At that time almost two million children were part of the workforce. Many were paid five or ten cents a day, and few attended school. (AP/Wide World Photos/Lewis Wickes Hine, Library of Congress)

Around the turn of the century, the women's movement revived, and although women's groups differed over agendas and tactics, together they pressed for the vote, birth control, social reform, and improved conditions for working women. Reformers worked to improve public health, housing, and sanitation. They made city governments more efficient and won control of many state governments. New thinking also extended to race but produced greater exclusion and discrimination under the name of reform.

WOMEN ORGANIZE The new reform mood swept over many American women. The newly elected president of the General Federation of Women's Clubs declared in 1904, "I have an important piece of news to give you. Dante is dead. He has been dead for several centuries, and I think it is time we dropped the study of his *Inferno* and turned our attention to our own." Her statement acknowledged what was already under way: Even organizations that had shunned public activism in favor of study and self-improvement now turned their energies to investigating and improving their communities. Involved in everything from public playgrounds to

For more than fifty years, Susan B. Anthony advocated women's rights, including the right to vote. Progress was slow, and the Nineteenth Amendment was adopted only in 1920, after Anthony's death. (Library of Congress)

federal legislation affecting women and children, women's clubs pushed forward the period's reforming spirit.

So, too, did other established groups. Many women campaigned against alcohol; the Woman's Christian Temperance Union (WCTU) attracted the widest support. Under the leadership of the dynamic Frances Willard (see chapter 19), the Methodist-oriented WCTU broadened its campaign against the sale of alcohol to include "home protection" against drunkenness, which broke up homes. By the 1880s, under a policy of "do-everything," the WCTU accepted woman suffrage as necessary to the passage of a federal constitutional amendment banning alcohol. The campaign for prohibition led women to lobby for prison reform, workingmen's centers, and public health. The WCTU also worked with Native Americans and African Americans.

Women involved in reform became part of a new constituency favoring woman suffrage. Once the most militant branch of the women's movement, woman suffragists had become divided after the Civil War. The Fourteenth Amendment had granted due process and voting rights to black males while effectively excluding white and black females. Opposition to the exclusion of women from the Fourteenth Amendment rights found its strongest voice in the National Woman Suffrage Association, headed by Elizabeth Cady Stanton and Susan B. Anthony. This position led to a bitter break in the women's movement when Lucy Stone and her husband, Henry Blackwell, formed the rival American Woman Suffrage Association based in New England.

These two groups remained divided until 1890, when they merged to become the National American Woman Suffrage Association. This new, unified organization concentrated on more than four hundred campaigns to place woman suffrage on state ballots. Women could already vote in Wyoming and Utah. In only two states did women gain the right to vote in statewide elections, Colorado (1893) and Idaho (1896). These state campaigns laid the groundwork for the national effort for woman suffrage that continued throughout the Progressive Era.

In 1909 Carrie Chapman Catt took the leadership of the merged organization, which worked both for national legislation and for campaigns in individual states. Her efforts coincided with the winning of woman suffrage in California, Arizona, Kansas, and Oregon. To some, mere state victories (and losses in other states in the early 1910s) promised slow progress and only partial justice. Alice Paul, a Quaker influenced by her counterparts in England, organized the Congressional Union to undertake more militant activity. Although much smaller than the two-million-member National American Woman Suffrage Association, Paul's Congressional Union attracted considerable attention with its insistence on direct confrontation. CU members pledged to support whichever party supported a national woman suffrage amendment, picketed the White House, and engaged in hunger strikes when arrested.

Activists for both woman suffrage and social reform trained their attention on working women. By 1900 more than five million women, nearly 21 percent of the female population, worked for wages. Most of these workers were young and unmarried. Nearly two million worked as domestic servants, another 900,000 were employed in clothing and textiles, and almost a half million were professionals, many of them teachers.

Women factory workers, in particular, were poorly paid and often worked in oppressive conditions. A number of groups campaigned to better the lives of working women. Leonora O'Reilly, a labor organizer, joined wealthy New York reformer Josephine Shaw Lowell to organize the New York Consumer's Society, which later became the National Consumers League (1891). The National Consumers League, under the able leadership of Florence Kelley, lobbied for laws limiting women's working hours and protecting women from unfair labor practices. Since labor unions had not been interested in the condition of working women (except to argue that, if men were paid a wage that could support a family, women would not have to work), reformers looked to government for help. The Progressives hoped that the Supreme Court would accept regulation for women, on the grounds that "fragile" women needed protection, even if it would not do so for most nonunionized men.

Leonora O'Reilly also played a key role in organizing the Women's Trade Union League (1903). She was joined by a group of other reformers, including William English Walling, Mary K. O'Sullivan, Jane Addams, and Lillian Wald. The Women's Trade Union League helped organize the Ladies' Garment Workers' Union in New York.

In 1909 attempts to organize women in the garment industry took a dramatic turn when women workers in New York spontaneously went on strike. Many of these women worked ten- to twelve-hour days for as little as $4 to $6 a week. Most were immigrants from eastern and southern Europe; many were Jewish. The citywide strike began in October when the female workers at the Triangle Shirtwaist Company walked out. Joined by Mary Drier and the Women's Trade Union League, the strike spread to other garment companies. By December, between twenty thousand and thirty thousand workers were on strike. Finally, in February 1910, garment factory owners agreed to a settlement proposed by Louis Brandeis, a lawyer representing the workers. The "Uprising of Twenty Thousand" changed the course of labor relations in New York by forcing the garment industry to recognize the union.

In 1911 the Triangle Shirtwaist Company gained further notoriety when a fire broke out at its new plant, taking the lives of 146 female workers. Firemen found the charred bodies of women piled up at doors that managers had locked to stop thefts. The public outcry against this tragedy led to the appointment of a commission composed of Frances Perkins (later to become secretary of labor in 1933 and the first woman cabinet member), Robert Wagner (later U.S. senator from New York), and Alfred E. Smith (later governor and Democratic Party presidential candidate). Based on their report, the state legislature passed new legislation protecting women workers.

Some female activists also attempted to change the family. By 1909 the traditional wife's promise to "obey" had been dropped from civil marriage vows and from some liberal Protestant vows. Margaret Sanger crusaded to introduce birth control devices in the form of diaphragms to working women. Trained as a nurse, Sanger argued that women had the right to determine for themselves "whether they shall become mothers, under what conditions, and when." She also saw in birth control a means to address social problems by allowing the poor to limit the size of their families. Influenced by Darwinian science and eugenics (the belief that "the race" could be improved through population control), Sanger believed that birth control could improve the American stock and liberate women. Although a rising divorce rate alarmed traditionalists, others welcomed these changes as a sign that women were finally gaining greater independence. In 1880 only one in twenty-one marriages ended in divorce; in 1900 one in twelve marriages failed; by 1915 the divorce rate had risen to one in nine. The divorce rate among working-class families nearly equaled that of the middle class.

REFORM BEGINS ON THE LOCAL LEVEL   The reform movement began on the local level and progressed through the state level to the federal government. New conditions seemed to require new responses; demands for more active government came from trade associations, professional groups, consumer leagues, women's groups, labor unions, and voters. The reform movement became a moral crusade even as it demanded greater efficiency in private and public activities.

Reform-minded businessmen rejected laissez-faire government and unfettered competition when they organized the National Civic Federation (1900), an association promoting industrial arbitration in labor disputes. This reform spirit was also found in the organization of the National Tuberculosis Association, the Boy Scouts of America, the Women's League for Peace and Freedom, and local and federal research organizations established in these years.

Newspapers and magazines stimulated reform (and sold more subscriptions) by revealing public corruption and abuses of power. "Muckraking" gained notoriety when journalist Lincoln Steffens documented business payoffs to city governments in a series of articles in *McClure's Magazine*. Later reissued as a book, *The Shame of the Cities* (1904) showed how business interests had corrupted local governments virtually everywhere. Other magazines became even more persistent. *Cosmopolitan*, a Hearst magazine, published David Graham Phillips's investigative reports, "The Treason of the Senate," revealing corporate influence in the federal government.

The efforts at reform on the municipal level included the settlement house movement. In 1889 Jane Addams, a wealthy social reformer, founded Hull House in a poor section of Chicago. Settlement houses sprang up in New York, Philadelphia, St. Louis, and other cities. Addams and other settlement house workers extended their efforts to improve public health, city sanitation, and public housing. Physicians and public health nurses fought against "the white plague," tuberculosis, by urging the public, especially the working class, to boil milk. Women's groups set up milk stations that provided inspected milk. Other reformers such as Frederic C. Howe launched the "City Beautiful" movement to improve cities through planning. During these years cities built civic centers, tree-lined boulevards, fountains, playgrounds, and parks.

Many urban reformers blamed the plight of the city on political bosses. Reformers maintained that bosses controlled government through ignorant immigrant voters who were marched to the polls on election day and told how to vote. City bosses then willingly subverted the public good by selling out to local business interests who were given government contracts, licenses, and franchises. Reformers also accused bosses of giving jobs to political supporters regardless of their competence to perform those jobs.

Some municipal reformers believed that control could be taken away from the bosses by bringing expertise to government. These reformers maintained that city governments should adopt a civil service under the direction of strong executive government instead of hiring of employees by favoritism. Other new forms of government were also tried. In 1901, when local government failed to respond to a giant tidal wave that wiped out the port city of Galveston, Texas, leading citizens instituted government in the form of a specially created commission, in which responsibility for city departments was divided among three to five elected commissioners. The Galveston plan spread to other cities and was refined into the city manager plan, in which a single administrator appointed by an elected city council operates the business affairs of the city. First adopted in Staunton, Virginia, the city manager plan was widely employed in other cities.

In city after city, reformers swept into office. Tom Johnson of Cleveland typified this reform sentiment. By the age of thirty, he had made a fortune in streetcar companies. Then he read Henry George's bitter critique of wealth, *Progress and Poverty* (1883). He sold his stock and ran for mayor on a campaign to reduce streetcar fares. During his nine years in office, starting in 1901, he introduced clean, well-lighted streets, public baths, market inspections, public parks, and better sanitation.

Johnson's program became a model for municipal reform in many cities. Progressivism in the cities improved municipal services and made city government more efficient. In many cities, public utilities and transportation services were taken over by publicly owned companies.

The expansion of public services, however, often brought increased property taxes that alienated middle-class voters. Divisions among reformers over such issues as prohibition often led to political defeat at the polls; as a consequence, political bosses often regained control of government. For example, ousted briefly in 1901, New York City's dominant Tammany Hall political machine, under Charles Croker and Charles Murphy, regained power in New York City in 1903. William Yare controlled Philadelphia; Edward Crump dominated the Democratic machine in Memphis into the 1930s; and the Pendergast brothers reigned in Kansas City.

REFORM MOVES TO THE STATE LEVEL   Problems they could not address at the city level reformers kicked up to the states. Reformers won control of many state governments. In California, Hiram Johnson became governor on a campaign to "Kick Southern Pacific Out of Politics." After heading an investigation of life insurance company abuses, Charles Evans Hughes became governor of New York in 1906. After enacting the first maximum–hour law for women workers, Oregon elected William Uren as governor. Uren also established the first state laws enabling voters to govern directly through ballot initiatives and referenda and to remove officials through recall. In 1904 Oregon adopted the first presidential primary election. In the South, James Vardaman of Mississippi and Hoke Smith of Georgia led white farmers against corporate interests. During his three terms as governor of Wisconsin, Robert La Follette introduced the "Wisconsin idea" to restore democratic government through party primaries and to replace corrupt party conventions with primaries. La Follette also imposed the first state income tax, improved civil service, and regulated corporations.

Progressive reformers agreed on the importance of returning government to the people. In striving for this goal, they sought to regulate economic activity, limit corporate influence in politics, and make government more economical and efficient. In many states, tax reform provided the funds for ambitious new programs by replacing states' reliance on property taxes with liquor, tobacco, inheritance, and corporate taxes, leaving property tax income to the cities and towns. Yet a strong moral element in the Progressive Movement divided reformers. For example, after coming into office in 1910, California Progressives achieved what Theodore Roosevelt described as the "greatest reform ever made by any state for the benefit of its people" through state constitutional amendments allowing the initiative and referendum, and through legislation adopting woman suffrage and public utility regulation. Yet when they tried to legislate public morality by banning saloons, racetracks, and prostitution, California Progressives became factionalized.

During these years, the prohibition movement gained momentum in other states, particularly in the South and West. From 1906 to 1917, twenty-one states passed legislation prohibiting the sale and consumption of alcohol. By the time the Eighteenth Amendment to the Constitution was ratified in 1919 prohibiting the "manufacture, sale, or transportation" of intoxicating liquors, half the population already lived in dry areas.

The control of narcotics was another outcome of these years of reform. Many patent medicines contained narcotics. For example, opium could be found in "Mrs. Winslow's Soothing Syrup" for crying babies. Cocaine was used for hay fever medicine and in small amounts in Coca-Cola until 1903, when it was replaced with caffeine. The Pure Food and Drug Act (1906) required most manufacturers to drop narcotics from their products. In 1909 Congress prohibited the importation of opium for smoking, and in 1914 the Harrison Narcotics Control Act brought narcotics in general under federal control.

RACE AND REFORM   Progressive Era reforms did little to benefit blacks. Most settlement houses in the North were segregated, as settlement leaders claimed that few white immigrants would use the facilities if the growing urban black population were included. Blacks lost the right to vote in the South through poll taxes, literacy tests, and outright intimidation. From 1900 to 1912, more than one thousand blacks were lynched or burned to death. Many Southern Progressive politicians linked reform to the disfranchisement of black voters. For example, Hoke Smith, a leading Georgia Progressive, ran for governor calling for primary elections, direct election of U.S. senators, and the prohibition of child labor—all Progressive causes—and taking the vote away from blacks.

The period also saw the outbreak of bitter race riots. Shortly after the 1906 gubernatorial election in Georgia, a riot broke out in Atlanta when rumors spread of black men attacking white women. A mob estimated at ten thousand to fifteen thousand white men roamed the city attacking any blacks found on the street; it was suppressed by the state militia. One white and twenty-five blacks were killed. That same year, an entire battalion of black soldiers stationed at Brownsville, Texas, was dishonorably discharged after being accused of firing on a crowd during a melee in town. The most shocking incident occurred in Springfield, Illinois. In August 1908, a white woman's allegation that she had been attacked by a black man sparked a three-day riot. The sheriff's transfer of the accused man out of town denied the white crowd's thirst for a lynching. The crowd turned its rage on the black community as a whole; they sacked black houses and business, lynched two blacks, and beat others.

White liberals might cluck their tongues at race riots in the South; this one, in the North and in the home town of Abraham Lincoln, no less, spurred action. A group of white liberals and prominent blacks assembled in New York City and formed the National Association for the Advancement of Colored People in 1911, dedicated "to promote equality of rights and eradicate caste or race prejudice. . . ." The founders included English Walling, a New York reformer and member of a wealthy Kentucky family; Mary White Ovington, who was compiling *Half a Man: The Status of the Negro in New York* (1911) and who opened a settlement house to work with black newcomers to New York; and Oswald Garrison Villard, another wealthy New York reformer and descendant of abolitionist William Lloyd Garrison. The only high-ranking black was W. E. B. DuBois, the editor of the influential newspaper *The Crisis*. By 1930, however, the NAACP was predominately black.

In its early years the NAACP targeted segregation and disfranchisement of black voters. In 1915 they persuaded the Supreme Court to overturn Oklahoma's grandfather clause, which prevented blacks from voting by setting difficult requirements that were waived if your grandfather had been a voter. (Because of slavery, most blacks did not have grandfathers who had voted.) Two years later the Court struck down Louisville's residential segregation ordinance. Still, these successes proved rather modest given the general climate for blacks.

Asians faced fierce discrimination as well, especially in the western United States. Legislation passed in 1882 prohibited the immigration of Chinese laborers, and because almost all of the early migrants were single men, the Chinese-American population gradually declined. Newly arriving Japanese farm workers replaced Chinese farm workers. Japanese immigrants tended to be more literate and came with their families. Work in the Hawaiian sugar fields first attracted the Japanese in the 1870s; from there they moved to the mainland, particularly to California. More than 130,000 Japanese arrived in California in the first decade of the 1900s.

The arrival of so many Japanese upset many Californians. In 1905 San Francisco labor union leaders formed an Asiatic Exclusion League to prevent further immigration. Under pressure from this league, the city board of education ordered all Japanese children to attend a segregated school. Protests from the Japanese government created a diplomatic crisis that forced President Theodore Roosevelt to involve himself in the affairs of the city. In 1907, in return for a compromise agreement with city officials, Roosevelt negotiated the Gentlemen's Agreement with Japan, which prevented any more Japanese laborers, unskilled or skilled, from migrating to the United States. Nevertheless, California Republican Progressives made barring Japanese immigration a major part of their political platform.

Conditions for Mexicans in the United States also worsened in these years. At the outbreak of revolution in Mexico in 1910, thousands fled north. Many Mexican refugees moved to cities and towns in the West, where they created *barrios*, or ghettos. Others became migrant farm laborers, only to encounter horrible working conditions. In California, Mexicans replaced Japanese farm workers after the Gentlemen's Agreement (1907) barred further Japanese immigration. In 1903 farm laborers conducted a bitter strike against California beet growers, one of the first agricultural strikes in the nation's history.

THEODORE ROOSEVELT BRINGS REFORM TO THE NATION, 1901–1909

Theodore Roosevelt's assertive leadership changed the nature of the presidency and made the federal government a more active player in the nation's economy. Although he accepted the existence of large corporations, Roosevelt opposed monopolistic control at the public's expense. He believed that, rather than serve the interests of industrialists, government should be a broker between labor and management. He brought food and drugs under federal regulation and established programs to conserve the nation's natural resources.

William Howard Taft succeeded Roosevelt in the White House in 1909, but proved a disappointment to some reformers accustomed to Roosevelt's exuberant leadership. Opposition to Taft split the Republican Party, enabling Democrat Woodrow Wilson to win the presidency in 1912. During Wilson's administration, the nation acquired the income tax, a central banking system, and increased regulation of industry.

THEODORE ROOSEVELT ENTERS THE WHITE HOUSE, 1901   When Theodore Roosevelt was catapulted into the presidency following the assassination of William McKinley in 1901, he focused the nation on Progressive reform. Roosevelt quickly brought a vigorous, assertive leadership to the Executive Mansion, which he soon renamed the White House. Roosevelt promoted antitrust prosecution, consumer protection, conservation, and new industrial relations.

Roosevelt differed in many ways from previous presidents. He had an exceptional personality, intellectual curiosity, and an expressed, conscious desire to be known in history as a prime mover. Afflicted as a child with a frail body and weak eyes, he was determined to prove himself the physical equal of any man and the intellectual superior of most. His well-publicized exploits and "charge" up San Juan Hill in Cuba during the Spanish-American War helped put him into the governor's mansion in New York, and then into the vice-presidency in 1901.

As president, Roosevelt proceeded cautiously in his reform efforts. The Republican Party was controlled by the "Old Guard," headed by Nelson Aldrich, senator from Rhode Island and an avowed spokesman for Wall Street, and Joseph G. Cannon, the autocratic Speaker of the House. The Old Guard sought to protect the industrial, financial, and railroad interests of the country and was more likely to support black civil rights than Progressives were. On issues of economics as well as racial justice, they harkened back to the nineteenth-century Republican Party.

One of Roosevelt's first actions was to strike a deal with Aldrich. Following a visit to Aldrich's summer home in Rhode Island, Roosevelt agreed to leave alone the protective tariff and the monetary structure. In return, he was allowed to propose railroad and antitrust legislation and enforcement. Roosevelt, who had earlier dismissed the trust question as Democratic partisan politics, understood that some action on this issue was necessary to appease an uprising in his own party by Midwestern congressmen, who later became known as Insurgents. Led by men such as Robert La Follette (Wisconsin), George Norris (Nebraska), Albert Cummins (Iowa), and William Borah (Idaho), these Progressive Republicans constituted a growing rebellion within the party.

Roosevelt immediately sought to strengthen the Interstate Commerce Commission (ICC), whose powers had been weakened in a series of court cases in 1896–1897 that limited its power to set rates. Roosevelt also moved to revise the Sherman Antitrust Act, which had also been weakened by the Supreme Court. In *United States v. E. C. Knight Company* (1895), the Court had ruled that the Sherman Antitrust Act did not apply to manufacturing. To redress this situation, Roosevelt's administration filed eighteen suits against trusts in the next few years. An investigation of Northern Securities, a holding company organized by J. P. Morgan that had brought together the Great Northern and Northern Pacific railroads, led to the first major antitrust suit. Shortly afterward, Roosevelt ordered the prosecution of the Swift, Armour, and Morris companies, the so-called Beef Trust, for organizing the National Packing Company. Successful antitrust actions were filed against Standard Oil in 1907 and the American Tobacco Company in 1908.

Even while conducting these actions against corporations, Theodore Roosevelt made a sharp distinction between good and bad trusts. He did not fear bigness per se. What he disliked was monopolistic control that thwarted what he confidently defined as the public interest. For this reason, Roosevelt negotiated a series of gentlemen's agreements with Morgan interests when he initiated investigations into U.S. Steel and International Harvester. In both cases, Morgan agreed to open corporate books to the government with the stipulation that the president would have final authority to release the material to the public. It was also agreed that antitrust violations would be pointed out to the companies first so they could correct the violation without going to court.

Roosevelt believed that government should serve the interests of neither labor nor capital. Rather, government was to be a broker between them. This attitude became evident in his first year in office when he confronted a national crisis brought about by a coal strike. In May 1902, 150,000 miners of the United Mine Workers' Union under John Mitchell struck to gain a pay increase, an eight-hour day, and union recognition.

Mine owners, engaged in a fiercely competitive business, stoutly resisted the union's attempts to break their hold on the coalfields of Pennsylvania, Ohio, and West Virginia. Represented by men such as George Baer, president of the Pennsylvania and Reading Railroad, they refused to bargain. Baer captured the attitude of his fellow owners when he told the press that capital had a religious duty to break the strike. "The rights and interests of the laboring men," he declared, "will be protected and cared for—not by labor agitators, but by Christian men to whom God in his infinite wisdom has given control of the propertied interest of the country."

Baer's obstinacy annoyed even fellow industrialists who had tried to mediate the dispute. Finally, by threatening to call in federal troops, Roosevelt forced mine owners to come to the table. A commission granted the miners a substantial pay increase and a shorter workweek. Although the union did not gain recognition, this episode marked the first time in the nation's history that a president had entered a dispute to defend the rights of labor.

In 1904 Roosevelt ran for the presidency in his own right by campaigning on what he described as a "square deal" for the American public. His task was made easier when the Democrats, tired of Bryan's defeats in 1896 and 1900, nominated conservative Alton Parker. Roosevelt's margin of victory was the greatest since Andrew Jackson's defeat of Henry Clay in 1832.

ROOSEVELT BUILDS ON AN APPETITE FOR CHANGE   The election was significant in another respect: The Socialist Party's nominee, Eugene Debs, increased his vote from 88,000 in 1900 to more than 400,000 in 1904. In 1911 Socialists won mayoral elections in eighteen cities and towns as well as state legislature seats in Rhode Island and New York. In all, 1,150 Socialists held office in thirty-six states. Socialist newspapers prospered. Julius Wayland's *Appeal to Reason,* published in Kansas, circulated 300,000 copies. Moreover, Socialist leaders gained control of a number of unions within the American Federation of Labor.

Eugene Debs, on the left side of politics but on the reader's right side on this button, ran for president as a socialist five times between 1900 and 1920. In 1912 he got six percent of the vote. Jailed for opposing World War I, he ran his 1920 campaign from prison. (© David J. & Janice Frent Collection/CORBIS)

The Socialist Party was nowhere close to unseating the major parties; its national vote was in the single-digit range, and its local pockets of strength were equally small. But the growth of radical politics in these years indicated a continuing political ferment, which produced policies that Roosevelt would happily claim as his own. Playing on the fear of more revolutionary demands for change, Roosevelt pushed reform legislation, including consumer regulation. In 1905 socialist Upton Sinclair wrote a series of muckraking articles exposing the sickening conditions in which sausages were processed (with the tasty addition of floor sweepings) and meat butchered in the Chicago packinghouses. Roosevelt capitalized on Sinclair's exposé, which was the basis of Sinclair's novel *The Jungle* (1906), in his arguments for the Meat Inspection Act (1906). The Pure Food and Drug Act (1906), through the establishment of the Food and Drug Administration, sought to end fraud in patent medicines and the sale of adulterated foods and drugs. Much of this effort to reveal the use of dangerous chemicals and false advertising in drugs was credited to Dr. Harvey W. Wiley, chief chemist in the Agriculture Department.

Roosevelt's love and appreciation of nature led him to undertake a program to conserve the nation's natural resources. A lifelong, avid bird-watcher and hunter, Roosevelt worried that the nation's timber and mineral resources were being rapidly depleted. In his first term he secured passage of the National Reclamation Act (1902), which allowed proceeds from public land sales to be used for irrigation projects in the Southwest. He also appointed his friend Gifford Pinchot, a wealthy Pennsylvania environmentalist, to head the U.S. Forest Service, which agency was moved from the Interior Department and the Land Office to the Department of Agriculture. The shift in departmental homes signaled a shift in mission. Rather than focus on development alone, Pinchot applied scientific resource management to federally owned lands. Following Pinchot's advice, Roosevelt designated more than 200 million acres of public lands as national forests, mineral reserves, and potential water power sites. Roosevelt rejected the more radical ideas of John Muir, the founder of the California Sierra Club, who sought to preserve wilderness areas from any commercial development.

Roosevelt's reform reputation was not harmed by his close ties to financiers. A wave of bank failures in 1907 created a financial panic on Wall Street. Only assistance from J. P. Morgan and his associates prevented a complete financial collapse. Roosevelt's association with Morgan did little to hurt his overall popularity with the American people.

TAFT EXPANDS REFORM AND ALIENATES REFORMERS   Roosevelt's great strength was as a politician who inspired his followers, grabbed media attention, and plainly enjoyed his office. This set him apart from his predecessors (and most of his successors) and translated into enormous personal popularity. Within the Republican Party he was able to name his choice for the nomination once he declined to run again. In 1908, William Howard Taft easily won the Republican nomination with Roosevelt's blessing and went on to defeat William Jennings Bryan.

Taft perceived himself to be a Progressive, but he was a departure from the Roosevelt style. Temperamentally, he was cautious and legalistic. He hated politics. Weighing well over three hundred pounds, Taft presented a much different figure from the athletic Theodore Roosevelt. For this reason many of Taft's contemporaries underestimated his abilities and later accomplishments. Although Taft misread the emotion of the reform movement and the ambitions of reformers, he agreed to take on the issue of the tariff. He proved to be more active than Roosevelt on the matter of antitrust suits. With the Mann-Elkins Act (1910), he extended ICC control over telephone and telegraph.

Taft alienated the Insurgents in his own Republican Party over the matter of tariff reform. He believed that the tariff should be lowered and supported a bill to reduce rates. The bill passed the House, but when it came before the Senate, Nelson Aldrich drafted an alternative bill that raised rates on hundreds of items. The final bill that was signed into law in 1909, the Payne-Aldrich Tariff, was clearly protectionist. Taft nonetheless praised it as the "best tariff bill that the Republican Party ever passed."

Taft's relations with the Insurgents became further estranged when Progressive Republicans in the House revolted against the poker-playing, Old Guard Speaker of the House, Joseph G. Cannon of Illinois. Underestimating the power of the Insurgents, Taft sided with Cannon, a mistake soon revealed when the House stripped Cannon of his powers to appoint members to committees.

Taft's final break with the Progressives came in 1910. Gifford Pinchot, head of the Forest Service, accused Taft's Secretary of the Interior, Richard A. Ballinger, of collusion with Morgan interests in the sale of public land in Alaska. Ballinger was a conservative Seattle lumber baron who favored private development of natural resources. Accusations of collusion involving Morgan immediately attracted national attention. Taft backed Ballinger and fired Pinchot. Theodore Roosevelt, now retired, openly broke with Taft. Any hope for reconciliation with Roosevelt disappeared when Taft filed an antitrust suit against U.S. Steel for the acquisition of the Tennessee Coal and Iron Company, an acquisition Roosevelt had personally approved during the Panic of 1907.

REPUBLICANS SPLIT; DEMOCRATS UNITE   The stage was set for an all-out fight between Taft and Roosevelt for the GOP nomination. Roosevelt formally entered the race in February 1912. He entered primaries in thirteen states, winning primary after primary against both Taft and Insurgent Robert La Follette. At the GOP convention that summer, however, Taft won the nomination by controlling delegates from New York, the South, and the nonprimary states (the same way Roosevelt had engineered Taft's nomination in 1908). Nearly three hundred delegates stormed out of the convention in protest. Shortly afterward, they met to form the Progressive Party.

The mood of the Progressives' convention was like that of a Protestant religious revival. The convention opened with the delegates, who included prominent women reformers like Jane Addams, as well as Roosevelt's male allies, singing "Onward, Christian Soldiers." The party pledged itself to a minimum wage for women, child labor legislation, social security insurance, woman suffrage, and national health insurance (which had been endorsed earlier by the American Medical Association).

Theodore Roosevelt accepted the Progressive Party's nomination, promising to roar like a bull moose during the campaign. "Bull Moose" stuck as a label for the newly formed party.

The Democrats also turned to a Progressive: Woodrow Wilson, the former president of Princeton University who had startled political insiders by winning the governorship of New Jersey in 1910. Wilson received the nomination on the forty-sixth ballot, only after Bryan threw his support to Wilson. A native Virginian raised in Georgia, Wilson appealed to the old Democratic South and the northern middle-class reform vote.

The Socialists turned to Eugene Debs, who advocated the restructuring of capitalism through government ownership of railroads, grain elevators, mines, and banks.

1912: THEODORE ROOSEVELT VERSUS WOODROW WILSON   The election of 1912 showed that the great majority of Americans were Progressive. With all four candidates favoring reform, the contest came down to Theodore Roosevelt versus Woodrow Wilson. At issue was the question of how to regulate corporate trusts. Theodore Roosevelt advocated a "New Nationalism," a phrase coined by the editor of the *New Republic*, Herbert Croly. Roosevelt accepted the emergence of large industry but called upon the federal government to regulate industry and protect consumers and workers. Wilson drew from the thinking of a young lawyer, Louis Brandeis, in proposing what he called a "New Freedom." This program called for the breakup of large industry and a return to a competitive market economy. Roosevelt denounced Wilson's program as "Rural Toryism."

On election day Wilson received only 42 percent of the popular vote but won forty-one of the forty-eight states. Wilson won approximately six million votes, while Roosevelt received four million, Taft three million, and Debs nearly 900,000. Wilson won a majority of the popular vote in only fourteen states, mostly in the South. The split in the Republican vote put the Democrats into the White House for the first time since Grover Cleveland.

WOODROW WILSON AND THE TRIUMPH OF PROGRESSIVISM   No other president had enjoyed such a rapid ascent as Woodrow Wilson, who rose from university president to governor of New Jersey and then to the presidency in three years. He now sought to use his good fortune to promote a Progressive agenda. Wilson pressed for tariff reform, signed into law a new income tax after the Sixteenth Amendment was ratified in 1913, sought to regulate industry through creation of the Federal Trade Commission, and established a central banking system, the Federal Reserve System.

On his first day in the White House, Wilson called a special session of Congress to revise the much-reviled Payne-Aldrich Tariff. When protectionists threatened to defeat the new tariff, Wilson lashed out against the lobbyists and threatened to force senators to reveal their personal corporate holdings. The resulting Underwood Tariff significantly lowered rates for the first time since the Civil War. To make up the lost revenue, Wilson turned to an income tax, made possible by the ratification of the Sixteenth Amendment. Through the efforts of a young congressman from Tennessee, Cordell Hull, a graduated income tax bill was enacted in 1913.

Wilson's next great reform measure was the Federal Reserve Act (1913). This act combined private control of local banks with federal regulatory supervision. It also established the banking system still in use today, consisting of a Federal Reserve Board and twelve district banks. This Federal Reserve System was given the power to issue paper currency. It also controls the nation's money supply by setting the amounts of money member banks must keep on hand and the interest rates at which member banks borrow from the system.

In 1914 Wilson turned to other questions of reform. The Clayton Antitrust Act (1914) prohibited competing firms from sharing holding companies and prohibited people from serving as directors of competing firms. That same year, Wilson's administration created the Federal Trade Commission to investigate unfair trade practices. During a threatened railroad strike, Wilson intervened to prevent a national shutdown of the lines and then signed the labor-supported Adamson Act, which provided an eight-hour day for railway workers.

Wilson's reform record did not extend to race. He supported segregationist policies toward African Americans. This was most evident in Wilson's support of his postmaster general, who issued orders to segregate black and white postal employees. Wilson also allowed his secretary of state, William Jennings Bryan, to appoint a white to the post of ambassador to Haiti, a post traditionally held by a black American.

As the election of 1916 approached, progressivism appeared to have spent itself. The outbreak of war in Europe in 1914 presented an ominous warning that foreign events were overwhelming domestic issues. Increasingly, Wilson's attention turned to international affairs, first in the Western Hemisphere and finally in Europe.

CONCLUSION

The activist years from 1901 to 1916 transformed Americans' expectations of government. During this period federal policy was actively extended in the areas of antitrust, consumer protection, conservation, banking, and industrial relations. In the process a new relationship developed between government and business.

The growth of government, with its coinciding growth of bureaucracy and expertise, appeared necessary to protect democratic government. Ordinary Americans supported and even demanded activist government. Yet the emergence of big government created a deep ambivalence on the part of many people toward a federal government that seemed distinctly remote.

Recommended Readings

DOCUMENTS: W. E. B. DuBois, *The Souls of Black Folk* (1903); William Allen White, *The Old Order Changeth* (1910).

READINGS: (GENERAL AND SOCIAL REFORM) Paul Boyer, *Urban Masses and Moral Order in America* (1978); Robert H. Bremmer, *From the Depths: The Discovery of Poverty in the United States* (1956); John D. Buenker, John C. Burnham, and Robert M. Crunden, *Progressivism* (1977); John Chambers II, *The Tyranny of Change: America in the Progressive Era* (1980); John Milton Cooper, Jr., *The Pivotal Decades* (1990); Susan Curtis, *A Consuming Faith: The Social Gospel and Modern American Culture* (1991); Allen Davis, *Spearheads for Reform: The Social Settlements and the Progressive Movement* (1967); Alfred Ekrich, *Progressivism in America* (1974); Samuel Hays, *Conservation and the Gospel of Efficiency* (1959); Richard Hofstadter, *The Age of Reform* (1955); Morton Keller, *Regulating a New Economy* (1990); Gabriel Kolko, *The Triumph of Conservatism* (1963); Richard L. McCormick, *Progressivism* (1983); William O'Neill, *The Progressive Years* (1975); James T. Patterson, *America's Struggle against Poverty* (1981); Martin J. Sklar, *The Corporate Reconstruction of American Capitalism* (1988); Robert Wiebe, *Businessmen and Reform: A Study of the Progressive Movement* (1962). (WOMEN) Paula Baker, *The Moral Frameworks of Public Life* (1991); Ruth Bordin, *Women and Temperance* (1981); Nancy F. Cott, *The Grounding of Modern Feminism* (1987); Aileen Kraditor, *Ideas of the Woman Suffrage Movement* (1965); David Morgan, *Suffragists and Democrats* (1972); Robyn Muncy, *Creating a Female Dominion in American Reform* (1991); William O'Neill, *Divorce in the Progressive Era* (1967). (PRESIDENTS) Donald Anderson, *William Howard Taft* (1973); John Blum, *The Republican Roosevelt* (1954) and *Woodrow Wilson and the Politics of Morality* (1954); John Milton Cooper, Jr., *The Warrior and the Priest: Woodrow Wilson and Theodore Roosevelt* (1983); Lewis Gould, *Reform and Regulation* (1978); Arthur Link, *Woodrow Wilson and the Progressive Era* (1954).

23

❧

Global Power and World War

OVERVIEW   The United States emerged from the Spanish-American War a world power. Theodore Roosevelt and William Howard Taft extended American influence in Latin America and Asia. Prior to the outbreak of World War I, the United States intervened militarily in Haiti, the Dominican Republic, Nicaragua, Panama, and Mexico. When war broke out in Europe, it was difficult for Woodrow Wilson to maintain American neutrality, and the United States was finally pulled into World War I.

War proved to be the nemesis of Progressive reform. Wilson had called for "New Freedom" to restore the free market, but with war the economy became more centralized and regulated instead. Wilson called for a "war for democracy," but the very brutality of war caused Americans to become disillusioned with reform at home and abroad. Wilson presided over the repression of civil liberties at home in 1919, the renewal of conflict between labor and management, and the worst race riots in the nation's history.

PROGRESSIVE FOREIGN POLICY
BEFORE THE FIRST WORLD WAR

After the Spanish-American War, the United States became increasingly involved in the affairs of Latin America and Asia. As a world trade power, the United States wanted to streamline international shipping by linking the Pacific and Atlantic Oceans by a canal in Central America.

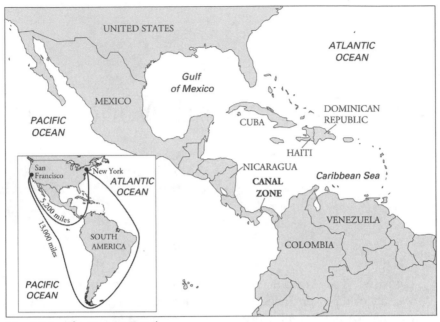

Map 23.1   The Panama Canal

When Central American authorities balked, Theodore Roosevelt encouraged a revolution in Panama and quickly made a deal with the new government to build a canal there.

His successor, William Howard Taft, used American investment to encourage stability in the Caribbean and Latin America but did not hesitate to intervene in a Nicaraguan civil war. The next president, Woodrow Wilson, intervened in a Mexican civil war; his inept pursuit of the rebel Pancho Villa in northern Mexico showed how unprepared America was for war.

THEODORE ROOSEVELT CARRIES A BIG STICK AND WINS A PEACE PRIZE   In the early 1900s American foreign policy focused increasingly on events in the Western Hemisphere. At the end of the Spanish-American War, the United States had acquired the Philippine Islands, Guam, Hawaii, and Puerto Rico and secured a protectorate over Cuba as well. In the ensuing years, the United States intervened in the affairs of Haiti, the Dominican Republic, Nicaragua, Panama, and Mexico.

America's place in the world seemed assured by the nation's economic position in international trade. In the two decades after the Spanish American War, American exports doubled. Manufactured goods outsold agricultural products, as sewing machines, typewriters, automobiles, tractors, electric machinery, cigarettes, and soft drinks were shipped to every corner of the world. American investments in foreign countries quadrupled in these years. So prominent were American firms in Europe that many worried about the "Americanization" of the Old World.

America's prominent economic position imparted new meaning to Theodore Roosevelt's call for the nation to become a world power. Although Roosevelt quoted an African proverb, "Speak softly and carry a big stick," to describe his foreign policy, he was given to saber-rattling rhetoric when discussing international affairs. In his first term, he proceeded cautiously in domestic affairs but moved boldly abroad. There he found a large enough arena to display his irrepressible energy, his need for action, and his vision of America as a global power.

The most dramatic episode in Roosevelt's presidency came in 1903, only two years after he entered the White House. The Spanish-American War had convinced many Americans of the need for a canal linking the Pacific and Atlantic Oceans; during the hostilities the battleship *Oregon* had taken sixty-eight days to steam from San Francisco around the horn of South America to Cuba. Most Americans believed that Nicaragua offered the best opportunity for such a canal, although some preferred the Isthmus of Panama, which then belonged to Colombia. In November 1901, Secretary of State Hay had negotiated a treaty with the British (the Hay-Pauncefote Treaty) that recognized American's plan to build a canal. (Britain also held claim to the territory through an earlier treaty).

The eruption of a volcano in Nicaragua confirmed the decision to build the canal in Panama. In 1881 a French company had started construction of a canal across Panama, but after the loss of twenty thousand lives and $300 million, the company proposed selling its holdings to the United States for $40 million. At this point Roosevelt ignored the French offer and completed negotiations with Colombia through the Hay-Harran Treaty to purchase a six-mile strip across the isthmus for $10 million in cash, along with a lease price of $250,000 a year. The U.S. Senate ratified the Hay-Harran Treaty, but the Colombian government balked under pressure from nationalists. An outraged Roosevelt organized an insurrection in Panama against the Colombians and sent a battleship to prevent Colombian troops from suppressing the revolution. In 1903 the State Department recognized Panama only forty minutes after hearing of the revolution. Twelve days later Panama's new ambassador to the United States signed a treaty stipulating that the United States pay $10 million in cash to Panama. The canal opened in 1914. Only after World War I did Colombia receive $25 million in compensation for the loss of the Canal Zone.

Roosevelt felt little need to justify his actions. Firmly believing that the nation should play a major role in world affairs, he asserted that the

United States had a special mission in Latin America. He articulated this role in what became known as the Roosevelt Corollary to the Monroe Doctrine. Speaking in response to a threat by European powers to invade the Dominican Republic, which had defaulted on its loans, Roosevelt declared that the Monroe Doctrine forbade European interference in Latin America. He emphasized that under certain circumstances the United States had the obligation to intervene in the internal affairs of Latin America if hemispheric interests were threatened. In this role the United States operated the Dominican Republic's customs service from 1905 to 1907.

Roosevelt also extended American influence in Cuba. Under the Platt Amendment (1901) to the original United States protectorate over Cuba, American troops occupied the country from 1906 to 1909 and from 1917 to 1923. By 1920 American investment in Cuba had grown to $500 million.

Although Roosevelt talked tough, his greatest legacy in foreign relations was as a peacemaker. In 1905 Roosevelt intervened on his own initiative to arbitrate the war that had broken out between Japan and Russia in 1904. Most observers believed that Russia, with its massive army and navy, would easily defeat Japan. Then Japan made a surprise attack on the Russian fleet at Port Arthur, Manchuria. European leaders began to worry that a Japanese victory would disrupt the balance of power in the Far East.

At this point, Roosevelt's personal diplomacy persuaded the Russians and the Japanese to sign a peace treaty in Portsmouth, New Hampshire, in 1905. The Portsmouth Treaty recognized Japan's sovereignty over Korea and ceded territory in Manchuria to Japan. For his efforts, Roosevelt won the 1906 Nobel Peace Prize. Roosevelt favored Japanese claims partly because he hoped to turn Japan's ambitions away from the Pacific; still, Japanese public opinion held that Roosevelt had sided with Russia during the negotiations. Lest the Japanese think America weak, the following year Roosevelt sent American battleships—the "Great White Fleet"—around the world as a show of force to the Japanese government. In 1907 Roosevelt sent American representatives to an international disarmament conference at The Hague, Netherlands, and agreed to American participation in establishing the Permanent Court of International Arbitration, the Hague Tribunal.

TAFT PURSUES DOLLAR DIPLOMACY   From 1909 to 1913, Roosevelt's successor, William Howard Taft, continued the policy of exerting American influence in world affairs. Taft's "dollar diplomacy" sought to link American business with pro-American economic elites throughout the Caribbean and Latin America. Taft believed that American investment would create political and economic stability.

Taft was even more willing than Roosevelt to use military power to protect American interests in the Caribbean and Latin America. When a revolt broke out in Nicaragua in 1909 against the anti-American government of Jose Zelaya, Taft supported the rebel Adolfo Diaz. Diaz overthrew the Zelaya government, but when the new legislature refused to allow the United States to manage its customs house and refinance its debt, Taft dispatched a warship to Nicaragua to ensure that the new government would be pro-American. When the "Zelayistas" launched a counterrevolution in 1912, Taft sent 2,500 marines to suppress them. When the marines finally withdrew twenty-one years later, in 1933, rebel resistance still had not been broken.

WILSON ESPOUSES IDEALISM IN FOREIGN POLICY   Woodrow Wilson sought to bring a new idealism to American foreign policy during his presidency (1913–1921). Wilson showed this idealism in his first term, when he denounced dollar diplomacy as a guise for imperialism. Wilson, however, was no less interventionist than his predecessors: He sent troops to Haiti in 1915, extended American financial supervision over the Dominican Republic, and renewed controls over Cuba in 1917.

He also intervened in the revolution in Mexico, where Americans had extensive investments. He sent warships to the waters off Veracruz in 1914 to halt arms shipments to the revolutionary government he opposed, then sent a detachment of marines to occupy the city. In March 1916, Mexican rebel General Pancho Villa led attacks against the U.S. cavalry stationed at Columbus, New Mexico, killing seventeen Americans. Wilson responded by ordering eleven thousand troops under General John Pershing to cross the Mexican border to pursue Villa. For nearly a year, Pershing chased Villa and his army around northern Mexico before the rebels withdrew further south.

The farcical American expedition revealed just how unprepared the United States was for war. Machine guns jammed, trucks and horse-drawn wagons were unavailable, and only two airplanes were in flying condition.

AMERICA RELUCTANTLY ENTERS THE FIRST WORLD WAR

When war erupted in Europe, Wilson chose neutrality, although the United States unofficially helped Britain and its allies. After Germany attacked American ships near Britain, the United States protested and forced Germany to place a moratorium on submarine warfare. Americans were sharply divided over whether to enter the war or stay out. Wilson tried to improve military preparedness without alienating peace activists. After barely winning reelection in 1916, he tried unsuccessfully to broker peace in Europe. Finally, in April 1917, the United States declared war on Germany.

WILSON PLEDGES NEUTRALITY   In June 1914 a Serbian nationalist named Gavrilo Princip assassinated the Archduke Francis Ferdinand, the heir to the Austro-Hungarian empire. A month later, Austria-Hungary declared war on Serbia. Soon every major power in Europe was in the war.

The nations of Europe divided into two warring alliances: the Triple Alliance, or Central powers, consisted of Germany, Austria-Hungary, and Turkey; the Triple Entente, or Allied powers, consisted of France, Great Britain, Russia, and Japan. Italy, initially linked with the Central powers, struck a bargain and joined the Allied powers in 1915.

German troops quickly drove through neutral Belgium to attack France. However, when the Germans failed to crush France, the war in western Europe became a bloody stalemate. At this point each side sought to destroy the war-making capabilities of the other. Britain imposed a naval blockade against Germany. Germany, realizing that Britain depended on overseas trade for military supplies and food, waged submarine warfare, sabotaging British shipping.

Wilson favored the Allies but wanted to keep America out of the war. He therefore urged the American people to maintain their neutrality "in thought as well as action"—easier said than done. The war cut heavily into American exports, and the situation worsened when English financial interests began to dump their American stocks, causing a drain on American gold reserves. Heavy trading forced the London Stock Exchange to close on July 31, 1914; this led to the closing of the New York Stock Exchange, which did not reopen until November. Unemployment, already high before the war, reached 11.5 percent by late 1914. By spring 1915, however, the Allies' demand for American supplies had created a wartime boom.

Wilson's policy of neutrality reflected deep divisions among the American people. Of the 92 million Americans in 1910, more than 32 million were of immigrant stock; either they or their parents had immigrated to the United States. Among those were 8 million German-Americans and 4 million Irish-Americans who shared deep-rooted animosity toward England. Three million Jewish-Americans had fled anti-Semitism in Russia and now distrusted that country's participation in the Allied cause. A number of neutrality groups were organized to keep America out of the war. They included the Friends of Peace, the American Embargo Conference, the American Neutrality League, and the American Truth Society.

Allied demands for American goods placed a strain on Wilson's policy of neutrality. Loans were needed to buy American goods. In October 1914 Wilson began approving credits to the British and French. By 1917 American investors had advanced more than $2 billion to the Allies but only $27 million to Germany.

THE WEB OF WAR TIGHTENS   Wilson believed that, even though the United States and Britain were tied together by a common culture and tradition, a policy of neutrality had to be maintained, especially regarding freedom of the seas. The principle of freedom of the seas had been deeply rooted in American foreign policy at least since the War of 1812. This principle was challenged, however, when the British declared the whole North Sea a war zone. As the war dragged on, Britain extended its embargo, warning that all ships suspected of carrying goods to enemy destinations would be liable to search and seizure. Britain also warned that vessels transporting goods by way of neutral ports were subject to being stopped. These actions provoked Wilson to declare, "I am, I must admit, about at the end of my patience with Great Britain."

In response to the British blockade, in February 1915 Germany declared that all ships entering the waters surrounding the British Isles were subject to attack by submarines, the German U-boats. Shocked by this new type of warfare that violated the traditional practice of stopping enemy vessels on the high seas and providing for the safety of passengers, Wilson warned that Germany would be held to "strict accountability" for any loss of American lives or property. In the spring of 1915, a series of German attacks on American ships created division in the administration about the proper response. Secretary of State Bryan believed that American citizens should be warned not to travel into the war zone. Other officials—including the State Department's Robert Lansing, Ambassador to Great Britain Walter Hines Page, and Wilson's advisor Colonel Edward House—demanded strong action, including the breaking off of diplomatic relations with Germany should U-boat warfare continue.

The sinking of the British passenger liner *Lusitania* on May 7, 1915, provoked a crisis. Among the 1,198 passengers lost were 128 Americans. The outraged American public called for a strong response. The United States demanded that Germany stop unrestricted submarine warfare and pay reparations to American families who had lost relatives on the *Lusitania*. Germany denied responsibility, citing a German advertisement in the New York newspapers that warned Americans not to sail on the ship. Germany also charged that the ship had secretly carried military provisions, a charge proven true decades later. Secretary of State William Jennings Bryan refused to send a message he thought would lead to war and resigned from the cabinet. His successor, Robert Lansing, showed no hesitation. Fearing war with the United States, the German government finally announced that vessels would not be sunk without warning. The crisis seemed to have passed. Wilson's strong stance won public confidence at a time when many doubted his understanding of international affairs because of the fiasco in Mexico.

Events in Europe prompted some Americans to champion "preparedness," meaning the building of a stronger army and navy and adoption of a universal draft. In December 1914 proponents of preparedness, including former Secretary of War Elihu Root and Theodore Roosevelt, organized the National Security League. Leading the charge, Roosevelt vociferously criticized Wilson's policy of neutrality and his reluctance to take a stronger stand against German imperialism. Once a close friend of Kaiser Wilhelm (the German emperor), Roosevelt now demanded that America enter the war on the side of the Allies to prevent autocratic rule in Europe. Bitterly assailing Wilson for his lack of leadership, Roosevelt suggested that moral cowardice lurked behind the proclamations of neutrality.

At the same time, antiwar sentiment gripped the rural South and West, while many northeastern liberals and pacifists opposed any measures that might lead to America's involvement in the European war. Playing a significant role in this peace movement was a group of women, including the social worker Jane Addams and the suffragist Carrie Chapman Catt. On August 29, 1914, these women organized the first significant peace march. Dressed in mourning, they paraded down Fifth Avenue in New York. Shortly afterward, they formed the Women's Peace Party.

The cause, however, drew public ridicule when Henry Ford, the automobile manufacturer, tried to bring peace to Europe. In November 1915 he joined Jane Addams and a group of one hundred men and women in chartering a peace ship, the *Oscar II*, to sail to Scandinavia in an attempt to mediate an end to the war. Newspapers lampooned the ill-fated cruise, and the warring Europeans ignored the earnest albeit naive Ford and his fellow passengers. Nevertheless, peace advocates were far from dismayed.

AMERICANS DIVIDE   As the 1916 election approached, the nation was divided on the issue of war. When Henry Ford ran for president as a peace candidate in the Michigan and Nebraska primaries and did well, peace activists were encouraged. At the same time, in Preparedness Day parades in Chicago and other industrial cities, thousands of workers marched, revealing strong support in the country for rearmament.

In the election of 1916, Wilson sought to steer a middle course between the peace and preparedness factions by pledging himself to a Progressive program of social legislation, neutrality, and reasonable preparedness. He failed to endorse woman suffrage but commended it to the states. Against his better instincts, he allowed his campaign managers to employ the antiwar slogan, "He kept us out of war." His Republican opponent, former Progressive governor of New York Charles Evans Hughes, ran as a Progressive, endorsed woman suffrage, and promised peace.

Wilson won the election, barely. He carried the far West and the South, winning the popular vote 9 million to Hughes's 8.5 million and the Electoral College 277 to 254. He was the first Democrat to succeed himself since Andrew Jackson.

WAR DECLARED, JUNE **1917**   Less than three months after the election, Germany announced a renewal of its policy of unrestricted submarine warfare. The German high command risked war with the United States to hurl a knockout punch in a major spring offensive against the Allies. On February 3, 1917, Wilson announced that the United States had severed diplomatic relations with Germany. Shortly afterward, the American press published a diplomatic note from the German foreign secretary, Arthur Zimmerman, to his minister in Mexico proposing an alliance between Germany and Mexico. The Zimmerman telegram, which British intelligence intercepted, promised financial aid and the return of Texas, New Mexico, and Arizona if Mexico would support Germany. Some who opposed American involvement in the war immediately denounced the Zimmerman telegram as a fraud—the product, not the discovery, of British intelligence. Most Americans, however, were shocked by the idea of the war expanding to the nation's border.

A short time later, another bombshell exploded when revolution overthrew Russia's czar. In America, Russian Jews, Poles, and Scandinavians came out in support of the war to defend the new democratic government in Russia. Economic interests, traditional alliances with Great Britain, a fear of German imperialism, and democratic sentiment moved Wilson toward the Allies.

On April 2, 1917, Wilson asked Congress to declare war against Germany. He declared, "The world must be made safe for democracy." The war resolution overwhelmingly passed the Senate by a vote of 82 to 6. The dissenting votes included Republican Progressives Robert La Follette and George Norris. The House concurred by a vote of 373 to 50. Among the opponents was Jeannette Rankin, a recently elected pacifist and feminist from Montana, a state that had enacted woman suffrage. Wilson signed the declaration of war on Good Friday, April 6. He privately admitted feeling depressed that the American people had so willingly entered into war.

AMERICA GOES TO WAR, 1917–1919

Once in the war, the United States went all out to win it. Millions of men volunteered for or were drafted into the military, but industrial and government inefficiency hampered the war effort. The government reorganized and centralized the economy. Women took jobs to fill labor shortages. Labor generally cooperated, but socialists and strikers were harassed. Dissent was forcibly suppressed through both legislation and vigilante groups.

James Montgomery Flagg's recruitment poster for World War I became a memorable example of the art of patriotic propaganda. (Library of Congress)

The arrival of 500,000 fresh American troops in Europe in 1918 broke the military stalemate, leading to the surrender of Germany. Wilson tried to ensure an enduring peace by establishing the League of Nations, but opposition frustrated his idealistic plan. Economic readjustment after the war led to a series of bitter labor strikes, fears of a communist conspiracy, and race riots following the migration of southern blacks to the North.

AMERICA MOBILIZES FOR WAR   In late June 1917 the United States sent a token force to France. Shortly after he arrived, American commander General John Pershing requested an additional million troops by the following spring. In order to supply this manpower, Wilson had accepted the necessity of conscription through the Selective Service Act of May 1917. In June registration for the draft began for 9.6 million men. More than 300,000 failed to register. Before the armistice agreement ending the war in Europe was signed in November 1918, the government had prosecuted 10,000 men for evading the draft.

The most dramatic instance of organized opposition to the draft was the "Green Corn Rebellion" in Oklahoma. Oklahoma was a hotbed of populism and western-bred socialism. On draft day a loosely organized army of nine hundred men, mostly poor black and white tenant farmers, gathered to march on Washington. They expected other "armies" of protesters to join them but were rounded up by a local posse before much happened.

More than four million men served in the armed forces of the United States during World War I. Some army regiments gained fame, such as the "Fighting Sixty-Ninth," a New York Irish regiment founded in the Civil War. African-American troops constituted 13 percent of those who served. Some black regiments, such as the Ninety-Second, were as well known as Irish and state regiments. General John Pershing, having commanded African-American troops in the Philippines, denounced racism; but black troops nevertheless experienced segregation and discrimination. A black officers' training program was created in May 1917 after students at black institutions like Howard University, Fiske University, and Tuskegee Institute demanded one.

Racism continued throughout the war. Black officers assigned to the Ninety-Second were prevented from rising above the rank of captain. Bringing together black troops and white southern troops also created tensions. On August 1917 members of the Twenty-Fourth Infantry's Third Battalion, an African-American unit, opened fire on white tormentors in Houston, killing seventeen of them. As a consequence, thirteen black soldiers were executed.

The United States committed huge numbers of men and quantities of resources to win the war. This was a total war involving armies, civilians, and industry. Approximately 2 million Americans crossed the Atlantic, and 1.4 million saw combat. To finance its armed forces, the government spent $33.5 billion: $23 billion from loans and $10.5 billion from taxes. The United States mobilized its industry and directed its resources for total war production.

In 1916 Congress moved to mobilize American industry, creating the advisory Council of National Defense, composed of six cabinet officers and seven civilian experts. Subsequently, the government began to extend its control to a wide range of industries, creating what some would later call "wartime socialism" (the coordination of industry by government during the war). Although such a description misconstrues the key role private enterprise played in the war effort, wartime controls did provide an experiment in government planning that would be remembered in the 1930s.

The federal government built ships through the United States Shipping Board, operated railroads through the Railroad War Board, managed agriculture through the Food Administration, and procured coal and oil through the Fuel Administration. Under Herbert Hoover the Food Administration encouraged farmers to expand production by guaranteeing high prices for their crops. During the war, land under cultivation increased by 203 million acres. Hoover's Food Administration also popularized the slogan "Food will win the war" by urging Americans to economize through "Wheatless Mondays," "Meatless Tuesdays," and "Porkless Thursdays." Through the Lever Act (1917), Hoover (who also served as head of the Fuel Administration) controlled the production, distribution, and price of coal and oil in the United States.

In early 1918 an alarming rise in prices, combined with production bottlenecks in certain strategic industries, led to more radical measures. Previously, in July 1917, Wilson had established the War Industries Board (WIB) to oversee the war effort; at the urging of Bernard Baruch, a Wall Street speculator, Wilson expanded the powers of the WIB to fix prices and to set priorities for the production and manufacture of goods. The War Industries Board became the most important agency created during the war because of its overall powers to allocate resources and coordinate production.

Wilson also established the War Labor Board to arbitrate wages. Organized labor made great strides during World War I. Membership in the American Federation of Labor increased from approximately 2 million members in 1914 to 3.2 million in 1919. While labor never relinquished its right to strike, the AFL's president, Samuel Gompers, tried to ensure cooperative relations with the Wilson administration to help win the war.

During the war, wages increased, but so did food prices. Some companies experimented with cost-of-living increases. This caused later tensions between labor and management as the war drew to a close, but generally cooperation prevailed.

Labor shortages triggered by the vast numbers of men who joined the armed forces created new opportunities for women, who made munitions, operated elevators, and took on increased clerical duties in offices. Still, female workers earned less than men. For example, males earned between $2.24 and $2.64 a day in munitions plants, while females doing the same job got $1.36 to $2.24 a day. Furthermore, gains in employment made by women workers disappeared at the end of the war when men returned to their civilian jobs. By 1920 fewer women worked for wages than in 1910.

The government also promoted the war effort through newspapers, newsreels, and public speakers. Wilson created the Committee on Public Information, headed by George Creel, a Progressive Denver newspaperman who initially had opposed the war. Creel hired a remarkable group of journalists, artists, and entertainers to sell the war to the public. More than 75,000 "Four-Minute Men" were organized to sell Liberty Bonds, plead for fuel conservation, and promote patriotism.

DISSENT SUPPRESSED   Shortly before America's entry into the First World War in 1917, President Wilson declared "Once lead this people into war and they'll forget there ever was such a thing as tolerance." Wilson's words proved prophetic. As war approached, there was a spontaneous outburst of patriotism throughout the nation. Theodore Roosevelt denounced the "hyphenated American," those Irish-Americans, German-Americans, and others who called for a policy of neutrality.

New patriotic groups were formed, including the American Defense Society, the National Security League, and the Boy Spies of America. More than 250,000 people volunteered to help the Justice Department watch immigrants from Germany, Austria, and Hungary. Fanatics randomly attacked German-Americans in Montana, Minnesota, and Wisconsin. German-sounding streets were renamed in Milwaukee, Chicago, and St. Louis. Bismarck, North Dakota, nearly lost its name. Public schools throughout the Midwest banned the teaching of German. Iowa outlawed speaking the German language. The New York Philharmonic stopped playing music by German composers. German measles became "liberty measles"; sauerkraut was renamed "liberty cabbage."

More drastic action came with the enactment of the Espionage and Sedition Acts (1917–1918), which made it unlawful to criticize the government or its war policies. Accordingly, government denied mail privileges to Socialist Party newspapers, including *The Masses* and the *Milwaukee Leader,* even though the party had split over the war. These laws also led to the prosecution of 1,500 dissenters for such acts as criticizing the Red Cross and the YMCA. One movie producer was sentenced to ten years' imprisonment for negatively portraying the English allies in a film about the American Revolution. In Chicago more than a hundred Industrial Workers of the World (IWW) leaders were put on trial for antiwar activity; most were convicted. While awaiting appeal, radical labor leader Big Bill Haywood jumped bail and fled to the new Soviet Union. In 1918 the leader of the Socialists, Eugene Debs, drew a ten-year sentence for declaring that wars were fought by the working class in the interests of the capitalist class. In 1920 Debs ran for president and received nearly a million votes—while still in prison. The Supreme Court upheld the Espionage and Sedition Acts in *Schenck v. United States.* Free speech, the Court ruled, could be restricted if it posed a "clear and present danger" to society.

AMERICAN TROOPS BATTLE IN EUROPE   The arrival of fresh American troops proved decisive. Russia's withdrawal from the war in November 1917 following the communist (Bolshevik) revolution allowed Germany to concentrate on the western front in France and Belgium. In mid-1918 the Germans launched an offensive against the French forces, the second Battle of

American doughboys manned a deadly machine gun behind barbed wire in a second-line trench in France in 1918. (© Hulton Archive/Getty Images)

the Marne. They failed, and in September more than 500,000 American troops began to roll back a crumbling German army at St. Mihiel, Belgium. Two weeks later, American divisions broke through the German line in the Meuse-Argonne district of France. This action cost 117,000 American casualties, including 26,000 dead. By November 1918, the Germans were in full retreat.

THE WAR ENDS IN DISILLUSIONMENT   As the end of the war approached, Wilson set forth his program for peace. Speaking before a joint session of Congress on January 8, 1918, Wilson articulated his Fourteen Points for an enduring peace. He called for freedom of the seas, free trade, arms reduction, and self-determination for various nationalities. Point 14 expressed Wilson's greatest hope, the establishment of a League of Nations composed of all countries, great and small. The League, in Wilson's farsighted view, was to provide both a forum for the peaceful resolution of disputes and a global alliance to punish wrongful aggressors.

By the early fall of 1918, the Central Powers had collapsed. The abdication of the German kaiser in November amid riots and revolutionary fervor finally brought an armistice on November 11, 1918. Only in Russia did war continue, where the Allied nations sent troops to aid the "White" forces attempting a counterrevolution against the Bolsheviks (the "Red" forces). Some 8,000 Americans joined the 100,000-troop Allied expedition, but this intervention failed. Not until April 1920 did Wilson withdraw American forces from Soviet territory.

Wilson insisted on attending the Paris peace conference that convened in January 1919. He became the first president to travel outside the United States while in office. Wilson wanted to ensure a lasting peace, but he became so absorbed in shaping the final peace treaty that he made crucial political mistakes. His relations with the Republicans in Congress were already strained. In 1918 Wilson had campaigned vigorously to keep a Democratic Congress, but the Republicans had won. He worsened matters when he selected a peace delegation that deliberately excluded prominent Republicans.

The huge European crowds that greeted Wilson upon his arrival in Paris in December 1918 also misled him. In Paris Wilson proved to be a skillful negotiator with the representatives of the leading victorious nations: Britain's David Lloyd George, France's Georges Clemenceau, and Italy's Vittorio Orlando. Wilson sought a forgiving peace, but to achieve his goals he first had to agree that Germany should pay high war reparations to Belgium and France, demilitarize the German Rhineland, and accept ten years of French control of the coal-rich German Saar Basin. In return Wilson gained self-determination for eastern European nations, including Poland,

Hungary, and Czechoslovakia. His greatest victory was winning support for establishing the League of Nations.

WILSON FAILS TO ACHIEVE A LASTING PEACE   Wilson returned home in February 1919 with a draft of the League charter. He seemed impervious to rumblings from Republicans led by the powerful chairman of the Senate Foreign Relations Committee, Henry Cabot Lodge, who stated that the League charter was unacceptable "in the form now proposed." Wilson returned to Europe a month later to finish the negotiations. In June the Germans reluctantly signed the final treaty at Versailles, formally ending the war.

In July Wilson returned to present the Versailles Treaty to the Senate. He expected the Senate to accept "this great duty." After all, a third of the state legislatures and thirty-three governors had endorsed the League of Nations. In his absence, however, the Republicans had been brooding. Lodge personally disliked Wilson. He wrote, "I never thought I could hate a man as I hate Wilson." Moreover, many ethnic groups—the Germans, Italians, and Irish—disliked the final peace that had taken so much from and given so little to their old countries. The Senate soon divided into three groups. Wilson loyalists backed the treaty, while the "irreconcilables" opposed any American participation in the League of Nations. Somewhere in the middle were the "reservationists," who called for amendments before acceptance of the treaty.

Wilson believed he spoke for the American people, and in September he decided to take his case directly to them. In a whirlwind speaking tour by train that covered eight thousand miles in twenty-two days, he gave thirty-two major addresses. He was driven by passionate idealism, but the strain began to show. Finally in Pueblo, Colorado, signs of exhaustion became apparent. Ordered by his doctor to return home, on October 2 Wilson suffered a severe stroke that slurred his speech and paralyzed his left side. His active political career effectively ended, and while the government drifted, his wife Edith managed most of Wilson's affairs. In March 1920 the Senate failed to muster the necessary two-thirds majority to ratify the treaty. Wilson, now a reclusive invalid, placed all hopes on the election of 1920.

AMERICA DEMOBILIZES, ONLY TO SEE RED   The end of the war created additional problems at home. Wilson's administration had not prepared for the massive influx of job seekers as the troops returned home. Cancellation of war contracts hurt many businesses. Although pent-up consumer demand and overseas trade created a brief economic boom in 1919, consumers seethed as prices began to rise sharply. That year more than four million workers went on strike. These economic problems led congress-men to warn Wilson that the domestic economy was "far more important than the League of Nations."

The first signs of labor discontent occurred in Seattle, Washington, when 35,000 shipyard workers walked off their jobs. By early February the city was paralyzed as 60,000 other workers, influenced by the locally powerful IWW, went out in support of the shipyard workers. Seattle came to a standstill, and the business community was terrified. The week-long general strike was finally broken by imported nonunion labor and the ve-hemently antilabor mayor of Seattle, Ole Hanson, who called the strikers "Bolsheviks."

Strike activity throughout the country heightened fears of a commu-nist conspiracy to incite labor violence. In September 1919 one of the most dramatic strikes took place in Boston when most of the police force walked out demanding a union. After two days of looting, Governor Calvin Coolidge called out the National Guard to restore order. When the striking police offered to return to work, the police commissioner fired them all. Coolidge declared, "There is no right to strike against the pub-lic safety by anybody, anywhere, anytime." These words brought him na-tional attention and later a vice-presidential nomination on the Republi-can ticket in 1920.

Also in September 1919, the steel workers went out on strike when Judge Elbert Gary, chairman of U.S. Steel, refused to discuss the union's demand for an eight-hour day. Led by a former Wobbly who had close ties to the newly organized Communist Party, more than 600,000 workers went out on strike. Steel firms retaliated brutally. Police and strikebreak-ers broke up strikers' meetings and picket lines. By January the union ad-mitted defeat and told its members to return to work.

The steel strike overshadowed developments in the railroad industry. Railroad unions had begun agitating for the "Plumb Plan," developed by union attorney Glenn Plumb, which called for federal ownership of the railways. The plan found few advocates outside the unions, and in 1920 Congress returned railroads to private operation under ICC regulation. With the defeat of the steel strikes and the failure of the Plumb Plan, unions began to decline in membership from more than 5 million work-ers in 1920 to a low of 3.4 million in 1930, a mere 6.8 percent of the non-agricultural workforce.

Many Americans believed these labor strikes showed communist con-spiracy at work. Following the Bolshevik revolution in Russia in 1918, American radicals split from the Socialist Party to form two rival com-munist parties. The emergence of a communist movement in the United States frightened authorities and the general public. In the spring of 1919, paranoia increased when bombs were mailed to Ole Hanson, the antilabor mayor of Seattle, and to a former senator from Georgia. Shortly afterward, postal workers discovered thirty-six similar bomb packages destined for high officials.

United States Attorney General A. Mitchell Palmer, a former Quaker who entertained presidential aspirations, warned the nation of a communist uprising. Such rhetoric encouraged members of the American Legion and other groups to break up Labor Day parades and attack meetings of leftist groups, including Socialist Party headquarters in many cities. In November 1919 Palmer launched his most dramatic assault against the "Reds." Directed by J. Edgar Hoover, head of the Justice Department's new "alien-radical" division, federal officers rounded up thousands of "radicals" as well as innocent aliens caught in the dragnet. In December 249 foreign-born radicals, including Russian-born anarchist Emma Goldman, were deported to the Soviet Union on a ship nicknamed the "*Soviet Ark*." Amid this excitement, the New York state legislature expelled those members who belonged to the Socialist Party.

ETHNIC AND RACIAL TENSIONS MOUNT   In addition to labor troubles and fears of communism, the nation also experienced heightened racial and ethnic tensions. Signs of these tensions had been evident even before America's entry into the war. Most notable was the case of Leo Frank in Georgia. A Jew from the North who had become superintendent of a southern textile mill, Frank was accused of raping and murdering Mary Phagen, a fourteen-year-old factory worker. The case attracted the attention of northern liberals such as Jane Addams, who protested the trial. Despite inconclusive testimony, Frank was sentenced to death.

After much protest, the governor of Georgia commuted the sentence. White supremacists were furious. Tom Watson, the former Populist vice-presidential candidate, linked the war against the Germans to protecting southern white women at home. He warned, "When 'mobs' are no longer possible, liberty will be dead." On a summer night in 1915, twenty-five men broke into the Georgia jail where Frank was being held, kidnapped him, drove him 175 miles across the state, lynched him, and then mutilated the body. Less than two weeks later, a Methodist minister and longtime salesman named William J. Simmons inaugurated a new Ku Klux Klan at a public ceremony on top of Stone Mountain, ten miles from Atlanta.

Tensions between whites and blacks became especially pronounced in northern industrial centers, which recruited heavily from the South to meet labor shortages. Between 1915 and 1917 close to half a million blacks moved from the South to the North. This migration followed the decline of cotton farming in the South, triggered largely by an infestation of boll weevils that destroyed the cotton crop. Those blacks who moved north aspired to better jobs and freedom from racial bondage. As one black wrote from Birmingham to a northern newspaper, "i am in the darkness of the south and i am trying my best to get out . . . o please help me get out of this low down county i am counted no more than a dog."

Most northern cities were ill prepared for this migration. Blacks could live only in certain segregated neighborhoods, but the new arrivals caused overcrowding and stimulated higher rents, which led some blacks to seek housing in white neighborhoods. Racial tensions sometimes erupted into fierce confrontations. In July 1917 a bloody race riot broke out in East St. Louis, Illinois, when whites, supported by the mayor and police chief, invaded the town's black district and burned houses with the tenants still inside. An estimated forty-eight men, women, and children died. Shortly afterward, a similar riot occurred in Chester, Pennsylvania.

The year 1919 brought new racial troubles. That summer as many as fifteen cities suffered race riots. The worst occurred in Chicago in July and claimed the lives of twenty-three blacks and fifteen whites. The riot began on a hot day when a black boy strayed into a customary "white" bathing area along Lake Michigan and was stoned to death by a mob of white youths. Federal troops were called in to end the rioting.

CONCLUSION

As his second term drew to a close, Wilson was broken in mind, body, and spirit, no longer a leader of his generation but a martyr for a future generation that was to emerge during a second world war. By 1920 the idealism of Wilsonian democracy had given way to disillusionment. The dream of a reformed society, with equitable distribution of wealth, harmony between the social orders, and peace in the world, had been displaced by a profound desire on the part of most Americans to return to what Republicans called "normalcy": the traditional American values of family, capitalistic enterprise, and individualism.

Recommended Readings

DOCUMENTS: Henry Berry, *Make the Kaiser Dance* (1978); e. e. cummings, *The Enormous Room* (1934); Addie Hunton, *Two Colored Women with the American Expeditionary Forces* (1971).

READINGS: (NEUTRALITY) John Coogan, *The End of Neutrality* (1981); John Cooper, *The Vanity of Power: American Isolationism and the First World War* (1969); Patrick Devlin, *Too Proud to Fight* (1974); Ross Gregory, *The Origins of American Intervention* (1977); Roland Marchand, *The American Peace Movement and Social Reform* (1973); Ernest May, *The World War and American Isolationism* (1959). (WAR) Arthur Barbeau and Henri Florette, *The Unknown Soldier: Black American Troops in World War I* (1974); Edward Coffman, *The War to End All Wars* (1968); Frank Freidel, *Over There* (1964); Paul Fussell, *The Great War and Modern Memory* (1975); Maurine Greenwald, *Women, War and Work* (1980); N. Gordon Levin, Jr., *Woodrow Wilson and World Politics* (1968). (HOMEFRONT) Valerie Conner, *The National War Labor Board* (1983); Robert Cuff, *The War Industries Board* (1973); Ellis Hawley, *The Great War and the Search for Modern Order* (1979); Robert Haynes, *A Night of Violence: The Houston Riot of 1917* (1976); David Kennedy, *Over Here: The First World War and American Society* (1980); Frederick Luebke, *Bonds of Loyalty: German-Americans and World War I* (1974); Paul Murphy, *World War I and the Origin of Civil Liberties* (1979); Barbara Steinson, *American Women's Activism in World War I* (1982). (PEACE) Robert Ferrell, *Woodrow Wilson and World War I* (1985); Lloyd Gardner, *Safe for Democracy: The Anglo-American Response to Revolution* (1984); Thomas J. Knock, *To End All Wars: Woodrow Wilson and the Quest for a New World Order* (1992); Arno Mayer, *Politics and Diplomacy* (1965); Charles Mee, Jr., *The End of Order, Versailles, 1919* (1980); William Widenor, *Henry Cabot Lodge and the Search for an American Foreign Policy* (1980). (AFTERMATH) David Brody, *Labor in Crisis* (1965); Stanley Coben, *A. Mitchell Palmer* (1963); William Tuttle, Jr., *Race Riot: Chicago in the Red Summer of 1919* (1970).

24

🙩

The Paradox of the 1920s

OVERVIEW   The 1920s appear full of contradictions and paradoxes. During this decade Americans supported the enactment of Prohibition, outlawing the sale of alcohol, yet a significant subculture emerged around distributing and drinking illegal alcohol. In this decade of rapid social and cultural changes, conservative ethnic enclaves flourished around urban neighborhoods, social clubs, and religious institutions. While social scientists welcomed the "modern age," the Ku Klux Klan and religious fundamentalism attracted wide support.

Paradox also marked the nation's politics. Despite a reputation for conservatism, the states and the federal government spent more than ever and launched new initiatives. The Harding administration (1921–1923) was marred by scandal yet achieved major domestic and foreign policy initiatives. President Calvin Coolidge (1923–1929) espoused the values of free enterprise yet extended federal regulatory powers over business. Herbert Hoover (1929–1933) called himself Progressive but left office in the midst of an economic depression, denounced as a reactionary.

AMERICANS ENJOY A DECADE OF PROSPERITY

Even though agriculture and certain industries suffered, the 1920s were a decade of prosperity. Americans enjoyed a higher standard of living and a better quality of life than ever before. Mass culture was spread by movies, radio, recorded music, and popular stage entertainment.

Though discrimination remained, minorities also found new opportunities. Women had won the right to vote and had begun to fill important positions in politics and society.

AMERICANS PROSPER   Americans enjoyed the 1920s with a heady confidence. Evidence in 1928 seemed to confirm this optimism. The gross domestic product rose 40 percent, per capita income rose 30 percent, and industrial production climbed 70 percent. Unemployment remained low, prices stable; as a result, real earnings increased 22 percent for the average American worker.

American consumers went on a buying binge. The availability of electricity allowed middle-class American households to use vacuum cleaners, refrigerators, and sewing machines. By 1929, 60 percent of all families owned a car. The automobile enabled people to live farther from downtown areas and thereby extended the suburbs. It gave rural people new mobility for work and fun. The automobile became a symbol of the decade, offering new freedom particularly to the nation's youth and women.

The extension of consumer credit allowed American families to buy new homes, automobiles, and appliances. By 1926, an estimated 15 percent of all retail goods sold annually were purchased on installment plans. "Enjoy while you pay" became the slogan of the day.

Although prosperity characterized the decade, not all groups participated equally. Many workers experienced sporadic unemployment because of seasonal layoffs. Agriculture did not prosper, nor did many industries, including cotton textiles, railroads, and coal mining.

Following a golden age that extended from 1897 through 1920, agriculture once again experienced depression. After expanding production during the First World War, American farmers faced declining prices for their crops. The loss of European markets from high tariffs and new competition in Europe only worsened matters. By 1929 the average per capita income of farmers stood at approximately $220, in contrast to $879 for the nonfarm population. With the assistance of the American Farm Bureau Federation, farmers tried cooperative marketing, aided in these efforts by antitrust exemptions from the federal government. The most successful of these marketing combines were the California citrus growers, who formed Sunkist.

During this period labor unions and collective bargaining also declined. Total union membership fell from 5 million to less than 3.5 million. Corporations encouraged the decline of unions by providing benefits to nonunion workers. They instituted pension plans, disability and health programs, savings and credit institutions, and educational and recreational activities for their employees.

Caught up in the frenzied prosperity, most Americans overlooked the period's failures. Bruce Barton's bestselling *The Man Nobody Knows* (1925) typified the obsession with success. Barton portrayed Jesus as a business-man who had "picked up twelve men from the bottom ranks of business and forged them into an organization that conquered the world." During this decade books of the "how to succeed in business" variety flourished. Dale Carnegie (no relation to Andrew) became a millionaire selling his public speaking program to aspiring businessmen. American advertisers played upon middle-class anxieties about getting ahead. President Calvin Coolidge expressed the sentiments of the age when he declared, "The business of America is business."

MINORITIES AND WOMEN FIND NEW OPPORTUNITIES   Critics easily parodied and satirized this emphasis on success, but for many it was no joke. The growth of managerial positions opened opportunities for many people to enter the expanding middle class. While the decade revealed deep-seated nativist and anti-Catholic prejudices within the culture, including the ex-istence of religious quotas at many colleges, Jews and Catholics began to enter the professions in large numbers. Blacks attended colleges and uni-versities in larger numbers, too, despite the wretched poverty in which most lived.

Women also enjoyed new opportunities. Although most women oc-cupied a separate sphere as traditional homemakers, an increasing num-ber joined the workforce and stayed in it even after marriage. The grow-ing number of college-educated women came to dominate new fields such as social work. Women also gained recognition in sports, business, education, and politics. In 1920, with the ratification of the Nineteenth Amendment to the Constitution, women finally gained the right to vote. Putting the new franchise to use, female political candidates made 1924 a banner year. In 1924 Nellie Taylor Ross became the first woman chief ex-ecutive when she won the governorship of Wyoming. Ross later became the first woman director of the United States Mint under Franklin D. Roo-sevelt. That same year Miriam "Ma" Ferguson won the governorship of Texas. The widespread perception that women would make up a solid bloc for reform eased the passage of the Sheppard-Towner Act (1921), which provided federal funds for health care for poor women and their children.

MEDIA RECREATES MASS CULTURE   The spread of a burgeoning mass culture through movies, radio, and advertising characterized this decade. Al-though mass culture tended to standardize the way Americans lived, it did not produce a fully homogenized society. Many working people and recent immigrant ethnic groups maintained older values and emphasized family relationships.

The popularity of movies was a key element in the emergence of mass culture. In 1922 more than 40 million movie tickets were sold each week. Seven years later, the introduction of sound, beginning with *The Jazz Singer* and *Don Juan,* attracted even larger audiences. Weekly attendance grew to 100 million. Blue-collar workers were particularly attracted to movies and spent a larger percentage of their incomes on "picture shows" than did the middle class.

Radio burst on the scene in 1920 when station KDKA in Pittsburgh broadcast the returns of the Harding–Cox presidential election. Few heard the broadcast, since only a handful of people owned receivers, but radio quickly became popular. Throughout much of the decade, small, independent radio stations dominated the market. Fundamentalists, those most opposed to modernism, ironically proved particularly aggressive in using the radio to evangelize the nation. The passage of the Radio Act of 1927 transformed the radio industry by requiring all radio stations to reapply for licenses under federal supervision, thereby driving out many of these independents. By the end of the decade, there were eight thousand broadcasting stations organized into two major networks, NBC and CBS, and two minor networks.

The growth of the record industry also characterized modern culture. Now all Americans could enjoy the same recording stars. The industry also allowed ethnic groups to preserve their heritage. For example, Italians listened to recordings of Italian opera sung by Enrico Caruso or folk songs recorded by ethnic musicians. Ties to regional culture were preserved by country, "hillbilly," and "race" records performed by southern musicians. Whites were introduced to jazz, a black music form that had migrated from the South at the turn of the century. Whites enthusiastically took up black dances like the Charleston.

Mass journalism also grew with the expansion of tabloid newspapers, syndicated features (including crossword puzzles and daily horoscopes), and news digests such as *Readers Digest* (1922) and *Time* (1923). Chain newspapers and national magazines encouraged mass advertising, which employed movie stars, radio personalities, and sports heroes to sell products to audiences who trusted and admired these popular figures. Advertising linked success and happiness to buying the right product. One ad told of how a businessman's career was held back because of "faulty elimination" until he discovered Post Bran Flakes. Producers of Listerine mouthwash invented the word *halitosis* (bad breath) to exploit anxiety about personal hygiene.

Mass media made it possible for many to become national celebrities. Baseball stars such Babe Ruth became household names. American hearts went out to young Gertrude Ederle, who courageously swam the English Channel. The greatest of heroes, however, was Charles Lindbergh, who became the first person to complete a solo, nonstop, transatlantic flight from New York to Paris.

AMERICA EXPERIMENTS WITH PROHIBITION

In 1920 the nation prohibited the sale and distribution of alcoholic beverages. This legislation received popular support, but Americans continued to drink. Widespread illegal drinking offered huge profits to the gangsters who provided alcohol, and organized crime permeated society. Although many complained about the failure of Prohibition, the law was not repealed until 1933.

AMERICANS OUTLAW THE SALE OF ALCOHOL—AND CONTINUE TO DRINK   The paradox of the decade was most evident in the era's boldest endeavor in moral reform, the prohibiting of alcoholic beverages. Prohibition started during the war, in 1917, and was written into the Constitution with the ratification of the Eighteenth Amendment. Although passed under a Democratic administration, Prohibition found its greatest support within the Republican Party, which campaigned throughout the decade on a platform of reducing the size of the federal government. Republicans did not see the contradiction in promoting Prohibition, which involved greater government intervention, while promising to reduce government.

In 1919 most Americans would have said that they favored Prohibition. Indeed, the decade of the 1920s witnessed a decline in alcohol consumption. Yet many Americans who favored Prohibition did so on the grounds that *other people* should not drink; they themselves intended to keep drinking. Moreover, they took pride in their rebelliousness.

Most Americans continued to support Prohibition with increasing reservations. The growth of organized crime and a popular culture that seemed to glorify drinking, gangsters, and good times caused many to change their minds about Prohibition, as did the intrusion of law enforcement into private homes later in the decade. Many of the old industrial elite opposed Prohibition, arguing that it restricted private enterprise. The financier J. P. Morgan put away a personal supply of a thousand cases of French champagne and prepared to wait out the law.

WOMEN DIVIDE OVER PROHIBITION   Women also split on the issue. Wives of many industrialists helped organize the Women's Organization for National Prohibition Reform, which sought to overturn Prohibition. The principal proponent of Prohibition, the Woman's Christian Temperance

Union (WCTU), found itself estranged from elite opinion. Once diverse, the WCTU's membership had come to be dominated by the small-town middle class. Yet the WCTU continued to uphold its Prohibitionist principles with a kind of feminism. One well-known WCTU tract, Ella Boole's *Give Prohibition Its Chance* (1929), proclaimed that Prohibition was women's opening to reorganize society.

The WCTU did not appeal to younger women, especially those in college and those who considered themselves part of the "smart" set. They saw Prohibition as an expression of what they considered the repressive Puritan tradition. Alcohol, speakeasies, and jazz represented freedom. Before Prohibition, women were barred from saloons, which were part of male culture; in contrast, speakeasies (illegal saloons) opened their doors to women. Opposition expanded beyond the young or adventurous. Some middle- and upper-middle-class women turned the WCTU's moral arguments on their heads with the thesis that Prohibition actually damaged public morals by substituting government power for family teaching about the dangers of alcohol and by encouraging disrespect for the law.

GANGSTERS THRIVE ON PROHIBITION   Behind the glamour of big-city nightclubs lurked gangsters and organized crime, which brought terror, murder, and corruption. Such sinister aspects of American society were not new, but "modern" gangsters, stimulated by huge profits, became better organized. All parts of society were tainted. The chief of police in Chicago declared that "sixty percent of my police are in the bootleg business." As gangs struggled for control of illicit markets, war broke out in the streets. In Chicago between 1922 and 1926, 215 gangsters were killed by rivals. Police killed another 160.

Symbolizing this new era was Chicago's Al Capone. By killing seven members of Bugs Moran's rival North Side Gang on Valentine's Day, 1929, Capone gained control of about 70 percent of Chicago's rackets. An estimated two-thirds of all labor unions paid Capone extortion money. Grossing over $105 million a year, Capone's organization became a potent force in Chicago business and politics. Capone finally was brought to justice when the federal Prohibition Bureau set up a special team called the Untouchables, headed by Eliot Ness. The Untouchables, so called because they could not be "touched" by bribery, gathered enough evidence to send Capone to prison for income tax evasion.

THE REJECTION OF TRADITION

The emergence of mass culture coincided with a rejection of traditional culture by many people, especially the young. The twenties became characterized by youthful rebellion. In their search for freedom, many of the young found sexual freedom. Disillusioned by war and progressivism, young writers and artists encouraged this sense of rebellion by expressing disillusionment with tradition and idealism.

AMERICANS WORSHIP YOUTH AND SEX   Mass culture emphasized youth and sophistication. Closely linked to this culture was sex. In the twenties the "new woman" emerged: Independent, spirited, and slightly rebellious, she rejected the roles of both homemaker and moral exemplar. Literary critic and essayist H. L. Mencken announced the arrival of the "American

In 1926 the flapper bobbed her hair, showed her knees, and danced the Charleston. In the Jazz Age, a boyish look and rebelliousness heralded the end of Victorian morality. Birth control techniques were still limited, however. (Library of Congress)

Flapper" in 1915, and in the twenties the flapper flourished. Noted for a distinct style that included blunt-cut, short hair left long at the front and often with bangs, dresses with hemlines above the knees and dropped waistlines, and cloche hats that came down over the ears, flappers captured the era's youthful rebellion.

The emergence of the new woman coincided with women's economic gains. During World War I nearly two million women held jobs; that number rose to ten million by 1930. Some women revolted against traditional roles and masculine possessiveness. For some women, freedom meant not sexual promiscuity but the right to control their bodies. Margaret Sanger, once sentenced to jail for advocating birth control (primarily condoms and diaphragms) now won approval for her promotion of birth control as a means of liberating women from the burdens of large families. Writer Charlotte Perkins Gilman warned, "Excessive indulgence in sex . . . has imperiled the life of the race."

For many younger women, and men too, the search for freedom was often superficial, meaning little more than the right to enter a speakeasy or smoke in public. Freedom became synonymous with sexual freedom. In throwing off Victorian restraint, Americans glorified sex.

WRITERS AND ARTISTS CHALLENGE TRADITION   The twenties were a period in which mass culture and high culture became closely intertwined. The level of mass culture was raised through the Book-of-the-Month Club, regional theater, and middle-class art groups. For the first time, hundreds of cities established symphonies, and major orchestras were established in smaller cities such as Minneapolis, Rochester, and Atlanta.

Already disillusioned by World War I, American writers expressed their alienation from modern society and the Progressive Era's earlier confidence in human progress. In a group that Gertrude Stein called the "Lost Generation," novelists such as William Faulkner, F. Scott Fitzgerald, Ernest Hemingway, Sinclair Lewis, and John Dos Passos wrote about the limits of human progress, the futility of modern life, and their fear of the machine age. Only art seemed to be worth living for, and the poet T. S. Eliot questioned even this conclusion in his poem "The Hollow Men" (1925).

The 1920s also brought fame and new audiences to a group of black writers, many of them associated with New York's Harlem. Langston Hughes, Claude McKay, Jean Toomer, and Countee Cullen were profoundly critical of American society. By writing about the lives of blacks in northern cities and the rural South and about race in America, they introduced the general reading public to the problems of blacks in modern America.

The other arts continued to bloom from experimental roots that had begun before the war. Modern painting flourished with cubists such as Stuart Davis and Charles Shelter and expressionists such as Georgia O'Keeffe, noted for her large flower canvases and New Mexican desert scenes.

American culture in the twenties, contrary to the opinion of its critics, was not a complete wasteland.

CHANGES SPARK A BACKLASH

While many Americans welcomed social and cultural change, others looked to traditional values. Some Protestants turned to religious revivals, others to fundamentalism and antimodernist religious values. Fundamentalist efforts to outlaw the teaching of evolution in public schools reached a climax with the Scopes trial. Some ethnic groups reacted to the homogenization of culture by asserting their ethnic identities. The Ku Klux Klan re-formed to terrorize blacks, Jews, and Roman Catholics. Indians organized to protect their cultures, and African Americans were inspired to promote their own businesses and culture.

TRADITIONALISTS DENOUNCE MODERNITY Although most Americans welcomed the rapid transformation of social, cultural, and intellectual life in the 1920s, a significant number resisted the change. They sought to restore traditional values even as they employed modern technology to spread their messages.

Religion was a focus of conflict in the 1920s. Since the heyday of the Social Gospel in the early twentieth century, mainstream Protestant churches had increasingly mixed sociology and psychology with their religious teachings. The doctrinal differences that had so sharply separated mainstream denominations in the early nineteenth century now appeared to be at best a quaint bit of history, at worst a dogmatism ill suited to enlightened people. While churches became community centers that offered a range of programs, church membership fell, especially among these mainstream Protestant churches.

Some of the decline was due to a more secular population choosing to do other things on Sundays, but some was due to Protestants who searched for denominations that provided less social engagement and more gospel. Pentecostal churches, whose followers were famous for dramatic, emotional conversions that included speaking in tongues, drew both black and white members, especially in the South and West. Others turned to fundamentalist and evangelical churches, both of which promised a more emotionally immediate experience than mainstream denominations offered. Fundamentalists also battled currents in modern culture and religious thought. While secular society celebrated a freewheeling youth culture, fundamentalists rejected drinking, dancing, and popular entertainment. Whereas current scholarship treated the Bible critically and historically, fundamentalists insisted on the literal truth of its words.

These views opened them to ridicule. Belief in the literal accuracy of the Bible set fundamentalists directly against the theory of Darwinian evolution, which they saw as a corrupting force in the nation. The Darwinian interpretation contradicted the Biblical view that the world was created in six days and cast doubt on God's direct hand in creation. Fundamentalists gained the help of William Jennings Bryan and won victories that restricted the teaching of evolution in Oklahoma, Florida, and North Carolina.

Their greatest success came in Tennessee in 1925, when the legislature passed a bill making it illegal for any teacher in a public school, including state universities, to teach a theory that denied the "divine creation of man as taught in the Bible." The American Civil Liberties Union searched for someone who would be willing to violate the law by using a standard science text that taught evolution (and also white evolutionary superiority over blacks). The organization found its volunteer in a high school biology teacher, John T. Scopes. The "Monkey Trial" in Dayton, Tennessee, gained national attention when two of the most prominent lawyers in the country, Clarence Darrow (representing Scopes) and William Jennings Bryan (representing the state), confronted one another. Reporters flocked to Dayton, and the trial was broadcast nationally on radio.

The jury convicted Scopes, who was fined $100, but the real victory went to Darrow and other modernists. During the trial Darrow made Bryan look foolish in the eyes of many Americans, especially when Bryan took the stand as an "expert witness" on the Bible. The sixty-five-year-old Bryan died shortly after the trial; fundamentalism, however, continued to thrive in parts of the South and the Midwest.

ETHNIC IDENTITIES ARE STRENGTHENED   The reemergence of the Ku Klux Klan, which had emerged immediately following the Civil War and then declined, revealed a pernicious desire on the part of some to maintain the old ways. Reorganized in 1915 by a Methodist minister, William J. Simmons, the Klan grew rapidly after it was joined by two professional organizers, Edward Clarke and Elizabeth Tyler. From 1920 to 1925, the KKK grew from two thousand to two million members, most of them in the Midwest and West, not the South. The rapid growth was due to sales tactics that resembled a pyramid scheme, in which organizers up and down the chain of command got a cut of the dues of new members and the proceeds from the sale of Klan paraphernalia. The pitch helped, too: The new Klan softened its image. Rather than emphasizing violence, it highlighted its support for such modern causes as woman suffrage and women's work outside the home. It claimed to be merely for the "100 percent" native-born, white, gentile American. It was anti-black, anti-Jewish, and anti-Catholic. Hiram Evans, who became head of the Klan, took the KKK into politics, where it gained a political foothold in many states and control of a few. The Klan strongly supported Prohibition. Financial and moral scandals involving Klan leaders severely damaged the organization, and membership dropped as fast as it had risen. By 1930 the KKK had dwindled to about 100,000 members.

While the Klan represented the worst aspects of an ethnic consciousness that swept the nation, other groups experienced ethnic reawakening. In the Southwest, Native American tribes in New Mexico organized to protect their culture from being weakened by white educators and missionaries. They protested the poor treatment of their children in government-run Indian schools and attempts by officials to outlaw native religious practices. They debated what it meant to be an Indian, and some rejected the leadership of mixed-blood individuals. Although federal law drastically limited the immigration of southern and eastern Europeans, entrepreneurs in those communities found that technology allowed them to encourage a stronger sense of ethnic identification. Radio programming in cities with large European ethnic populations targeted specific language groups, as did grocery stores and social clubs.

An ethnic reawakening also occurred within the black community. Most prominent in this regard was Marcus Garvey, a Jamaican-born leader who promoted black nationalism through his Universal Negro Improvement Association (UNIA). Garvey's UNIA sponsored black-run commercial enterprises, including the Black Star steamship line, a hotel, a printing plant, a black doll factory, grocery stores, restaurants, and laundries. His "Back to Africa" movement attracted tens of thousands of followers, particularly in the North, as well as large donations.

Garvey's program appeared radical, but it embraced capitalist standards of success. He promised "every Black Man, Woman, and Child the opportunity to climb the greater ladder of industrial and commercial progress." Garvey was convicted of mail fraud and deported in 1922; he had sold tickets for trips on a nonexistent steamship line.

Black capitalism continued to expand in the African-American community, especially in the larger northern cities. Campaigns were launched

President-General of the Universal Negro Improvement Association, Marcus Garvey was thirty-three when this photo was taken at a Harlem parade. Garvey influenced other black nationalist leaders, including Malcolm X, in the 1960s. (AP/Wide World Photos)

to encourage blacks to shop at black-owned stores. This campaign benefited undertakers, barbers, and beauticians in particular but also encouraged the creation of black-owned banks and insurance companies.

PARADOX IN POLITICS, 1920–1928

According to some critics, the 1920s brought a conservative turn in the nation's foreign policy and domestic politics. Yet, staying out of the League of Nations did not mean that the United States decided to ignore foreign affairs. And although the popular mood favoring reform in domestic policies had faded, governments continued to spend, often considerably more than in earlier decades, on social services and transportation improvements.

Republicans controlled national politics through the 1920s. The party's candidates promised stability and prosperity, and they built on the base established in the election of 1896. Limited to steady support only in the South and in a few large northern cities, Democrats were divided and dispirited.

HARDING ELECTED, 1920   Woodrow Wilson had not succeeded either in constructing a new Democratic coalition or in sustaining a coalition for new reform initiatives. In 1920 conditions looked good for the Republicans, but they too were divided between Progressive and conservative wings. The convention deadlocked and finally picked a weak compromise candidate, Senator Warren G. Harding of Ohio, who called for lower taxes, smaller government, and a "return to normalcy." He condemned the Democratic candidate James Cox and his running mate, Franklin D. Roosevelt, for their support of "Wilson's League." Instead, he proposed a new association of nations, a vague proposal that appealed to pro- and anti-League of Nations forces alike. On election day Harding won in a landslide, getting nearly twice as many votes as Cox.

Corruption overwhelmed Harding's administration. The president was jovial and a friend to everyone; he simply could not say no. This inability proved to be his downfall. His administration was pulled into the spotlight after the suicide of the assistant to Attorney General Harry Daugherty. He ran a private house on K Street in Washington, where the so-called Ohio Gang (Harding and his associates) met to play poker and drink bootleg whiskey. The suicide prompted congressional investigations, which revealed the depth of corruption in the administration. Investigators discovered that the attorney general had allowed the Department of Justice to sell hundreds of pardons to bootleggers, wartime profiteers, and tax evaders. The Office of Alien Property had arranged for confiscated property to be transferred to a bogus claimant. The director of the Veterans Bureau, Charles Forbes, was indicted for embezzling $200 million in department funds.

In the midst of these scandals, Senate investigations revealed that Secretary of the Interior Albert Fall had received payoffs in the form of "low-interest loans" from oil executives who were leasing Navy-owned oil reserves. The Senate probe showed that oil executive Edward Doheny had given Fall a $100,000 "loan" shortly before he gained drilling rights to federal land in Elk Hills, California. In the case of Teapot Dome, Wyoming, Harry Sinclair had given Fall $223,000 in government bonds and $85,000 in cash. Although Sinclair and Doheny escaped conviction, Secretary of the Interior Fall went to prison.

The depth of the scandals shocked even the president, who told a confidant, "I have no trouble with my enemies . . . but my damn friends . . . they're the ones that keep me walking the floor nights!" In July 1923, just as these scandals were breaking, the deeply worried and depressed Harding suffered a heart attack and died. His death unleashed a flood of exposés about his drinking, gambling, and sexual affairs. A former mistress claimed that Harding had made love to her in a White House clothes closet and had fathered her illegitimate child.

COOLIDGE OFFERS STABILITY   Republicans scrambled to dissociate themselves from Harding. Vice President Calvin Coolidge, who stepped into the White House following Harding's death, appeared to be perfect for this task. Raised in Vermont, Coolidge seemed almost a caricature of rural New England reserve. The honest, simple Coolidge believed that the duty of the citizen was to serve God and society and that big business offered American society prosperity, social stability, and opportunity for individual advancement.

Coolidge moved quickly to clean up the scandals within the administration by forcing Harry Daugherty to resign as attorney general. Under Coolidge, income tax rates were reduced. So was military spending, although domestic spending took up the slack.

In 1924 Coolidge sought the presidency in his own right. Easily nominated, he defeated both Democratic rival John W. Davis, a conservative Wall Street lawyer who was nominated in a bitter fight after 104 ballots, and the Progressive candidate, Robert La Follette, senator from Wisconsin.

AMERICA ENGAGES THE WORLD ON ITS OWN TERMS

Warren G. Harding swept into the White House in 1920 with his call for a "return to normalcy." The United States had become the world's leading economic power, and Harding's administration reflected the nation's prevailing desire to engage foreign powers on the terms the United States would set. Harding played an instrumental role in international arms reduction and also arranged to reduce Germany's war reparations. The Coolidge administration also pursued disarmament through treaties while also intervening in Central America.

HARDING PURSUES INTERNATIONALISM   The United States could not have removed itself from international problems even if the nation had wanted it. World War I had left America the world's leading economic power; by 1920 the United States had replaced Great Britain as creditor to the world, and American trade accounted for some 30 percent of all international trade. In October 1921, with the ratification of the Treaty of Berlin, German–American relations were normalized. In the following years the

United States developed an unofficial system of cooperation and consultation with the League of Nations, which had been organized without America's formal participation.

In foreign policy Harding sought peace and cooperation without involving America in the League of Nations. President Harding's greatest accomplishment in international affairs came in 1921, when Secretary of State Charles Evans Hughes brought the major world powers to Washington for a conference on arms reduction. Hughes called for scrapping warships and maintaining fixed naval ratios. As one observer remarked, in thirty minutes Hughes sank "more ships than all the admirals of the world had sunk in a cycle of centuries." By the close of the Washington Conference, three treaties had been signed pledging that the five leading naval powers (the United States, Great Britain, Japan, France, and Italy) would restrain the naval arms race by limiting the construction of battleships over 10,000 tons for ten years. The five powers also agreed to a fixed ratio that left the British and American navies at 525,000 tons each, the Japanese navy at 315,000 tons, and the French and Italian navies at 175,000 tons each.

The Four Power Treaty pledged Britain, the United States, Japan, and France to respect each others' Pacific possessions. The Nine Power Treaty (the five major powers plus China, Belgium, Portugal, and the Netherlands) promised that the leading powers of the world would respect Chinese sovereignty and maintain an "Open Door" policy toward Chinese markets. Later critics found much to criticize in these treaties, especially after the outbreak of World War II, but at the time Americans welcomed Harding's peacekeeping efforts.

Among the most serious problems confronting the Harding and subsequent Republican administrations in the 1920s were the issues of war debts and war reparations. Allied war debts amounted to some $26.7 billion, mostly owed to the United States and Britain. France remained the principal debtor nation. To ease their debts, the Allies, contrary to Wilson's wishes, had imposed heavy war reparations on Germany. In 1922–1923, however, Germany found itself unable to make its reparation payments. Finally, in January 1923 France and Belgium sparked an international crisis when they marched into the German Ruhr district to seize the coal mines.

In this crisis American and British pressure forced France and Belgium to withdraw their troops. Hughes then convened a commission headed by Charles Dawes, a Republican with close ties to Wall Street. After months of negotiations, France, Britain, and Germany accepted the Dawes Plan, which reduced Germany's annual reparation payments and set a new payment schedule. American financial interests also agreed to extend loans to Germany. The United States still insisted on debt payments from the Allies, even though it maintained high tariff barriers that restricted their ability to sell goods to earn money to pay their debts. This created a circular arrangement: Americans extended loans to Germany, Germany made reparation payments to France and Great Britain, and France and Great Britain continued to make payments to the United States, which maintained high tariff barriers.

COOLIDGE SEEKS WORLD PEACE   President Coolidge's greatest "triumph" came in the late summer of 1928, shortly before he left office, when his new secretary of state, Frank Kellogg, negotiated a treaty with France and fourteen other nations to renounce war as an instrument of national policy except in cases of self-defense. The Kellogg-Briand Pact (1928) outlawed war. Coolidge rejoiced, as did isolationists such as Senator William Borah of Idaho. Republicans appeared to have fulfilled Wilson's dream of a world safe for democracy, without American participation in the League of Nations.

In Latin America, Coolidge sought to develop a pan-American alliance. But revolutionary upheavals in Mexico and Nicaragua led to calls for Coolidge to send in the Marines. Coolidge finally capitulated to this pressure in 1927 and ordered five thousand Marines into Nicaragua to put down a civil war. Coolidge's action unleashed a storm of criticism in the United States and Latin America, but a special diplomatic mission headed by Henry L. Stimson, who had been secretary of war under Taft, negotiated a truce and Nicaragua's agreement to hold democratic elections. Only one small rebel band, under Augusto Sandino, refused to lay down their arms and accept the election results. American troops began withdrawing from Nicaragua in 1931.

REPUBLICANS INSTITUTIONALIZE PROGRESSIVISM

Republican administrations sought to reduce the income tax from its wartime levels while maintaining high tariffs. Together with other efforts to help old and new businesses, such policies were intended to expand American prosperity. The thrust of many Republican policies was to extend Progressive Era and wartime policy initiatives even without a Progressive Movement pressing for reform.

TAXES AND SPENDING   Harding's economic policies focused on reducing wartime debts and sought to reduce wartime tax rates. The debt did decline from $26 billion in 1919 to less than $16 billion by 1930. Cuts in some government expenditures contributed to this. Nonetheless, public activities were expanded in a number of areas. For example, Secretary of Commerce Herbert Hoover's department was enlarged substantially, and federal mail subsidies of the fledgling airline industry were increased. Federal aid for state and local highway construction grew from $20 million in 1920 to $90 million in 1929. The trend continued under Coolidge. Despite his professed belief in limited government, Coolidge supported federal regulation of Alaskan fisheries, coastal water pollution, radio broadcasting, and aviation. His administration supported additional funds for highways and reforestation. He also proposed to privatize the postal system.

Secretary of the Treasury Andrew Mellon actively advocated federal tax cuts. The wartime excess profits tax was repealed in 1921 (President Wilson had advocated its repeal in 1919). Taxes on personal income, corporations, and estates were reduced in 1921 and again in 1924, 1926, and 1927. This trend led the Democrats to accuse the Republicans of following a policy of soaking the poor to finance big business. Mellon argued, however, that reduced taxes for the rich meant further capital investment in production and the creation of new jobs. Because the economy prospered, government revenues actually increased slightly over the 1920s.

There were few demands for new federal spending in the 1920s. Coolidge vetoed one, a plan for creation of an administration to bring cheap power to the Tennessee valley. Agriculture was another exception. Although California and Florida citrus farmers prospered, as did Northeastern farmers who supplied fresh produce to urban markets, many American farms foundered after the war. Farm debts doubled from 1915 to 1922, while prices for staples such as wheat, corn, and cotton remained soft. Farmers on marginal land—especially in the northern Great Lakes states, the Ozarks, and Appalachian areas—bore the brunt of depressed conditions.

As American farming failed to come out of the doldrums, a "farm bloc" in Congress, drawn mostly from Midwestern agricultural states, began to press for more radical measures to save agriculture. They pressed for a remedy that came to be called "McNary-Haugenism." Proposed by Senator Charles McNary (Oregon) and Representative Gilbert Haugen (Iowa), the plan called for the federal government to support domestic farm prices by purchasing surplus agricultural goods at "parity" with (equivalence to) the pre-World War I price. These surpluses were to be sold abroad at lower prices. Although Congress passed McNary-Haugen Bills in 1927 and 1928, Coolidge refused to sign them into law. Instead, Coolidge advocated government help to farmers in marketing their produce and in forming cooperatives that could reduce their costs.

Although Harding had not reduced military spending significantly, Coolidge proposed bigger defense cutbacks. From the point of view of Colonel Billy Mitchell, an advocate of air power, defense expenditures fell so low that the government was guilty of "incompetency, criminal negligence, and almost treasonable administration of national defense." Mitchell was court-martialed for these statements and discharged from the service.

Most of the burden of new spending fell, as it traditionally had, upon the states. While the federal government had begun to support road building, states shouldered most of the responsibility. And it was substantial: States that had not spent much in the first two decades of the twentieth century now found themselves spending large portions of their budgets (Tennessee, Illinois, and Nevada spent half or more) on highways in the 1920s. Spending on schools, hospitals, and urban transportation also mounted. Although states experimented with new ways of raising income, such as income, gasoline, and sales taxes, the income of most states still came from property taxes. Those taxes increased and were a special irritation for struggling farmers in the Midwest and West and for middle-class homeowners in free-spending cities. By the late 1920s tax revolts were brewing in a number of cities and states.

SOCIAL POLICIES   Harding's probusiness policies embodied a general hostility to labor. In 1921 Harding approved the use of federal troops to restore order following a strike in West Virginia's coal mines. The following year the nation's railroads were shut down by a strike. Attorney General Harry M. Daugherty obtained sweeping court injunctions prohibiting strike activity.

Nevertheless, Harding's administration was far from reactionary. Harding opposed peacetime sedition laws and pardoned Eugene Debs, who had been convicted of sedition during World War I. Harding also refused to support white supremacy within the Republican Party in the South. He chided southerners for their discriminatory practices toward blacks and urged the passage of a federal antilynching law. Yet he declined to use the federal government to stop the terrorism of the Ku Klux Klan. President Coolidge, however, called for the "prevention and punishment against the hideous crime of [Negro] lynching," but Southern congressmen presented a united barrier against any such legislation. Coolidge also asked Congress to expand agricultural and medical education for blacks. He appointed few blacks to federal offices, even though African Americans continued to actively support the Republican Party.

As recognition of their new clout as voters, women gained some federal appointments. Under Harding, Mabel Willebrandt became assistant attorney general for Prohibition enforcement. Lucille Anderson became the first woman to enter the diplomatic service. Harding opposed the equal rights amendment, which would have explicitly recognized equal rights for women under the U.S. Constitution. So did many feminists, who supported legislation that protected women workers and single women left to support children.

Those who had worked for immigration restrictions since the late nineteenth century got their wish with the passage of the National Origins Act (1924). Based upon a belief that the Anglo-Saxon stock was being weakened by immigration from eastern and southern Europe as well as Asia, the law set ethnic quotas according to the composition of the American population in 1890. The act precluded Asian immigration altogether. Outraged, the Japanese in Tokyo declared the day the act passed, July 1, 1924, "Humiliation Day."

There were signs of change in the government's Indian policy. After a well-organized campaign by Native Americans, Coolidge ordered an investigation of the federal Indian Service. The investigation's final report called for major reforms in Indian education, governance, and aid. This marked the beginnings of a major shift in Indian policy for the first time in fifty years.

HOOVER ELECTED: PROSPERITY COLLAPSES

In the presidential election of 1928, Herbert Hoover defeated his Democratic opponent, Al Smith, in a landslide. Smith, a Roman Catholic, a New York Democrat, and "wet," proved a poor match for Hoover, a Protestant, a midwestern Republican, and "dry," running in a boom year for the economy. Within a year, however, the good times had ended: The stock market crashed, marking the beginning of the Great Depression.

HOOVER WINS THE 1928 ELECTION   Finally, after six years in office, the taciturn Coolidge announced, "I do not choose to run in 1928."

The Democratic convention was raucous. The party remained divided between its urban and rural wings, between North and South, between "wets" (those who opposed Prohibition) and "drys" (those who favored it). After a bitter floor battle, the party nominated Al Smith, who was outgoing governor of New York, Irish Catholic, and "wet." The Republicans turned enthusiastically to Secretary of Commerce Herbert Hoover.

Hoover personified the American success story. Orphaned at an early age, he grew up on a farm in Iowa and later lived in Oregon. Educated at public schools, he entered Stanford University, became a mining engineer, and amassed a fortune building hydroelectric dams. During World War I, Hoover won a reputation as a humanitarian when, as chairman of the American Relief Committee, he worked to provide food to Belgium and other war-ravaged countries. As secretary of commerce, Hoover prevailed upon industry to standardize, simplify, and become more efficient. In 1928, many people saw Hoover as an engineer with a heart, a man of vision with a sense of the possible.

The religious issue haunted the campaign. In the fundamentalist Bible Belt, opponents organized "Southern Protestants Against Smith." Protestant ministers denounced "Al-cohol Smith." He confronted a revived KKK that had gained strength in the South, Indiana, Ohio, Oklahoma, Oregon, and California. When Smith traveled to Billings, Montana, his train passed a fiery display of burning crosses that extended for miles outside the town.

On election day Herbert Hoover's 21.3 million votes swamped Al Smith's 15 million. Still, Smith won the traditional Republican states of Massachusetts and Rhode Island and carried the urban vote for the Democratic Party for the first time since 1896, suggesting a permanent shift among voters.

Hoover had little time to enjoy his victory. Within a year after his election, the American economy began a frightening spiral downward. Beginning on October 29, 1929, the stock market crashed. The crash abruptly shifted American's attention from the politics of culture and the pursuit of individualism to economic concerns. The worst depression in modern history had begun.

CONCLUSION

As the economy declined and America slipped into the Great Depression, Americans began to reassess the 1920s. Many viewed the period as marred by corruption and self-indulgence.

History is a stern judge. The onset of the Great Depression and the push for reform that followed allowed critics of American culture and society to have their day. Assuredly, Americans had been too complacent in celebrating economic growth, Republican political success, and cultural renaissance in the twenties. Still, there had been much to celebrate: The economy had boomed, the political order had remained stable, and the arts had flourished as never before. The crash of 1929, however, made it hard to celebrate.

Recommended Readings

DOCUMENTS: Frederick Lewis Allen, *Only Yesterday* (1931); Bruce Barton, *The Man Nobody Knows* (1925); Malcolm Cowley, *Exiles Return* (1934).

READINGS: (GENERAL) Paul Carter, *The Twenties in America* (1968) and *Another Part of the Twenties* (1977); Lynn Dumenil, *The Modern* Temper (1995); John D. Hicks, *Republican Ascendancy* (1960); Morton Keller, *Regulating a New Economy* (1990); William E. Leuchtenberg, *Perils of Prosperity* (1970); Donald McCoy, *Coming of Age* (1973); Geoffrey Perrett, *America in the Twenties* (1982); David Shannon, *Between the Wars* (1979). (SOCIAL) Lois Banner, *American Beauty* (1983); Irving Bernstein, *The Lean Years: A History of the American Worker* (1960); David M. Chalmers, *Hooded Americanism* (1965); Norman H. Clark, *Deliver Us from Evil: An Interpretation of Prohibition* (1976); Robert Crunden, *From Self to Society: Transition in Modern Thought* (1972); James Flink, *The Car Culture* (1975); James Gilbert, *Designing the Industrial State* (1972); Nathan Huggins, *Harlem Renaissance* (1971); Kenneth T. Jackson, *The Ku Klux Klan in the City* (1967); J. Stanley Lemons, *The Woman Citizen: Social Feminism in the 1920s* (1973); Roland Marchand, *Advertising the American Dream* (1985); George Marsden, *Fundamentalism and American Culture* (1980); Lacy May, *Screening Out the Past* (1980); Leslie W. Tender, *Wage Earning Women* (1979); Robert Zieger, *Republicans and Labor* (1969). (POLITICS) Kristi Andersen, *The Creation of a Democratic Majority* (1979); Robert Murray, *The Politics of Normalcy* (1973); Burl Noggle, *Teapot Dome* (1962); Eugene Trani and David Wilson, *The Presidency of Warren G. Harding* (1977).

25

❧

The Great Depression
and the New Deal

OVERVIEW The economic downturn that began in 1929 shook American confidence, weakening traditional beliefs in progress, historic destiny, and providential mission. The Depression led to a restructuring of the American economy and new relations among government, business, and labor. President Franklin Roosevelt's program, the New Deal, modified democratic capitalism by placing new government regulations on business, labor, and society. The New Deal provided work for the unemployed, security for the elderly, legal rights for workers, and better lives for farmers.

American political life underwent a profound transformation as Roosevelt shaped the Democratic Party into a majority coalition built around ethnic and racial minorities, organized labor, blue-collar workers, and large segments of urban dwellers and farmers. At the same time, American social life underwent deep alterations.

HOOVER FACES DEPRESSION

The stock market of the 1920s drew record levels of investment—reckless speculation, some charged. The underlying weakness of the market, however, lay not in the investor dollars it attracted but in the fact that so many of those dollars were borrowed. Anxious to get in on a good thing, people put up as little as 20 percent of purchase prices in the hope of selling at a profit later. Such gambles worked as long as the market continued to climb. But the house of cards collapsed in October 1929; the stock market crash liquidated many Americans' savings. The crash alone was hardly enough to cause what followed. Industrial production and sales dropped sharply, forcing businesses to lay off workers. Unemployment reached 25 percent. Newly in office, Herbert Hoover faced the worst depression of modern times, one that affected the whole industrialized world; and like his critics and leaders in other industrialized nations, he groped for explanations and ways to fix it.

Hoover believed in local solutions and American individualism, so he called on state and local governments and the private sector to help, but they were soon overwhelmed by the severity of the Depression. Despite his reputation as a visionary, Hoover's responses revealed political ineptness in a crisis.

THE BUBBLE BURSTS   In early 1929 some were concerned about the stock market and the overall economy, but few suspected trouble. Sales of big-ticket consumer goods were softening, and industrial production in turn began to slow. The stock market dipped but rose again. The ability of investors to borrow—to buy on margin—lent instability to the market. So did "stop-loss" agreements, in which investors arranged to sell their holdings if prices dropped below a certain level. The emergence of vast investment holding companies (parent companies that held stock in smaller companies) added to the explosive situation on Wall Street. These huge companies, which often controlled dozens of smaller companies, issued millions of dollars' worth of stock, in the process building large paper pyramids that appeared attractive but were structurally flimsy. It all collapsed in October 1929.

Hoover had just entered office when the system began to unravel. By the summer of 1929, industrial production had gone into a slump, although the stock market remained strong. By autumn, however, the market had begun to wobble. The first signs of the portending crash occurred on October 21, 1929; on Thursday, October 24, the market fell into complete disorder that soon gave way to panic as an unprecedented 12.9 million shares were traded. The volume was so heavy that the reporting system completely broke down. People could not find out what had happened until hours after the market closed. Rumors added to the confusion.

Finally, leading New York financiers stepped in, pledging $20 million to $30 million to bolster the market and calm fears. Thomas Lamont, a senior partner of J. P. Morgan and Company, assured reporters in a classic understatement, "There were technical difficulties, but these have been addressed." The market remained fairly calm until "Black Tuesday," October 29. By the end of that day, stock prices had fallen forty-three points, more than 10 percent. Investment houses, brokers, and small investors were devastated. Tens of thousands of accounts were wiped out.

AMERICANS FIND NEITHER WORK NOR RELIEF   The crash weakened the confidence and erased the assets of many but was hardly sufficient to send the economy into a tailspin. What had was a matter of urgent debate at the time and is still a question in economic history. Possible culprits include the uneven distribution of wealth in the 1920s, which prevented the growth of a class of consumers large enough to support an economy increasingly reliant on consumer goods; the high protective tariffs that choked international trade; the Federal Reserve's inept handling of interest rates; and the long-term instability of major European economies still not completely recovered from World War I. Economists debated the causes at the time and continue to debate them today. People knew for

In 1933 surplus potatoes and cabbage were distributed in Cleveland by the Federal Relief Agency. The worst year of the Great Depression saw one-quarter of Americans out of work. (AP/Wide World Photos)

certain only what they saw around them. Industrial production fell to nearly half of what it had been. This downward spiral was made worse by the policy of the Federal Reserve Bank, which withdrew funds and shrank the money supply at the exact moment when additional liquidity was needed. As sales dropped, businesses began to lay off workers. By 1932 an estimated thirteen million to seventeen million workers, about a quarter of the labor force, had been laid off.

Unable to find regular jobs, casual work, or even relief, the unemployed became desperate. As many as two million young men (and a few women) took to the railroads and highways as tramps. Tens of thousands of the homeless slept in city parks, subways, and abandoned buildings; others gathered in makeshift camps that sprang up on the outskirts of towns. These rough settlements of primitive tarpaper shacks were sardonically referred to as "Hoovervilles."

As conditions worsened, many families turned to private or local government charities for aid. Yet government at all levels lacked the administrative infrastructure to deal with the problems facing the nation. As a result, public officials relied on volunteer relief efforts to handle the growing numbers of those seeking relief. The numbers themselves reveal the scale of the problem: More than half the families on unemployment relief were located in eight states; and more than a third were in the four highly industrialized states of Pennsylvania, New York, Ohio, and Illinois. Forty percent of all persons on relief were children. Exact numbers are unknown because the government had never tried to collect unemployment statistics.

Initially, most social workers opposed federal involvement in local relief efforts. As people began to go hungry, social workers sought federal aid. Hoover refused. He saw America at a crossroads, declaring that the "American system" limited government "to protect the people." Hoover feared "that we shall directly or indirectly regiment the nation, the people, and the state."

The severity of the Depression made the world seem irrational. Hamburgers sold at two for five cents, and people still could not afford to buy them. Men worked for only ten cents an hour, yet many businesses were unable to make a profit. Interest rates fell to below 1 percent, but few were willing to invest. Unable to sell their crops at decent prices, farmers allowed them to rot in the field while people went hungry. The world seemed topsy-turvy, and after a decade of general prosperity, Americans simply were not prepared to cope with economic collapse.

HOOVER RESPONDS RELUCTANTLY   In 1930 many Americans naturally looked to President Herbert Hoover, the great engineer and the great humanitarian, to duplicate his past feats, which had prevented Europe from starving at the end of World War I. As a result of these earlier experiences, however, Hoover held fast to his belief that local voluntary cooperation, community effort, and federal encouragement would address the problems of the emergency.

Hoover had a reputation as a visionary. Like other Progressives, he believed that economic stability and efficiency could be introduced through the formation of business and community associations. According to this associational vision, voluntary groups of business, labor, and social leaders could use rational, scientific planning to cope with the complex problems of an industrial society. These associations were touted by Hoover as the beginning of a new era in American capitalism. Destructive competition through unfair business practices, he argued, was a thing of the past.

Hoover addressed the national economic crisis in 1929 by calling on businessmen and labor leaders to maintain employment, prices, and wages. In 1930 he appointed an emergency commission to review unemployment, but when the commission recommended a federal public works program, Hoover disbanded it and formed the new President's Organization on Unemployment Relief. This committee also failed. Hoover encouraged businessmen to undertake campaigns to "Buy American and Spend American." In 1931 Hoover persuaded Congress to pass the Smoot-Hawley Tariff, which raised import duties to the highest levels ever seen. Foreign trade almost stopped as other nations pursued similarly foolish policies by raising their tariffs to protect their markets in the midst of what had become a worldwide depression.

Protectionism also extended to the domestic front. By late 1932 half the states required their governments to buy goods from their own states and employ only residents of their states in public works contracts. Such policies, however, caused trade to decline, introduced inefficiencies, raised costs, and did little to revive a plummeting economy.

Hoover resisted instituting a concerted federal program to address problems, even as those problems grew worse each day. Finally, in the summer of 1932, he capitulated to Congress and a distressed nation. About to stand for reelection, Hoover accepted a relief bill that allowed the newly created Reconstruction Finance Corporation to lend $1.8 billion to states and municipalities for relief and public works. Hoover continued to insist, however, that federal money should not undermine local relief efforts and American individualism.

As the Depression worsened, Hoover reluctantly increased government spending. Money was appropriated to build Boulder Dam (later renamed Hoover Dam) along the Colorado River. The Emergency Relief and

Construction Act gave federal grants to states for highway construction. The Reconstruction Finance Corporation continued to provide loans to banks and insurance companies. As a consequence, federal expenditures increased from 3 percent ($3.3 billion) of the gross national product in 1929 to 9 percent ($4.6 billion) of a smaller gross national product in 1932.

As federal expenditures increased and revenues fell (with declining corporate and individual earnings), the federal budget went into the red. A strong supporter of a balanced budget, Hoover hiked business taxes in 1932, a policy that dampened an already weakened economy.

FRANKLIN D. ROOSEVELT LAUNCHES THE NEW DEAL

Franklin Delano Roosevelt easily defeated Herbert Hoover for the presidency in 1932. In his first hundred days in office, FDR targeted industrial and agricultural recovery through legislation that gave the government the power to control agricultural production and to set industrial prices and wages. These measures challenged fundamental American assumptions about the government's proper role in society and drew intense criticism. The economy recovered somewhat, but only temporarily.

FRANKLIN DELANO ROOSEVELT ELECTED, **1932**   For the presidential election of 1932, the desperate Republicans renominated a demoralized Hoover, while the Democrats, sensing that the Depression would bring them victory, turned to Franklin D. Roosevelt, the governor of New York.

Roosevelt brought to the campaign a bright personality and a cheerful manner that generated confidence wherever he traveled, and his fight against his own physical disability gave courage to Americans. In 1920 political insiders saw Roosevelt as a future leader of the party when he won the Democratic nomination for vice president. But when polio struck him the following year, Roosevelt's political career appeared to be over. He was only thirty-nine. His mother urged him to retire, but his wife Eleanor encouraged him to fight his disability. From 1921 to 1928, she kept her husband's name alive by writing hundreds of letters to leading politicians. She also established key contacts with women's groups, social welfare activists, and human rights advocates. Franklin Roosevelt eventually turned his disability into a strength. His fight against polio became a symbol of the nation's fight against a sick economy. His hearty laugh and cigarette dangling jauntily from a long holder became symbols of the nation's defiance of the Depression.

While he attacked Hoover's spendthrift policies, which had led to budget deficits, Roosevelt also called for the federal government to put

The secret of President Roosevelt's political success was a combination of confidence, optimism, cunning, experimentation, and infectious enthusiasm. His smile said it all: charm. (Library of Congress)

people back to work. For example, in a speech in Pittsburgh, he declared, "I regard the reduction in federal spending as one of the most important issues of this campaign." Still, he pleaded on behalf of the "forgotten man at the bottom of the economic pyramid" and called for "bold, persistent experimentation."

Meanwhile, Hoover further offended people by his bungled handling of a protest in the summer of 1932. Hundreds of World War I veterans marched on Washington to demand that Congress give them pensions they were not due to receive until 1945. Some veterans set up a crude shantytown of tents and shacks at the edge of Washington, while others occupied unused lots along Pennsylvania Avenue. Feeling besieged and fearful of an angry mob, Hoover ordered the White House put under guard, the gates chained, and the streets cleared of people. Warned that communists had infiltrated this makeshift "Bonus Army" of protesters, Hoover ordered the military to drive the veterans away. General Douglas

MacArthur led six tanks, four troops of cavalry with drawn sabers, and a column of steel-helmeted infantry to clear the camps. A thousand veterans and their wives and children fled as troops attacked the colony and burned the shacks. Fires lit Washington that night, and Hoover's bid for reelection went up in smoke. (Roosevelt, too, would refuse the petitions for bonuses, but instead of having the army clear the protesters, First Lady Eleanor Roosevelt served the protesters hot coffee.)

Roosevelt's election was a foregone conclusion. He received 22.8 million votes to Hoover's 15.7 million. FDR, as Roosevelt became popularly known, swept thirty-two states, carrying cities in the Northeast and the Midwest, the farm vote in the Midwest and the West, and the reliably Democratic South. Roosevelt's victory was the worst defeat for the Republicans since 1912. Memories of "Hoover's Depression" kept the Republicans out of the White House until 1952.

ROOSEVELT JUMP-STARTS THE NEW DEAL   Roosevelt faced a nation in crisis. In the four months between his election in November 1932 and his inauguration on March 4, 1933, the nation's entire banking system collapsed. (The Constitution's Twentieth Amendment changed inauguration day to January 20, beginning in 1937). By the eve of the inauguration, thirty states had closed or restricted their banks to discourage runs by depositors. In early 1933 business activity reached an all-time low, half the 1929 level. In the Appalachian Mountains of Kentucky, unemployed coal miners ate wild greens from the fields and forests. Unemployment among blacks in Harlem, Philadelphia, Detroit, and Chicago reached 50 percent. In the Midwest, under the leadership of Milo Reno and his National Farm Holiday Association, farmers protested low prices and declared a farmers' holiday. Corn was so cheap in South Dakota that one county courthouse burned it as fuel. In an attempt to drive up farm and dairy prices, armed bands of farmers blockaded highways. In the cities communists successfully organized protest marches of unemployed. A thousand hungry men attacked two bakery trucks in New York. In Oklahoma three hundred unemployed men raided food stores.

At his inauguration Roosevelt reassured the American people. "The only thing we have to fear is fear itself, nameless, unreasoning, unjustified terror which paralyzes needed efforts to convert retreat into advance." These were brave words, but Roosevelt knew that more than words were needed. The people, the nation, demanded action. FDR's plan of action was called the "New Deal."

In the next hundred days Congress, called into session by Roosevelt, furiously enacted laws concerning banks, industry, agriculture, Wall Street, unemployment relief, and home mortgages. What emerged was neither planned nor comprehensive but a series of practical responses generally informed by Progressive concerns.

Roosevelt's first action was to resolve the banking crisis. On March 5, 1933—the day after his inauguration—the president declared a "bank holiday" and closed all banks. Although Progressives within Congress called for nationalization of the banking system, Roosevelt signed the Emergency Banking Act, which provided federal loans to distressed banks and set guidelines for reopening those banks considered solvent. Later banking legislation separated commercial banks providing checking and saving accounts from investment banks handling stocks and bonds, and established the Federal Deposit Insurance Corporation (FDIC) to insure deposits in individual banks up to $5,000.

The keystones of the early New Deal were two measures aimed at agricultural relief and industrial recovery. Secretary of Agriculture Henry A. Wallace, son of Harding's former secretary of agriculture, cooperated with economists Rexford Tugwell and M. L. Wilson in 1933 in drafting an agricultural relief measure, the Agricultural Adjustment Act (AAA). This act transformed American farm policy by controlling the supply of agricultural goods placed on the market. Through a tax on food processing plants, farmers received subsidies *not* to plant certain crops (because oversupply of a given crop would drive prices down, and limiting the supply would hold prices up). At the same time, new credit measures allowed farmers to receive funds to improve their farms. Shortly after the enactment of the AAA, Wallace ordered farmers to slaughter 6 million pigs and plow under 100 million acres of cotton, one-fourth of the entire 1933 crop. Few within the administration seemed to worry about plowing crops under while people went hungry. Nor did many worry about the long-term costs of subsidizing a special class of citizens, farmers.

The second keystone of the New Deal was the National Industrial Recovery Act (NIRA). Drafted by Raymond Moley, the NIRA called upon industry and labor to meet to set wage and price controls through cooperative codes overseen by a federal board, the National Recovery Administration (NRA). Modeled on the War Industries Board of 1919, the NRA oversaw the establishment of more than five hundred industrial and trade associations to draft codes of fair competition. These codes determined production quotas, hours, business practices, standards of quality, and methods of competition. The act thus granted the federal government extensive and previously unheard-of powers to set prices and wages in a peacetime economy.

That New Dealers often compared the Depression to the nation's struggle during World War I seemed natural to many at the time. Yet NRA practices raised serious constitutional questions. Moreover, few within the administration seemed to notice the apparent contradiction of a policy that sought to maintain industrial wages through the NRA while driving up agricultural prices through the AAA. Higher food prices inevitably meant higher costs for the industrial worker.

An important feature of the National Industrial Recovery Act, Section 7A, gave employees the right to form labor unions; it also set minimum wages and maximum hours for all employees. Section 7A pleased the American Federation of Labor and offered organized labor a chance to regain ground lost during the 1920s.

The NIRA also appropriated $3.3 billion for the Public Works Administration (PWA), to be formed under Harold Ickes, Secretary of the Interior. A former Progressive Republican, Ickes, like many New Dealers, remained cautious about spending government money. Because the PWA only undertook large projects, such as highways, bridges, and dams, that involved meticulous and time-consuming planning, its funds were disbursed slowly and did little immediately to relieve the unemployed.

THE NEW DEAL TARGETS THE UNEMPLOYED   Roosevelt sought more direct relief for the unemployed with the Federal Relief Act of May 1933, which appropriated $500 million for the states for relief through the Federal Emergency Relief Administration (FERA). Headed by New York social worker Harry Hopkins, the FERA confronted an unemployment problem of historic magnitude: More than 4.7 million Americans were on relief by 1933. Impatient with bureaucratic red tape, within a month Hopkins disbursed over $51 million to states in matching grants. To manage the program and to control the aid, Hopkins created regional staffs throughout the country to oversee state and local agencies.

Federal relief dented the massive unemployment problem only slightly. As winter approached, Hopkins worried about the 12.5 million Americans still without work. In November 1933, he convinced Roosevelt to establish a temporary Civil Works Administration (CWA) to undertake short-term, light construction in the public sector. Diverting funds from the PWA, the CWA put 4 million people to work. In its brief existence during the winter of 1933–1934, the CWA built 500,000 miles of roads, 40,000 schools, 3,500 playgrounds, and 1,000 airports.

For all its successes, the CWA drew political fire from conservatives within the administration, including Vice President John Nance Garner, Budget Director Lewis Douglas, and others. Southern congressmen, in particular, complained that the program was luring black workers off farms. The CWA policy of paying equal wages to black and white workers also drew resentment from some whites. As one small farmer wrote his senator, "The CWA's paying sorry no-account Negroes 45 cents per hour . . . and I can't get any job." Concerned about these political attacks as well as the high costs of the program, in the spring of 1934 FDR ordered Hopkins to start disbanding the program.

The Civilian Conservation Corps (CCC), established in 1933 to put the nation's unemployed youth to work, drew less political criticism. The CCC recruited 250,000 youths, including many blacks and Indians, to camps in national parks and forests. CCC members built roads, trails, campgrounds, and ranger stations, planted trees, cleared brush, and improved the environment. Paid $1 a day, the same as army wages, CCC workers were housed, fed, and clothed in uniforms. Most mailed their pay home to their desperate families. The CCC proved to be one of the New Deal's greatest success stories.

Other legislation created the Home Owners Loan Corporation to provide refinancing for homeowners facing foreclosure on mortgages, and the Tennessee Valley Authority (TVA) to bring federally sponsored electricity and flood control to the Tennessee River valley.

The fight over establishing the TVA had pitted Progressive Republican Senator George Norris of Nebraska against conservative Republican administrations from Harding through Hoover. The federal government's entry into public utilities proved to many Republican and conservative opponents of the emerging New Deal that Roosevelt planned to take the

In the 1930s millions of Americans worked at public service jobs. Here the Civilian Conservation Corps lines an irrigation ditch. The CCC, which catered to single young men, provided room and board plus $30 a month. Men sent most of the money home to help unemployed relatives. (Library of Congress)

country down the path of socialism. Conservatives were even more dismayed when Roosevelt announced that he was taking America off the domestic gold standard. The price of gold was to be set at $35 an ounce, but Americans could no longer exchange their dollars for gold.

The accomplishments of Roosevelt's first hundred days offered some relief to a nation demoralized by the Depression. Eventually the gross national product rose from $56 billion in 1933 to $72 billion in 1935. Wholesale prices jumped a third. People began to speak of an NRA recovery. In the congressional elections of 1934, Americans showed their enthusiasm for the New Deal by electing 322 Democratic congressmen, a gain of thirteen seats for Roosevelt's party. The recovery proved only temporary, however. Early in 1935 the economy began to lapse again, and by midsummer it was clearly stagnant.

LEFT AND RIGHT REACT

Despite its early success, the New Deal came under increasing criticism from those who thought it went too far and from those who thought it did not go far enough. In 1935, the NIRA and the AAA were declared unconstitutional. As the Depression wore on, Americans became more receptive to calls for radical action. A drive for old-age pensions won wide support. Senator Huey Long challenged FDR with a plan for a guaranteed income for everyone. Conservatives and big business opposed the New Deal but attracted little popular support.

THE NRA AND AAA COME UNDER FIRE   In these circumstances critics on both the left and the right voiced discontent. Once the symbol of success, the National Recovery Administration drew criticism from all sides. The NRA, under its director Hugh Johnson, had been launched with much fanfare; businesses that had helped draft the production codes willingly displayed the blue "NRA Eagle" emblem. But problems soon became apparent within the agency. Johnson, who suffered from a severe drinking problem, often disappeared for days, leaving the office in charge of his secretary (and mistress).

Discontent also arose concerning the program itself: Small business owners felt disadvantaged by big business, which played a key role in drafting the NRA's six hundred production codes. Organized labor felt betrayed by the promise of the NRA when businesses formed company unions to keep out organized labor. Protesting that the NRA allowed discriminatory codes to be instituted, blacks denounced the NRA as the "Negro Run Around," the "Negro Removal Act," and the "Negro Rarely

Allowed." Roosevelt's embarrassment over the NRA was finally relieved when the Supreme Court in *Schechter v. United States* (1935) ruled the NIRA act unconstitutional.

The Agricultural Adjustment Administration also drew fire. Early AAA efforts to cut food production had been aided by a drought that swept through the Great Plains in 1934. Without rain much of the plains became a desert, scoured by severe winds that blew blinding dust storms. Thousands began a mass exodus out of the Dust Bowl. Weather and the AAA caused wheat production to fall and prices to rise. Farmers' share of the nation's income rose from 11 percent in 1933 to 15 percent in 1935.

While the AAA benefited many farmers, the program hurt tenant farmers in the South. Large cotton planters, as major beneficiaries of the program, took federal money to remove land from production and then ordered tenant farmers to leave. Particularly hard hit were black farmers. Some experts estimated that the AAA displaced 200,000 black tenant farmers. Liberals in Congress and the AAA protested, while tenant farmers formed, under communist influence, the Southern Tenant Farmers Union. Pressure led President Roosevelt to increase the share of AAA payments to tenant farmers, but in early 1936, in *United States v. Butler*, the Supreme Court ruled the AAA unconstitutional because of its tax on food processors.

Some critics of the New Deal found it too tame. The first signs of popular discontent came in the governor's race in California in 1934, when socialist and novelist Upton Sinclair, best known for his book *The Jungle*, won the Democratic nomination on a campaign to "End Poverty in California" (EPIC). Sinclair's call to establish cooperative farms and state-run industries frightened conservatives like movie mogul Louis B. Mayer of Metro-Goldwyn-Mayer and young Oakland district attorney Earl Warren (later chief justice of the Supreme Court), who conducted a vicious media campaign against Sinclair. Sinclair lost the general election to the Republican candidate, but EPIC indicated widespread discontent among the electorate.

Others turned to Francis Townsend, a dentist from South Dakota who had retired to California. Townsend devised a scheme to provide a federally funded monthly payment of $200 to any unemployed person over the age of sixty on the condition that this money be spent within the month. By 1935 the Townsend movement claimed 3.5 million supporters, helped win seats in Congress, and assisted lobbying efforts for state old-age pensions.

Another radical, the Roman Catholic priest Charles Coughlin, reached nearly thirty million listeners each week on a nationally syndicated religious radio program. He demanded inflation through a free silver policy. His increasingly vitriolic attacks charged that Roosevelt's Brain Trust (which he called the "Drain Trust") had been infiltrated by communists and Jews.

A more serious threat came from Louisiana's Huey P. Long. Although Long supported Roosevelt in 1932, by 1934 he had broken with the New Deal. Entertaining presidential aspirations of his own, Long proposed a "soak the rich" tax program that would enable every man to have a homestead worth $5,000 and an income of $2,500. He promised everyone a college education and a guaranteed income. His "Share Our Wealth Clubs" swept the nation, claiming 27,000 clubs with a mailing list of 7.5 million supporters. The Long threat ended on September 8, 1935, when he was assassinated in Baton Rouge by a relative of a recently discharged state judge.

Radicalism also led to a revival of the Communist Party. In 1932 the party had backed William Z. Foster for president on a Stalinist platform that called for nationalizing all private enterprise and abolishing all political parties except its own. By 1935, however, the party had adopted the slogan "Communism Is Twentieth-Century Americanism" and had formed coalitions with liberal groups through what were called "popular fronts." For example, the Communist Party sponsored the 1935 American Writers Congress, which attracted such distinguished authors as John Dos Passos, Theodore Dreiser, James T. Farrell, Richard Wright, and Ernest Hemingway. The Writers Congress issued a public statement declaring that "communism must come and must be fought for."

Documents from the United States government and intelligence files obtained from the former Soviet Union in the 1990s reveal that that approximately two hundred Communist agents and spies penetrated the Roosevelt administration in the 1930s and 1940s. While most of these spies operated at low and middle levels of government, evidence shows that presidential advisor Lauchlin Currie and Assistant Secretary of the Treasury Harry Dexter White worked for Soviet intelligence. Alger Hiss, a high-ranking State Department official, appears to have been a Soviet agent as well. Although these agents illegally conveyed highly secret information to the Soviet Union, their exact influence on American policy remains uncertain.

CONSERVATIVES ORGANIZE AGAINST THE NEW DEAL   The Right appeared less well organized than the Left. The American Bund, a fascist organization, found support among a small group of German Americans. Fascism, however, attracted few followers, although Lawrence Dennis, a Harvard graduate and former Foreign Service officer, drew considerable attention with his book *The Coming of Fascism* (1936).

Mainstream conservatives opposed fascism and communism as differing forms of big-government collectivism. Conservatives feared that the American tradition of individualism, limited government, and property rights were being subverted by the New Deal. Opposition to the New Deal led to formation of the Liberty League in 1935, financed by members of the DuPont family and New York financiers Winthrop Aldrich and Felix Warburg. Although membership remained small, the Liberty League was significant as an indicator that much of big business had broken with the New Deal. Roosevelt had become a "traitor to his class." On the other hand, Roosevelt made the Liberty League into a symbol of big business and its selfish opposition to the New Deal. While conservatives remained isolated throughout most of the 1930s, anti-New Deal opposition gained some strength in the late 1930s through local tax revolts, opposition to Roosevelt's scheme to reorganize government and "pack" the Supreme Court, and, when Nazi Germany invaded Poland in 1939, fear that America would become involved in another war in Europe.

ROOSEVELT SECURES THE NEW DEAL

Roosevelt responded to attacks from the Left and the Right by pushing the New Deal forward. In doing so, he transformed the nature of the American welfare state. The Social Security Act (1935) became the centerpiece of the second New Deal. Roosevelt also moved to secure new farm, public works, and labor legislation. After winning reelection in 1936, however, he found his administration embattled over his scheme to reform the Supreme Court and his failure to address another downturn in the economy.

ROOSEVELT TACKLES UNEMPLOYMENT   Under political attack from both the Left and the Right, Roosevelt moved to redefine the New Deal. Denouncing the dole as a "narcotic, a subtle destroyer of the human spirit," Roosevelt disbanded the temporary Federal Emergency Relief Administration in December 1935. In its place he established a $5 billion employment program called the Works Progress Administration (WPA), directed by Harry Hopkins. In doing so, he returned 1.5 million people, including the aged, disabled, and orphaned, to state and local welfare agencies. The other 3.5 million "employables" were put to work on federally sponsored WPA projects, building more than 2,500 hospitals, 13,000 playgrounds, and 1,000 airports. The WPA also hired artists to decorate post offices with murals, actors to perform free plays in parks, and writers to turn out tourist guidebooks. Among the young authors employed were John Cheever, Richard Wright, and Conrad Aiken.

Congress also authorized the creation of the National Youth Administration (NYA). This agency paid stipends to half a million college students and offered part-time employment to 1.5 million needy high school students. Another two million youths received stipends in state-sponsored programs.

Nevertheless, of the ten million unemployed, the WPA and the NYA employed a few more than three million. Even at its height the WPA never employed more than one-third of the nation's jobless.

SOCIAL SECURITY AND LABOR LEGISLATION ENACTED, **1935**   State governments were ill equipped to meet the needs of the so-called unemployables: the aged, the disabled, and the sick. For this reason Roosevelt called for a social security program. The Social Security Act (1935) marked a turning point in the history of social policy in the United States by extending federal responsibility for care to the elderly, the poor, and the disabled. The act established a contributory system that provided pensions to all over age sixty-five. The program also offered relief for the elderly poor, allowed matching grants-in-aid to states to assist the physically disabled and mothers raising children without a male provider. In addition it established a federal–state system of unemployment insurance.

Roosevelt also moved to address the problems created for organized labor and farmers by the Supreme Court's overturning of the National Industrial Recovery Act. The Court's ruling meant that the right to collective bargaining embodied in Section 7A no longer had a basis in law. To redress this situation, the Wagner Act (1935) granted collective bargaining rights to organized labor and established the National Labor Relations Board (NLRB) to oversee relations between labor and industry.

The Wagner Act came just in time. Workers were restless. In 1934 the nation had been rattled by a series of violent strikes, many led by radicals. Taxi drivers rioted in Philadelphia and New York; communist-led farm workers struck in California's Salinas valley; textile workers in twenty states had walked out; violence broke out in Minneapolis when a Trotskyist-controlled truckers' union went on strike. Harry Bridges, a follower of the Communist Party, launched a general strike in San Francisco to support dock workers.

The Wagner Act protected workers' rights to collective bargaining, while creating a more stable environment for labor and management. Shortly after the passage of the act, John L. Lewis, who believed in organizing unskilled workers, led the United Mine Workers' Union into the newly formed Committee for Industrial Organization (CIO). Supported by representatives of various garment workers' unions, including Sidney Hillman, David Dubinsky, and Max Zaritsky, the Committee for Industrial Organization tried to unionize the unorganized. Expelled by the AFL in the summer of 1936, the committee formally changed its name into the Congress of Industrial Organizations as it moved to organize unskilled workers in auto, rubber, textile, steel, and other heavy industries.

Congress also passed laws regulating public utilities. The Holding Company Act (1935) broke up many utility holding companies, while the Federal Power Act (1935) created the Federal Power Commission to regulate interstate rates for electricity and natural gas. More important, the Rural Electrification Act (1935) encouraged loans to local farm cooperatives to build electric lines. This law alone transformed the American farm, especially in the South. In 1933 only 10 percent of southern farms had electricity, but by 1943 more than 80 percent of the region's farms did.

ROOSEVELT REELECTED, 1936   Roosevelt entered the 1936 presidential race in a strong position. Although the Depression continued, the federal government had moved aggressively to provide work for the unemployed, security for the elderly, legal rights for organized labor, and improvement in the lives of farmers. Republicans fumed that these measures were socialistic and antibusiness, and they nominated Alf Landon, the governor of Kansas, to head the Republican ticket. Landon lost. In fact, Roosevelt carried every state except Vermont and Maine. In winning, he forged a new Democratic coalition that added urban white ethnics in the industrial Northeast, organized labor, and blacks to the party's traditional white southern base. The election revealed sharp polarization along class lines; upper-income groups overwhelmingly voted Republican, while those with lower incomes, especially the poor on relief, voted Democratic.

ROOSEVELT BATTLES THE COURT AND ECONOMIC RECESSION   Victory gave Roosevelt a mandate to move forward with the New Deal, but he quickly made a key mistake: He tried to change the composition of the Supreme Court. The Supreme Court's overturning of the National Industrial Recovery and Agricultural Adjustment Acts, as well as unfavorable rulings against other New Deal measures, caused Roosevelt great consternation. The president feared that the Court might overturn the Wagner Act, which protected workers' rights to collective bargaining, and perhaps even the Social Security Act. Confident that he had the support of the people, the president proposed the Judicial Reorganization Bill (1937), which would have allowed him to appoint a new judge to the Supreme Court for each present justice over the age of seventy. Under this bill Roosevelt would have been able to add six handpicked justices to the nine-member Court, enough to ensure support for his programs.

Roosevelt's "court-packing" scheme caused a fury. Newspapers warned of dictatorship, protesters marched, citizens signed petitions, and Republicans described Roosevelt as another Mussolini (the Italian fascist leader). Many prominent Democratic congressional leaders opposed the measure, and Roosevelt withdrew it. Ironically, within two years four justices died or retired, which allowed Roosevelt to appoint replacements and gain control of the court.

Roosevelt's second mistake was attempting to balance the budget by cutting government spending when the economy remained weak and dependent on federal expenditures. Although in his first term Roosevelt had reluctantly accepted budget deficits as necessary, he remained essentially a fiscal conservative. Roosevelt believed, however, that the economy was recovering and that continued deficit spending might release runaway inflation. As a consequence, in late 1935 and early 1936 Roosevelt began systematically to slash the federal budget, including funds for the WPA. The WPA had come under attack by Republicans who denounced the program as creating makeshift, undemanding jobs for people who really did not want to enter the labor force. Moreover, the middle class had turned against the program. Humor of the day captured the general mood; even Roosevelt told WPA jokes. Telling Alf Landon about a WPA poison, the president said, "We don't guarantee it to kill rats, but it'll make them so damned lazy you can catch' em."

Just as the budget appeared to be nearing balance, economic disaster struck: The rapid decline in income and production in the nine months from September 1937 to June 1938 was without precedent in American economic history.

Roosevelt once again took the offensive. He rejected fiscal conservatives and accepted the advice of a group of young economists (followers of the English economist John Maynard Keynes) who urged the government to undertake a deliberate policy of deficit spending during economic slumps. Roosevelt proposed a $4.5-million package to finance public housing, highway construction, and agencies that had been targeted for cuts the previous year. A new farming bill, the Agricultural Adjustment Act (1937) was passed, which allowed the federal government to pay farmers not to plant crops, under the guise of preventing soil erosion. The government made it possible for tenant farmers to borrow money to buy and improve their own farms. The Fair Labor Standards Act (1938) set minimum wages and maximum hours for the nation's workers.

ROOSEVELT SWINGS TO THE LEFT   Swinging to the Left, Roosevelt openly targeted big business. On the advice of Supreme Court Justice Louis Brandeis and Harvard law professor Felix Frankfurter, Roosevelt revitalized the Antitrust Division of the Justice Department. He appointed a commission to investigate monopolies in the nation's major industries and imposed new federal regulations on the trucking and airline industries. The Fair Trade Act (1937) required retailers to sell products at prices set by manufacturers. Finally, the government imposed new corporate taxes and increased taxes on upper-income groups.

With the outbreak of war in Europe on September 1, 1939, when Germany invaded Poland, the president accelerated the American buildup, pressuring a reluctant Congress to increase defense appropriations. Later, it would become common wisdom that the war had brought America out of the Depression; of course, what people meant was that *spending* on the war effort had ended the economic slump. Roosevelt's spending program had begun before the war, but the war did allow him to accelerate the government's spending program.

THE CULTURAL FABRIC OF DEPRESSION

American writers and artists remained social critics but celebrated American culture and American themes. At the same time, social life changed for women and minorities during the Depression years. Women entered the workforce and politics in increasing numbers. The New Deal's record on behalf of Mexican Americans proved mixed. During the Depression years thousands of immigrants from Mexico entered the United States, where they often met hostility and violence. The New Deal promoted tribal control of Indian lands, but life on reservations remained deplorable for most Native Americans.

DEPRESSION CULTURE   The best-selling novel of the decade was Margaret Mitchell's *Gone With the Wind* (1936), a romantic epic about the Old South far removed from the Great Depression. Still, social criticism found expression in such works as James T. Farrell's trilogy, *Studs Lonigan* (1932–1935), which described Irish-American working-class life; John Dos Passos's trilogy *U.S.A.* (1930–1936), which satirized American capitalism; and Nathaniel West's *Miss Lonelyhearts* (1933) and *Cool Million* (1934), which told of alienation in modern America. Leftist writers such as Mike Gold, Jack Conroy, Howard Fast, and Josephine Herbst explored the theme of class struggle, but their works found a limited audience.

By the mid-1930s writers, while remaining critical of society, displayed a more affirmative mood. For example, John Steinbeck, in *The Grapes of Wrath* (1939), his moving story of an uprooted Dust Bowl family, has Ma Joad declare, "They ain't gonna wipe us out. Why, we're the people—we go on."

The American stage also reflected a shift from radical social criticism to a celebration of American culture. Clifford Odets's *Waiting for Lefty* (1935) ended with the audience shouting "Strike! Strike! Strike!" but Thornton Wilder's *Our Town* (1939) celebrated small-town life at the turn of the century.

Composers also celebrated American themes in their music. For example, George Gershwin turned to black life in Charleston for his enthusiastically received opera *Porgy and Bess* (1939). Although white and Jewish, Gershwin decreed that only African Americans could be in the cast; this was the first time an all-black cast appeared on Broadway.

SOCIAL LIFE IN THE DEPRESSION   The American family proved particularly resilient during the Depression, even though the divorce rate began to climb in the mid-1930s. The role of women also showed signs of continuing change. During the Depression women entered the workforce and politics in increasing numbers. Enrollments of female college students grew throughout the period, reaching one-quarter of those attending. The number of single women increased, and the birth rate declined. Abortion rates also appear to have increased during this period.

Women took an active part in the New Deal. The Women's Division in the Democratic Party, headed by Molly Dewson, lobbied for women to receive key positions within the New Deal. Secretary of Labor Frances Perkins gained high visibility as the first female cabinet officer, and other women attained leadership in the Federal Emergency Relief Administration and WPA. Grace Abbott, director of the Children's Bureau, played a key role in shaping social policy. The black educator Mary McLeod Bethune, a college president, served as Director of the Office of Negro Affairs for the National Youth Administration. In 1935 Bethune organized the National Council of Negro Women to coordinate the work of a hundred black groups representing 800,000 women.

During the 1930s women continued to be sport stars. The most notable sports figure was Babe Didrikson Zaharias, who won two Olympic gold medals in track in 1932 and later became a professional golfer. Figure skater Sonja Henie won fame as an Olympic champion and became a popular movie star. Pilot Amelia Earhart, the first woman to fly solo across the Atlantic, led other women to follow her pioneering example.

THE NEW DEAL BENEFITS MINORITIES   During these years the Supreme Court showed growing liberalism on the issue of civil rights for African Americans. In 1935 the Supreme Court questioned the absence of African Americans from juries in court cases involving black defendants and reexamined the "separate but equal" doctrine upheld in *Plessy v. Ferguson* (1896). In 1938 the Court, under Chief Justice Charles Hughes, ruled in *Missouri ex rei Gaines v. Canada* that a black law school applicant must be admitted to the University of Missouri given the absence of a state-supported black law school.

In contrast to the Supreme Court, the New Deal's record on black civil rights was mixed. In large part because of his need to win southern congressional support for his programs, FDR refused to back the new civil rights legislation or the antilynching bills brought before Congress in 1933 and 1939. Secretary of the Interior Harold Ickes desegregated the cafeteria at the Department of the Interior and insisted that the Public Works Administration reserve one-half of the housing projects for African Americans. Moreover, all PWA construction contractors were required to hire blacks.

Some African Americans grew increasingly militant. In 1934 the National Association for the Advancement of Colored People (NAACP) split when W. E. B. DuBois resigned as editor of the association's newspaper, *The Crisis,* over his belief that blacks should pursue a militant nationalist program. In many American cities strong nationalist tendencies became especially evident in "Buy Black" campaigns. At least thirty-five cities experienced pickets and boycotts organized by "Don't Buy Where You Can't Work" campaigns. Some of these campaigns lasted for years, often engaging large segments of the black community and eventually securing a significant number of jobs for blacks. In Chicago and New York, nationalist leaders such as Sufi Abdul, Ira Kemp, and Arthur Reid conducted fairly successful campaigns to pressure white merchants to hire more African Americans. This campaign often increased tensions between the black community and Jewish merchants, leading Jews to charge blacks with anti-Semitism.

Hispanics, although a less organized force than other ethnic groups in the 1930s, benefited from New Deal programs. The Mexican-American population increased rapidly during the Depression as many Mexicans migrated to the United States. This migration occurred mostly in the West but extended to Kansas, Illinois, and Michigan. As a result, many Hispanics enrolled in the Civilian Conservation Corps in Texas, New Mexico, and California. Mexican-American agricultural workers tried to organize labor unions in California, which often led to violent confrontations with local authorities and with well-financed owners' organizations such as the Associated Farmers of California and the California Fruit Growers Exchange (which markets Sunkist citrus).

Newly arrived Mexicans faced ethnic hostility in cities like Los Angeles, where white welfare officials offered to pay transportation costs to send them back to Mexico. In 1931 alone an estimated seventy thousand Mexicans left Los Angeles to return home. Nevertheless, the first signs of the growing political power of Hispanics came in 1934 with New Mexico's election of Dennis Chavez to the U.S. Senate.

The New Deal also helped Native Americans when the Commissioner of Indian Affairs, John Collier, persuaded Congress to enact the Indian Reorganization Act (1934). Although Collier's program sparked opposition in western states as well as from some Native American leaders, this law shifted American policy away from cultural assimilation of Native Americans and individual land ownership to tribal government and tribal control of Indian lands. Collier also encouraged the hiring of Native Americans by the Bureau of Indian Affairs.

Even with this progress, however, most Native Americans continued to live in abject poverty. Infant mortality remained the highest of any group in the nation, life span the shortest, and educational levels the lowest. Suicide and alcoholism continued to be prevalent on Indian reservations.

CONCLUSION

The New Deal marked a major turning point in American politics. FDR forged a new coalition, while the federal government assumed new responsibilities for maintaining economic prosperity and caring for the elderly and the poor. At the same time, the federal government extended its economic powers.

The New Deal accomplished much, even though its record on reform remained uneven. If its record on civil rights was poor, new hope had been offered to blacks, Hispanics, and Native Americans. Women had been given new roles in government. American democracy had been preserved, and capitalism had survived. The nation did not experience an economic revolution, as some liberals claimed it would, nor did it take the road to socialism, as some conservatives warned it might.

Recommended Readings

DOCUMENTS: Robert S. McElvaine, *Down and Out in the Great Depression: Letters from the "Forgotten Man"* (1983); Studs Terkel, *Hard Times: An Oral History of the Great Depression* (1970); Twelve Southerners, *I'll Take My Stand: The South and the Agrarian Tradition* (1937).

READINGS: (GENERAL) Frederick Lewis Allen, *Since Yesterday* (1939); Alan Brinkley, *Voices of Protest: Huey Long, Father Coughlin, and the Great Depression* (1982); James Burns, *Roosevelt: The Lion and the Fox* (1956); Lester Chandler, *America's Greatest Depression* (1970); Paul Conkin, *The New Deal* (1967); Frank Freidel, *Franklin D. Roosevelt* (4 vols., 1952–1976); John Kenneth Galbraith, *The Great Crash* (1960); John Garraty, *The Great Depression* (1937); Barry Karl, *The Uneasy State* (1983); David M. Kennedy, *Freedom from Fear* (1999); William E. Leuchtenburg, *The FDR Years* (1997) and *The Supreme Court Reborn* (1995); Richard Lowitt, *The New Deal in the West* (1984); Robert McElvaine, *The Great Depression* (1984); Arthur Schlesinger, Jr., *The Age of Roosevelt* (1957–1960). (SOCIETY AND CULTURE) Irving Bernstein, *Turbulent Years: A History of the American Worker, 1933–1941* (1969); Lizabeth Cohen, *Making of a New Deal* (1990); Sidney Fine, *Sit-Down: The General Motors Strike* (1969); Abraham Hoffman, *Unwanted Mexican-Americans in the Great Depression* (1974); Laurence Kelly, *The Assault on Assimilation: John Collier and the Origins of Indian Policy Reform* (1983); John Kirby, *Black Americans in the Roosevelt Era* (1980); Richard Pells, *Radical Visions, American Dreams* (1973); Harvard Sitkoff, *A New Deal for Blacks* (1970); Raymond Waiters, *Negroes and the Great Depression* (1970); Susan Ware, *Beyond Suffrage: Women and the New Deal* (1981). (COMMUNISM IN THE NEW DEAL) Harvey Klehr, *The Heyday of American Communism: The Depression Decade* (1984); Allen Weinstein and Alexander Vassiliev, *The Haunted Wood: Soviet Espionage in America: The Stalin Era* (1999).

26

❧

A Global Nation: World War II and the Origins of the Cold War

OVERVIEW   Roosevelt entered the White House at a time when the western democracies were confronted with the rise of ruthless dictators who threatened the world order.

Economic depression in the 1930s, however, only reinforced non-interventionist sentiments as Americans turned to domestic problems. Reflecting this general sentiment, Congress sought to isolate the United States from international events. The outbreak of World War II in Europe in 1939 led Roosevelt to tacitly support England and its democratic allies, against the wishes of a well-organized isolationist movement. Japan's attack on the U.S. Pacific fleet at Pearl Harbor, Hawaii, in 1941 ended the debate; America entered the war in full force.

In fighting a war for democracy, American society was transformed, as a new era of prosperity began, one characterized by the emergence of a military-industrial complex. Women and ethnic minorities were called to enter the armed services and the workforce at home. The war led to the emergence of the United States as an international power that would face a powerful foe, the Soviet Union.

THE UNITED STATES ISOLATES ITSELF FROM WORLD EVENTS

Preoccupied with the Depression at home, Roosevelt tried to avoid involvement in international affairs. He pledged not to intervene in Latin America and kept that pledge even after Mexico seized American oil holdings. He worked to grant Philippine independence and responded with only a protest when Japan invaded China. He also opened relations with the Soviet Union. Still, the nation—and Congress—remained deeply isolationist.

ROOSEVELT LIMITS INTERNATIONAL INVOLVEMENT   In the 1930s Franklin Roosevelt favored reducing the nation's involvement in international affairs. As a result, he tempered his earlier commitment to internationalism. Although he ran as the Democratic Party's vice-presidential candidate in 1920 on a platform that supported Wilson's League of Nations, once in the White House in 1933, Roosevelt retreated from Wilsonian internationalism.

Clear evidence of Roosevelt's backtracking came in 1933, when he undermined an international economic conference in London. During the conference he instructed Secretary of State Cordell Hull, who was representing the United States in London, to oppose any currency stabilization proposals, thereby derailing the conference. The message sent a clear signal to the European delegates: The United States would take care of its own problems; Europe should do the same.

Roosevelt did not retreat fully into isolationism, however. In November 1933 the United States recognized the Soviet Union. Although FDR's official recognition of the communist government caused great consternation among conservatives, Roosevelt believed that the Soviet Union should be brought back into the family of nations, that it offered new business opportunities for depressed American industry. Nevertheless, the Soviet Union failed to live up to its promise to grant religious freedom in Russia, nor did it curb its international communist propaganda.

Roosevelt moved to establish new relations with Latin America when he announced the Good Neighbor policy and formally pledged the United States to pursue a noninterventionist policy in Latin America. He sought to lower tariff barriers through reciprocal trade agreements, and he established the Export-Import Bank in 1934 to help stabilize the currencies of South American trading partners. (Roosevelt's willingness to stabilize Latin American currencies contrasted sharply with his refusal to participate in European monetary stabilization.) As a result, U.S. exports to Latin America rose more than 14 percent.

In pursuit of the Good Neighbor policy, Roosevelt abrogated the Platt Amendment, which had given the United States the right to intervene in the internal affairs of Cuba. In 1934 Roosevelt withdrew U.S. marines from Haiti, ending nineteen years of military occupation. This noninterventionist policy was extended in 1936 when the United States signed a nonintervention treaty with twenty-one Latin American nations at the Inter-American Conference in Buenos Aires, Argentina.

The nationalization of American oil holdings by the Mexican government in 1938 tested Roosevelt's noninterventionist resolve, but the United States remained steadfast, despite the urging of one congressman to annex the Gulf of California and the call by American Catholic bishops for reprisals against the anticlerical Mexican government. As one Mexican magazine lamented, "Poor Mexico! So far from God, and so close to the United States."

In Asia, Roosevelt moved to grant the Philippines their independence. In 1934 Congress enacted the Tydings-McDuffie Act, which established the Commonwealth of the Philippines and offered full independence after a transition period of ten years. American sugar interests supported Philippine independence in order to place tariff restrictions on Philippine sugar. In this way American policy in the Philippines reflected altruism carefully interwoven with economic self-interest.

Elsewhere in Asia, the United States confronted an increasingly aggressive Japan. In 1933, Japan seized disputed territory in northern China. The Japanese government ignored American protests against this clear violation of the Nine-Power Pact (1921) and the Kellogg-Briand Pact (1928). Isolationist sentiment in Congress, however, constrained Roosevelt from pursuing a stronger course of action.

ISOLATIONISTS CONTROL CONGRESS   During the Depression, Americans withdrew deeper into isolationism. Ironically, the rise of militarism in Europe and Japan seemed to offer the American public further proof of World War I's failure. Pacifism ran high on college campuses and in intellectual and religious circles. Within Congress, isolationists such as Senators Hiram Johnson (R-California), Gerald Nye (R-North Dakota), and William Borah (R-Idaho) dominated the Senate Committee on Foreign Relations. In 1934 Nye chaired a special Senate committee that alleged a link between America's entry into World War I and the self-interests of the banker J. P. Morgan and the munitions-making DuPont Corporation. Nye concluded that World War I had been fought "to save the skins of American bankers. . . ."

In 1935, when Roosevelt proposed that the United States join the World Court, thousands of hostile telegrams flooded into Washington. One senator declared, "To hell with Europe and the rest of those nations." Congress defeated Roosevelt's modest proposal.

Instead, isolationists passed the Neutrality Act (1935). The measure purported to be a compromise between Roosevelt and Congress over trade embargoes. Actually, the act favored Congress by limiting executive power. It prohibited American munitions sales to any nation at war. Roosevelt preferred a limited embargo applied only to aggressor nations;

nevertheless, he reluctantly signed the bill and quickly implemented it by placing an arms embargo on Italy when Mussolini invaded Ethiopia in October 1935. Roosevelt also called for a "moral embargo" restricting all trade with Italy, but this failed. Indeed, oil exports to Italy tripled within a matter of months.

Further troubles came in the summer of 1936 when civil war broke out in Spain. There, rightist General Francisco Franco led the army's revolt against the leftist democratic-Loyalist government. Aided by fascist Germany and Italy, by 1939 Franco's army had overwhelmed the Loyalists, supported by the Soviet Union. The three-year Spanish Civil War divided American public opinion. The hierarchy of the Roman Catholic Church supported Franco, while liberals and those close to the Communist Party backed the Loyalists. American leftists organized the Abraham Lincoln Brigade, which sent two thousand to three thousand volunteers to fight in Spain. The majority of Americans remained neutral, but when Roosevelt imposed a U.S. embargo on Spain, the effect favored Franco, who continued to be well supplied by his allies, especially Germany.

In 1937 Congress passed a stricter neutrality act that provided an embargo on sales of oil and other products to nations at war, extended neutrality laws to cover civil wars, and banned American loans to warring nations. The act also imposed a "cash-and-carry" clause that forced belligerents who did buy American war goods to pay for them in cash and transport their purchases on their own vessels. Shortly afterward, in July 1937, Japan invaded China. Outraged by the invasion, Roosevelt favored imposing a "quarantine" on aggressor nations through trade sanctions on all goods, but the isolationists forced him to retreat. As a consequence, Japan's invasion went unchecked.

Indeed, isolationists sought stronger measures to keep the United States out of war. In late December 1937, Indiana Representative Louis Ludlow introduced a resolution calling for a constitutional amendment that would require a national referendum before war could be declared. Only Roosevelt's intervention prevented Congress from approving the measure. That same month, Japanese war planes attacked an American patrol boat, the USS Panay, and three Standard Oil tankers along the Yangtze River in China. A crisis was averted when the Japanese government agreed to pay an indemnity for the attack.

Despite such provocation, antiwar sentiment continued to run high in Congress. Isolationists refused to increase defense appropriations. From 1933 to 1937, the armed forces received on average only $180 million annually. Experts rated the American army equal to Poland's. Poverty-stricken units were forced to drill with wooden rifles.

WORLD WAR ERUPTS IN EUROPE, 1939

Before the outbreak of World War II, French and British leaders sought to appease Hitler by giving in to his demands for the restoration of German territory lost during the First World War. He soon revealed his brutality by seizing all of Czechoslovakia, and, on September 1, 1939, invading Poland. In the spring of 1940, Hitler swiftly conquered most of western Europe, leaving only England to oppose him.

After winning election to an unprecedented third term, Roosevelt increased aid to England. Meanwhile, American-Japanese relations deteriorated. On December 7, 1941, Japan bombed America's Pacific fleet at Pearl Harbor, Hawaii. The United States entered the Second World War on the side of the Allies.

BRITAIN AND FRANCE SEEK TO APPEASE HITLER, 1938–1939   In the immediate aftermath of World War I, antiwar sentiment ran high in Europe too. As a result, European leaders sought to avoid war through a policy of appeasement that recognized Adolf Hitler's claims to formerly German territory lost in the Versailles peace treaty that ended World War I. British Prime Minister Neville Chamberlain and French Premier Édouard Daladier became Europe's most eloquent and avid spokesmen for appeasement. Although Chamberlain and Daladier sought peace, Hitler saw weakness.

Appeasement had tragic results when Chamberlain and Daladier met with Hitler in Munich in September 1938 amid a crisis caused by Germany's demand to annex the Sudeten region of Czechoslovakia. Hitler's troops had already rolled into Austria earlier in 1938. Chamberlain fervently believed that appeasement might contain Hitler's appetite for expansion. He therefore accepted Hitler's "right" to the Sudetenland.

Chamberlain's hopes were short-lived. That November, Hitler launched a vicious attack against Germany's Jews that included burning and looting synagogues and shops. This campaign of terror led to an exodus of Jewish and non-Jewish intellectuals, scientists, and artists. Still, Congress refused to open the immigration quota system to allow more Jewish refugees into the United States. As a result of this policy, thousands of Jews remained in Germany. Most were destined to die in wartime Nazi extermination camps.

Less than six months after the Munich Conference, Hitler launched a full-scale invasion to annex the remainder of Czechoslovakia. Nevertheless, Chamberlain continued to espouse appeasement, even as Mussolini invaded Albania, Franco won in Spain, and Japan proclaimed its intention to create a Greater East Asia Co-Prosperity Sphere in China and Manchuria.

On August 23, 1939, the Soviet Union and Germany—previously bitter enemies—shocked the world by entering into a defense pact. The pact included a secret agreement to divide Poland between them. Yet many European leaders continued to believe that war could be prevented.

Hitler's invasion of Poland on September 1, 1939, shattered this illusion. Two days after the invasion, England declared war on Germany; six hours later the French government reluctantly followed. The Poles valiantly resisted, but their fate was sealed when the Soviet Union's Red army attacked from the east. Warsaw fell in less than a month.

ROOSEVELT HELPS ENGLAND BUT AVOIDS WAR, 1940   After Poland's defeat, a six-month lull in the war occurred, which the press quickly called the "Phony War." The Soviet Union's treacherous attack on Finland on November 30, 1939, still did not convince everyone that war had come to Europe. Following this winter of illusion, Hitler quickly conquered most of western Europe, beginning with his invasion of Norway and Denmark in early April 1940. The next month, Hitler's tanks surprised French, Belgian, and British troops when they rolled through the hilly and wooded Ardennes, an area the Allied High Command had considered impassable by tanks. Caught from behind, the British army barely escaped by sea from Dunkirk, France. A week later, on June 22, 1940, the remaining French forces surrendered. Britain now stood alone against Nazi Germany.

Germany's rapid conquest of most of western Europe swung American public opinion in favor of the Allies, but isolationist sentiment remained strong. As a consequence, Roosevelt pursued a cautious policy of aiding England while promising to keep America out of the war. Three weeks after the invasion of Poland, FDR asked a special session of Congress to replace the arms embargo with a cash-and-carry policy to provide munitions and raw materials to England. Roosevelt's request set off a storm of criticism. Thousands of telegrams flooded into Congress pleading to "keep America out of the blood business." After six weeks of bitter debate, Congress finally agreed to allow England to buy munitions with cash and to transport it on British ships.

With England tottering at the brink of defeat, Roosevelt now called for an additional $1 billion for a massive defense program, including the production of fifty thousand airplanes a year. (The urgency of the program was all too apparent: The army had only 350 serviceable infantry tanks, 2,806 mostly outmoded aircraft, and no antiaircraft ammunition). Under fierce air attack, England pleaded for American aid. Chamberlain had been replaced as prime minister by Winston Churchill, who warned Roosevelt that the situation was critical. On September 2, 1940, Roosevelt

A radio announcer points to his own number in America's first peacetime draft lottery in 1940. The unlucky few were supposed to serve for one year but were not discharged until 1945. By then, sixteen million men and women had been in uniform in World War II. (Library of Congress)

offered Britain fifty rusting World War I navy destroyers in exchange for a ninety-nine-year lease on naval and air bases in Newfoundland and the Caribbean. In October, Congress enacted the first peacetime conscription law in American history.

ISOLATIONISTS OPPOSE ROOSEVELT   These military measures outraged noninterventionists, who found support among Irish and German ethnic groups, college students, and elements in the Republican Party. Opponents of American support of intervention in the European war called themselves noninterventionists, not isolationists. The noninternventionists claimed they were not isolationists, because they believed that, if the United States were attacked, the nation should defend itself. The movement included pacifists, anticommunists, socialists, communists (until the Soviet Union was attacked in 1941), Republican conservatives, and Republican Progressives. Many called for building a "Fortress America" through a strong air force and navy. Many worried that American intervention would enable the Soviet Union to become the major power in Europe following a defeat of Germany.

In the summer of 1940, isolationists organized the America First Committee to oppose Roosevelt's defense program. Led by a group of midwestern businessmen including Robert Wood of Sears, Roebuck, the meat packer Jay Hormel, and Robert McCormick, publisher of the *Chicago Tribune*, the America First Committee found its most eloquent spokesman in the aviator hero Charles Lindbergh. Lindbergh's wife, Anne Morrow Lindbergh, had revealed pro-fascist sympathies in her widely read book, *The Wave of the Future* (1939). Charles Lindbergh drew thousands to America First rallies throughout the nation, filling California's Hollywood Bowl and stadiums throughout the Midwest. Lindbergh's accusations that America was being led into war by a Jewish conspiracy caused a backlash in mainstream America, but isolationist passions continued to find expression in Congress, especially as the election of 1940 approached.

ROOSEVELT WINS, LENDS AID TO ENGLAND, 1940   To ensure Republican support for his program and to counter the isolationists, Roosevelt appointed two Republicans to his cabinet, Henry Stimson as secretary of war and Frank Knox as secretary of the navy. Roosevelt's appointments stole thunder from the Republicans on the eve of their national convention. Believing that FDR would conform to the time-honored tradition of serving not more than two terms, the Republicans nominated former Democrat and anti-New Dealer Wendell Willkie to head their presidential ticket. In a bitter campaign, Roosevelt won, but with only 55 percent of the vote.

After the election Roosevelt confidently pursued a forthright policy of aiding the Allied cause. In December 1940 Churchill reported to Roosevelt that Britain faced its darkest hour. Financially ruined, Britain could no longer afford to purchase war materials. Roosevelt acted swiftly. In the spring of 1941, Roosevelt requested Congress to establish a lend-lease program to provide $7 billion for the production and export of military supplies. The Lend-Lease Act (1941) empowered the president to lend Britain the money to lease military arms. When the bill was passed, Roosevelt announced that the United States was determined to become the "arsenal of democracy."

JAPAN ATTACKS PEARL HARBOR, 1941   In late 1940, Roosevelt increasingly shifted his attention to Japanese imperialism in Asia. In September 1940, Japan entered into the Tripartite Pact with Germany and Italy to create the Axis alliance.

The Axis's opportunity for expansion came in June 1941 with Germany's invasion of the Soviet Union. Expecting England's imminent surrender, Hitler broke Germany's nonaggression pact with the Soviet leader Stalin and launched a surprise attack on the Soviet Union on June 22, 1941.

Japan took advantage of Allied problems in Europe by occupying the southern portion of French Indochina. Japan's wanton attack on Indochina outraged Roosevelt, who placed an embargo on the export of aviation oil and scrap metal to Japan. As U.S.-Japanese relations deteriorated, a faction within the Japanese government advocated avoiding war through negotiation.

American and Japanese negotiators, however, found little common ground. For example, Japan offered to refrain from armed aggression in Southeast Asia if the United States restored trade and recognized its position in China. The United States, on the other hand, demanded that Japan withdraw from China and Indochina. By September 1941 negotiations appeared stalemated. Japanese militarists began to draft secret war plans, and in October an extremist faction headed by Admiral Hideki Tojo took over the government. Final negotiations were under way in Washington when Japan launched a surprise attack on the Pacific fleet stationed at Pearl Harbor, Hawaii, on December 7, 1941. Within hours Japanese aviators had disabled or sunk eight battleships, three cruisers, and three destroyers. Simultaneously, Japan attacked the Philippines, Hong Kong, Thailand, Malaya, and Wake and Midway Islands.

The next day—December 8, 1941—President Roosevelt appeared before Congress. "Yesterday, December 7, 1941—a date which will live in infamy—the United States of America was suddenly and deliberately attacked by naval and air forces of the empire of Japan," he declared. "We will gain the inevitable triumph, so help us God." After Congress declared war on Japan, Italy and Germany brought the Axis pact into play by declaring war on the United States. The United States had entered the Second World War.

THE WAR TRANSFORMS THE HOME FRONT

Once the United States entered the war, it went all out to win. Roosevelt created numerous federal agencies to manage the war effort. As production boomed, so did the economy. Despite their resentment of rationing, Americans widely supported the war effort. The government sought to protect the civil liberties of dissenters, but its record was marred by the relocation of Japanese Americans into special camps.

The war created labor shortages and hence new employment opportunities for African Americans and women. Blacks moved north to take jobs but found discrimination and racial hostility. Native Americans and Mexican Americans joined the war effort.

AMERICANS MOBILIZE FOR WAR   The global nature of the war entailed the total mobilization of the United States as a military and industrial power. More than 16 million men and women served in the armed services during the war: 11.2 million in the army, 4.1 million in the navy and the coast guard, 670,000 in the marines, and 216,000 women in the auxiliary services. Of those 16 million who served in the armed services, 291,000 died in battle—less than half the number killed in the Civil War.

The war wakened an industrial giant that had slept through the Great Depression. American production skyrocketed. In 1944 the United States produced more munitions than all of the Axis nations combined. America supplied 45 percent of the total arms used by all nations during the war.

ROOSEVELT ORGANIZES WARTIME GOVERNMENT   Roosevelt pursued the war in much the same way he had confronted the Depression. He created myriad agencies (more than forty-five), which often competed with one another for resources and power. Before the outbreak of war, he created the War Resources Board (WRB) and the Office of Production Management (OPM). Without extensive powers to mobilize war production, the agencies faced massive shortages of steel, copper, rubber, and other vital raw materials. Finally, in January 1942 Roosevelt established the War Production Board (WPB), headed by the Sears, Roebuck marketing executive Donald Nelson.

The government's war effort proved to be a remarkable success. Although war profiteering occurred (which led to congressional investigation by a special Senate committee chaired by Missouri Senator Harry S. Truman) war production boomed. By 1944 unemployment had fallen to 1.2 percent. In many cities skid rows vanished overnight.

With war production in full swing by 1943, there was a shortage of labor. Consequently, pay rates soared, as average weekly wages increased from $24.96 in 1940 to $45.70 in 1944. Workers changed jobs frequently. Strikes were kept to a minimum, however, through the cooperation of organized labor. Unions expanded from ten million to nearly fifteen million members, primarily among industrial unions organized by the Congress of Industrial Organizations (CIO). The demand for labor drew women, blacks, and older workers into the workforce.

AMERICAN CONSUMERS COPE WITH RATIONING   American industrial capability was so vast that, even in wartime, half its production was consumer goods. Unlike their counterparts in England and Russia, American civilians experienced little rationing. In April 1941, Roosevelt established the Office of Price Administration (OPA) to set prices and wages. By imposing wage and price controls, wartime inflation was kept at a minimum, well below the inflation rate of the First World War. Controls also created lucrative black markets.

Nevertheless, even limited rationing created an undercurrent of resentment in the American electorate. Because there was a shortage of the imported rubber used to make tires, the government sought to conserve tires by imposing gasoline rationing, setting a national speed limit of twenty-five miles per hour, and setting up roadblocks to stop Sunday driving. A shortage of leather forced the government to limit consumers to three pairs of leather shoes a year. War also forced the rationing of nylon hosiery, sugar, coffee, and meat.

The planting of twenty million "Victory Gardens" by homeowners, city officials, and businesses produced nearly 40 percent of all vegetables grown in the country and created an excess of green vegetables for the American consumer. Also, the emergence of a "black market," on which goods could be bought at higher prices without ration cards, made most goods available. Yet it also encouraged crime. Hijackings of trucks carrying liquor, nylon stockings, and shoes became common, and in the West cattle rustling revived.

Despite their resentment of limited rationing, Americans generally rallied to the war effort and purchased more than $156 billion in war bonds, accounting for nearly half of the $389 billion spent by the government during the war. The other half of the war's cost was paid from significantly higher taxes. Many more people had to pay income tax, and the top bracket was raised to 98 percent. To expedite tax collection, the government instituted a "pay-as-you-go" taxation scheme, withholding income tax from paychecks. Before the war, income taxes had been due in one annual, lump-sum payment.

ROOSEVELT LEAVES A MIXED RECORD ON CIVIL LIBERTIES   The war saw the American nation unified as never before. In the war against fascism, few Americans dissented. Fewer than one-fifth of one percent of the thirty-four million who registered for the draft declared themselves conscientious objectors who opposed war on religious grounds. These were mostly members of Quaker, Mennonite, and Brethren sects. Although some Jehovah's Witnesses went to jail for refusing involvement in the war, most conscientious objectors were treated fairly.

The Office of War Information, headed by newsman Elmer Davis, promoted American patriotism through radio broadcasts, pamphlets, and posters. Unlike the Creel Committee, the government information agency of the First World War, the Office of War Information did not suppress dissent or target "un-American" antiwar opponents.

Furthermore, the Supreme Court showed a strong determination to uphold the right of free speech. Court decisions upheld the right to criticize the draft and the war effort. When the government tried to prosecute twenty-five members of the fascist German-American Bund (a pro-German political organization), the Court threw out the case.

This fine civil liberties record, however, was severely tarnished by the federal government's actions against people of Japanese ancestry in California, Oregon, and Washington. In flagrant disregard of civil liberties, the government ordered the evacuation without trial of Japanese Americans, citizens and aliens alike, to "relocation" camps in the interior of the nation. The Japanese evacuation was undertaken under executive orders signed by Roosevelt in early 1942. More than 112,000 Japanese Americans were forced, under great emotional and economic stress, to leave their homes and farms and move into military-run camps surrounded by barbed wire. The Supreme Court upheld this relocation policy in the *Hirabayashi* case (1943) and the *Korematsu* and *Endo* cases (1944). In his dissent to the *Korematsu* case, however, Justice Frank Murphy argued that this interpretation pushed constitutional power to the "ugly abyss of racism."

AFRICAN AMERICANS EXPERIENCE THE WAR AT HOME   The employment of blacks and women created new demands for equality and fair treatment in the workplace, portending the transformation of postwar life and society.

New economic opportunities encouraged many African Americans to move north. Once there, however, they found employers often reluctant to hire them. Confronted by seemingly impenetrable racial barriers, black leaders demanded federal intervention to ensure that the war against fascism meant democratic participation for all races at home. In the summer of 1941, the black socialist and labor leader A. Philip Randolph called for a march on Washington to pressure FDR to take action. Under mounting political pressure, Roosevelt issued an executive order establishing the Fair Employment Practices Committee, with powers to investigate complaints of employment discrimination. By 1942 African Americans were entering the northern urban workforce in large numbers.

Black migration transformed northern cities. The massive influx northward created a volatile situation in many cities. For example, more than half a million people flooded into Detroit between 1940 and 1943. Here, sixty thousand African Americans found themselves living in some of the worst housing in the nation. Local white ethnic groups, mainly Poles and Irish, bitterly resented the new arrivals. Tensions reached a boiling point when rumors spread, among both blacks and whites, of incidents of rape and assault. On June 23, 1943, black and white teenagers clashed at a Detroit recreation park. Blacks then attacked unsuspecting white workers returning from the night shift, and bands of whites poured into the street to randomly attack blacks. The next day, full-scale rioting erupted as whites rampaged through the black community. With violence spreading, Governor Frank Murphy called out six thousand national guardsmen to quell the riot. The episode left twenty-five blacks and nine whites dead.

That August a riot in Harlem left six blacks dead and three hundred people injured. To restore order, the New York police deputized fifteen thousand blacks, who quickly contained the riot. These incidents shocked the nation and became ready propaganda for the Nazis, who broadcast reports of the riots to Allied troops.

Nevertheless, the war brought new opportunities to many black Americans. More than 800,000 African Americans served in the armed forces during the war. The fight for democracy abroad encouraged African Americans to seek civil rights at home. In 1942 militant black leaders formed the Congress of Racial Equality (CORE), which sponsored nonviolent protest to achieve civil rights. In 1943 CORE staged a series of sit-ins in a number of major cities to integrate restaurants and movie theaters. At the same time, the National Association for the Advancement of Colored People (NAACP) quadrupled its membership. Young lawyers like Thurgood Marshall developed legal strategy to challenge the "separate but equal" doctrine that had been used to justify segregation and had shaped racial policy since the end of the nineteenth century.

HISPANICS AND NATIVE AMERICANS AT WAR   The war brought changes to other ethnic minorities as well. Native Americans actively supported the war effort. At the outbreak of war, the Pueblo Indians retreated to their ancient shrine, where they prayed for victory. The Indians of the Six Nations of the Iroquois Confederacy declared war on the Axis. More than 29,000 Native Americans joined the armed services. A contingent of Navajo fighting in the Pacific formed a special communications unit, the Code Talkers, who used their native language to communicate on the battlefront. More than 100,000 Native Americans migrated to cities to take war jobs.

Hispanics displayed deep patriotic feelings by volunteering in the armed forces in disproportionate numbers. Mexican Americans gained fame fighting in the 200th and 515th Coast Artillery in the campaign for the Philippines. During the war, seventeen Mexican Americans won Congressional Medals of Honor.

Mobilization also opened new opportunities for Hispanics at home. Discrimination against Mexican Americans in the copper mines of Arizona and in shipyards and oil refineries on the Pacific Coast led FDR to appoint Carlos Castaneda, a prominent political leader, as assistant to the chairman of the Fair Employment Practices Committee. The Office of Inter-American Affairs created a Spanish-speaking division to confront problems of discrimination against Hispanics. This office played a key role in reducing segregation in public schools in Texas and California.

The labor shortage during the war prompted the federal government to renew the importing of Mexican farm labor to the United States through the *bracero* (worker) program. These guest workers alleviated the shortage of agricultural workers during the war. The war, however, worsened ethnic tensions, especially in large western cities. In Los Angeles some young Mexican Americans formed *pachuco* (a slang term meaning "newcomers") gangs that got into fights with soldiers and sailors on leave. Noted for their "zoot suits"—distinctive suits with large shoulder pads, trousers that ballooned at the knee and were pegged at the ankle, worn with broad-brimmed felt hats—*pachuco* gangs often roamed the streets, engaging in vandalism and assault. Following a series of attacks on servicemen, a group of angry sailors stationed at the Chavez Ravine Naval Base entered East Los Angeles and attacked the gangs. The attack sparked a two-day riot that involved one thousand youths before order was restored. During the spring of 1943, smaller disturbances erupted in San Diego, Long Beach, Chicago, Detroit, and Philadelphia.

WOMEN CHALLENGE TRADITION   At the war's outset, many employers hesitated to hire women. Labor shortages and efforts by the Women's Bureau of the Department of Labor soon overcame this initial resistance. From 1940 to 1945, the number of women in the workforce spiraled upward from 12 million to 18.6 million, making women workers a third of the workforce. Women performed every job, from welding to operating heavy equipment. As a result, many unions promoted women to leadership positions, called for federal child care centers, and demanded "equal pay for equal work."

The federal government responded positively to these demands. The War Production Board and the War Manpower Commission accepted an equal-pay policy. Under the Lanham Act (1940) the federal government established federally funded day care centers for children of working mothers.

Because many women took jobs formerly held by men, they presented an implicit challenge to traditional notions about women. At the same time, disruptions of family life caused by the war reinforced beliefs that women should subordinate personal ambition for the benefit of the family. Nonetheless, the war marked a turning point, making it acceptable

Women provided much of the factory labor that enabled the United States to win World War II. Building and maintaining an airplane engine was no longer a man's job. After the war, many women remained in the workforce. (Library of Congress)

for women to combine their role in the home with paid employment. Three-fourths of working women were married. After the war, many women quit their jobs, but by 1950 29 percent of women worked outside the home, a higher number than a decade earlier.

The war also encouraged greater involvement of women in government. The number of women entering the civil service rose from 200,000 in 1939 to one million in 1944, 38 percent of all federal office workers. Women's groups, such as the American Association of University Women and the National Federation of Business and Professional Women's Clubs, lobbied for legislation to prevent discrimination. State campaigns were launched to protect women from job discrimination, to make women eligible for jury duty, and to eliminate legal restrictions on married women. Although women were divided on the issue of an equal rights amendment to the Constitution, eleven states endorsed such an amendment.

Women also entered political office in greater numbers. By 1945, 228 women had been elected to state legislatures, up from 144 the previous year.

Nevertheless, poor housing, inadequate child care services, long working hours, and single-parent households strained the American family. Juvenile delinquency increased, leading many experts to decry the breakdown of the American family. Everywhere, school truancy and juvenile arrests for loitering and petty crimes appeared on the rise. Sexual promiscuity and venereal disease rose dramatically. Teenage girls, called "Victory girls" by the press, provided "companionship" to lonely servicemen.

THE UNITED STATES FIGHTS IN EUROPE AND THE PACIFIC

The United States fought on five fronts: a vicious war in the Pacific, a fierce naval war in the North Atlantic, an involved campaign against the Germans in North Africa, an air war over Europe, and a major military operation in western and central Europe.

The war occurred in three phases from 1942 through 1945. The first phase, in 1942, was primarily defensive in the Pacific and in Europe. The second phase, during 1943, turned the Allied tide with a costly island campaign in the Pacific, massive bombing raids on German industry, and a Middle East campaign. The last phase brought victory in Europe, beginning with the Allied landing in France on June 6, 1944, and the final defeat of Japan.

THE UNITED STATES ON THE DEFENSIVE, 1942   Following the attack on Pearl Harbor, the Japanese swept through the Pacific. In March 1942, the Japanese navy inflicted heavy losses on an Allied fleet in the Battle of the Java Sea. Two months later, in May 1942, the Japanese army finally broke the valiant resistance of American troops under Generals Douglas MacArthur and Jonathan B. Wainwright in a well-executed campaign in the Philippines. The Japanese onslaught was stopped only by American victories in the battles of the Coral Sea and Midway. The loss of four Japanese aircraft carriers at Midway Island, which the U.S. located by breaking Japanese radio codes, ended the Japanese army's control of the air and spelled Japan's ultimate doom.

In the Atlantic, German submarines, called U-boats, sank Allied ships seemingly at will throughout 1942. The Allies lost an average of three boats a day, which kept vital supplies from reaching Europe. Ships were sunk faster than shipyards could replace them. Only the introduction of newly developed British sonar equipment, which could detect lurking

Map 26.1   World War II in Europe

German submarines, and the use of elaborate convoys of hundreds of Allied vessels restored Allied shipping in early 1943. As the year drew to a close, the United States had cut its losses to less than 1 percent of its traffic in the Atlantic.

The German Afrika Korps under General Erwin Rommel (known as the "Desert Fox") swept through North Africa and threatened to seize the Suez Canal, which was crucial to Allied shipping and oil supplies. An extended American, British, and Free French offensive finally forced Rommel's withdrawal from North Africa in the spring of 1943.

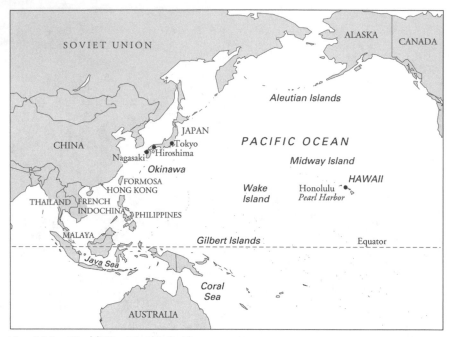

Map 26.2   World War II in the Pacific

THE ALLIES TURN THE TIDE, 1943   In 1943 the Allies took the offensive. American industrial production, now in full swing, provided the ships, planes, tanks, trucks, and munitions that overwhelmed both Japan and Germany. Beginning in 1943, British and American air forces initiated massive bombing raids on German industrial centers. Employing from 1,000 to 1,500 bombers, these raids rained destruction on Germany.

Despite Allied efforts, German production increased throughout 1942. In January 1943, the Allied command ordered intensified raids on Germany, to undermine the "morale of the German people." The destruction wrought by Allied air attacks was horrendous. In that year, 200,000 tons of bombs destroyed city after German city.

THE ALLIES ENTER THE FINAL PHASE OF WAR, 1944   By 1944 the defeat of Germany and Japan was certain; the only question was when. On the eastern front, the Soviet army courageously withstood the German siege of Stalingrad (now called Volgograd) from September 1942 to February 1943. Thousands died and the city was devastated before the German forces finally withdrew. The Red army then began a long offensive that drove the Germans back. By 1944 the Russian army moved at will, limited only by its own supply lines. The Russians launched their final offensive against the Germans in June 1944 to coincide with the British-American landings in Normandy, France. By late July the Russian army had driven the Germans back to Warsaw, Poland. There the Russians halted their advance, allowing the Germans to crush a rebellion by the Polish resistance. By autumn 1944 the Russians were once again on the march.

On June 6, 1944—D-Day—American and British forces under the Supreme Allied Commander Dwight D. Eisenhower launched their long-awaited campaign on the European mainland with massive landings of troops on the beaches of Normandy, France. More than two million troops stormed Hitler's "Atlantic Wall," including a force of fifty-eight divisions in the west of France, among them ten panzer tank divisions. Within weeks the American army had broken through German lines and sped to liberate Paris on August 25, 1944.

In the spring of 1945, the Russian and American armies met inside Germany. As the American army under General George Patton approached Berlin, Eisenhower ordered it to withdraw to Prague, Czechoslovakia, to allow the Soviets to enter Berlin first, an agreement reached by FDR, Churchill, and Stalin. On April 30, as the desperate German army resisted the entering Russian army street by street, Hitler and his recent bride, Eva Braun, committed suicide. On May 8, 1945, the war in Europe officially ended with Germany's unconditional surrender.

The liberation of Germany revealed the stark horror of the Nazi regime and its program to exterminate the Jews. Reports of death camps had first arrived in Washington in late 1942, but nothing could have prepared American soldiers for what they discovered when they entered these camps. In mid-April 1945, Eisenhower visited an extermination camp. Accompanied by top staff officers, Eisenhower moved in silent horror through the barracks where naked and emaciated bodies of Jewish inmates were piled. Following the tour, Eisenhower told his officers, "I want every American unit not actually in the front lines to see this place. . . . Now, at least, he will know what he is fighting against."

As other camps were liberated by Allied troops, the full extent of the extermination program became obvious. Of the 8 million Jews living in German-occupied territory, only 2.3 million escaped. Six million non-Jews, including Polish Catholics, gypsies, communists, homosexuals, or anyone else the Nazis disliked, also died in the camps.

PLANNING THE POSTWAR WORLD

Roosevelt, Churchill, and Stalin coordinated strategy for ending the war and shaped the postwar order. Roosevelt held fast to his overriding priority: to create a new international organization, the United Nations. To secure Roosevelt's assent to Soviet influence in eastern Europe, Stalin withheld his acceptance of the United Nations until late in the war. These wartime compromises became the basis of the cold war, which would dominate world affairs for the next forty-five years. Roosevelt died before both the end of the war and the founding of the United Nations.

DESIGNING A GREAT ALLIANCE   Roosevelt began to prepare for the postwar world even before the United States entered the war. In August 1941, Roosevelt and Churchill met off the coast of Newfoundland. The meeting concluded with a joint declaration known as the Atlantic Charter, which promised a world without war "after the final destruction of the Nazi tyranny." The Atlantic Charter envisioned a new postwar international organization to replace the League of Nations and affirmed democracy's adherence to the Four Freedoms: freedom from want, freedom from fear, freedom of speech, and freedom of religion.

Soon after the attack on Pearl Harbor, Roosevelt announced the formation of the United Nations alliance, composed of nations opposed to the Axis powers. These nations pledged themselves through the Declaration of the United Nations, issued on January 1, 1942, to support the principles of the Atlantic Charter (1941) and not to conclude a separate peace with the Axis powers. (Even so, rumors circulated throughout the war that the Soviet Union was prepared to sign a separate peace with Hitler.)

Both Roosevelt and Churchill shared a profound faith in the British–American democratic tradition. During the war this sense of cooperation had led the United States and Britain to establish the Combined Chiefs of Staff, composed of ranking military commanders of each nation. This body shaped military strategy, conducted joint operations, and allocated supplies and resources. Although inevitable tensions arose between rival commanders, the Combined Chiefs of Staff functioned remarkably well.

Roosevelt believed that China, under military dictator Chiang Kai-shek, should be treated as an equal power, but Chiang often seemed more interested in resuming the civil war against the communists than in engaging the Japanese. General Joseph W. Stilwell reported widespread corruption in Chiang's army, including sales of American supplies to the Japanese. Nevertheless, FDR authorized more than $4 billion in lend-lease aid and an additional $100 million in loans to China.

COMPROMISING WITH STALIN   The most difficult member of the alliance was the Soviet Union. The Soviet regime continued to be tightly controlled by its ruthless dictator, Josef Stalin. Stalin remained fiercely nationalistic and suspicious of the western democracies. Nevertheless, in order to gain American supplies through the lend-lease program, Stalin agreed to mute communist propaganda against the West. As a consequence, the United States sent more than $11 billion in supplies to help the Soviet Union in its war against Hitler.

Relationships became severely strained in 1942, however, when Stalin insisted that a western front be opened in France. At Churchill's urging, however, Roosevelt postponed an Allied landing in France and instead launched an invasion of North Africa in January 1942. Shortly afterward, British, American, and Free French leaders met in Casablanca, Morocco, to discuss the next phase of the military campaign. Here, Churchill, Roosevelt, and France's Charles DeGaulle decided to invade Europe through Italy. This decision precluded a second major front against Germany. To assuage the angry Stalin, Roosevelt and Churchill agreed to meet with Stalin in Teheran, Iran, in late November 1943.

The Teheran meeting marked the height of Allied cooperation. Churchill, Roosevelt, and Stalin reached an accord on a number of key points. The United States and Britain accepted a date for an invasion of France. The Allies also agreed to the principle that Germany would never again be a military power. At Stalin's urging, Roosevelt agreed to send military aid to the communist underground leader Tito in Yugoslavia. Churchill and Roosevelt also accepted Stalin's demand that Poland's western and eastern borders be radically shifted to the west. Questions concerning democratic elections in Poland divided the Allies, however. In particular, Churchill sought recognition of the London-based Polish government in exile, while Stalin wanted recognition for his communist-controlled Polish government. As a bargaining chip, Stalin refused to make a commitment to the new international organization that Roosevelt and Churchill wanted.

THE BIG THREE BARGAIN AT YALTA In February 1945, shortly after his election to a fourth term, Roosevelt flew to Yalta, a city in the Russian Crimea, where he met once again with Churchill and Stalin. The looming defeat of Germany set the context for the final meeting of the Big Three. Roosevelt came to Yalta with one primary goal, the creation of a new international organization, the United Nations. Roosevelt seemed willing to subordinate all other issues to achieving Stalin's acceptance for a postwar United Nations.

The Big Three turned first to the German question. Stalin proposed dividing Germany into three separate states. He stated bluntly that Germany's heavy industry should be destroyed and that Germany should pay a huge reparation of $20 billion (half to the Soviet Union). The final resolution of reparations and other questions concerning postwar Germany, however, were left to a later joint commission.

Before Yalta, British, American, and Soviet representatives had agreed on a basic structure for the new United Nations but could not agree on voting procedures. Soviets wanted veto power over the Security Council (the executive committee of the organization) and demanded that the sixteen Soviet republics each be given a separate vote in the organization's general body, the General Assembly. At Yalta, Roosevelt now conceded the principle that each permanent member of the Security Council hold veto power. In return, Stalin dropped his demand for General Assembly representation from sixteen seats to three seats (Ukraine, White Russia, and the Soviet Union). With Stalin's acceptance of the United Nations, Roosevelt felt he had achieved a major diplomatic victory.

Next came the issue of a postwar government in Poland. Roosevelt and Churchill accepted Stalin's claim to land in eastern Poland. There was little choice: Stalin's army had been there since 1939. In return, Stalin agreed to free Polish elections, although the mechanics of these elections were never decided. One aide warned Roosevelt that the Polish agreement was "so elastic that the Russians can stretch it all the way from Yalta to Washington without technically breaking it."

Finally, Stalin agreed to declare war on Japan "in two or three months after Germany surrendered." (The Soviet Union and Japan had agreed tacitly not to fight, so that each could avoid fighting on a second front.)

Shortly after the Yalta conference, on April 12, 1945, Roosevelt died of a cerebral hemorrhage. Throughout the war, Roosevelt had kept foreign policy in his own hands. His death brought into the White House his vice president, Harry S. Truman, a man of little experience in world affairs.

THE UNITED STATES DEFEATS JAPAN

Despite decisive Allied victories in the Pacific and the deadly firebombing of Toyko, Japan refused to surrender. In order to avoid a bloody land invasion of Japan and end the war quickly, the new American president, Harry Truman, ordered atomic bombs—the most powerful weapons ever invented—to be dropped on the Japanese cities of Hiroshima and Nagasaki. Japan surrendered.

JAPAN CONTINUES TO FIGHT   With Germany's surrender and a new president, Americans turned their efforts to defeating Japan. The war in the Pacific was especially fierce. By early 1944 the Japanese had been driven from the central Pacific islands but showed no signs of surrendering.

Chief of Staff George C. Marshall and Pacific Commander General Douglas MacArthur concluded that only an invasion of Japan could end the war. Calculations indicated that such an invasion would be costly, perhaps as high as one million American casualties. On March 9, 1944, an American air raid on Tokyo using incendiary bombs took approximately 185,000 lives and destroyed 267,000 buildings. In the battle for Okinawa, an island between Formosa and Japan that the Japanese considered part of their homeland, the Japanese had put up a fierce defense from April 1 through mid-May 1945. In the battle for Okinawa, Japanese planes undertook "kamikaze" suicide attacks, sending 700 pilots to crash their planes on American ships. During the three-month campaign, Japan lost an estimated 110,000 soldiers, while America experienced 49,000 casualties.

THE WAR ENDS   Japan's continued resistance created deep anxiety among Truman's military chiefs. Although Tojo's militarist government had been replaced, signs of surrender still had not appeared. Seeking a quick end to the war, Truman turned to atomic weapons, developed by American and British scientists at Los Alamos, New Mexico. These weapons were more powerful than any in human history. Although leading American scientists expressed opposition to using the bomb, military advisers felt that the bomb offered a "merciful abridgment of the slaughter in the East." Concerned about further loss of American lives, Truman ordered the bomb dropped.

On August 6, 1945, a single atomic bomb leveled the city of Hiroshima, causing casualties of 130,000. When the Japanese military leaders did not immediately surrender, Truman ordered a second bomb dropped on the city of Nagasaki, wounding and killing approximately 75,000 people on August 9. On August 15th a stunned Japanese nation listened to their emperor announce the end of the war.

In the context of war, in which an estimated 45 million people lost their lives, the atomic bomb appeared to be just another weapon, one that had mercifully ended a terrible war. The bomb also revealed the extent of American military power to a Soviet Union whose relations with the United States already appeared strained.

CONCLUSION

The Second World War taught Americans an important lesson: Never again would the United States be caught with its guard down, unprepared for war. Never again would the nation turn its back on world events. Never again would aggression be appeased. This new conscious-ness would lead the United States to counter the Soviet Union at every turn in the postwar world. The nation had entered a new era.

Recommended Readings

DOCUMENTS: Omar N. Bradley, *A Soldier's Story* (1951); Dwight D. Eisenhower, *Crusade in Europe* (1948); Phillip McGuire, ed., *Taps for a Jim Crow Army: Letters from Black Soldiers in World War II* (1982).

READINGS: (GENERAL) A. Russell Buchanan, *The United States and World War II* (2 vols., 1964); Robert A. Divine, *Roosevelt and World War II* (1969); B. H. Liddell Hart, *History of the Second World War* (1970); Martha Byrd Hoyle, *A World in Flames: The History of World War II* (1970); Gordon Wright, *The Ordeal of Total War* (1968). (COMING OF WAR) Robert Dallek, *Franklin D. Roosevelt and American Foreign Policy* (1979); Robert Divine, *The Reluctant Belligerent* (1979); Justus D. Donecke, *Storm on the Horizon* (2000); Frederick W. Marks, *Wind over Sand: The Diplomacy of Franklin Roosevelt* (1988); Gordon Prange, *At Dawn We Slept* (1981); John Toland, *Infamy* (1982); David Wyman, *The Abandonment of the Jews* (1984). (MILITARY) John Dower, *War without Mercy: Race and Power in the Pacific War* (1986); Kent R. Greenfield, *American Strategy in World War II* (1963); Akira Iriye, *Power and Culture: The Japanese-American War* (1981); John Keegan, *Six Armies in Normandy* (1982); Robert Leckie, *Delivered from Evil* (1987); Charles B. MacDonald, *The Mighty Endeavor* (1969); Bernard C. Nalty, *Strength for the Fight: A History of Black Americans in the Military* (1986); Richard Rhodes, *The Making of the Atomic Bomb* (1986); Ronald H. Spector, *Eagle against the Sun: The American War with Japan* (1984); and John Toland, *The Rising Sun* (1970). (HOME FRONT) Robert Abzug, *Inside the Vicious Heart: Americans and the Liberation of Nazi Concentration Camps* (1985); Karen T. Anderson, *Wartime Women* (1981); John M. Blum, *"V" Was for Victory* (1976); David Brinkley, *Washington Goes to War* (1988); Roger Daniels, *Concentration Camps U.S.A.* (1971); Leonard Dinnerstein, *America and the Survivors of the Holocaust (1982);* Susan Hartman, *The Home Front and Beyond: American Women in the 1940s* (1982); Clayton Koppes and Gregory Black, *Hollywood Goes to War* (1986); Nelson Lichtenstein, *Labor's War at Home* (1982); Richard Lingeman, *Don't You Know There's a War On?* (1970); Mauricio Mazon, *The Zoot Suit Riots* (1984); Gerald Nash, *The American West Transformed* (1985); Richard Polenberg, *War and Society* (1972); Harold Vatter, *The American Economy in World War II* (1984).

27

❧

The Cold War Haunts the "Fabulous Fifties"

OVERVIEW The postwar years after 1945 brought renewed prosperity to the American people. Looming over this era of abundance, however, was the threat of the Soviet Union. The development of nuclear weapons and the emergence of the Soviet Union as a world power affected nearly every aspect of American politics, foreign and domestic. The ideological conflict between the Soviet Union and the United States, and the ensuing arms race, became known as the "cold war."

President Harry S. Truman (1945–1953), who had stepped into the White House following Franklin Roosevelt's death, sought to extend New Deal reform at home, in what he called the Fair Deal, and to contain communism abroad. His Republican successor, Dwight D. Eisenhower (1953–1961), undertook moderate domestic reform while continuing Truman's policy of containment. American popular culture, too, reflected this mix of complacency and anxiety. Prosperity brought new leisure time, greater consumption, higher standards of living, and better prospects for education and worldly success. As the "fabulous fifties" drew to a close, however, Americans once again began to question where their society was headed.

TRUMAN CONFRONTS COMMUNISM ABROAD AND AT HOME, 1945–1952

Following the death of Franklin Roosevelt, Harry S. Truman came into the presidency under the shadow of his predecessor. In international relations,

Truman was slow to find his own voice. He shifted American foreign policy toward containment of Soviet expansionism; he also called for rebuilding Europe through the Marshall Plan and for organizing regional defense through the North Atlantic Treaty Organization (NATO).

In 1950 Truman's attention turned to Asia when the communist North Korean army invaded South Korea. Truman persuaded the United Nations to pass a resolution sending troops to Korea in a "police action." The Korean War still had not been resolved by the time Truman left office.

Concern about communism abroad led to anticommunist sentiment at home. Republican Senator Joseph R. McCarthy of Wisconsin became a leading force in this anticommunist crusade by attacking opponents, often without any evidence of communist involvement.

FACING THE SOVIET UNION, **1945**   On hearing of Roosevelt's death, Truman told reporters, "The moon, the stars, and all the planets fell on me." Truman stepped into the White House as World War II was drawing to a close. FDR, as was his style with subordinates, had kept his vice president generally uninformed about his plans for the postwar world.

Many in Washington viewed Truman as a small-time politician who lacked the ability or stature to lead the nation. Cabinet members remained loyal to FDR and compared Truman unfavorably to him. (All but three cabinet members were gone by the end of 1945.) As Truman stumbled from one diplomatic problem to another, many perceived him as a failure.

No doubt a large part of Truman's problems came from a personal style that clashed with eastern New Deal liberals. He was from Missouri, a state that combined the characteristics of the Midwest and the South. (Truman's mother was an unreconstructed Confederate.) Although Truman had won election to the U.S. Senate in 1938 as a loyal New Dealer, he was placed on the 1944 presidential ticket as a running mate to Roosevelt at the insistence of mainstream Democrats who disliked FDR's liberal vice president, Henry Wallace. (The popular Wallace became secretary of commerce in early 1945 during Roosevelt's fourth term.) The Democrats won an unprecedented fourth term in 1944 against a Republican ticket headed by the New York reformer Thomas Dewey. Truman had just come into the vice presidency when Roosevelt's death in 1945 placed him in the White House.

As Truman surveyed the postwar world, he saw an America unrivaled in economic and military power. Western Europe had been shattered by the war. England no longer stood as a preeminent imperial power; Germany was devastated. The only threat to world order came from Josef Stalin's Soviet Union. Tensions between the United States and the Soviet Union were already evident before FDR's death in April 1945.

The struggle between Russia and the United States soon assumed global dimensions.

Liberals hoped to continue the wartime alliance of the Big Three: the United States, Great Britain, and the Soviet Union. Truman, too, wanted to maintain cordial relations with the Soviet Union. At the same time, however, he saw clear signs of Stalin's willful disregard of agreements reached at Yalta, especially those pertaining to Eastern Europe. Most apparent was the Soviet Union's brazen suppression of political opposition in Poland. The Soviet Union dominated coalition governments in Bulgaria and Hungary. Only in Finland did the Soviets accept genuinely independent leaders.

Other problems between the United States and the Soviet Union exacerbated tensions. At first the Soviets refused to withdraw their occupation troops from northern Iran, an issue made even more significant by Iran's strategic location in the oil-rich Middle East. The Soviet Union finally agreed, under pressure from the United States, to withdraw from northern Iran in May 1946, but by then relations had already deteriorated.

In Asia, Truman confronted a full-scale civil war between the reactionary and corrupt nationalist government of Chiang Kai-shek and communist insurgents led by Mao Zedong. Americans supported the nationalists but called for Chiang to institute meaningful political and economic reform. In late 1945 Truman sent General George Marshall as a special envoy to settle the conflict. By the spring of 1946, negotiations had collapsed. At home many liberals believed that a Red Chinese victory was for the best. Misunderstanding the nature of Chinese communism, one liberal journalist declared that the Red Chinese were no more communistic "than the farmers of Minnesota and North Dakota."

Liberals sensed a hardening toward the Soviet Union within the administration that included Chief of Staff Admiral William D. Leahy, Secretary of the Navy James V. Forrestal, and ambassador to the Soviet Union W. Averell Harriman. From mid-July through August 1, 1945, Truman met with Britain's Prime Minister Clement Atlee (the Labor Party leader who had just defeated Churchill in the general election) and Stalin at Potsdam, Germany, to discuss postwar problems. The code name of the conference, TERMINAL, proved appropriate; it was the last time top leaders of the three countries would meet together for a decade.

TRUMAN DECIDES TO CONTAIN THE SOVIET UNION, 1946–1949   In early 1946 relations only worsened. In February, George F. Kennan, a long-time State Department official stationed in Moscow, sent Washington officials a ten-thousand-word telegram containing a closely reasoned analysis of Soviet foreign policy. The "long telegram," as it was called, argued that the Soviet

Union remained historically and ideologically hostile to democratic government and expansionistic by nature. Appeasement would not work; instead, the United States should keep Soviet expansionism in check through a policy of containment. Kennan warned, however, that the United States should only defend those places vital to American strategic interests. A shorter version of Kennan's memorandum was later published in the influential *Foreign Affairs* magazine, under the pseudonym "X" so as not to reveal Kennan's official status in the State Department. Containment remained the general American policy toward the Soviet Union for the next four decades.

Shortly after the Kennan memorandum, former prime minister Winston Churchill, speaking at Westminster College in Fulton, Missouri, asserted that an "iron curtain" had fallen across Eastern Europe, dividing the Soviet bloc from Western Europe. Many Americans, however, were not ready to accept a prolonged cold war with the Soviet Union. Liberal Senator Claude Pepper (Democrat-Florida) denounced Churchill's speech as a lame attempt "to make America the great defender of [British] imperialism." Liberals became further alarmed in September 1946 when Truman fired Henry Wallace as secretary of commerce after Wallace spoke in favor of recognizing the Soviet domination of Eastern Europe.

With relations between the two nations rapidly deteriorating, Truman attempted to ease Stalin's suspicions by offering to place America's atomic weapons under the control of the United Nations. Stalin, calculating that he could build bombs better than he could control the pro-American United Nations, immediately rejected the proposal. Only Stalin knew how close the Soviets were to becoming a nuclear power.

U.S.-Soviet tensions escalated in 1947, setting the course of relations between the two nations for the next forty years. Responding to a direct threat to Greece, where communist insurgents had launched a civil war against a military government, Truman appeared before Congress on March 12, 1947, to enunciate the Truman Doctrine, the United States' commitment to support democratic nations threatened by communist aggression. Truman requested $450 million in aid to help Greece and Turkey resist such aggression. Although conservative Republicans led by Robert Taft (Ohio) questioned this massive foreign aid package, the Greek–Turkish aid bill was narrowly passed by Congress. Truman continued to worry that war-devastated Western Europe was ripe for a Soviet-backed communist revolution.

In response to Truman's concern, Secretary of State George C. Marshall announced a bold economic recovery program for the democracies of Western Europe. The Marshall Plan called for massive economic assistance to Europe, to bolster Europe's economies while providing important market and investment opportunities for American business. Predictably, the Soviets denounced the program as "imperialistic."

In February 1948, communists ruthlessly seized power in Czechoslovakia. The Soviet takeover shocked many in the West. Czech foreign minister Jan Masaryk, son of the founder of the republic and a much-admired figure, mysteriously "fell" from a window in his apartment, probably a victim of assassination. The coup in Czechoslovakia confirmed Truman's worst perceptions of Stalin's intentions.

Truman moved to unite American, British, and French military zones in occupied Germany into the Federal Republic of Germany (West Germany). A politically and economically strong West Germany could present a powerful buffer against further Soviet expansion into Europe. In spring 1948 a unified West Germany was created. Berlin now stood divided physically and symbolically into noncommunist West Berlin and communist East Berlin.

The Soviet Union retaliated by blockading all surface traffic into West Berlin. This challenge prompted Truman to initiate a massive airlift of food and provisions to West Berlin. Nearly a year later, in May 1949, the Russians finally lifted the blockade; two days later the formation of a West German democratic government was announced. Americans now spoke of a "cold war" between the United States and the Soviet Union.

Truman pressed for stronger defensive measures against the Soviet Union. Shortly after the 1948 election, the United States and twelve other nations formed the North Atlantic Treaty Organization (NATO), a regional defense alliance that linked Europe and America. In 1949 Truman substantially increased the defense budget and approved the development of the hydrogen bomb. The arms race was on.

TRUMAN SENDS TROOPS TO KOREA, 1950   In the Far East, Truman's attention remained focused on China. By 1949 communist forces led by Mao Zedong had defeated the American-backed nationalist government, forcing its leader, Chiang Kai-shek, to retreat to the island of Taiwan. The new Chinese communist government quickly aligned itself with the Soviet Union. At home the loss of China created a backlash; conservative Republicans denounced Truman and State Department "liberals" for "losing" China. Fearing further losses in Asia, Truman began to aid the French in their war against a communist insurgency in Vietnam.

Truman's fears of further communist intrusion in Asia were confirmed when the communist North Korean army launched a full-scale invasion of South Korea in June 1950. (At the end of World War II, Korea had been taken from Japanese control and divided at the thirty-eighth

Map 27.1   Asia in the 1950s

parallel into zones of occupation by the Soviet Union and United States). The Soviet-backed leader of North Korea, Kim Il Sung, had informed Stalin of his intentions and had not been discouraged from attacking. Stalin believed that American involvement in Korea would distract the United States from affairs in Europe. Although the invasion caught the Americans by surprise, Truman moved within hours to prevent the total collapse of South Korea. He ordered additional American troops to Korea and then secured a United Nations Security Council mandate for a "police action." (The Soviet Union failed to veto the U.N. resolution as expected, because their ambassador had undertaken a poorly timed boycott of the Security Council just at that moment).

In the war's first weeks, the North Koreans overwhelmed Americans fighting under the United Nations banner and led by General Douglas MacArthur. Surrounded at Pusan, at the southeastern corner of the Korean peninsula, MacArthur executed a brilliant maneuver with an amphibious landing behind enemy lines on the west coast of Korea. Within a week the North Korean army was routed. Of 400,000 North Korean troops sent south, at least 280,000 were killed.

Overjoyed by the victory, Truman approved MacArthur's request for permission to drive north to unseat the Soviet-backed North Korean government and reunify Korea. MacArthur crossed the thirty-eighth parallel, which divided North and South Korea, and by mid-October 1950 had captured the North Korean capital of Pyongyang. He boasted, "The boys will be home by Christmas." Disobeying presidential orders, MacArthur decided to advance further north toward the Yalu River, bordering China. MacArthur seemed oblivious to reports of a Chinese buildup. On October 27, 1950, waves of Red Chinese troops (previously assembled for an invasion of Taiwan) crossed into North Korea. The Americans retreated, attacked, and retreated again. Only the use of massive air bombing saved American forces from disaster.

By the spring of 1951, Americans and North Korean–Chinese troops had entered into a prolonged stalemate. When MacArthur denounced the administration's handling of the war, an outraged Truman relieved MacArthur of his command. MacArthur returned home a hero among conservatives, but a movement to draft him as the Republican presidential nominee in 1952 soon fizzled. "Old soldiers," said MacArthur, "never die. They just fade away."

Meanwhile, truce talks, which opened in July 1951, bogged down over America's refusal to send back to the north those communist prisoners who wished to remain in South Korea. Republicans charged that Truman's unwillingness to expand the war encouraged North Korea, supported by the Soviet Union, to prolong it.

THE COMMUNIST SPECTER HAUNTS THE NATION, 1947–1950 The struggle with the Soviet Union created profound fears of communist subversion at home. While genuinely concerned with the communist issue, Republicans also astutely saw the political advantages of an anticommunist crusade that targeted liberal groups once tied to communists. The House Un-American Activities Committee (HUAC) opened hearings on communist influence in the United States. Witnesses were instructed to disclose known communist associates; the uncooperative found themselves harassed at work and home by HUAC and the FBI.

In March 1947, under increasing pressure, Truman ordered the FBI to investigate all federal employees. During this probe more than three hundred employees resigned, many for personal reasons, such as homosexuality, which they did not want publicly revealed. Others quit because they had leftist ties and felt their careers would be ruined if this became public. So began the great witch hunt, which soon extended to Hollywood, universities, labor unions, and industry. For those questioned, the only way to prove their loyalty was to "name names." Many reputations and livelihoods were lost as gossip and lies multiplied.

The Communist Party also came under attack; a dozen of the top party leaders in America went to prison for their political beliefs. The party was infiltrated by the FBI and all but destroyed.

In the summer of 1948, former Communist Party members Elizabeth Bentley and Whittaker Chambers shocked the nation by testifying that they had been involved in a Russian spy ring in Washington. Chambers, a *Time* magazine editor, identified Alger Hiss, a former high-ranking State Department official who had accompanied Franklin Roosevelt to Yalta, as a key figure in this ring. Working with Richard Nixon, a young congressman from California, Chambers led the committee and journalists to his farm in Maryland and produced microfilm, hidden in a hollow pumpkin, that appeared to many to implicate Hiss in a scheme to transmit secret government documents to the Russians. A technicality prevented a charge of espionage, but the "pumpkin papers" led to Hiss's conviction for perjury.

Other accusations of communist infiltration followed. In late 1949 the British intelligence service uncovered a spy ring headed by Klaus Fuchs, a German-born atomic scientist with British citizenship who had worked at Los Alamos, New Mexico, on the Manhattan Project (the name given to the project to build the first atomic bomb) during World War II. Fuchs's trail led to New York, to the arrest of Julius and Ethel Rosenberg, who were then charged with transmitting nuclear secrets to the Soviet Union. Convicted, the Rosenbergs were executed in 1953, despite intense controversy over the fairness of their trial, although later evidence from Soviet archives proves Julius's guilt.

In the 1990s the United States government released radio messages it had intercepted between the Soviet embassy in Washington, D.C., and Moscow. These intercepts—called the Venona Project—showed conclusively that Julius Rosenberg was the head of a Soviet spy ring that had penetrated the Manhattan Project. The Venona documents, as well as the release of documents from the archives of the former Soviet Union, revealed extensive spy infiltration of the United States government. Although this evidence does not exonerate Senator Joseph McCarthy of the abuse of power, it casts a different light on the debate over communist infiltration of the government.

TRUMAN ANNOUNCES THE FAIR DEAL, 1945–1953

At the conclusion of World War II, American policymakers undertook the conversion of a wartime economy into a peacetime one by providing veterans with loans to attend college and buy homes. Truman also proposed a Fair Deal program to extend the New Deal social program. Republicans countered by passing legislation such as the Taft-Hartley Act (1947) that restricted union activity. Truman won the 1948 election, but his proposal for national health insurance failed. Congress did enact new Social Security legislation, however.

EXTENDING BENEFITS TO RETURNING G.I.S   When Truman became president in April 1945, he faced the major problem of converting the basis of the economy from war to peace. Policymakers worried that a depression could be caused by returning World War II soldiers flooding into the labor force. The GI Bill cleverly kept millions of veterans out of the labor market and sent them to college. The bill also provided low-interest loans to help veterans buy houses, which created jobs in construction and started a postwar suburban housing boom.

Congress sought to extend federal economic power with the Employment Act (1946), which established the Council of Economic Advisers and vaguely committed the federal government to maintaining high employment.

Truman also called for a permanent Fair Employment Practices Commission (FEPC), an agency temporarily created in wartime to end employment and housing discrimination. However, the race riots of 1943 had created a backlash against civil rights legislation; when the FEPC measure came before Congress in 1946, a group of southern legislators filibustered and forced the bill's withdrawal.

Republicans countered the Fair Deal with their own agenda, which included anti-union legislation. In 1947 a coalition of Republicans and conservative southern Democrats pushed the controversial Taft-Hartley Act through. Enacted over Truman's veto, Taft-Hartley authorized use of antistrike court injunctions against labor unions. The legislation also outlawed secondary union boycotts (in which one union pickets a business that is involved in a dispute with another union) and closed shops (an agreement between union and employer that the employer will hire only union members). This new law also allowed states to adopt "right-to-work" laws, which prohibited union contracts from requiring employees to join the union. Most southern states quickly adopted such laws to lure industry from the North. Denouncing Taft-Hartley as a "union busting" measure, liberals and organized labor launched a campaign to repeal it, but the campaign was not successful.

TRUMAN WINS THE ELECTION OF 1948   In 1946, capitalizing on war weariness and campaigning under a slogan of "Had Enough? Vote Republican!" Republicans gained control of both houses of Congress for the first time since 1928. Amid a wave of strikes and rising prices, they looked forward to winning the White House in 1948. As the 1948 presidential election approached, however, Truman revealed unexpected political tenacity.

Harry Truman entered the 1948 election hampered by a divided Democratic Party. Indeed, liberals had asked war hero General Dwight D. Eisenhower to run. He declined. (The general had not yet publicly declared himself a Republican.) When Truman won renomination, the former vice president, Henry Wallace, led a new third party, the Progressive Party, as an anti-cold-war alternative. In turn, conservative southern Democrats bolted to support South Carolina's Governor J. Strom Thurmond and his States' Rights ("Dixiecrat") Party in their opposition to the party platform on civil rights. Truman's defeat appeared inevitable when the Republicans nominated the popular New York reformer, Governor Thomas Dewey.

Truman's opponents underestimated his resolution. As his thirty-thousand-mile railroad tour wound its way across the country, Truman began to hear cries of "Give 'em hell, Harry!"

On election night, contrary to the polls and pundits, Democrat Truman squeaked past Republican Dewey. Truman polled 24.1 million votes to Dewey's 22 million, while Dixiecrat Strom Thurmond won 1.1 million votes and carried only four southern states. Henry Wallace's Progressive Party, which called for friendly relations with the Soviet Union, failed to win a single state. Still, Truman received less than half the total vote.

After the election Truman proposed a far-reaching legislative agenda. The centerpiece of his Fair Deal was comprehensive national health insurance. Although a majority of the public initially favored the idea, the bill's passage was stalled in Congress when the American Medical Association denounced it as "socialized medicine." On the other hand, Truman's proposal to expand the Social Security system found widespread support among both Democrats and Republicans, who extended coverage to ten million additional workers in 1950. On the whole, Truman's call for a fair deal became, in effect, a small deal.

DWIGHT D. EISENHOWER SEEKS MODERATION, 1952–1960

Dwight D. Eisenhower assumed the presidency in 1953 as one of America's most popular figures. Still in the midst of a brutally stalemated war in Korea, the country turned to the former military commander of the Allied forces in Europe. In foreign policy, Eisenhower and Secretary of State John Foster Dulles sought to turn back communism in Eastern Europe, Asia, the Middle East, and Latin America.

In domestic policy the moderate Eisenhower, critical of the welfare state, favored limited expansion of federal activity in housing, medical care, education, and highway construction. In 1957 his administration enacted the first civil rights legislation since Reconstruction. In the end Eisenhower's administration offered an interlude rather than a new beginning.

THE ELECTION OF 1952   While the Democrats nominated Adlai E. Stevenson, a relatively unknown liberal governor of Illinois, in 1952, the Republicans picked the immensely popular Dwight D. Eisenhower, a moderate. In doing so, the party rejected conservative senator Robert Taft ("Mr. Republican"). After being out of the White House for twenty years, the GOP cared more about victory than ideology.

Eisenhower's appeal was broad and deep. His own modest beginnings in Abilene, Kansas, and his success as a West Point graduate who had become commander of the Allied forces during World War II made Eisenhower a hero. In order to appease the Right, Eisenhower selected Richard Nixon, the well-known anticommunist senator from California, as his running mate.

Nixon was almost bumped from the vice president slot on the Republican ticket because of a controversial political bank account. He successfully defended himself on television in what became known as the "Checkers speech," in which he asked for sympathy by declaring that his family would not return one particular gift, a puppy named Checkers, even if the dog proved to be an illegal campaign donation. Other than this, the campaign offered little excitement. Eisenhower won by a landslide, carrying every state except a few border states and the Deep South. Moreover, the Republicans regained control of Congress.

EISENHOWER ADDRESSES FOREIGN POLICY, **1953–1960**   Eisenhower and his secretary of state, John Foster Dulles, promised a new foreign policy. Whereas Truman had pursued a policy of Soviet containment, Eisenhower and Dulles claimed they would liberate communist-dominated countries in Eastern Europe. They also shifted American defense policy toward nuclear weapons development, which they called the "new look." In practice Eisenhower's foreign policy differed little from Truman's. Eastern Europe was not liberated, and the United States continued to be involved in limited, often covert engagements against perceived communist threats.

By threatening nuclear war, Eisenhower was able to end the war in Korea on July 27, 1953; the final truce once again divided North and South Korea near the thirty-eighth parallel. After three years of fighting, the United States had prevented the communist takeover of South Korea, but more than thirty-five thousand American lives had been lost.

Eisenhower believed firmly that communist aggression must be thwarted, that a communist takeover of one country could lead to a "domino effect" involving nearby countries. Eisenhower especially worried about Vietnam, where the French colonial army was engaged in an eight-year struggle (1946–1954) against a communist nationalist insurgency led by Ho Chi Minh. The situation became critical in 1954, when communist forces surrounded a French garrison at Dien Bien Phu. The French pleaded for direct American military assistance, but Eisenhower declined to commit troops to another Asian war.

Peace negotiations opened in Geneva, Switzerland, in April 1954. Shortly after the conference convened, the French surrendered at Dien Bien Phu. This defeat led the French and the Vietnamese to sign the Geneva Accords, which partitioned Vietnam at the seventeenth parallel between the communist North and the pro-French South. Reunification of the country was to be achieved through democratic elections, but the United States refused to sign the agreement, fearing that Ho Chi Minh would win such a nationwide election. Instead, the United States sought to strengthen South Vietnam by arranging for Ngo Dinh Diem, a fiercely anticommunist Catholic, to head a new government in South Vietnam.

At the same time, Secretary of State Dulles organized a regional defense alliance, the Southeast Asia Treaty Organization (SEATO), which eventually included the United States, Britain, France, Australia, New Zealand, the Philippines, Pakistan, and Thailand. Dulles also instructed the Central Intelligence Agency (CIA) to become more active in the region.

The Korean peace might have led to better relations with communist China, but Dulles adamantly refused, unlike Britain and France, to recognize Red China, which he described as "demonstrably aggressive and

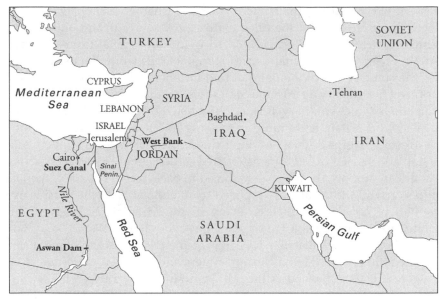

Map 27.2   The Middle East in the 1950s

treacherous." Tensions worsened in 1955, when mainland China began to shell islands off its coast that were controlled by Taiwan. Eisenhower acted decisively to align the United States with the nationalist government on Taiwan through a mutual defense treaty. The crisis passed when the Chinese abruptly ended the shelling.

The Middle East presented Eisenhower with another series of crises. Shortly before Eisenhower came into office, nationalist forces in Iran under Mohammed Mossadeq overthrew the repressive government headed by Shah Mohammad Reza Pahlavi. The British and the French, concerned with Mossadeq's nationalization of western oil interests, undertook an economic boycott of the country. Viewing the action as naked colonialism, Truman had refused to join the boycott, but Eisenhower reversed American policy and sided with the British and French. On his instructions the CIA orchestrated a coup against the Mossadeq government and returned the shah to power in 1954. Ironically, even as Mossadeq was being overthrown, his party was engaged in a campaign against the small Iranian Communist Party.

By the mid-1950s nationalism had emerged as a potent force in Middle Eastern politics. The creation of Israel in 1948 fueled much of this nationalism. In Egypt, Gamal Abdel Nasser flamed anti-Zionist, nationalist passions. When it was discovered that Nasser had undertaken an adventurist policy of accepting American aid while purchasing weapons from eastern bloc countries, the United States punished Nasser by withdrawing its promise to build the huge hydroelectric Aswan Dam on the Nile River. Nasser boldly retaliated by seizing the Suez Canal from a private Anglo-French company and declaring that its tolls would be used to pay for the construction of the dam. In mid-October 1956, in the midst of an uprising in Hungary against the communist regime, Egypt, Syria, and Jordan entered into a military alliance. Frightened by the new Arab alliance, Israel joined Britain and France in retaking the canal in the same month.

To the chagrin of its allies, the United States refused to support this action and instead called for a negotiated settlement of the crisis. Without American support, the allies were forced to back down. Nasser remained in power, and the canal was reopened to all nations, with the notable exception of Israel. Nonetheless, many in the Middle East viewed the United States as the leader of pro-Israeli western imperialism.

In January 1959, Eisenhower confronted a crisis closer to home when Fidel Castro overthrew the corrupt, American-supported government of Fulgencio Batista in Cuba. Although Castro initially criticized the Cuban Communist Party for not supporting his guerrilla war against Batista, the Eisenhower administration refused to meet with Castro when he came to New York in April 1959 to address the United Nations. Castro's nationalization of the sugar industry and other American-owned companies in Cuba further convinced Eisenhower that Castro was a threat to American interests. When Castro signed trade agreements with the Soviet Union and China, Eisenhower approved covert plans to overthrow the Castro government.

MCCARTHY ACCUSED, 1953–1954   While confronting communism abroad, Eisenhower faced a powerful conservative wing in his own party that demanded an even stronger anticommunist stance. The right focused much of its attention on China, forming the "China Lobby," which called for the "liberation" of the mainland. A potent force in ultraconservative circles was Wisconsin's Senator Joseph R. McCarthy. By 1952, McCarthyism was in full swing, and the politically cautious Eisenhower refused to confront the volatile senator.

By 1953 many believed McCarthy himself was a threat to the nation, although he continued to have strong support in many segments of the American population. The end came when McCarthy accused the army of harboring communists. (He made the accusation after army officials revealed that McCarthy had sought special privileges for his former aide, Private G. David Schine). The Senate decided to hold special televised hearings concerning McCarthy's charges. For thirty-five days, nearly twenty million Americans watched the Army–McCarthy hearings and witnessed McCarthy's bullying tactics. In November 1954, the Senate voted 64 to 25 to censure McCarthy. Three years later he died of alcoholism.

EISENHOWER QUIETLY SEEKS LIMITED GOVERNMENT   Many Americans continued to equate "big government" with socialism. In this atmosphere, Eisenhower accepted a limited role for the federal government. He endorsed the Saint Lawrence Seaway Act (1954) for a canal system to link the Atlantic Ocean with the Great Lakes. He supported the Federal Highway Act (1956) to construct forty thousand miles of interstate highways and freeways across the nation. In other matters Eisenhower believed that federal responsibilities should be given back to the states and private interests. He approved a measure to return offshore tideland oil wells to states bordering the Gulf of Mexico. His proposal to privatize the Tennessee Valley Authority, however, failed when it came under public scrutiny. Only in 1957, when the cold war spilled over to a debate on education after the Russians launched the world's first space satellite, *Sputnik,* would the administration show strong support for federal aid to public education.

Although Eisenhower warned of "creeping socialism," he nonetheless accepted enlargement of the welfare state. The number of people receiving Social Security increased dramatically, from 1.3 million in 1945 to 14.8 million in 1960. The number of women and children receiving welfare benefits through Aid to Families with Dependent Children (AFDC) nearly tripled. The percentage of poor people fell in the 1950s, however, because the economy expanded.

LEARNING TO LIVE WITH THE BOMB

American society in the 1950s reflected both the fears of the atomic age and the smugness promoted by economic abundance. Following the war, the nation experienced the longest sustained period of economic prosperity in its history. During the war the gross domestic product more than doubled. Even minor recessions during the decade did little to dispel a sense of never-ending affluence.

ANXIETY RADIATES IN THE ATOMIC AGE   The cold war introduced new fears to America as the arms race accelerated. Atmospheric testing of atomic weapons was conducted openly. During the 1950s the United States tested 122 nuclear bombs; the Soviet Union, 50 bombs; and Great Britain, 21 bombs.

Military authorities, overseen by the Atomic Energy Commission, did not realize the seriousness of this testing. They conducted the first tests in Nevada without warning the small populations in surrounding areas. One rancher later said it was quite common on test days to wake up at the break of dawn to see a "nuclear sunrise," as a bomb exploded. Sometimes soldiers and sailors were less than thirty miles away from a bomb site.

While military officials developed new nuclear weapons, civil authorities prepared the nation to protect itself from nuclear attack. One government pamphlet, "You Can Survive" (1950), told Americans to "know the bomb's true dangers; know the steps you can take to escape them." In the event of nuclear attack, Americans were advised to take refuge inside a house or get inside a car, "rolling up the window." Those who could not find a shelter, the pamphlet said, would get sick to their stomachs, and then, two weeks later, their hair might fall out, but in spite of it all they stood a good chance of making a complete recovery.

Only a few publicly opposed the arms race. Scientists such as Linus Pauling, a Nobel Prize winner, became a leading spokesmen for a "ban the bomb" movement that called for nuclear disarmament. The "ban the bomb" movement was joined by a group of religious and moral pacifists led by A. J. Muste.

DEFINING THE GOOD LIFE   Most Americans learned to live with the threat of nuclear war. They found security in well-paying jobs, in home ownership in the suburbs, and in family life. At no other time had middle-class values done more to shape the country than in the years after World War II.

Ignoring contemporary problems was made easier by the extraordinary affluence enjoyed by average Americans. Life was to be enjoyed, along with hard work. America went on a shopping spree; people filled their homes with the latest labor-saving devices, including dishwashers, electric can openers, and garbage disposals. By 1960 most American households had television sets. Suburbanites might have as many as two roomy cars, often with electric-powered windows, power brakes, and power steering.

Some of this good life resulted from federal efforts on behalf of veterans. The GI Bill, as it was popularly called, provided educational grants and home and business loans, imposed employment preferences for veterans, and encouraged the immense expansion of higher education following the war. By 1948 the Veterans Administration had paid the college expenses of about half of all male students enrolled in college. Approximately 2.5 million students attended college under the first GI Bill; in turn, returning veterans changed campus life.

Veterans' loans also changed how Americans lived. These loans financed nearly one out of every five houses sold in the 1950s. At the start of World War II, about 45 percent of American families owned their own homes; by the end of the 1950s, more than 60 percent did.

This rise in homeownership paralleled the shift in population to the West and South. The good life also meant moving to the suburbs. Large, old cities like Detroit, Baltimore, St. Louis, and Washington, D.C., lost population in the 1950s. In the process, suburbs gained almost four million jobs, while central cities lost three million jobs, mostly in manufacturing. This movement from the city also meant that large cities lost much of their tax bases.

Americans lived not only better but longer in the postwar years. In 1940 the average life expectancy was about 61 years for men and 65 for women. After the war, better medical treatment contributed significantly to longevity, largely due to the invention of antibiotics like penicillin. By 1950 average life expectancy had risen to 65.5 years for men and 71 for women. These figures remained significantly lower for black Americans— 59 years for men and 63 years for women—but during the 1950s the average life span of this group increased as well.

AMERICANS FOCUS ON FAMILY   Although Americans lived longer, they also married more readily and at younger ages than ever before in modern history. The United States had one of the highest marriage rates in the world. By 1950 almost 70 percent of males and 67 percent of females over fifteen were married. Furthermore, the divorce rate dropped to only 10 percent in 1950. Because of this marriage boom, more children were born. The rising birth rate reflected economic prosperity; people could afford children, and the middle class wanted more children. Surveys showed that most Americans thought three or four children was the "ideal" number.

The happy housewife became a symbol of postwar America; she was featured prominently on television comedies such as *I Love Lucy* and in advertising. In part this ideal was a reaction to the women who had worked at men's jobs during the war, when approximately five million new women workers had joined the labor force. Although the war effort had encouraged "Rosie the Riveter," Rosie was told she was a temporary expedient, needed only until her husband returned from the war. As one unenlightened government pamphlet declared, "A woman is a substitute— like plastic instead of a metal."

Surveys showed that many women did not want to give up their jobs after the war, and as the war drew to a close, many women lobbied for equal pay for equal work and federally funded child care centers. This movement for job equality led the Democrats to endorse an equal rights

When television was new in the 1950s, an entire family usually gathered around the black-and-white set to watch the same show. In many towns this togetherness was promoted by the fact that there was only one station. (© Hulton Archive/Getty Images)

amendment in 1944, backed earlier by the Republicans in 1940. As male veterans returned home, however, many women were forced out of their jobs.

Still, contrary to the idealized vision of the happy housewife, many women continued to work. Indeed, the decade of the 1950s marked one of the largest increases in female employment. This did not mean better careers for women, however; except in the low-paid professions of teacher, nurse, and social worker, women generally could not gain higher-level positions in most professions. Many worked part time as secretaries or sales clerks. The percentage of postgraduate degrees obtained by women fell in the 1950s from a high point in the 1930s; for example, in the 1950s only 10 percent of the Ph.Ds in History were awarded to women.

During this decade, American society nevertheless saw a significant rise in single-parent households headed by women. The number of women under fifty-five who headed households jumped from 2.5 million in 1940 to 4.4 million in 1962. Nearly half of these families were poor, and many were black.

OF SEX AND GOD   In the 1950s a new sexual consciousness occurred, even as Americans expressed greater feelings of religiosity. This clash between changing sexual mores and traditional values indicated mounting tensions within American culture.

Americans showed a new awareness about sex, as many states repealed laws prohibiting homosexual activity between consulting adults. Moreover, the publication of Alfred Kinsey's *Sexual Behavior in the Human Male* (1948) introduced the public for the first time to a broad portrait of American sexual behavior. Crammed full of charts, tables, and graphs, this study gave every appearance of being dry and scientific but quickly became a bestseller. Later, historians discovered that Kinsey had knowingly falsified much of his evidence in order to pursue a social agenda opposed to traditional sexual mores. Other changes in attitude were evidenced in 1953 with the publication of Hugh Hefner's *Playboy* magazine, which offered readers revealing photographs of Playboy "Bunnies." From 1940 to 1970, out-of-wedlock births nearly quadrupled. The number of abortions, rarely legal, increased in the 1950s.

During this same decade, many contemporary observers were struck by what they described as a religious revival. In 1942 fewer than 50 percent of the population belonged to churches; by 1956, 65 percent did. Evangelists such as the Baptist Billy Graham organized revivals that drew tens of thousands of people to his rallies, which were often held in football stadiums. Bible sales skyrocketed 140 percent between 1949 and 1953. Vendors reported that one out of every ten books sold was religious.

THE SOCIAL ORDER STARTS TO CRACK

For all the signs of stability, society revealed deep anxieties about where the culture was headed. African-American civil rights leaders demanded an end to segregation. In 1954 the Supreme Court declared segregation unconstitutional in *Brown v. Topeka Board of Education*. This decision unleashed a black civil rights movement that openly protested segregation and struggled to integrate schools, buses, and other public facilities. Signs of discontent with society also appeared among writers, artists, and intellectuals. Teenagers too showed a youthful discontent with American society. As the decade drew to a close, Americans had begun to reevaluate their society.

THE BLACK CIVIL RIGHTS MOVEMENT BEGINS, **1953–1957**   The transformation of the American economy in the immediate postwar period laid the groundwork of the civil rights movement that emerged in the late 1950s and early 1960s. The high demand for labor in a burgeoning economy opened new opportunities to African Americans. A new, although small, black middle class emerged, created largely by the GI Bill and housing loans to World War II veterans, and soon demanded political rights and equal treatment before the law. At the same time, however, a poor urban class emerged among blacks in the inner city.

In these circumstances the National Association for the Advancement of Colored People (NAACP) undertook a legal campaign to overturn the "separate but equal" doctrine embodied in *Plessy v. Ferguson* (1896; discussed in chapter 18). Their opportunity came in 1952 when the Supreme Court decided to hear a school case involving a suit by Reverend Oliver Brown against the school board of Topeka, Kansas. Because of the crazy-quilt system imposed to ensure segregation, Brown's daughter was forced to travel more than two miles to school, even though her home was only five blocks from an all-white grade school. The NAACP was represented by Thurgood Marshall, later the first black appointed to the Supreme Court.

On May 17, 1954, reporters were called into the Court chambers. Here newly appointed Chief Justice Earl Warren read the opinion, only ten pages long. He read tonelessly for fifteen minutes and then concluded, "We come then to the question presented: does segregation . . . deprive the children of the minority group of educational opportunities? We believe that it does." *Brown v. Topeka Board of Education* (1954) marked a historic moment in the Court's history and in the country's race relations.

Eisenhower worried that the ruling would create a white backlash. Nevertheless, he deplored segregation and ordered federal agencies to end the financial support of segregated facilities. He pushed the armed services to speed up integration and appointed Vice President Richard Nixon to draft new civil rights legislation. In 1957, largely through the efforts of Senate Majority Leader Lyndon Johnson, Congress enacted the Civil Rights Act (1957), the first civil rights legislation since 1875. The act established the Civil Rights Commission and a civil rights division of the Justice Department. The act proved modest in its powers but significant in its symbolism.

The emergence of a black civil rights movement showed that change had arrived. By the 1950s black Americans were earning four times more than in 1940. Yet the black median income was $3,000, well below the white median of $5,000. Despite *Brown v. Topeka Board of Education,* school integration moved slowly. Southern states devised schemes to delay or stop integration. In many parts of the South, segregationists organized White Citizens' Councils to intimidate black activists. A campaign of terror spread across the South.

African Americans fought back. In 1955 the struggle for black civil rights gained national attention when civil rights activists launched a campaign to end segregation on city buses in Montgomery, Alabama. That campaign was sparked on December 1, 1955, when a well-dressed black seamstress, Rosa Parks, a long-time local civil rights activist, refused to give up her bus seat to a white man and was arrested. Local black religious leaders launched a boycott of the Montgomery bus system, which mostly served black patrons.

Leadership quickly fell to a twenty-six-year-old Baptist minister, Dr. Martin Luther King, Jr. The boycott lasted nearly a year before the Supreme Court ruled that segregation on Montgomery buses was unlawful.

President Eisenhower hesitated to interject federal power into local conflicts; however, events in Little Rock, Arkansas, forced Eisenhower's hand. In September 1957 the federal courts ordered Central High School integrated. Hoping to win reelection on the issue, Governor Orval Faubus ordered the state-controlled National Guard to prevent the "forcible" integration of the school. When a lone black child mistakenly appeared at the school, a white mob attacked her. The ensuing national outcry forced Eisenhower to put the guard under federal control and send a thousand army troops to Little Rock to protect the nine black children who entered Central High that year.

Massive resistance to integration continued in much of the South, but blacks countered this opposition. Martin Luther King, Jr., the socialist Bayard Rustin, and Ralph Abernathy organized the Southern Christian Leadership Conference (SCLC) to press for an end to segregation. As King crossed the nation to organize communities and students, especially those in black colleges, the nation sensed that a new era was about to dawn.

INTELLECTUALS REBEL   Intellectual circles showed signs of rebellion. Writers criticized conformity and praised rebellion. Playwrights such as Arthur Miller and Tennessee Williams wrote about humanity's tragic struggle against the norms of society.

A new generation of "beat" poets and writers in New York and San Francisco proclaimed their disgust with American civilization—its values, its obsession with materialism, and its legacy of puritanism. Jack Kerouac's *On the Road* (1957) became a bible for many of these beat writers. The romantic ethos of the beat poets, who spoke in the language of free verse, was captured in Allen Ginsberg's collection, *Howl and Other Poems* (1955). Ginsberg wrote of individualism and sexual liberation.

Liberal society came under criticism from the Right and the Left. Friedrich von Hayek, an Austrian émigré economist, warned that the liberal welfare state offered *The Road to Serfdom* (1944). As the end of the 1950s approached, radical leftists also attacked the liberal society. One of the most notable critics was Texas-born sociologist C. Wright Mills, a Columbia University professor who zoomed around New York on his motorbike. In *The Power Elite* (1956) and other books, he laid the intellectual foundation for the New Left, which would emerge in the 1960s.

REBELS WITH A CAUSE   Tensions were evident in the emerging teenage subculture, which was based on rock-and-roll music, fast cars and motorcycles, and a unique style of dress. Rebellious males wore ducktail haircuts, low jeans with the cuffs rolled up, white tee-shirts, and motorcycle boots. Females put on bright lipstick and low-cut blouses; the most daring wore tight skirts and high heels. For music, teens turned to the pulsing beat of Elvis Presley, the frenetic sounds of Jerry Lee Lewis, and black performers like Little Richard and Chuck Berry. For the first time, black music found a large white audience, and white pop music was almost entirely derived from black rhythm and blues. While parents listened to "The Man Upstairs," teenagers turned to "Blueberry Hill," "Great Balls of Fire," and "Honey Love."

CONCLUSION

The Truman–Eisenhower years hid the profound changes taking place in American society: changes in the family, in the roles of women and youth, in sexual consciousness, and in race relations. As the 1950s closed, Americans began to reevaluate where they were and where they were headed as a nation. Many people sensed profound changes to come.

Recommended Readings

DOCUMENTS: Dean Acheson, *Present at the Creation* (1969); Daniel Bell, *The End of Ideology* (1960); George Kennan, *Memoirs,* 2 vols. (1967 and 1972); David Riesman, *The Lonely Crowd* (1950); William Whyte, *The Organization Man* (1956).

READINGS: (GENERAL) John P. Diggins, *The Proud Decades* (1988); John Gaddis, *We Now Know* (1998); James Gilbert, *Another Chance* (1981); Eric Goldman, *The Crucial Decade and After* (1960); Alonzo Hamby, *The Imperial Years* (1976); Godfrey Hodgson, *America in Our Time* (1976); Martin Jezer, *The Dark Ages* (1982); William Leuchtenburg, *A Troubled Feast* (1979); William O'Neill, *American High* (1986). (FOREIGN POLICY) Stephen Ambrose, *The Rise to Globalism* (1983); John L. Gaddis, *The United States and the Origins of Containment* (1982) and *Strategies of Con-*

tainment (1982); Gregg Herken, *The Winning Weapon* (1980); Michael Hogan, *The Marshall Plan* (1987); Hugh Thomas, *Armed Truce: The Beginnings of the Cold War* (1987); Adam Ulam, *The Rivals* (1983); Daniel Yergin, *Shattered Peace* (1977). (ANTI-COMMUNISM AT HOME) David Caute, *The Great Fear* (1978); Harvery Klehr and John Haynes, *Venona: Decoding Soviet Espionage in America* (1999); Stanley I. Kutler, *The American Inquisition: Justice and Injustice in the Cold War* (1982); Michael Oshinsky, *A Conspiracy So Immense: The World of Joe McCarthy* (1983); Ronald Radosh and Joyce Radosh, *The Rosenberg File* (1983); Ellen Schrecker, *Many Are the Crimes: McCarthyism in America* (1998); Athan Theoharis, *Seeds of Repression* (1971); Allen Weinstein, *Perjury: The Hiss–Chambers Case* (1978). (POLITICS IN THE TRUMAN–EISENHOWER ERA) Stephen Ambrose, *Eisenhower the President* (1984); Larry Burt, *Tribalism in Crisis: Federal Indian Policy* (1982); Robert Donovan, *Conflict and Crisis* (1977); Fred Greenstein, *The Hidden Hand Presidency: Eisenhower as Leader* (1965); Alonzo Hamby, *Beyond the New Deal* (1973); Donald McCoy, *The Presidency of Harry S. Truman* (1973); Elmo Richardson, *The Presidency of Dwight D. Eisenhower* (1979). (AMERICAN SOCIETY) Erik Barnouw, *Tube of Plenty* (1975); Paul Carter, *Another Part of the Fifties* (1983); William Chafe, *The American Woman* (1972); Carl Degler, *At Odds* (1980); John D'Emilio and Estelle Freedman, *Intimate Matters: A History of Sexuality in America* (1988); James Gilbert, *A Cycle of Outrage* (1986); Kenneth Jackson, *Crabgrass Frontier* (1985); Elaine May, *Homeward Bound* (1987); Richard Pells, *The Liberal Mind in a Conservative Age* (1985); Jon C. Teaford, *The Rough Road to Renaissance: Urban Revitalization in America* (1990).

28

🌿

The Decade of
Illusion, 1960–1969

OVERVIEW   The 1960s, which began with high hopes for John F. Kennedy's presidency, were soon marred by growing controversy over race and civil rights and took an abrupt, alarming turn with Kennedy's assassination in 1963. Suddenly elevated to office, President Lyndon Baines Johnson launched the Great Society, which included a "war on poverty"; new civil rights laws; and federal aid to education, welfare, and health care.

Johnson's programs failed to meet the rising tide of black expectations and anger, which became militant by the decade's end. Other racial and ethnic groups, women, and homosexuals soon joined in to demand rights. Radicalism within black communities and on college campuses created a backlash among the white middle class and in blue-collar families; politics became increasingly polarized. Meanwhile, the United States had gradually become involved in a large, growing, and controversial war in Vietnam. By the end of 1965, some young people had adopted radical politics. A new youth subculture emerged—a "counterculture" based on drugs, rock music, and easy sex.

KENNEDY FIGHTS THE COLD WAR ON
THE NEW FRONTIER, 1961–1963

Young, charismatic John Fitzgerald Kennedy won the presidency in 1960 by narrowly defeating his Republican rival, Richard Nixon. A staunch cold warrior, Kennedy believed that communism fed on poverty, and so he advocated new foreign assistance programs.Crises in Cuba, Berlin, and Laos nearly ruined the administration; the Cuban missile crisis in 1962 almost touched off a nuclear war. At home Kennedy proposed an ambitious, liberal domestic program called the "New Frontier," but his proposals stalled in Congress. The growing momentum of the civil rights movement worried Kennedy, and only in 1963 did he propose a civil rights bill. His administration ended abruptly with his assassination.

THE ELECTION OF 1960   In 1960 Americans appeared restless, ready for change. Eisenhower's "middle way" had brought economic prosperity to many and political stability to the nation, but anxieties were triggered by mild economic recessions in 1957–1958 and 1960–1961. Many also feared that America was losing the arms race and the space race. The Republican nominee, Richard M. Nixon, who had loyally served Eisenhower through two terms, offered political continuity. Kennedy, a cold warrior in foreign policy and a tempered liberal domestically, conveyed youthful energy, wit, and the promise of change.

From the outset the race was close. Nixon made a strategic mistake by promising to campaign in all fifty states. While he exhausted himself flying all over the country, Kennedy focused on key states that held large blocs of electoral votes. In hindsight, Nixon's greatest mistake was to accept Kennedy's challenge to meet him in four nationally televised debates. The first debate proved crucial. More than seventy million Americans, the largest audience in history thus far, tuned in to the nation's first televised encounter between presidential candidates. Many believed that Nixon, an experienced college debater, would trounce his rival; but the photogenic, energetic Kennedy more than held his own against the perspiring and tired-looking Nixon.

Kennedy gained further momentum when he called the wife of the civil rights leader Martin Luther King, Jr., who had been sentenced to prison by a Georgia court on a trivial charge. Kennedy's supportive call stopped the erosion of black votes, which had begun to drift to the Republicans in 1956.

Kennedy's popularity among Catholics and blacks proved crucial. Kennedy barely won. A shift of fewer than 33,000 votes in both Illinois and Texas would have brought Nixon to the White House. Charges of massive Democratic voter fraud in Chicago, Texas, and Missouri clouded the election, but Nixon chose not to challenge the outcome.

Table 28.1   The 1960 Presidential Election of 1960

Candidates	Parties	Popular Vote	Percent	Electors	States
Kennedy	Democrat	34,227,096	49.9	303	23
Nixon	Republican	34,107,646	49.7	219	26
Byrd	Independent	285,820	0.4	15	1

MEETING THE COLD WAR CHALLENGE, **1961**   When Kennedy took office in 1961, the cold war was at its iciest. The Soviet Union, headed by the truculent Nikita Khrushchev, had emerged as a superpower and had begun to pursue an aggressive foreign policy in Latin America, Africa, and Asia. As a committed cold warrior, Kennedy prepared to meet the Soviet challenge.

Believing that communism fed on poverty, Kennedy sought to promote a "peaceful revolution" in the world's developing countries by creating the Peace Corps. Established in 1961, the Peace Corps offered young Americans a way to put idealism into practice: two years' service as teachers, engineers, agricultural experts, and health workers in forty developing nations. Kennedy also established the Agency for International Development (AID) to oversee foreign aid to these countries and established a foreign assistance program, the Alliance for Progress, for Latin America.

TESTING IN CUBA, BERLIN, AND LAOS, **1961**   Kennedy tended to view foreign policy as a series of tests posed by the Soviet Union, mainland China, and other communist countries. The first foreign policy test came in April 1961, when the United States Central Intelligence Agency (CIA) trained a group of 1,400 anti-Castro exiles to invade Cuba and overthrow Fidel Castro's communist government. The exiles landed at Cuba's Bay of Pigs, but when Kennedy refused to provide the outnumbered invasion force with American air support, they were forced to surrender within days. Although the Eisenhower administration had planned the Bay of Pigs invasion, Kennedy took full responsibility for the fiasco. After this episode, he was suspicious of the CIA and the foreign affairs bureaucracy within the State Department.

Kennedy's next test involved Berlin. The Soviets were determined to stop the flood of East German refugees seeking asylum in West Berlin. When Kennedy met with Khrushchev in Vienna in June 1961, the Soviet leader crudely demanded that the United States immediately withdraw its troops from West Berlin. Kennedy refused to budge, returned home, and called up 150,000 reservists and national guardsmen, increased the defense budget, scheduled maneuvers, and started a crash program to build nuclear fallout shelters.

In mid-August 1961 this tense atmosphere worsened when the Soviet-backed East German government began to build a wall between East Berlin and West Berlin. Adding to the tension, the Soviets withdrew from a voluntary agreement to ban nuclear testing. The Berlin Wall came to symbolize a world divided by superpowers capable of destroying the other with their nuclear arsenals.

Meanwhile, Kennedy confronted another crisis in the Southeast Asian nation of Laos. In this small, landlocked country bordering China, a communist insurgent movement, the Pathet Lao, appeared near victory. Shortly before leaving office, Eisenhower had encouraged Kennedy to intervene militarily, but Kennedy concluded that intervention would be a mistake logistically and diplomatically. Instead, he supported a Soviet proposal for negotiations between the unpopular rightist government in Laos and the Pathet Lao. Finally, both sides agreed to restore a neutralist government to power, although the insurgents continued to make headway in the countryside. Deciding that the communists should not be allowed to make any further gains in Southeast Asia, Kennedy resolved to provide military assistance to South Vietnam, which also faced a communist-backed insurgent movement in North Vietnam. Ironically, the Laos settlement convinced the North Vietnamese that American resolve to protect South Vietnam was weak.

FACING THE CUBAN MISSILE CRISIS, **1962**   In August 1962, rumors began to circulate that the Soviet Union was installing offensive nuclear missiles in Cuba. In October, intelligence photos taken by America's high-flying U-2 spy planes revealed the construction of medium- and intermediate-range missile sites in Cuba.

On October 22, Kennedy appeared on national television to reveal knowledge of the missile sites in Cuba. He demanded the missiles' immediate removal and ordered a naval blockade of Cuba to prevent Soviet ships from carrying missiles to Cuba. For the next five days, with the American military on full alert, the world teetered on the edge of nuclear war. Anxious Americans hoarded canned goods in preparation for war. After a week of confusing diplomatic messages, proposals, and counter-proposals, Radio Moscow announced on October 28, two days before Kennedy's deadline, that the Soviet Union was withdrawing its missiles from Cuba. The Soviets and the Americans had confronted one another, "eyeball to eyeball," and the Russians had blinked first. Kennedy appeared to have won a diplomatic victory. Privately, Kennedy had promised the Soviets to remove American missiles from Turkey in exchange for the Cuban withdrawal; he had also pledged that the United States would not invade Cuba. The crisis led to the ousting of Khrushchev two years

With his trademark beard and military fatigues, Fidel Castro addressed a Cuban workers' rally in 1961, two months before the United States launched the invasion at the Bay of Pigs. (© Hulton Archive/Getty Images)

later because of his "adventurist" foreign policy. Humiliated, the Soviet Union began a massive armaments buildup to gain parity with America's nuclear arsenal.

The Cuban missile crisis caused the administration to reevaluate American defense policy. During the presidential campaign, Kennedy had criticized the Eisenhower administration for allowing the United States to fall behind the Soviet Union in production of nuclear missiles. In reality, there was no "missile gap," and the United States held a technological lead. Following the missile crisis, defense strategists such as Secretary of Defense Robert McNamara convinced Kennedy that nuclear war could best be avoided if the Soviet Union developed nuclear parity with the United States. According to the Mutually Assured Destruction theory (called "MAD"), if both superpowers were equally capable of destroying each other, the threat of nuclear holocaust would cause each side to think twice about launching a first strike against the other.

On McNamara's advice, Kennedy proposed that *both* sides enter *mutually* into a formal treaty banning nuclear testing. In July 1963, Kennedy sent a delegation headed by W. Averell Harriman to Moscow to negotiate the test ban treaty. The final treaty, ratified in September 1963, banned only atmospheric testing, not underground testing; but other agreements set up a direct telephone "hot line" between the White House and the Kremlin and provided for American wheat to be sold to the Soviet Union. Kennedy, the cold warrior, had eased tensions between the two rival nations.

KENNEDY QUARRELS WITH CONGRESS, 1961–1963   Kennedy failed to develop good relations with key congressional members. Kennedy's style, while winning public approval, proved ineffectual with powerful committee chairmen, many of whom were older, conservative southerners who noted the president's inexperience, his tiny margin of victory, and the rumored sexual escapades. His vice president, Lyndon Baines Johnson, a politician with strong ties in Congress, felt underutilized, observing that the White House won the support of the congressional minnows but not the whales.

As a result Kennedy's major proposals for education, health, and welfare became stalled in Congress. So Kennedy focused his attention on a proposed tax cut instead. Having inherited a recession that raised unemployment to 6.7 percent in 1961, Kennedy needed to show that he could offer a program that would promote a high rate of economic growth without causing inflation. Kennedy moved to stimulate the economy by lowering top tax rates and providing an investment credit to give corporations a generous tax break. By the time the measure passed Congress, economic recovery was well under way, but the tax break further stimulated economic growth. This tax cut measure became a hallmark of Kennedy's administration.

Kennedy also enjoyed success with environmental legislation. In 1963 Rachel Carson's book *Silent Spring* became a bestseller with its sobering account of the toxic effects of DDT and other pesticides on wildlife in America. Carson's exposé set off a national furor that prompted Kennedy to establish an advisory committee on pesticides, which eventually produced tough new federal regulations. In 1963 Congress passed the first major Clean Air Act to regulate automobile and industrial emissions. These measures marked the awakening of a new environmental consciousness among Americans.

CIVIL RIGHTS HAUNT KENNEDY, 1961–1963   Civil rights troubled Kennedy. He correctly feared that new civil rights legislation would split the Democratic Party. While he appointed an unprecedented number of African Americans to high office and encouraged the Department of Justice to speed desegregation of southern schools, he named well-known white racists to federal judgeships in the South. During his campaign he had argued that

On August 28, 1963, at the March on Washington, Martin Luther King, Jr., greeted the crowd just before he gave his famous "I have a dream" speech. The event was broadcast around the world on the new Comsat satellite. (© Francis Miller/Time Life Pictures/Getty Images)

discrimination in federally financed housing could be eliminated with "a stroke of the pen," but not until his second year in office did Kennedy issue a weak executive order to remedy housing discrimination.

Black and white civil rights activists became increasingly impatient with Kennedy's timidity. In 1961 the Congress of Racial Equality (CORE) undertook courageous "freedom rides" to integrate buses and bus terminals throughout the Deep South. Attacks on the freedom riders by hostile white mobs forced Kennedy to send federal marshals to end the violence. In the fall of 1962, a riot broke out when James Meredith, a black air force veteran, attempted to enroll at the University of Mississippi. Backed by defiant Governor Ross Barnett, a mob attacked the federal marshals escorting Meredith; in the ensuing riot two died and hundreds were injured.

Each incident left civil rights leaders more determined to push Kennedy toward action. In early 1963 a confrontation between civil rights activists, led by Martin Luther King, Jr., and officials in Birmingham, Alabama, finally moved the conscience of the nation. This episode began when more than fifteen thousand blacks and activists attempted to march on city hall to demand the end of segregation. The police commissioner, Eugene "Bull" Connor, unleashed state troopers armed with fire hoses, dogs, and nightsticks. After images of this savage assault were broadcast on national television, Kennedy went on the air to declare, "Are we to say to the world that this is the land of the free, except for the Negroes? . . . Now the time has come for this nation to fulfill its promise." He called for a civil rights law to protect blacks.

In August 1963 the movement's leaders organized the March on Washington to support civil rights legislation. Martin Luther King, Jr., electrified the audience. "I have a dream," he declared, that someday "all of God's children, black men and white men, Jews and gentiles, Protestants and Catholics, will be able to join hands and sing the words of the old Negro spiritual: Free at last, free at last, thank God almighty, I'm free at last." That next summer, under Lyndon Johnson, the Civil Rights Act (1964) was passed, outlawing discrimination on the basis of race, creed, sex, or age.

Kennedy's actions hurt him politically in the South, although national polls rated his popularity high in the fall of 1963. In November 1963, the president traveled to Dallas, Texas, to shore up his southern political support. On November 22, as Kennedy rode with his wife in an open car past the cheering crowds, shots burst through the air, leaving the president mortally wounded. Two days later, a stunned nation witnessed on television the shooting of the accused assassin, Lee Harvey Oswald, by a Dallas bar owner with underworld connections. These events caused many to suspect a conspiracy, although no conclusive proof has ever been offered to confirm this. Stunned by this event, the nation turned to Vice President Lyndon Baines Johnson, upon whom the burdens of leadership now fell.

LYNDON JOHNSON LAUNCHES
THE GREAT SOCIETY, 1964–1965

Following Kennedy's death, President Lyndon Johnson launched a crusade to bring racial equality and economic opportunity to all Americans. He called his program the "Great Society." In his five years in office, Johnson saw more legislation enacted than had any other president. Bills were passed regarding civil rights, education, and medical care for the elderly and the poor. Johnson presided over the further expansion of the welfare state, but when his programs failed to fulfill the high expectations he had raised, the national mood turned to one of resentment.

JOHNSON DECLARES WAR ON POVERTY, 1964   "We have suffered a loss that cannot be weighed," Johnson told the nation on the day of Kennedy's assassination. "I will do my best. That is all I can do." The new president swore to carry on the Kennedy legacy, but his predecessor's image haunted him.

After three years of neglect and humiliation in the Kennedy administration, Johnson remained resentful and defensive. Johnson knew that many on Kennedy's staff, including his brother, Attorney General Robert Kennedy, had opposed Johnson's selection as vice president.

Johnson represented the old Democratic Party with its base in the South and the congressional committee system. Johnson had risen through Congress to become the Senate majority leader in 1953 by carefully cultivating older, more powerful men such as Speaker of the House Sam Rayburn, a fellow Texan.

An obsessive man, Johnson alternatively flattered and badgered other politicians. He rarely slept, and wore down opponents with late-night phone calls and ample supplies of liquor. A large man physically, Johnson intimidated fellow senators and was so hard on his staff that most quit from exhaustion within a year.

When Johnson stepped into the presidency, he found approximately fifty pieces of Kennedy's legislation stalled in Congress. He quickly moved to cajole a sympathetic Congress to fulfill the Kennedy dream. After pushing through a Kennedy-proposed tax cut, Johnson led Congress to enact the most comprehensive civil rights bill since Reconstruction, despite a fifty-seven-day filibuster by a group of southern Democrats. The Civil Rights Act (1964) provided safeguards for voting; prohibited discrimination in public places; offered assistance for the desegregation of public schools; and outlawed discrimination in employment on the grounds of race, color, religion, sex, or national origin. Although Congress was assured that the law did not require quotas, the Equal Employment Opportunity Commission, established under the legislation, later defined "equal opportunity" in such terms, thereby provoking further legal and political argument.

A former history teacher, Johnson sought to impart historic meaning to his administration by waging a "war on poverty." He remained convinced that poverty could be eliminated in his lifetime. At his urging, Congress voted to establish the Office of Economic Opportunity (OEO), the centerpiece of the war on poverty. Headed by Sargent Shriver, Kennedy's brother-in-law and the former director of the Peace Corps, the OEO was charged with the oversight of job training, work relief, remedial and adult education, rural assistance, small business loans, a domestic Peace Corps, and a Community Action Program (CAP) to enlist the poor in the war on poverty.

The Community Action Program became the most visible program in the war on poverty through its mandate to organize poor communities.

Community organizing, however, generated political factionalism among the groups who claimed to represent the poor, and antagonized vested interests. It quickly became a lightning rod for attacks from both the Right and the Left.

Middle-class whites reacted with hostility to a program they thought fostered welfare and radicalism. By 1965, less than a year after declaring this war, increased racial tensions and growing involvement in the war in Vietnam had led the politically astute Johnson to distance himself from his own war on poverty.

JOHNSON WINS, RAISES EXPECTATIONS   In 1964 Johnson seemed certain to win a second term when the ideologically divided Republican Party nominated Barry Goldwater, a conservative Arizona senator. Promising "a choice, not an echo," Goldwater chose as his campaign slogan "In Your Heart You Know He's Right." Critics replied, "You Know He's Too Far Right," or "In Your Head You Know He's Nuts."

With Goldwater on his right, Johnson moved toward the political center by downplaying his support for the welfare state and civil rights, even though his running mate, Senator Hubert Humphrey of Minnesota, was a well-known liberal. The president portrayed Goldwater as a danger to the world, a man who would not hesitate to use atomic weapons if necessary. On election day, Johnson won more than 43 million votes (61.1 percent) to Goldwater's 27.1 million (38.5 percent). Johnson's landslide victory provided coattails as Democrats gained thirty-seven seats in Congress, ensuring that liberals would dominate both ends of Pennsylvania Avenue.

In 1965 Congress passed unprecedented social legislation, including Medicare and Medicaid, which provided national health insurance for the elderly and the needy. Other legislation provided massive federal aid to education, from kindergarten to graduate school; funds for urban development, housing, and transit; and established the National Endowments for the Arts and the Humanities to promote culture, public television, and public radio. Congress also liberalized immigration and approved the Voting Rights Act (1965), which provided federal examiners to register voters in the South.

The rhetoric of the Johnson administration only raised expectations further. Johnson promised to eliminate poverty in ten years, to rebuild America's cities and beautify its highways (a special project of Johnson's wife, Lady Bird), to educate all Americans, to provide meaningful jobs to everyone who desired work, and to improve race relations. He thus offered dreams that left the impatient unfulfilled and the realistic skeptical.

AMERICANS STRUGGLE FOR EQUALITY, 1961–1971

After 1963 many African Americans became increasingly militant. While Martin Luther King, Jr., continued to press the Democratic administration for new civil rights legislation, young blacks, influenced more by Malcolm X and the Black Muslims, turned to black nationalism and separatism. Militant black leaders such as Stokely Carmichael and H. Rap Brown denounced nonviolent protest. Race riots in 1965 and 1966 caused white backlash and further exacerbated racial tensions. Inspired by black activism, Native Americans, Hispanics, and Asians likewise asserted their ethnic identities and rights. Women, too, organized their own liberation movement.

THE BLACK CIVIL RIGHTS MOVEMENT MARCHES, 1965   Following passage of the Civil Rights Act (1964), Johnson felt that further civil rights legislation should be delayed, to give Americans a chance to assimilate the profound changes brought about by that bill. Social conditions for African Americans had improved; between 1947 and the late 1960s, for example, black household income more than doubled. With segregation in the South on the verge of collapse, Martin Luther King, Jr., and other civil rights leaders demanded a new voting rights bill that would extend federal protection to the polling place.

To apply political pressure, King targeted Selma, Alabama, as the focus of the Southern Christian Leadership Conference (SCLC) campaign to register black voters. Local white officials resisted, and in March 1965 civil rights marchers faced a brutal attack by state troopers swinging clubs from horseback. More than ninety blacks were hospitalized after the attack. Shocked by the brutality of "Bloody Sunday," as the day came to be called, ABC Television interrupted its Sunday night movie, *Judgment at Nuremberg,* to report the assault. The events at Selma moved the nation and the president, and in August 1965 Johnson signed the Voting Rights Act.

MILITANTS SPEAK OUT, 1963–1966   Many African Americans, however, turned militant. In an increasingly tense atmosphere, some looked to the Black Muslims, also called the "Nation of Islam." The Nation of Islam had been founded in 1931 in Detroit by Elijah Muhammad, who urged blacks to practice self-discipline and reject integration. In the early 1960s Malcolm X, who had rejected his "slave name" of Malcolm Little, gained national attention as a spokesman for the Muslims. He called upon African Americans to separate from "white devil" culture and to free themselves "by any means necessary." He told audiences that, with John F. Kennedy's violent death, "the chickens have come home to roost" because whites had perpetuated centuries of violence on blacks. After a pilgrimage to Mecca, Saudi Arabia, however, Malcolm X declared that cooperation among people of different races was possible, but in 1965, shortly after this startling reversal, he was assassinated.

In August 1965 a confrontation between police and young blacks in the Watts section of Los Angeles led to six days of rioting. Thousands of rioters battled police officers, firefighters, and national guardsmen. In the end, an estimated $30 million worth of property was destroyed, thirty-four people killed, nine hundred injured, and nearly four thousand arrested. Riots followed in Chicago and in Springfield, Massachusetts.

The following summer, in 1966, race riots broke out in thirty-eight cities. Cleveland experienced the most sustained outbreak, but police and national guardsmen were also called out in San Francisco, Chicago, Dayton, and Milwaukee. Cries of "Get whitey" and "Burn, baby, burn" were heard through the conflagrations.

Young militants in the civil rights movement espoused "Black Power." The main black youth group, the Student Nonviolent Coordinating Committee (SNCC), expelled that organization's whites. Its leader, Stokely Carmichael, declared, "The only way we are gonna stop them white men from whuppin us is to take over. . . . What we gonna start saying now is Black Power." Carmichael's successor in SNCC, H. Rap Brown, used even more inflammatory language by declaring, "Don't be trying to love that honky [white man] to death. Shoot him to death."

In Oakland, California, Huey Newton and Bobby Seale organized the Black Panther Party in 1967 to urge blacks to undertake "armed self-defense." They quoted the Chinese communist leader Mao Zedong's statement that "political power comes through the barrel of a gun."

RACIAL PRIDE GROWS   As the Black Power movement spread, other ethnic communities took up the call for "Red Power," "Brown Power," and "Yellow Power." Militant Native American leaders organized protests that moved from the reservations into the cities.

Native-American activists clashed with state officials in Washington over fishing rights on the Columbia River and Puget Sound. A group of Native Americans from various tribes invaded the recently closed federal prison on Alcatraz Island in San Francisco Bay and claimed the island as their own. This intertribal cooperation led to the organization of the militant American Indian Movement (AIM), which battled tribal elites, entrenched interests, and the Bureau of Indian Affairs.

Mexican Americans took up the cry of "Brown Power." Farm workers, led by Cesar Chavez and his United Farm Workers union, called a strike in the grape fields of California in 1965. When growers hired strike-breakers, Chavez and other labor leaders organized a nationwide boycott of grapes that eventually forced growers to recognize the union. Still, fewer than 20 percent of farm workers were ever organized.

Mexican-American militants demanded that bilingual and bicultural education be instituted in public schools. In response the Bilingual Education Act (1968) provided funds for bilingual education to public schools. In New Mexico, Hispanics organized the militant and sometimes violent Alianza movement. Emphasizing that their ancestors had lived in New Mexico for four hundred years, they demanded the return of the territory they alleged the Anglos had taken from them. Mexicanos organized the Crusade for Justice in Colorado and La Raza Unida in Texas.

REDEFINING GENDER RULES AND ROLES, 1963–1971   A new feminist movement also reflected the emergence of a radical consciousness concerning self-identity. Kennedy assisted the new feminist awareness when he established the President's Commission on the Status of Women. The commission's final report, *American Women* (1963), documented that women were still denied many rights and opportunities enjoyed by men. As a consequence, many states established commissions on the status of women.

During this same time, Betty Friedan published *The Feminine Mystique* (1963), a bestseller that questioned the cultural assumption that women could find fulfillment only as wives and mothers. This "mystique," argued Friedan, left women feeling trapped without independent careers. In 1966 Friedan helped organize the National Organization for Women (NOW).

More militant feminists called for "women's liberation" by openly criticizing the Black Power movement and the New Left for their "male chauvinism." Across the country, radical feminists organized "consciousness-raising" groups to discuss ways in which women were oppressed and ways to overcome their oppression. Feminists established health groups, day care centers, abortion counseling services, and a range of collectives. In August 1970 feminists organized the largest women's rights demonstration in American history; tens of thousands of women across the nation paraded under the banner of the Women's Strike for Equality. Demonstrations called for equal employment opportunities and legal abortions. Underneath this appearance of solidarity, however, an ideological rift became evident between liberals and radicals within the movement.

Some feminists announced their lesbianism and demanded rights as homosexuals. By the early 1970s female and male homosexual lifestyles had become somewhat fashionable in certain circles, and "coming out" became more frequent as homosexuals discovered that they, too, could claim to be a minority long discriminated against by majority culture. In 1969 male homosexuals rioted against abusive police officers at New York's Stone Wall bar. The Stone Wall riot marked an important turning point in the homosexual liberation movement.

These liberation movements challenged the traditional vision of the American "melting pot" in which all groups are assimilated into one culture. Later critics, however, accused these radical movements of heading toward a "cult of otherness" that envisioned a society made up of subgroups: African Americans, Hispanics, Asians, women, and homosexuals who identified only with their own minority cultures. Proponents of these new movements responded by arguing that American society needed to acknowledge and encourage the existing diversity of cultures within it.

VIETNAM: THE UNITED STATES BEGINS ITS LONGEST WAR, 1961–1968

In the early 1960s the United States sent a few thousand military advisers to South Vietnam to help suppress communist guerrilla insurgents (the Vietcong) in that country. In August 1964, though, following an alleged attack on two American ships patrolling in North Vietnam's Gulf of Tonkin, Johnson escalated the war. Although Johnson pledged to limit America's involvement, he launched a military campaign in Vietnam.

Reports of atrocities by Americans intensified domestic opposition to the already unpopular war. The Tet offensive, a major campaign mounted by the Vietcong and North Vietnamese in 1968, discredited Johnson's assurances that the United States was on the verge of victory. When antiwar Democrats challenged Johnson for the 1968 presidential nomination, he was forced to announce his retirement.

AMERICA GETS ENTANGLED IN VIETNAM, **1961–1964**   When Kennedy took office, two thousand American military "advisers" were in South Vietnam aiding the government in its efforts to suppress a well-organized guerrilla group, the Vietcong. Kennedy hoped to avoid American involvement in a full-scale land war in Southeast Asia by means of a counterinsurgency program organized around "strategic hamlets." This strategy called for peasants to be relocated to fortified villages by South Vietnamese troops. Americans also urged South Vietnam's government, headed by the Catholic leader Ngo Dinh Diem, to undertake serious social and economic reform. Continued corruption and political repression by Diem's government, however,

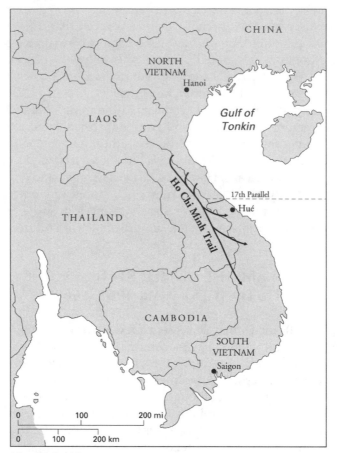

Map 28.1   Vietnam

brought other groups into open opposition, especially among the country's Buddhist majority.

In October 1963, with American encouragement, South Vietnamese generals finally staged a coup and executed Diem. Three weeks later John F. Kennedy was assassinated in Dallas. By then the United States had sixteen thousand "advisers" in Vietnam.

Johnson came into the White House with a reputation as a "hawk," that is, one who sought greater American involvement in Vietnam. In August 1964, the president found an opportunity to widen the war when two American destroyers patrolling in the Gulf of Tonkin off North Vietnam's coast were allegedly attacked by North Vietnamese patrol boats. (Due to fabricated evidence, the real nature of the incident remains unclear.) Johnson asked Congress for a resolution granting authority to "take all necessary measures to repel any armed attack against the forces of the United States." The Senate passed the so-called Gulf of Tonkin Resolution 88 votes to 2. The House passed the resolution without a single dissenting vote.

In lobbying for the Gulf of Tonkin Resolution, Johnson assured Congress that he sought to contain the present conflict, but in fact he used the resolution to justify a rapid escalation of United States involvement. In doing so, Johnson failed to anticipate a prolonged and brutal conflict that would severely divide public opinion.

Although the leader of North Vietnam, Ho Chi Minh, was a ruthless communist who had his opponents killed, many American antiwar dissenters saw him as the George Washington of his country, a nation conceived in revolution against a colonial power. On the other hand, various leaders in South Vietnam *were* corrupt and incompetent.

JOHNSON EXPANDS THE WAR, 1965–1967   What began as a limited engagement in a distant land soon escalated into a full-scale war that lacked both clear objectives and a firm moral basis. During early 1965 Americans remained confused as the war continued, several South Vietnamese governments fell, and American casualties rose. In 1965 Johnson ordered sustained bombing of North Vietnam through "Operation Rolling Thunder." Johnson hoped that bombing selective sites in North Vietnam would force Ho's government to negotiate. From 1965 to 1968, the United States dropped eight hundred tons of bombs daily on North Vietnam. When North Vietnam refused to talk, Johnson sent additional American troops into Vietnam. There were 184,000 troops there by the end of 1965.

By 1967 the United States had nearly half a million troops in Vietnam. General William Westmoreland, the American commander, asserted that the United States was winning the war. Seeking to draw the highly mobile, lightly equipped enemy into open battle, Westmoreland evacuated huge areas, declaring them "free fire zones" and all remaining inhabitants hostile. Bombing sorties caused an estimated half-million civilian casualties. Surrounding areas were cleared by spraying defoliants such as Agent Orange that caused the lush green jungles to turn brown. Crops, livestock, and homes were systematically obliterated. One American officer commented, after surveying the destruction of one such village, "We had to destroy the town in order to save it."

By its guerrilla nature the war meant that both sides terrorized peasants. While insurgents undertook land reform in villages they controlled, the Vietcong also conducted a systematic campaign of brutal assassination of enemies. Village chiefs who opposed the communist-controlled National Liberation Front (NLF) were often beheaded and dismembered.

The destruction and burning of Vietnamese villages by American soldiers was also brutal. Americans used deadly napalm, a flammable gel that stuck to clothing and skin. Finding it impossible to distinguish between "friendlies" and the Vietcong, some American soldiers fired indiscriminately at Vietnamese peasants. One of the worst cases of indiscriminate slaughter occurred on March 16, 1968, when an American combat unit captured the small village of My Lai and systematically executed four hundred civilians, mostly old men, women, and children. The My Lai massacre fueled further outrage at home against the war.

TET TOPPLES JOHNSON, 1968   Still, Johnson believed the war was being won. Then, on January 30, 1968, the beginning of the Vietnamese New Year (Tet), North Vietnam's regulars and their allies the Vietcong launched a major offensive that startled the Americans. Attacking thirty-six of forty-four provincial capitals, the communists seized the old imperial capital of Hue and occupied it for a month. In Saigon a suicide squad penetrated the American diplomatic–military compound before being driven off. The Tet offensive was contained in a matter of weeks. An estimated 42,000 communists were killed during it.

Afterward, General Westmoreland claimed a military victory, but the communists nevertheless had won an important political one. The offensive revealed their unexpected strength and determination throughout South Vietnam. Even reports of the massacre of two thousand Vietnamese civilians by communist troops in Hue did little to persuade increasingly disillusioned Americans that the war was worth fighting. The Johnson administration's rosy portrayal of a quick, easy victory was completely discredited; even Johnson's top advisers, including Secretary of Defense Robert McNamara, until then a hawk, concluded that the United States needed to extricate itself from the Vietnam quagmire. McNamara's opposition to the war led to his replacement by Clark Clifford. The Tet offensive bolstered the political strength of the "doves" (opponents of the war) within the Democratic Party.

While liberal senators such as William Fulbright of Arkansas and Robert Kennedy of New York denounced the war, other leaders, including Martin Luther King, Jr., and the influential pediatrician, Benjamin Spock, called for draft resistance. Increasing draft calls in 1965 had ignited a protest movement on American college campuses. In the spring of 1965, some twenty thousand people—far more than organizers expected—attended the first major antiwar rally in Washington, D.C. Opposition to the war spread from pacifists and leftists to members of the clergy, liberal Democrats, and the general public. As the war escalated, the antiwar movement itself split; some segments turned radical and violent. Many spoke not of changing the system but of overthrowing it. Protest led some into revolutionary rhetoric or violence.

Opposition to the war spilled over into the Democratic Party. Johnson's approval rating dropped to 35 percent, the lowest since Truman. By the spring of 1968, polls showed the nation equally divided between "doves" and "hawks." This antiwar sentiment allowed Senator Eugene McCarthy of Minnesota to challenge Johnson in the Democratic presidential primary in New Hampshire. McCarthy's campaign drew five thousand students from across the country, who cut their long hair and shaved their beards to ring doorbells on his behalf. This "clean for Gene" campaign paid off; McCarthy won nearly half the votes cast in the March primary. At this point Robert Kennedy, who had hesitantly stayed on the sidelines, entered the presidential race.

On March 31, 1968, Johnson appeared on evening television to announce a halt of bombing in the North as a first step to end the conflict. He then added, "I shall not seek and I will not accept the nomination of my party." Johnson left office a disappointed man who realized that war in Vietnam had marred his presidency. Years later he explained in his homespun way that the Great Society was a beautiful lady and his true love, yet he had felt compelled to embrace war, ugly old whore that she was.

YOUNG PEOPLE SEEK SOLUTIONS

"Something's happening here / What it is ain't exactly clear. . . ." The refrain from Buffalo Springfield's popular rock song "For What It's Worth" (1967) captured the mood of the times. It was clear to most people, radicals and traditionalists alike, that something was indeed happening to popular culture, especially among the youth. On college campuses angry students turned to New Left radical politics to change society and stop the war in Vietnam.

Many youths expressed political cynicism, rejected materialist values, and searched for intensity of experience through alternatives such as drugs, mysticism, and sexuality. The result was a loosely defined counterculture based on inarticulate feelings and unclarified sentiment.

ORGANIZING THE NEW LEFT   In the late 1950s a number of college students had protested against nuclear weapons testing. Many of these student leaders sought to create a new radical politics that broke with cold war alignments. In 1962 several dozen students sponsored by the socialist League for Industrial Democracy met at Port Huron, Michigan, to draft a

Angry antiwar protestors clashed with police on the University of Wisconsin campus in 1967. Demonstrators needed to prove to themselves that cowardice was not the basis for their opposition to the Vietnam War. (AP/Wide World Photos)

charter for a new organization, Students for a Democratic Society (SDS). Written mostly by Tom Hayden, a student at the University of Michigan, the Port Huron Statement rejected both American capitalism and Soviet-style communism for an envisioned "participatory democracy" in which citizens would directly control political decisions affecting their lives.

Two years later, in the fall of 1964, students at the University of California, Berkeley, organized a massive protest against the university's decision to ban political groups from setting up tables on campus to distribute their literature. Organized into the Free Speech Movement (FSM), the students held a massive sit-in that led to nearly eight hundred arrests and conducted a strike that closed down classes. The strike garnered sufficient faculty support to pressure the university administration to back down and open the campus to political activity.

In January 1966 the government abolished automatic draft deferments for college students, a move that mobilized campus protest across the country. Activist students burned draft cards, disrupted Reserve Officers' Training Corps (ROTC) classes, and protested war-related corporate recruiting efforts on campus. Dow Chemical Corporation, the manufacturer of napalm, was singled out for angry protests. In 1967 the SDS urged more militant resistance through open acts of civil disobedience. That spring nearly half a million antiwar protesters, mostly young and long-haired, converged on New York's Central Park in the largest demonstration against the war. As protesters chanted, "Hell, no, we won't go," and "Hey, hey, LBJ, how many kids did you kill today?" many waved signs reading "Make love, not war."

Not all American youth participated in the protest movement. Indeed, most students remained middle-of-the-road politically. Surveys at the time revealed that the vast majority of college students believed that the United States should either win the war or get out. Antiwar sentiment was strongest at the most elite colleges and universities. Furthermore, the number of students who identified themselves as conservatives, members of such organizations as Young Americans for Freedom, equalled the number of radicals on campus.

MAKING THE COUNTERCULTURE   Most political activists separated themselves from the larger youth counterculture represented by "hippies," youths who chose an alternative life style by rejecting political involvement, taking drugs, wearing their hair long, and living communally. Most middle-class adults failed to distinguish between hippies and activists, however, especially since many activists also wore long hair, listened to rock music, and took drugs. Hippies followed a path of noninvolvement, heeding to varying degrees the dictum of counterculture's high priest, Timothy Leary, a former Harvard psychologist, to "tune in, turn on, drop out." The widespread use of drugs contributed to this ethic.

In the early 1960s young people listened to antiwar and civil rights protest songs by folksingers like Joan Baez; Peter, Paul, and Mary;and Bob Dylan. In 1964, the English rock group the Beatles swept the United States with such innocuous songs as "I Want to Hold Your Hand." At the top of the charts for more than two years, the Beatles' music took a decidedly different turn with the album *Sgt. Pepper's Lonely Hearts Club Band* (1967). This album, some believed, glorified drugs; for others it opened a whole new musical world, challenging traditional culture in fundamental ways. Other boldly innovative performers were Jimi Hendrix, Janis Joplin, and Jim Morrison, all three of whom died of drug overdoses.

Closely associated with youth culture was a sexual revolution that changed sexual practices and perceptions. Promiscuity became common, and increasing numbers of young couples chose to live together outside of marriage. Homosexuality became more open and accepted. Although many welcomed the new sexual liberation, others feared that the erosion of traditional values would lead to the decline of the family, a rise in divorce and abortion, and erosion of the social order. Ironically, while many proponents of the counterculture decried the negative influence of technology and mass society, they also benefited from technology. The sexual revolution was made possible by the development of artificial contraception: "the pill."

CONCLUSION

As the decade drew to a close, Americans appeared polarized over politics and culture. The idealism of American youth in the first part of the decade had given way to anger, frustration, and despair. Americans in general and young people in particular found political involvement meaningless, distrusted politicians, and considered participation in the "establishment" (American business and government) as "selling out." In these circumstances, many felt that American society was coming apart and that Americans had lost control of their future.

Recommended Readings

DOCUMENTS: Joan Didion, *Slouching Towards Bethlehem* (1968); Todd Gitlin, *The Sixties* (1987); Anne Moody, *Coming of Age in Mississippi* (1968); Theodore Roszak, *The Making of a Counter Culture* (1969).

READINGS: (GENERAL) John Morton Blum, *Years of Discord* (1991); William Chafe, *Unfinished Journey* (1986); Godfrey Hodgson, *America in Our Time* (1976); Allen Matusow, *The Unraveling of America* (1984); Charles R. Morris, *A Time of Passion: America, 1960–1980* (1988). (KENNEDY AND JOHNSON) James N. Giglio, *The Presidency of John F. Kennedy* (1991); Paul Conkin, *Big Daddy from the Pedernales: Lyndon Baines Johnson* (1986); Greg Davis, *Years of Poverty, Years of Plenty* (1984); Hugh Davis Graham, *Uncertain Trumpet* (1984); Jim Heath, *Decade of Dillusionment* (1975); Lyndon Johnson, *Vantage Point* (1971); Doris Kearns, *Lyndon Johnson and the American Dream* (1976) and *JFK: The Presidency of John F. Kennedy* (1983); Walter McDougall, *The Heavens and the Earth: A Political History of the Space Age* (1985); Charles Murray, *Losing Ground: American Social Policy* (1984); W. J. Rorabaugh, *Kennedy and the Promise of the Sixties* (2003); Tom Wicker, *JFK and LBJ* (1968). (FOREIGN POLICY) Graham Allison, *Essence of Decision: Explaining the Cuban Missile Crisis* (1971); Loren Baritz, *Backfire: A History of How American Culture Led Us into Vietnam* (1985); Larry Berman, *Planning a Tragedy* (1982); Frances Fitzgerald, *Fire in the Lake* (1972); Leslie Gelb and Richard Betts, *The Irony of Vietnam*; Mike Gravel et al., *The Pentagon Papers* (1975); David Halberstam, *The Best and the Brightest* (1972); George Kahin, *Intervention: How America Became Involved in Vietnam* (1986); Stanley Karnow, *Vietnam* (1983); Gabriel Kolko, *Anatomy of a War* (1985); Kathryn Marshall, *In the Combat Zone: An Oral History of Women in the Vietnam War* (1987); Norman Podhoretz, *Why We Were in Vietnam* (1982); Al Santoli,

Everything We Had: An Oral History of the Vietnam War (1981); Neil Sheehan, *A Bright Shining Lie* (1988); Harry Summer, Jr., *On Strategy: A Critical Analysis of the Vietnam War* (1981); Wallace Terry, *Bloods: An Oral History of the Vietnam War by Black Veterans* (1984); James S. Olson and Randy Roberts, *Where the Domino Fell* (1991); Glen Seaborg, *Kennedy, Khrushchev, and the Test Ban* (1981). (CIVIL RIGHTS) Michael Belknap, *Federal Law and Southern Order* (1987); Taylor Branch, *Parting the Waters* (1988); Carl Brauer, *John F. Kennedy and the Second Reconstruction* (1980); Stokely Carmichael and Charles Hamilton, *Black Power* (1967); Clayborne Carson, *In Struggle: SNCC and the Black Awakening* (1981); William Chafe, *Civilities and Civil Rights* (1980); David Garrow, *Bearing the Cross* (1986); Steven Lawson, *Black Ballots* (1976) and *In Pursuit of Power* (1985); Malcolm X (with Alex Haley), *The Autobiography of Malcolm X* (1966); August Meier and Elliot Rudwick, *CORE* (1975); Harvard Sitkoff, *The Struggle for Black Equality* (1981); Nancy J. Weiss, *Whitney M. Young, Jr., and the Struggle for Civil Rights* (1989). (SOCIETY AND CULTURE) John Patrick Diggins, *The Rise and Fall of the American Left* (1992); David Farber, *Chicago,'68* (1988); Maurice Isserman, *If I Had a Hammer* (1987); James Miller, *Democracy Is in the Streets* (1987); William O'Neill, *Coming Apart* (1971); Kirkpatrick Sale, *SDS* (1973); Ed Ward et al., *Rock of Ages: The Rolling Stone History of Rock and Roll* (1986); Lawrence Wittner, *Rebels against the War* (1984).

29

🐾

The Tumultuous Years: Nixon–Ford–Carter, 1968–1980

OVERVIEW   In 1968 the Vietnam war raged and violence erupted at home. Martin Luther King, Jr., and Robert F. Kennedy were assassinated. That summer at the Democratic national convention in Chicago, police battled protesters. Republican Richard Nixon defeated Democrat Hubert Humphrey for the presidency, campaigning on the promise to restore law and order and end the war.

Nixon pressured the North Vietnamese into a negotiated settlement while he pursued a policy of détente with the Soviet Union and opened diplomatic relations with China. At home he proposed to reform the welfare system, to give federal funds to the states through "new federalism," and to control inflation. Nixon easily won reelection in 1972, but the Watergate scandal, involving a break-in at the Democratic National Committee headquarters during the 1972 campaign, forced his resignation from office. His successors, Gerald Ford and Jimmy Carter, failed to win public confidence. By 1980 many Americans believed that the "American century"—the promise of continued American prosperity and international leadership—had ended in dismal failure.

1968: THE YEAR OF DISARRAY

In 1968 unprecedented violence haunted the nation. Martin Luther King, Jr., and Robert F. Kennedy were assassinated; race riots and violent protest became commonplace. With King's death, advocates of black violence became more influential. Radical students at elite universities turned increasingly to violence. Political protest climaxed at the Democratic convention in Chicago, where vicious police attacks on protesters eclipsed Hubert Humphrey's nomination. Repelled by the turmoil and the extremist rhetoric of young radicals, the white middle class and blue-collar workers deserted the Democratic Party to elect Richard Nixon, who promised "peace with honor" in Vietnam and "law and order" at home.

VIOLENCE ESCALATES   The year 1968 brought escalating and often seemingly pointless violence to American cities and political life. In March 1968, the National Advisory (Kerner) Commission on Civil Disorders reported on the race riots that had occurred during the previous three years. Blaming "white racism," the commission called for a "massive" economic program targeted at the inner city to relieve tensions within the black community. Less than a month later, on April 4, 1968, the civil rights leader Martin Luther King, Jr., was assassinated in Memphis, Tennessee.

King went to Memphis to support a group of black sanitation workers who had been on strike for nearly a month. The night before he was slain, King prophetically announced in a speech to supporters that his struggle on behalf of civil rights had placed his life in danger. He passionately declared, "I've seen the Promised Land. I may not get there with you. But I want you to know tonight that we as a people will get to the Promised Land."

Following news of the assassination, rioting broke out in cities across America. In Washington, D.C., flames of burning buildings crackled only three blocks from the White House. In Chicago, Mayor Richard Daley ordered police to "shoot to kill" looters. By week's end, forty-six people had died in rioting across the nation. From 1964 through 1968, riots destroyed an estimated $200 million in property and left two hundred dead, seven thousand injured, and forty thousand arrested.

King's death was a major setback for the civil rights movement. Many within the movement now rejected King's strategy of nonviolence and denounced King for not being militant enough. In certain circles the rhetoric of revolutionary violence replaced King's message of nonviolent resistance. H. Rap Brown proclaimed that violence was "as American as cherry pie." Other black militants spoke ominously of robbery and rape as "revolutionary" acts against oppressive white society.

Following the Tet offensive in late January 1968, the antiwar movement became increasingly militant. Students for a Democratic Society (SDS), the principal radical student group, splintered into warring factions, each claiming to be truly revolutionary. In the spring of 1968, student protest turned violent. Much of this activity involved only a small number of students at elite universities such as Harvard, Cornell, Columbia, Berkeley, Michigan, and Stanford.

In April 1968 radical students at Columbia University, led by SDS leader Mark Rudd, seized control of the administration building to protest the construction of a student gymnasium in a park in neighboring Harlem. When police (who were mostly from the outraged working class) brutally attacked the students and recaptured the buildings, other students staged a general strike that closed the campus. The Columbia strike inspired student radicals across the country.

THE ELECTION OF **1968**   The presidential election of 1968 focused on the war in Vietnam. After the antiwar candidate Eugene McCarthy showed surprising strength in the New Hampshire primary, Robert Kennedy entered the race. President Johnson withdrew as a candidate, leaving McCarthy and Kennedy bitterly struggling for the peace vote. Vice President Hubert Humphrey made it a three-way race.

McCarthy embodied the moral fervor and idealism of the peace movement. A devout Catholic given to reading philosophy and writing poetry, he appeared to eschew politics. Robert Kennedy also spoke of peace but appealed to working-class ethnic voters and minority groups. McCarthy was a one-issue candidate, but Kennedy was cheered by blacks in New York, Hispanics in Phoenix, poor whites in Appalachian West Virginia, and Irish Americans in Chicago. He appeared about to gain the Democratic nomination when tragedy struck. After winning the important California primary on June 5, Kennedy was assassinated by an Arab nationalist.

The nation was shocked by the death of another Kennedy within five years and the second major assassination in 1968. Humphrey stepped forward to claim his party's nomination. Embittered and frustrated by the democratic process, students in the antiwar movement turned to the politics of the streets. When the Democrats met in Chicago for their convention, antiwar protesters gathered outside the convention hotels to battle the police. While Chicago's Mayor Richard Daley shouted obscenities at delegates protesting on the floor of the convention hall, his police went after the protesters outside with a viciousness that appalled the country. As television cameras whirred, the bloodied protesters chanted, "the whole world is watching." After the convention, Humphrey's nomination elicited little excitement from an alienated and hostile electorate. The disarray of the Democratic Party opened the way for a third-party candidate, conservative Democrat Governor George Wallace of Alabama, to run on the American Independent ticket. Wallace appealed to less educated white

Table 29.1   The 1968 Presidential Election

Candidates	Parties	Popular Vote	Electoral Vote
Richard M. Nixon	Republican	31,785,480 (43.4)	301
Hubert H. Humphrey	Democrat	31,275,166 (42.7)	191
George C. Wallace	American Independent	9,906,473 (13.5)	46

voters who welcomed his attacks on "pointy-headed intellectuals and bu-reaucrats," black militants, hippies, welfare mothers, and "bearded anar-chists." His running mate, retired Air Force General Curtis LeMay, terrified many when he spoke of dropping "nukes" on Vietnam. Nonetheless, Sep-tember polls estimated Wallace's support among the electorate at more than 20 percent, close to Humphrey's 28 percent.

The Republicans, turning back to their center, nominated former Vice President Richard Nixon. Many believed that Nixon's political career had ended with his failed presidential bid in 1960 and unsuccessful run for the governorship of California in 1962. Nevertheless, Nixon won the 1968 Re-publican nomination on the first ballot.

Nixon hoped to cut into the Democratic majority by courting south-ern whites, working-class white ethnics, and the suburban middle class. This strategy entailed support of law and order, reform of the "welfare mess," and the promise of a "secret plan" to end the war in Vietnam.

By 1968 the white working class and poor whites alike identified the Great Society with black militants and race riots. As a result, Humphrey received just 38 percent of the white vote. Instead, former Democratic loy-alists, including white southerners, ethnic Catholics, and union members, switched to either Wallace or Nixon. The Sun Belt, including the South, shifted toward the GOP as well. Concerned with law and order, disdain-ful of welfare programs, and opposed to forced busing, these voters de-clared themselves ripe to become Republicans. In so doing, they gave the Republicans a chance to build a clear majority that would dominate American presidential politics for the next two decades.

NIXON PURSUES A PRAGMATIC
FOREIGN POLICY, 1969–1973

Richard Nixon sought to end America's involvement in Vietnam through a negotiated settlement that would save as much face as possible for the United States. He intensified air strikes while withdrawing American ground troops. He increased bombing to pressure North Vietnam to ne-gotiate and tried to replace American troops with South Vietnamese troops. Seeking to break the back of communist forces, in the spring of 1970 he launched a major offensive in Cambodia, which unleashed violent protests at American colleges. Finally, secret negotiations conducted in Paris by foreign policy adviser Henry Kissinger led to a breakthrough that brought peace to Vietnam in late 1972. Two years later, North Vietnam conquered South Vietnam.

By resolving the war in Vietnam, Nixon also sought to stabilize relations with the Soviet Union and China. In securing nuclear arms reduction agreements with the Soviet Union and the diplomatic recognition of mainland China, Nixon the anticommunist showed his instinct for diplomatic compromise.

NIXON: THE MAN AND THE FOREIGN POLICY LEADER   Nixon's diplomatic skills reflected an instinctive political cunning, a sharp sense of himself as a poor boy who had fought his way to the top, and a knowledge of the world and international relations unequaled by most other presidents of the twentieth century.

Nixon had built a political career as an anticommunist crusader. He had defeated liberal Democrat Helen Douglas for the U.S. Senate, and he had led the prosecution of Alger Hiss; both efforts earned him the enmity of liberals. Nixon was far less conservative than portrayed by his opponents, but his role in the Hiss–Chambers investigation in the 1940s earned him a following among the Republican Right.

Although secretive, obsessed with politics, and concerned with his place in history, Nixon was a masterful politician, more often given to political opportunism than to strict ideology. Nixon came to the presidency in 1969 intent on making a name in foreign policy. He viewed himself as a "tough guy" who needed to take an aggressive line against the North Vietnamese. He appointed William Rogers to head the State Department and Henry Kissinger, a former adviser to Nelson Rockefeller, to chair the National Security Council. In the end, Kissinger eclipsed Rogers and later became secretary of state.

THE WAR IN VIETNAM GRINDS ON, **1969–1973**   By the time Nixon came to office in 1969, the war in Vietnam had become a major moral issue. Nixon, however, was far too pragmatic to view the war in terms of morality; he sought to get the United States out of Vietnam as expeditiously as possible at minimal cost to American prestige. To do so, he upgraded South Vietnam's military capacity through a policy of "Vietnamization." This entailed gradually turning the fighting over to the South Vietnamese and withdrawing American ground troops while at the same time intensifying the bombing of the North to bring Ho Chi Minh to the negotiating table.

Despite the intensified bombing, Nixon realized that LBJ's air offensive, Rolling Thunder, had failed to break the back of the North Vietnamese. He therefore sought a new option, a major offensive directed at the Ho Chi Minh Trail in Cambodia. Kissinger had reported that the communists were using the trail through Cambodia to bring a steady stream of replacement troops and supplies into Vietnam. Additionally, army intelligence told Nixon of a secret central headquarters in Cambodia used by the communists to prepare a major offensive in the South.

On April 30, 1970, Nixon announced a major U.S. ground offensive and air raids into Cambodia. The Cambodian invasion provoked furious protest on American college campuses. Radicals smashed windows and attacked police; campus leaders organized a nationwide student strike.

In Ohio, Governor James Rhodes ordered three thousand national guardsmen to restore order at Kent State University. On May 4 a squad of inexperienced and nervous guardsmen fired wildly into a group of rock-throwing protestors, killing two demonstrators and two bystanders. Reports of the Kent State killings only heightened tensions on campuses. Eleven days later state police killed two black students and wounded eleven at Jackson State College in Mississippi. Most campus demonstrations remained nonviolent, but the Cambodian invasion encouraged ultraradicals to undertake acts of terrorism. There were firebombings on at least ten campuses. Sixteen governors called out the national guard to quell unrest on twenty-one campuses. In California, Governor Ronald Reagan closed the twenty-eight campuses in the state university and college systems.

The war ground on. In February 1971 the South Vietnamese army invaded Laos to cut off the flow of supplies to communists in the South. The North Vietnamese army easily routed the invaders, who fled in disarray back to South Vietnam.

Negotiations with the North Vietnamese dragged on. Nixon sent Henry Kissinger to Paris to negotiate secretly with North Vietnam's foreign minister, Le Duc Tho. In Paris, Kissinger faced an intransigent North Vietnam. Le Duc continued to reject various proposals made by Kissinger, and in the fall of 1971 the North Vietnamese launched an offensive in the South that led to the fall of the provincial capital of Quang Tri. An American counteroffensive recaptured the city, but negotiations in Paris still proceeded slowly.

The war entered its final phase in 1972. Negotiations between Kissinger and Le Duc moved forward ever so slowly. By October 1972, with the American presidential elections fast approaching, Kissinger and Le Duc reached a secret agreement. It provided for a cease-fire, the formation of a coalition government in South Vietnam, free elections, the withdrawal of remaining American troops, and the release of all prisoners. However, the South Vietnamese refused to accept the peace plan, and the North Vietnamese angrily broke off negotiations. Following his reelection in November, Nixon put additional pressure on the North with massive bombing from December 18 to 29. The "Christmas bombing" strategy brought Le Duc Tho back to the table.

Finally, on January 22, 1973, the day Lyndon Johnson died of a heart attack on his Texas ranch, Nixon announced that a cease-fire agreement had been signed in Paris that would allow U.S. troops to withdraw. Kissinger and Le Duc Tho won Nobel Peace Prizes for their efforts. Nixon had extricated America from Vietnam, but at a heavy cost. Nearly 60,000 Americans had been killed, more than half during Nixon's presidency; 300,000 had been wounded, and $146 billion had been spent on the war. In April 1975, the war finally ended in a communist victory when the North Vietnamese captured Saigon (soon renamed Ho Chi Minh City) and quickly absorbed South Vietnam into the single country of Vietnam.

NIXON SEEKS DÉTENTE WITH COMMUNIST POWERS, 1969–1973   During the Vietnam negotiations, Nixon also sought peaceful coexistence with the Soviet Union and recognition of mainland China, a policy called *détente*. Nixon felt that ideology should be subordinated to the pragmatic acknowledgment of both the United States' and the communist countries' self-interest in maintaining a competitive balance of power in the world.

In 1968 relations between the United States and the Soviet Union worsened when Russian tanks rolled into Prague, Czechoslovakia, to suppress local communist-led liberalization. Soviet leader Leonid Brezhnev asserted the "Brezhnev Doctrine," which upheld the right of unilateral Soviet intervention in any "socialist" state in Eastern Europe. United States–Soviet tensions did not improve when American intelligence discovered that the Soviets were building a naval base for atomic submarines in Cuba. The Soviets ceased construction of the base only after strong U.S. protests.

Nixon believed that a balance of power entailed mending relations with mainland China, the People's Republic of China. Nixon and Kissinger believed that rapprochement with China would pressure the Soviet Union to stabilize relations with the United States. The Sino-Soviet dispute had become particularly ominous with China's development of nuclear weapons. (On a number of occasions, Russian officials had suggested to their American counterparts that a preemptive strike by the Soviet Union against China's nuclear facilities would be desirable.)

President Richard Milhous Nixon surprised liberal opponents when he renewed trade with communist China. In 1972, while the war in Vietnam continued, he visited China for a week, meeting with Chinese leader Mao Zedong. (AP/Wide World Photos)

Since the Truman administration, the United States had refused to extend diplomatic recognition to the People's Republic. This refusal had been made easier by Chinese leader Mao Zedong's devout adherence to communist revolutionary ideology and by China's vituperative anti-American propaganda. The widening Sino-Soviet split, however, created a diplomatic opening for Nixon to establish relations with Mao. Armed clashes in 1969 between Soviet and Chinese troops along their common border further encouraged reestablishing relations with China.

Nixon journeyed to communist China on February 22, 1972. American television showed Nixon touring the Great Wall and toasting Mao Zedong and the Chinese premier, Zhou Enlai. Although full diplomatic relations were not established until 1979, Nixon's visit marked a milestone in cold war history. The idea of a monolithic, global communism gave way to the recognition that the Soviet Union and China were rivals who could be played against one another.

American public opinion of communist China seemed to shift overnight. Shortly after Nixon's visit, actress Candice Bergen, returning from a carefully supervised tour of the mainland, declared that she had been most impressed by the pervasive respect for human life she encountered in China. During the next several years, this praise of mainland China was joined by a chorus of serious journalists and government officials who returned from similar tours.

The road to détente (the establishment of peaceful relations with the Soviet Union) proved rocky. While relations with the Soviet Union proceeded in fits and starts, Nixon's boldest stroke was the 1972 agreement to sell American wheat and technology to the Soviet Union. Nixon and Brezhnev then signed the first Strategic Arms Limitation Talks (SALT I) agreement, limiting both nations to two hundred antiballistic missiles (ABMs) and two ABM systems. A separate agreement froze for five years the number of intercontinental ballistic missiles (ICBMs) and submarine-launched missiles. These treaties formalized a strategy of mutual deterrence, the view—adopted by both sides—that the surest protection against nuclear attack was parity.

In pursuing the SALT agreement, Nixon pressured reluctant liberals in Congress to support the development of new weapons systems. Nixon gave the go-ahead to develop a new kind of missile called a multiple independently targeted reentry vehicle (MIRV), which allowed multiple warheads on missiles. Each of these missiles carried three to ten separately targeted warheads, so fewer missiles could launch more bombs.

Some defense hawks within the Republican Party and a few in the Democratic Party felt that Nixon's foreign and defense policies were too accommodating. The SALT I agreement, they argued, gave the Soviet Union an advantage in nuclear weapons, recognized the Soviet Union's control of Eastern European–bloc countries, discouraged dissidents in those countries, and supported the continuation of a brutal regime in the Soviet Union by offering wheat and western technology to the Brezhnev government. Furthermore, the Brezhnev government was providing military and strategic support to liberation movements in Africa and Latin America.

Nixon's belief that American foreign policy needed to be realistic, not ideological or idealistic, sometimes led the United States to support repressive regimes considered important to American economic and strategic interests. The Nixon administration enthusiastically supported the brutal government of Iran, headed by the shah Reza Pahlavi. The administration also backed the corrupt Ferdinand Marcos in the Philippines and the repressive white-only government of South Africa. Nixon also backed repressive regimes in Argentina, South Korea, Brazil, and Nigeria. Nixon's foreign policy came under criticism in 1973, when he used the Central Intelligence Agency to help overthrow Chile's Marxist president, Salvador Allende, who had been democratically elected in 1970.

NIXON BAFFLES LIBERALS AND CONSERVATIVES IN DOMESTIC POLICY

Though liberals despised Nixon, he turned out to be a reformer. His proposal to transform the welfare system failed, but he did push through a variety of measures to help the poor, aged, blind, and disabled. A record volume of environmental legislation was passed during his administration. His New Federalism program aimed to shift power back to states and local communities. A restructuring and subsequent elimination of the draft in 1972 took the steam out of the antiwar movement. Nixon's record on civil rights and women's issues was mixed.

REFORMING WELFARE, ENVIRONMENT, AND THE ADMINISTRATION, 1969–1970
Although Nixon remained less interested in domestic affairs, he sought new policy initiatives in welfare, health care, federal aid to states, and executive reform. At the same time, ever the politician, Nixon believed that Republicans could emerge as the majority party by luring white southerners and blue-collar voters away from the Democrats. He therefore espoused "law and order," appointed conservatives to the federal courts (including the Supreme Court), and opposed busing children to achieve school integration.

During the presidential campaign of 1968, Nixon attacked the "welfare mess." He knew that many Americans disliked the Great Society's welfare measures, but he also wanted to beat the liberals at their own game. In 1969 he proposed to transform the welfare system by offering direct benefits to welfare recipients through the Family Assistance Plan (FAP). The centralized program, however, drew fierce opposition from liberals and fiscal conservatives alike. Liberals conducted a "ZAP–FAP" campaign that denounced Nixon's proposal as the "Family Annihilation Plan."

Nixon withdrew the proposal and replaced it with a food stamp program that allowed the poor to purchase food with vouchers. In October 1972, Nixon signed the Supplemental Security Income Act, which led the government to assume responsibility for aid to the aged, the blind, and the disabled. The act also increased Social Security benefits, extended subsidized housing, and expanded the Job Corps program.

The Nixon administration also extended the federal government's role in protecting the environment. When an oil well off the California coast at Santa Barbara burst, spewing tons of sludge on the beaches in 1969, environmentalists demanded new legislation. Congressional Democrats led by Senators Edmund Muskie (Maine) and Henry Jackson (Washington) pushed for support of the National Environmental Policy Act

(1969). Declaring that the environment must be protected and restored, this historic law required an environmental impact study of every federal construction project before work was begun.

Shortly after the passage of this act, Nixon consolidated all antipollution programs under a new Environmental Protection Agency (EPA). The EPA, under William Ruckleshaus, became an activist agency that brought scores of criminal actions against polluters. Nixon also called for drinking-water standards, mass transit, stronger land use policies, the protection of coastal wetlands, and the preservation of endangered species. The National Oceanic and Atmospheric Agency (NOAA) consolidated research in these areas. The Clean Air Act (1970) established national emission standards for automobiles and factories, while the Occupational Safety and Health Administration (OSHA) protected worker safety.

Congress pushed the environmental agenda further, enacting legislation over Nixon's veto that provided funds for cleaning the nation's polluted waterways. More environmental legislation was passed during Nixon's time in office than during any previous presidency.

Following the 1970 congressional elections, Nixon moved to cut federal expenditures, vetoing dozens of bills passed by a Democratic-controlled Congress. When these vetoes were overridden, Nixon refused to spend ("impounded") the funds authorized by Congress. The Supreme Court eventually outlawed impounding. Nixon announced a New Federalism that promised to shift power back to the states and local communities. To fulfill this objective, Nixon pushed through a revenue-sharing act in October 1972 that reallocated certain federal revenues to the states, with no strings attached. At the same time, the federal government used revenue sharing to consolidate 130 grants concerned with urban community development, education, law enforcement, and manpower training.

A MIXED RECORD ON CIVIL RIGHTS AND WOMEN'S ISSUES   An essential part of Nixon's strategy to keep the white southern vote was to maintain a low profile on civil rights.

The Nixon record on civil rights, however, was more mixed than his rhetoric implied. While his administration challenged "forced" busing, the Justice Department quietly presided over the desegregation of southern schools, which lowered the proportion of southern black children attending all-black schools from 68 percent in 1968 to 8 percent in 1972. At the same time, under Nixon the Equal Employment Opportunity Commission (EEOC) imposed targets for the hiring of minorities and women on federal projects. In 1972 Congress passed an equal employment practices law covering all federal, state, and municipal governments, educational institutions, and businesses or unions with more than eight employees.

The inclusion of women in federal hiring guidelines set by the EEOC followed legally from civil rights legislation passed in the Johnson administration. In 1968 women accounted for only 8 percent of scientists, 7 percent of physicians, 3 percent of lawyers, and 1 percent of engineers. Progress in the professions was slow, but the number of women appointed to military academies, embassies, and the federal courts increased rapidly.

In 1970 Congress passed the Equal Rights Amendment (ERA) to the Constitution, which had first been suggested by Alice Paul in the 1920s. The ERA ran into strong opposition, especially in the Sun Belt states. Many fundamentalist Christians campaigned against the amendment, as did Phyllis Schlafly, an antifeminist activist who argued that it would destroy the American family. In the end, thirty-four states ratified it, but the amendment failed to win the thirty-eight states needed for ratification.

During the presidential campaign of 1968, Nixon had promised to fill the Supreme Court with conservatives. In late May 1969, Nixon nominated and the Senate quickly confirmed federal judge Warren E. Burger as chief justice, following Earl Warren's retirement. Nixon also appointed Harry Blackmun, Lewis F. Powell, and William H. Rehnquist to the Court; among these appointments only Rehnquist proved to be consistently conservative.

This Supreme Court issued one of its most important decisions in 1973: *Roe v. Wade* struck down a Texas law that made abortion a crime except to save the life of the mother. In the 1960s a number of states, including California under Ronald Reagan, had legalized abortion. In *Roe*, Justice Harry Blackmun wrote the majority opinion that made abortion within the first three months of pregnancy a constitutional right. Later Court cases restricted this right, but *Roe* marked an important turning point in American constitutional law.

CONSERVATIVES AND LIBERALS REACT   Nixon's record left most liberals and many conservatives baffled. Liberals felt that Nixon's policies did not go far enough, and they suspected Nixon of supporting civil rights, environmental, and social programs just to take away important issues from the Democratic Party. In this regard, they were right; Nixon was a political opportunist. At the same time, some conservatives were shocked by Nixon's foreign policy—détente with the Soviet Union and recognition of mainland China—and his domestic policy, which appeared to expand federal powers in areas of regulation and environment, to extend civil rights into unprecedented areas such as affirmative action, and to enlarge the welfare state through a guaranteed national income program, FAP.

NIXON'S EXCESSES AND ECONOMIC FAILURES

Facing a deteriorating economy in 1971, Nixon announced a variety of sweeping economic reforms. These reforms proved to be rigid and unworkable. To win over the conservative South and the white working class, Nixon emphasized law and order, but he launched a campaign of harassment, infiltration, and sabotage against dissidents, using an assortment of legal and illegal tactics.

CURING STAGFLATION WITH WAGE AND PRICE CONTROLS   Nixon approached the 1972 election convinced that only a weak economy could cost him reelection. The war in Southeast Asia had led to an inflationary spiral that seemed uncontrollable. By 1970 inflation had risen to an annual rate of more than 5 percent and was still growing, while unemployment reached 6 percent, partly because of the winding down of the war's defense contracts. The Democrats blamed Nixon for the worst of all possible worlds: stagnant employment and high inflation, dubbed "stagflation."

The state of the economy continued to deteriorate through 1971. Under pressure, Nixon went on television on August 15, 1971, to announce his reshaping of the economic system. He took the United States off the gold standard. In the 1930s Roosevelt had pegged the dollar at $35 to one ounce of gold; now, Nixon declared, the dollar would no longer be tied to gold. This move resulted in pressure to increase the money supply and greatly increased inflation during the rest of the 1970s. For the first time since the late 1940s, Nixon also placed the dollar on the international market, allowing the exchange rate of the dollar and foreign currencies to be set by market conditions. This had tremendous implications for world trade and prices.

He also announced a ninety-day freeze of wages and prices. In November 1972 Nixon announced Phase II of the wage- and price-control strategy, which established firm federal guidelines for increases in wages, prices, and interest rates. There was lingering suspicion among business executives that exemptions from the guidelines could be obtained in exchange for large campaign contributions to Nixon, however. Although economic conditions improved only marginally (indeed, inflation soared 9 percent in 1972), the American electorate was temporarily reassured.

NIXON PREACHES LAW AND ORDER BUT VIOLATES CIVIL LIBERTIES, 1969–1973

Nixon knew that the middle class feared the breakdown of law and order in America. New Left revolutionaries, hippie counterculturists, pornography, and crime in the streets seemed to be inexplicably linked. Thus, while Nixon had campaigned in 1968 on the slogan "Bring us together," he used the presidency to denounce protesters, attack crime, and promote "law and order." Nixon worked to win over southern and suburban Americans to the Republican Party.

Nixon encouraged Attorney General John Mitchell to pursue a "war on crime" and take a tough stand on drugs. The Justice Department also attacked domestic dissidents through the use of wiretaps without court approval, a practice the Supreme Court prohibited in 1971. Meanwhile, the Justice Department obtained conspiracy indictments against several groups of radical political activists. Working closely with local police, the FBI and the Justice Department targeted the militant Black Panthers in a number of police raids. Shoot-outs with the police led to the deaths of more than forty Black Panthers.

The Central Intelligence Agency (CIA), in violation of its charter, was instructed in 1970 to compile dossiers on thousands of American dissidents. Nixon wanted to intensify this antiradical campaign through a scheme known as the Huston Plan, which proposed using the CIA and FBI in an extensive program involving wiretaps, electronic surveillance, break-ins, and covert operations against radical groups. Although many were indicted, convictions were rare.

These indictments were part of a larger policy of harassment, infiltration, and sabotage of organized dissent called COINTELPRO (counterintelligence program). Never had civil liberties been so systematically violated by the United States government. Activities included destroying dissenters' property, planting lies in the media to ruin reputations, and controlling political nominations.

Concerned with government "leaks" to the press, the White House established a secret group, the "plumbers," to ensure that sensitive information remained secret. Headed by ex-FBI agent G. Gordon Liddy and former CIA agent E. Howard Hunt, the plumbers undertook a campaign to discredit radicals. Their first target was Daniel Ellsberg, a former analyst for the Defense Department who had turned over to the press the Pentagon's secret history of the Vietnam War. In the summer of 1971, when the *New York Times* began to publish the *Pentagon Papers,* as they were called, the administration obtained a court injunction preventing further publication. After the Supreme Court lifted the injunction on First Amendment grounds, Nixon ordered the Justice Department to indict Ellsberg. In August 1971, the plumbers broke into the office of Ellsberg's psychiatrist in hopes of finding information that could be used to discredit the antiwar movement's new hero.

While attacking antiwar dissenters and student radicals, the administration sought to defuse confrontations by undertaking a long-overdue reform of the Selective Service System. The military draft was modified through a national lottery system that in effect excused young Americans from military service. The goal, however, was an all-volunteer army, finally achieved in 1972. The decline and subsequent end of the draft effectively took the steam out of the student antiwar movement.

NIXON WINS REELECTION AND LOSES THE PRESIDENCY, 1972–1974

Although his opponent, George McGovern, appeared to have little chance of beating him in 1972, Nixon undertook a "dirty tricks" campaign that resulted in an attempted break-in by his campaign workers, without his knowledge, to tap the phones at the Democratic headquarters in Washington's Watergate office complex. When the burglars were caught by the police, Nixon and his aides attempted to cover up White House involvement. Nixon's illegal obstruction of justice became a more important issue than the original crime. In 1974, when presidential tapes of recorded conversations in the White House were released (after much resistance on Nixon's part), he resigned from the presidency under threat of impeachment.

THE ELECTION OF 1972   Approaching the 1972 election, the Democrats remained in disarray. They nominated the liberal senator from South Dakota, George McGovern, who capitalized on the prevailing antiwar sentiment within the party. At the convention, new party rules required every state delegation to include a proportionate number of minorities, women, and youth, which startled television audiences used to seeing conventions dominated by older, affluent, white males. This convention stood well to the left of the American electorate.

McGovern proved an easy target for Nixon. When third-party candidate George Wallace withdrew from the race in the spring of 1972, after a would-be assassin's bullet left him paralyzed, Wallace's "law and order" vote was left to Nixon. McGovern called for defense cuts, immediate withdrawal from Vietnam, amnesty for draft dodgers who had fled to Canada, and income redistribution. Nixon attacked McGovern as an inept radical who wanted "abortion, acid [LSD], and amnesty." When it became known that McGovern's vice-presidential running mate, Thomas Eagleton, had received electroshock therapy for mental depression, McGovern confirmed this image of incompetence by first declaring his "one thousand percent" support for Eagleton and then dumping him.

In these circumstances, Nixon's reelection seemed certain. Nevertheless, he left nothing to chance. His Committee to Reelect the President (CREEP), operating independently of the Republican Party, raised millions of dollars (which were often delivered in briefcases stuffed with untraceable cash) by targeting corporations and executives with ties to government contracts. The chairman of CREEP, former Attorney General John Mitchell, also approved a "dirty tricks" campaign against the Democrats. The extent of these tricks became known after agents of Nixon's reelection committee, supervised by G. Gordon Liddy and E. Howard Hunt, were arrested on July 17, 1972, while breaking into the Democratic National Committee headquarters in the Watergate office complex in Washington. Shortly afterward, the police arrested James McCord, the security coordinator of CREEP, for his involvement in the break-in.

Nixon's White House immediately began to cover up its links with the break-in by announcing that "no one in the White House staff, no one in this administration . . . was involved in this bizarre incident." Nixon also ordered that the White House telephone directory be changed to delete the name of E. Howard Hunt. Moreover, Nixon secretly provided $400,000 to buy the silence of those arrested. The administration pressured the FBI to halt its investigation of the Watergate break-in, using national security as a pretext. By these actions, Nixon committed an illegal act by trying to cover up a crime.

McGovern's campaign was in such a shambles that the Democrats could not capitalize on the issue. The *Washington Post* was one of the few newspapers that even mentioned Watergate. Nixon swamped both the popular vote, polling over 60 percent, and the Electoral College, with 520 votes to 17. McGovern won only Massachusetts and the District of Columbia.

WATERGATE FORCES NIXON TO RESIGN, 1973–1974   The Watergate scandal, however, continued to haunt Nixon. The trial of the Watergate burglars in spring 1973 brought further troubles to Nixon when federal judge John Sirica encouraged James McCord to confess that highly placed White House aides knew of the break-in. Then, two young, enterprising *Washington Post* reporters, Bob Woodward and Carl Bernstein, wrote a series of front-page stories linking the Nixon administration with the break-in. Using an unnamed informant in the Nixon administration nicknamed "Deep Throat" (after the then-popular pornographic film), Woodward and Bernstein kept the Watergate story alive.

In February 1973, the Senate established the Special Committee on Presidential Campaign Activities under Democratic Senator Sam Ervin of North Carolina to investigate the matter. Feeling the heat, Nixon forced top White House aides John Ehrlichman and H. R. Haldeman to resign; he also fired John Dean, the president's special counsel, who had engineered the original cover-up. Pledging "no whitewash at the White House," Nixon appointed a new attorney general, Elliot Richardson, to oversee the investigation and named Archibald Cox, a Democrat and Harvard Law School professor, as special prosecutor to conduct it.

In May 1973, the Ervin committee began nationally televised hearings. When the Senate committee and the special prosecutor learned that Nixon had installed a secret taping system in the White House that recorded all conversations in the Oval Office, they demanded the tapes. Claiming "national security," Nixon resisted Cox in court and, after losing, ordered Attorney General Richardson to fire Cox. When Richardson and his deputy, William Ruckelshaus, refused to do so, Nixon fired both of them and ordered Solicitor General Robert Bork to dismiss Cox. The firings, timed too late to make the Sunday newspapers, were dubbed the "Saturday Night Massacre." Thousands of telegrams pushed the House Judiciary Committee to initiate impeachment proceedings against Nixon.

Later that October Vice President Spiro Agnew was forced to resign in a plea bargain after being charged with income tax evasion and with accepting bribes while governor of Maryland. Members of Congress from both parties forced President Nixon to select Representative Gerald R. Ford, a Republican, to replace the disgraced Agnew.

In April 1974 Nixon released edited transcripts of many tapes but withheld the tapes themselves. Far from restoring confidence, the transcripts showed Nixon to be foulmouthed, mean-spirited, anti-Semitic, manipulative, and cynical. His approval rating plunged. Nixon did not release everything; the new special prosecutor, Leon Jaworski, then persuaded the Supreme Court (who voted 8 to 0) to order Nixon to turn over additional tapes, and the jig was up. The end became certain when congressional Republicans led by Barry Goldwater informed Nixon that he would be convicted in the impeachment proceedings. On August 9, 1974, Nixon became the first president of the United States to resign from office.

GERALD FORD TRIES TO HEAL A TROUBLED NATION, 1974–1977

As president, Gerald Ford attempted to end the Watergate saga by pardoning Nixon. An Arab oil embargo made a bad economy worse, driving up inflation and contributing to a severe recession. Ford's handling of the economy showed him to be an inept leader.

He continued Nixon's foreign policy course and generally served as little more than a caretaker. The war in Vietnam had drained the public's interest in Southeast Asia, so Ford could do little when communists took control of Cambodia and South Vietnam. By 1976, voters were fed up with Washington and replaced Ford with an outsider, Jimmy Carter.

FORD FUMBLES DOMESTIC POLICY   Gerald Ford was sworn in on August 9, 1974, the first president to hold office without having been elected either president or vice president. Ford brought to the presidency a calm, reassuring manner, a sense of confidence, and a deep faith in traditional values. A former football player on a winning team at the University of Michigan, Ford enjoyed success in Republican politics, working his way up through the ranks to become minority leader in the House.

As president, Ford sought desperately to reconcile a divided nation. One of his first acts, just thirty days after assuming the presidency, was to pardon Richard Nixon for "any and all crimes" committed while in office. This action did little to restore confidence in Washington and severely hurt Ford politically. He defended his decision, made with little input from advisers, as being in the best interest of the nation.

The economy remained Ford's greatest concern, and his actions further reinforced his image as an inept leader. Arab oil producers imposed an embargo against the United States in early 1973, then raised prices through the Organization of Petroleum Exporting Countries (OPEC). This sent oil prices spiraling upward, which in turn produced runaway inflation. Ford attempted to thwart inflation through persuasion, by promoting a voluntary program of wage and price freezes called "Whip Inflation Now" (WIN). The president frequently wore a WIN button. The Federal Reserve Board tried to cool inflation by raising the discount rate (the rate at which banks borrow money). The resulting high interest rates led to a severe economic recession in 1974–1975 as money became tight. By 1974 unemployment had reached nearly 11 percent, the highest rate since the Great Depression of the 1930s.

Faced with high gasoline prices, consumers increasingly bought the more fuel-efficient, imported cars, thereby hurting the American auto industry. Domestic producers were slow to respond to changing demand with competitive models. As domestic automobile sales plunged, General Motors, Ford, and Chrysler were forced to lay off more than 200,000 workers.

FORD CONTINUES NIXON'S FOREIGN POLICY   In foreign policy, Ford sought to continue Nixon's initiatives by retaining Henry Kissinger as secretary of state (a position Kissinger had taken following Nixon's 1972 reelection). In his first year in office, Ford faced the final collapse of anticommunist resistance in Southeast Asia. In April 1975 Cambodian communists under Khmer Rouge leader Pol Pot defeated the pro-American government. The ensuing campaign by the communist Pol Pot government forced millions of Cambodians from the towns to the countryside and led to genocide on a scale unseen since the Nazi holocaust. More than a million Cambodians died.

In the spring of 1975, the North Vietnamese openly violated the 1973 truce and invaded South Vietnam, whose army and corrupt government quickly collapsed. In March the North Vietnamese communists took Saigon, imposing a harsh rule on those who had opposed them.

By this time, most Americans did not want anything more to do with Southeast Asia. This widespread sentiment limited Ford's response to the communist takeover of Cambodia and South Vietnam. This became evident when the new communist government of Cambodia seized a U.S. merchant marine ship, the *Mayaguez*, shortly after the fall of Saigon. Ford ordered a military rescue of the thirty-nine crewmen, and a massive bombing of Cambodia, but the raid cost the lives of forty-one U.S. marines.

Ford also drew criticism from the right wing of his party for his diplomacy with the Soviet Union. Meeting with the Soviet leader Leonid Brezhnev in Vladivostok, Siberia, in late 1974, Ford made progress toward a new arms control treaty, SALT II. The following year Ford and Brezhnev signed an accord in Helsinki, Finland, with thirty-one other nations, recognizing Europe's post-1945 political boundaries and agreeing to respect human rights. The Helsinki agreement drew further criticism from conservatives who felt that Ford had given the Soviets too much for too little. Even Kissinger expressed doubts about the agreement.

CARTER WINS THE ELECTION OF 1976   Ford's strength among conservatives was challenged when the former governor of California, Ronald Reagan, entered the Republican primaries. Ford barely defeated Reagan for the nomination, and the contest left the GOP severely divided.

Vietnam and Watergate had shaken the public's faith in Washington and anyone associated with it. As a result, the Democrats turned to an outsider, Jimmy Carter, an engineer, Annapolis graduate, ex-nuclear submarine officer, former governor of Georgia, and wealthy peanut farmer. Proclaiming opposition to "politics as usual," Carter promised to restore virtue and trust to government. He pledged a government as good as the American people. Cynics worried about any government that "good."

Carter narrowly won the election, receiving 49.9 percent of the popular vote to Ford's 47.9 percent. The Georgian swept the South but gained only 297 votes to Ford's 240 votes in the Electoral College. As a consequence, Carter entered the White House without strong Washington ties, without much party support, and without a strong mandate to lead the nation.

CARTER DISAPPOINTS A NATION IN MALAISE, 1977–1981

Jimmy Carter brought to the White House a welcome down-home style but no clear vision of where to lead the nation. His inability to work with Congress sank many of his proposals and convinced Americans that he was the wrong person for the job. Inflation reached record levels, and Carter's measures to fight it were ineffective. His greatest achievement was brokering a peace treaty between Israel and Egypt in 1979. He signed a new arms control treaty with the Soviet Union, but Congress refused to ratify it.

Carter entered the 1980 election campaign having made many enemies and few friends. His chances for reelection declined further when Islamic militants took over the U.S. embassy in Iran and held its diplomats hostage. For more than a year, Carter was unable to free them by either diplomacy or military rescue. Few should have been surprised when Carter was trounced in the election by Ronald Reagan.

CARTER FLUNKS POLITICAL SCIENCE   Carter entered the White House as an outsider. His promise to change the "imperial presidency" that marked the Johnson–Nixon years was reflected in the down-to-earth style he brought to the office. On inauguration day he and his wife, Rosalynn, walked more than a mile from the Capitol to the White House to demonstrate the beginnings of a "people's presidency." He insisted on being called Jimmy Carter, not James Earl Carter, Jr. He brought to the White House a group of young advisers from Georgia who prided themselves on their lack of experience in Washington.

At first the public welcomed the down-home Carter style, but his inability to work with a liberal Congress only accentuated his growing image as a nice man out of his depth. He seemed to be overly concerned with the details of government, including such matters as assigning times at the White House tennis courts, and to lack the breadth of vision to set an agenda or guide his administration along a particular path. As a result, Americans began to view his unpretentiousness as staged and indicative of a man unable to lead the nation.

In 1977, the administration persuaded Congress to enact a tax cut and a public works program, which by late 1978 had reduced unemployment to 5 percent. Yet Carter's attempts to reform welfare by reactivating Nixon's FAP proposal failed miserably, as did his proposal for national health insurance.

Inflation haunted Carter's administration even more than it had Nixon's or Ford's. A boost in oil prices by the OPEC nations further worsened the inflation rate, which had climbed to more than 13 percent by 1979. Carter relied, as had Ford, on voluntary curbs of prices and wages. To slow the spiral, the Federal Reserve Board also pushed interest rates higher, so that by 1980 the rate for mortgage and business loans had reached an unheard-of 20 percent.

Carter created a new Department of Energy to deal with oil prices. He also proposed a comprehensive energy bill, but due to his poor relations with Congress, his initiative was watered down in 1978. By 1979, Carter's approval rating had fallen below Nixon's mid-Watergate level.

In the midst of growing political despair, Carter retreated to the presidential country house at Camp David in Maryland to consult with some 130 public figures. He emerged from the retreat to deliver a remarkable television address in which he proclaimed that Americans were suffering from a "malaise" and a "crisis of confidence." By 1979, however, most Americans concluded that the problem lay not with the national spirit but with Carter himself.

THE REVIVAL OF THE RIGHT   The emergence of social issues—abortion, the Equal Rights Amendment (ERA), and prayer in school—energized a growing conservative movement and activated evangelical and fundamentalist Christians to become involved in politics. Traditionally-minded women got involved on a grassroots level to oppose ERA and abortion and also supported legislation or a constitutional amendment to allow prayer in public schools. The grassroots campaign that emerged over these social issues showed the Republican Party that Catholics (traditionally aligned with Democrats) and non-aligned evangelical Christians could be won over to the GOP. This mobilization of the pro-life and antifeminist Right created what later became known as the "gender gap"; that is, the difference in the voting patterns of white men and white women. The real gap, however, was not between men and women but between single white women, who tended to vote Democratic, and white men and married women, who tended to vote Republican.

FOREIGN POLICY DOOMS CARTER   Carter enjoyed some success in foreign policy. He made human rights a priority. Through Secretary of State Cyrus Vance, the administration applied pressure on the governments of Chile,

Argentina, Ethiopia, South Africa, and the Philippines to correct human rights violations.

Carter successfully persuaded a reluctant Congress to ratify a treaty gradually transferring the Panama Canal and the Canal Zone to the Panamanians. He also established full diplomatic relations with the People's Republic of China in early 1979.

His greatest achievement was in the Middle East, when he invited Israeli Prime Minister Menachem Begin and Egyptian President Anwar al-Sadat to Camp David in September 1978 to hammer out a peace treaty between the two antagonistic nations. After thirteen days of prolonged negotiations, the three leaders announced a "framework" for a peace treaty. Carter's moral fervor, especially regarding the Biblically significant Middle East, gave him confidence in the power of personal diplomacy. The president saw his own generosity and will, rather than political calculation, as the basis of this foreign policy success. In March 1979, Begin and Sadat signed a formal peace treaty at the White House, establishing diplomatic relations between the two nations.

The Middle East accord marked a high point in the Carter administration. It was quickly followed by SALT II, a new arms control treaty with the Soviets. His image as a peacemaker seemed assured. When Carter submitted this treaty to Congress, however, he ran into strong opposition from conservatives who argued that the Soviets had not lived up to either the earlier SALT I agreement or the Helsinki Accords. Warning that the treaty offered the Soviets a means to achieve nuclear supremacy, Senate conservatives blocked SALT II's ratification.

In December 1979 the Soviet Union invaded neighboring Afghanistan to support a weak pro-Soviet regime against anti-Soviet rebels. Washington felt obliged to demonstrate its outrage. Carter withdrew the SALT II agreement from the Senate and ordered American athletes to boycott the summer Olympic games scheduled to be held in Moscow in 1980. Acting on the advice of his national security adviser, Zbigniew Brzezinski, Carter endorsed the development of a very expensive nuclear missile system, the MX. (Although SALT II was never ratified, the United States and the Soviet Union informally agreed to abide by it anyway.)

As the 1980 election approached, Carter was in political trouble. Matters only worsened in January 1979, when America's long-time ally, Reza Pahlavi, the shah of Iran, was overthrown by the militant Islamic leader Ayatollah Ruhollah Khomeini. Less than a year later, zealots seized the American embassy in the Iranian capital, Tehran, and held more than fifty Americans hostage. For the next 444 days, American television showed angry Iranian mobs parading blindfolded American hostages through the streets. While running for reelection, Carter desperately explored every

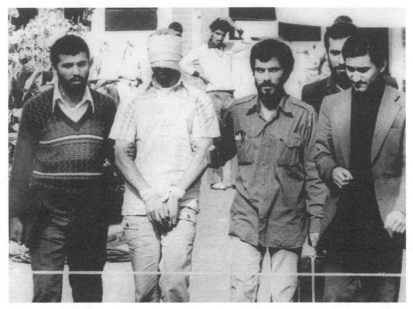

In November 1979 radical Iranian students seized the American embassy in Tehran and demanded that the United States extradite the deposed shah to Iran. For more than a year, Iranians held Americans from the embassy hostage. The crisis helped elect Ronald Reagan, who secured the prisoners' release in January 1981. (AP/Wide World Photos)

diplomatic avenue to secure the release of the hostages. Finally, in April 1980, Carter ordered a secret military mission to rescue them. The mission failed disastrously when an American helicopter and a transport plane crashed, leaving eight servicemen dead. Carter's approval rating sank to the lowest of any president since polling began in the 1930s.

REAGAN ELECTED IN 1980   By 1980 Carter's presidency was in deep trouble. Although the president fought off a challenge in the Democratic primaries by Senator Edward Kennedy, the youngest brother of John and Robert, the Democratic Party was unenthusiastic about Carter. However, few predicted the severity of his defeat at the hands of his Republican challenger, Ronald Reagan, an ex-Hollywood actor, former governor of California, and long-time presidential hopeful. In a single presidential debate, Reagan challenged Carter by asking the American voter, "Are you better off now than you were four years ago?" For most the answer was no.

On election day the voters soundly rejected Carter. Reagan received almost 51 percent of the popular vote to Carter's 42 percent. John Anderson, a moderate Republican running as an independent, got 7 percent. Reagan received 489 electoral votes to Carter's 49. For the first time since 1925, a self-proclaimed conservative stepped into the White House. Jimmy Carter became the fifth consecutive president after Dwight D. Eisenhower to fail to gain and complete two terms.

CONCLUSION

The 1970s appeared to have ended in political and economic failure. The early confidence Americans had placed in the Nixon presidency had been betrayed, and the Ford and Carter presidencies seemed only brief and disillusioning interludes in a downward spiral. The office of president was left tarnished and weakened. Both at home and abroad, America seemed less vital, less confident, and less certain of its place in history than ever before.

Recommended Readings

DOCUMENTS: Henry Kissinger, *The White House Years* (1979) and *Years of Upheaval* (1982); Bob Woodward and Carl Bernstein, *All the President's Men* (1974) and *The Final Days* (1973).

READINGS: (GENERAL) Stephen Ambrose, *Nixon: The Triumph of a Politician, 1962–1972* (1989); Edward D. Berkowitz, *The American Welfare State* (1991); Peter Calleo, *The Imperious Economy* (1982); Donald T. Critchlow, *Intended Consequences: Birth Control, Abortion, and the Federal Government* (1999); Steven F. Hayward, *The Age of Reagan: The Fall of the Old Liberal Order* (2001); Jim Hougan, *Decadence: Radical Nostalgia, Narcissism, and Decline in the 1970s* (1975); Christopher Lasch, *The Culture of Narcissism* (1978); J. Anthony Lukas, *Common Ground* (1986); Martin Melosi, *Coping with Abundance* (1985); James T. Patterson, *Grand Expectations* (1996). (NIXON–DOMESTIC) John Dean, *Blind Ambition* (1976); John Ehrlichman, *Witness to Power* (1982); Stanley I. Kutler, *The Wars of Watergate* (1990); Daniel Patrick Moynihan, *The Politics of a Guaranteed Income* (1973); Richard Nixon, *RN* (1978); Leon Panetta and Peter Gall, *Bring Us All Together* (1971); Jonathan Schell, *The Time of Illusion* (1975); Garry Wills, *Nixon Agonistes* (1970). (NIXON–FOREIGN POLICY) Seymour Hirsh, *The Price of Power: Kissinger in the Nixon White House* (1983); Roger Morris, *Uncertain Greatness: Henry Kissinger and American Foreign Policy* (1977); William Shawcross, *Sideshow: Nixon, Kissinger, and the Destruction of Cambodia* (1978). (FORD–CARTER) Zbigniew Brzezinski, *Power and Principle* (1983); Jimmy Carter, *Keeping the Faith* (1982); Erwin C. Hargrove, *Jimmy Carter as President* (1988); Charles O. Jones, *The Trusteeship Presidency: Jimmy Carter and the United States Congress* (1988); Clark Mollenhoff, *The President Who Failed* (1980); Richard

Pipes, *U.S.–Soviet Relations in the Era of Détente* (1981); James Reichley, *Conservatives in an Age of Change: The Nixon and Ford Administrations* (1981). (SOCIETY AND CULTURE) Mary Frances Berry, *Why ERA Failed* (1986); John D'Emilio, *Sexual Politics, Sexual Communities: The Making of a Homosexual Minority in the United States* (1983); Alice Echols, *Daring to Be Bad: Radical Feminism in American Society* (1989); Sara Evans, *Personal Politics: The Roots of Women's Liberation in the Civil Rights Movement and the New Left* (1979); Jo Freeman, *The Politics of Women's Liberation* (1975); David Frum, *How We Got Here: The 1970s* (2000); Samuel Hayes, *Beauty, Health, and Permanence: Environmental Politics in the United States* (1977); Steven Mintz and Susan Kellogg, *Domestic Revolution: A Social History of American Family Life* (1988); Marc Reisner, *Cadillac Desert: The American West and Its Disappearing Water* (1986); Robert Stobaugh and Daniel Yergin, *Energy Future* (1979); Donald Worster, *Rivers of Empire* (1985).

30

❧

The Reagan Revolution and Its Aftermath

OVERVIEW   In the 1980s the United States presented many contradictions. The decade witnessed astonishing technological and social changes accompanied by political and, to a lesser extent, cultural conservatism. Presiding over this paradox was Ronald Reagan (1981–1989), who redefined the tone and nature of political discourse in this period.

During his first term Reagan initiated a rapid arms buildup that challenged détente with the Soviet Union, as well as arms control and mutual nuclear deterrence. In his second term Reagan used the strengthened American military position to reopen negotiations with the Soviet Union. These negotiations preceded the breakup of the Soviet bloc and the collapse of communism in Russia and Eastern Europe. At the same time, Reagan pursued aggressive policies in the Middle East, Central America, and the Caribbean. Swapping arms for hostages in Iran and waging a covert war in Nicaragua led to the Iran–Contra affair, which rocked the administration in 1986–1987.

Reagan's popularity was so high that he was able to pass the presidency on to his vice president, George Bush (1989–1993). Bush sought moderation in domestic policy and a strong foreign policy that led to American involvement in Panama and the Middle East. A lingering economic recession that continued into the 1992 election led to Democrat Bill Clinton's victory over Bush that year.

PEOPLES OF PARADOX

The 1980s saw striking economic and social changes that contrasted with the political conservatism of the decade. The computer revolution, demographic changes, the transformation of the traditional American family, rising ethnic consciousness, and foreign immigration characterized the period.

OF COMPUTERS AND CONTRADICTIONS   No change affected Americans' lives in the 1980s more than computer-based technology. During the 1980s new companies such as Apple Computer and Microsoft joined the Fortune 500. "Silicon Valley," an area south of San Francisco, became a major high-tech center with more than 400,000 computer-related manufacturing jobs, more than in steel and autos combined. The rise of the computer industry accelerated a shift of jobs, profits, wealth, and power to the southwestern Sun Belt.

Computers changed the way the country did business. Large corporations, insurance companies, banks, and retail merchants laid off thousands of middle managers. Decisions could now be made directly by senior management employees or sales staffs who had access to the relevant data on computers.

The decade of the 1980s was a contradictory mix of high-tech advances, social progress, and social decay. For example, the communications revolution brought on by cable television, satellites, and computers allowed unprecedented access to information, yet illiteracy rose to historic levels.

WOMEN IN THE 1980S: DIFFERING SPHERES   Women entered the workforce in greater numbers and in better jobs than ever before, but at the same time, growing numbers of women also entered the ranks of the poor, a process described as the "feminization of poverty." By 1988 approximately 60 percent of women worked outside the home, although much of this work remained part-time. Most significantly, women now held more than a third of all corporate management positions and accounted for nearly one-fourth of all doctors and lawyers. Half of the students in law school were women, while close to 40 percent of university graduate students were women.

As a result of these economic gains, women were the big winners in the 1980s. While median annual salaries of men slid 8 percent in the 1980s, comparable salaries for women rose 10 percent, although women still made less, on the whole, than men. Unlike World War II, when women achieved temporary increases in pay, gains in the 1980s and 1990s reflected solid, enduring trends. Women have chosen to stay in school

In 1980 supporters and opponents of the proposed equal rights amendment to the U.S. Constitution met inside the Illinois State Capitol. Both sides lobbied the Illinois legislature, which failed to ratify the amendment. Thirty-four states ratified, four short of the required thirty-eight. (© Bettmann/CORBIS)

longer and train for higher-paying occupations. Since the mid-1980s more women than men have received bachelor of arts degrees. Moreover, women entered male-dominated professions such as law, medicine, law enforcement, and construction. Yet women's wages remained only 70 percent of men's.

By 1990 the divorce rate had risen to nearly 50 percent. Associated with this increase was the growing number of single-parent households headed by women. By 1990 close to half of all women workers were single, either because they had never married or because they were divorced. At the same time, almost 25 percent of the nation's children were growing up in single-parent households.

AFRICAN AMERICANS GAIN AND LOSE   The 1980s also marked a period of upward mobility for many African Americans. During the decade large numbers of African Americans entered the middle class as professionals. More than 40 percent of African-American workers held white-collar jobs, and nearly half owned their own homes. Moreover, the median family income of African Americans rose in the 1980s, while the number of poor African Americans fell.

Although social conditions had improved, many blacks remained poor, unemployed, and vulnerable to violence. More than one in three blacks remained in poverty, compared to one in ten whites. Moreover, the inner city created an environment of social isolation for African Americans. Middle-class blacks moved to the suburbs, leaving behind a hard core of inner city poor. Unemployment in poor neighborhoods often reached 60 percent or more, and nearly half the residents failed to graduate from high school. This environment created its own pathology, an underclass plagued by joblessness and lawlessness.

In this world, violence prevailed. Murder became the leading cause of death among young black males. Blacks were responsible for about half of all crimes of violence. The growth of black gangs such as the Bloods and the Crips of Los Angeles further contributed to the problem of violence in the city.

AMERICA DIVERSIFIES   In the 1980s the United States experienced a significant influx of Hispanic and Asian immigrants. Hispanics became the fastest-growing ethnic group, as Mexican Americans settled in the Southwest and West, Puerto Ricans and Dominicans migrated to the East Coast, and Cubans made homes in Florida. Newcomers from Vietnam, Thailand, Korea, Hong Kong, Taiwan, and the Philippines created new communities, especially in California. Demographers predicted that by the year 2010 whites of European ancestry would be a minority in California. During the 1980s the number of residents for whom English was a foreign tongue jumped by more than a third, to 31.8 million. About 14 percent of all residents grew up speaking a language other than English.

American religion reflected this growing ethnic diversity. Although the majority of Americans remained within the Judeo-Christian tradition, this tradition revealed greater variety. By 1990 Roman Catholics, reflecting in part the growing Hispanic immigrant population, constituted 24 percent of the American population. At the same time, Protestantism became more diverse as evangelical sects attracted new followers.

By 1990 Islam had become the eighth largest denomination in the United States, larger than the Episcopal Church, the Presbyterian Church, and the Assemblies of God. Quasi-Christian movements, such as the Korean-based Unification Church (the Moonies) under the leadership of Sun Myung Moon, also drew wide attention.

Even as religion grew more diverse, many Americans declared themselves secularists, answering "none" when questioned about religious preference, thereby making secularists the fastest-growing segment within American religion.

REAGAN CHARTS A DOMESTIC REVOLUTION, 1981–1988

As a presidential candidate, Reagan had promised Americans a "new sunrise." As president, he cut taxes, reduced social spending, and placed greater reliance on state, local, and community efforts. Easily reelected in 1984, Reagan reformed taxes but faced criticism for his role in several scandals.

REAGAN UNLEASHES A CONSERVATIVE REVOLUTION   After a career as a movie actor in Hollywood from the 1930s through the 1950s, Reagan entered politics in the 1960s as a conservative Republican, promising less government and lower taxes. He served two terms (1966–1974) as governor of California while he continued to build a conservative following. He won the Republican nomination for president in 1980 on the promise to implement his conservative agenda.

Reagan promised to unleash American capitalism by cutting taxes and deregulating business. During his administration inflation abated, unemployment fell, and the economy experienced the longest peacetime expansion in history. The government also ran record budget deficits. By

President Ronald Reagan and his wife Nancy on inauguration day, 1981. Reagan set a conservative agenda and confronted the Soviet Union, which he called "the evil empire." (© CORBIS)

1986 a series of tax cuts had benefited the wealthy by reducing top personal income tax rates to 28 percent and lowering capital gains, inheritance, and gift taxes.

To compensate for the lost revenue, Reagan proposed massive spending cuts. Conservatives argued that the nation could no longer afford the expensive social programs established in the 1960s. Conservative southern Democrats, nicknamed "boll weevils," joined Republicans in slashing more than $40 billion from domestic spending in 1981. Reagan's Omnibus Budget and Reconciliation Act (1981) proved to be a milestone in welfare policy. It shifted more responsibility to state and local governments for maintaining social programs. Between fiscal years 1981 and 1984, Reagan drastically cut spending for youth training, school lunches, child nutrition, food stamps, preventive health, and Aid to Families with Dependent Children (AFDC).

Reagan and his advisers believed that tax cuts and deregulation would spur economic growth. Growth, it was argued, in turn would increase government revenues and thus make up for money lost due to lower tax rates. Cutting taxes to increase federal revenues appeared paradoxical, but a similar policy had been followed in the Kennedy administration. Reagan's tax strategy, labeled "supply-side economics," called for unprecedented tax cuts. The theory assumed that, freed from the burden of taxes, consumers could both spend and save more and businesses could both invest and produce more, leading to overall greater economic activity and hence larger tax revenues. Reagan also tried to shift spending from social programs to the military. The defense budget burgeoned, but Congress refused to cut social spending by enough to offset the increase. As a result, by 1986 the budget deficit had soared to more than $200 billion.

Reagan's new environmental policies drew the most criticism. In his campaign Reagan appealed to a strongly anti-environmental segment of western ranchers, miners, lumber interests, and farmers. This "sagebrush rebellion" called for an end to regulatory control of the western states, where the federal government owned the majority of the land, timber, and mineral resources. Reagan's first secretary of the interior, James Watt, proposed selling public lands. He also favored oil and gas exploration off the California coast and placed a moratorium on further federal land purchases.

Environmental groups filed dozens of lawsuits against federal agencies for not enforcing environmental regulations and laws. More damaging, however, was the criticism Watt's program drew from conservatives. Sagebrush ranchers wanted grazing rights on federal land, not land auctions in which they would compete with wealthy oil and mineral companies. Conservatives attacked Watt's land sale program as economically improvident and environmentally unsound.

These criticisms took their toll on Watt. Then in 1983, Watt's appointee to the Environmental Protection Agency, Anne Gorsuch Burford, resigned following disclosure of her mishandling of the $1.6 billion "superfund" intended to clean up toxic waste sites. She was replaced by William Ruckelshaus, a pro-environmentalist. The final nail was put in Watts' political coffin when he made a derogatory racial remark and was forced to resign.

Environmentalists generally blasted Reagan and Watt, although the administration scored some notable environmental successes, including a renewed Endangered Species Act (1982) and several dozen wilderness laws (1984). Still, environmentalists remained sorely disappointed by Reagan's international record, which included reduced support for the United Nations' environmental and population control programs. He also opposed international treaties on global cooperation for environmental protection of the seas and the atmosphere.

Reagan quickly began to deregulate the economy. Deregulation had begun in the Carter administration with the airline industry. Reagan accelerated this movement by reducing federal regulatory power in areas such as broadcasting, transportation, and occupational safety and health. Early in Reagan's administration, Secretary of Transportation Drew Lewis eased automobile safety and pollution regulations.

In the summer of 1981, Lewis confronted the Professional Air Traffic Controller's Organization (PATCO) when they illegally went on strike. Reagan broke this walkout by firing all 11,500 striking workers and hiring replacements. Reagan's victory set a tone for the rest of his administration, and the destruction of PATCO was a devastating defeat for organized labor.

Reagan's administration also sought to change federal policy on civil rights. Conservative Republicans believed that many white Americans resented affirmative action and preferential hiring programs for minorities. As a consequence, the Justice Department opposed school busing and sought to overturn prohibitions against tax deductions for contributions to nonintegrated religious schools. The budget of the Civil Rights Division of the Justice Department was cut, and the number of African Americans appointed to major government positions declined.

Reagan's record on appointing women to federal positions was marginally better. Women served in the cabinet and in the Republican Party. He named Jeane Kirkpatrick ambassador to the United Nations. His most notable appointment came in 1981 when he nominated Sandra Day O'Connor to the Supreme Court, the first female justice in the Court's history.

In late 1981 Reagan faced his greatest challenge: The economy went into a severe recession. The Federal Reserve Board, trying to fight the double-digit inflation plaguing the country, allowed interest rates to soar. Rates for home mortgages shot up to double-digit figures. Very high interest rates created an abrupt and deep slowdown of the economy. By late 1982 unemployment had risen to 10 percent, the highest in forty-five years. A decline in American exports led to a worsening trade deficit fueled by huge increases in imports of Japanese televisions, stereos, and automobiles. The trade deficit rose from $31 billion in 1981 to $111 billion in 1984.

Reagan's program appeared doomed. In the 1982 midterm elections, Democrats gained twenty-six House seats, although the Republicans held on to a narrow Senate majority. The breakup of the Middle East's oil cartel (OPEC) and a decline in world oil prices, however, fueled a recovery. Inflation dropped to 4 percent; unemployment fell, and the gross domestic product rose nearly 10 percent. American auto manufacturers reported record sales. This economic boom lasted until 1990.

REAGAN REELECTED, 1984   Reagan's personality seemed to mesmerize the American people. His aura was enhanced on March 30, 1981, when a mentally disturbed man shot him. Wounded in the chest, Reagan was rushed to the hospital. As he was wheeled into surgery, he told the physicians, "Please tell me you're all Republicans." This jaunty ability to joke under pressure ingratiated him with the public. He possessed a natural ability to communicate with the American people. Opponents called him the "Teflon president" because nothing negative seemed to stick to him. Supporters called him "the Great Communicator."

In 1984 Reagan enjoyed the highest popularity rating of any president since Dwight D. Eisenhower. He brought to his reelection campaign an economy that was booming. As promised, Reagan had revived the economy, conquered inflation, rebuilt the military, and helped America to once again "stand tall" in the world. Reagan said it was "morning in America." In the 1984 election he and Vice President Bush beat Democrat Walter Mondale, Carter's former vice president, and his running mate, Representative Geraldine Ferraro, the first woman on a major party presidential ticket. In a landslide, Reagan swept forty-nine states, with 525 of the 538 electoral votes. He won the popular vote, garnering 59 percent to Mondale's 41 percent.

CONSERVATISM AT HIGH TIDE, 1986–1988   Reagan entered his second term intent on a major overhaul of the tax system. The president's main goal was to reduce tax rates, especially on higher incomes. He achieved that goal with the Tax Reform Act (1986), the first fundamental reform of the modern federal income tax system since World War II. The act both lowered rates and simplified the tax code, closing many loopholes and eliminating a variety of tax shelters. Moreover, the law removed six million poor Americans from the federal income tax rolls. The act also lowered the tax burden for the majority of taxpayers, although those with high incomes benefited the most. Some of the tax burden was shifted to corporations by the elimination of some tax write-offs and exemptions.

Reagan promised that this supply-side tax reform would bring a booming economy and control a mounting federal deficit. This proved half right; the economy prospered, with growth rates averaging 3 to 4 percent annually. Corporations enjoyed record sales and profits, the stock market reached new heights, and consumer spending and confidence remained high. Nevertheless, federal deficits continued to soar, reaching a high of $200 billion in 1986 and settling at $150 billion by 1988. Congress attempted to balance the budget with the Gramm-Rudman Act (1985), which tried to limit spending. Gramm-Rudman failed to balance the budget, however, when Congress found myriad ways to circumvent the law and the Supreme Court declared key provisions unconstitutional.

Next to tax reform, Reagan believed that his most enduring legacy might be to remake the Supreme Court in a conservative fashion. His appointment of moderate Sandra Day O'Connor in 1981 pointed in this direction. Following the retirement of Chief Justice Warren Burger in 1986, Reagan elevated conservative William Rehnquist to chief justice and appointed the equally conservative Antonin Scalia to the bench. In 1988, after a bitter fight that led to the rejection of Robert Bork, a well-known judicial conservative, California federal judge Anthony Kennedy joined the court.

Reagan also tackled the difficult problem of illegal immigration. In October 1986 Congress enacted a landmark immigration bill. The law offered amnesty for current illegal aliens and required employers to verify the citizenship of job applicants. Designed to stem the tide of illegal immigration by cutting illegals' access to jobs, the law nonetheless failed to halt the thousands of illegal aliens entering the United States, especially from Mexico and Central America. Often employers neglected to enforce the rules, and illegal immigrants forged citizenship documents.

SCANDALS PLAGUE REAGAN'S SECOND TERM   Reagan promised new integrity in government, but a series of scandals tarnished his second term. After a two-year investigation, in June 1988 the Justice Department revealed widespread corruption in the Pentagon involving bribes taken from defense contractors. Other officials came under investigation. In July 1988 Attorney General Edwin Meese, a close friend of Reagan's, resigned after allegations that he had used his influence to help friends secure a billion-dollar contract to build an oil pipeline in Iraq. After leaving their positions in the White House, Reagan advisers were convicted of influence peddling. One of the worst scandals occurred in the Department of Housing and Urban Development, where developers paid hundreds of thousands of dollars in bribes for federal contracts.

While Reagan remained personally and politically immune from these charges, critics maintained that the get-rich-quick atmosphere of the Reagan years had contributed to influence peddling and corruption in government.

THE REAGAN REVOLUTION AROUND THE WORLD, 1981–1988

Ronald Reagan entered the White House convinced that détente with the Soviet Union had failed and that communism remained a threat to international stability. Taking a hard line, he ordered a massive defense program while adopting a tougher stance toward arms control with the Soviet Union. Reagan displayed a willingness to use American military force, as evidenced when U.S. marines were sent to Lebanon in early 1983. The Reagan administration provided covert support to rebels in Soviet-occupied Afghanistan and to rebels seeking to overthrow the leftist government in Nicaragua. The involvement in Nicaragua led to the Iran–Contra scandal when it became public that administration officials had entered into a secret deal to supply the Iranian government with arms.

While foreign policy under Reagan often appeared blundering, his administration witnessed the end of the cold war as major arms treaties with the Soviet Union were reached and the Soviet Union began to withdraw from Eastern Europe.

REAGAN CHOOSES MORE MUSCLE, LESS TALK   Reagan and his advisers found détente wanting. They believed the Soviet Union had taken advantage of America's goodwill and desire for cooperation and had given little in return. The Soviet Union had invaded Afghanistan; Soviet and East German generals commanded Cuban troops in Ethiopia; and the Soviet Union was supplying and encouraging a revolutionary, anti-American regime in Nicaragua. Reagan denounced the Soviet Union as an "evil empire" intent on undermining American power around the globe.

Under Reagan the Pentagon's budget swelled from $171 billion in 1981 to more than $300 billion in 1985. Secretary of Defense Caspar Weinberger warned that the Soviet Union might be able to undertake a first-strike nuclear attack against the United States. This sort of advice pushed Congress to approve the MX missile system, a new strategic bomber, and an expanded navy with six hundred ships. In 1983, the United States deployed more than five hundred Cruise and Pershing II missiles in Europe to counter the Soviet Union's intermediate missiles in Eastern Europe. The placement of these missiles set off peace demonstrations in both the United States and Europe. Activists called for a unilateral "nuclear freeze" to halt the new arms race.

Reagan showed little faith in arms control. Nevertheless, his administration proposed to the Soviet Union a dramatic "zero option" plan, which offered to cancel the U.S. deployment of intermediate missiles in Western Europe if the Soviets withdrew missiles from Eastern Europe. When this proposal was rejected, the United States entered into new negotiations, called START, with the Soviet Union. Meeting in Geneva, American negotiators proposed that both sides scrap one-third of their nuclear warheads. The Soviet Union rejected the proposal outright. When intermediate missiles sent from the United States began to arrive in Great Britain and West Germany in 1983, the Soviet Union broke off the START talks.

Following the breakdown of the START talks, Reagan approved the Strategic Defense Initiative (SDI), a complex antimissile system that would use high-powered lasers in space to destroy Soviet missiles launched at the United States. Quickly denounced as a fanciful and impractical "Star Wars" by critics, SDI was seen as an expensive and destabilizing escalation of the arms race that could encourage a preemptive first strike.

Reagan's tough stance appeared to have little effect on the Soviet Union. In late 1981 the Soviet Union ordered a crackdown in Poland against the militant Solidarity trade union movement. Following the declaration of martial law by the communist government, Reagan sought to isolate the Soviet Union by imposing an economic boycott on Poland. In 1982 Reagan tried to block the building of a natural gas line linking the Soviet Union and Western Europe, but Reagan's efforts were stymied by western European leaders.

Efforts to aid anti-Soviet rebels in Soviet-occupied Afghanistan proved more successful. The Central Intelligence Agency arranged to supply high-tech weapons to the rebels through an extensive covert operation based in Pakistan. Rebel forces were able to bog down Soviet forces in a guerrilla war reminiscent of America's involvement in Vietnam a decade earlier.

EXPANDING TRADE WITH ASIA   The Reagan administration worked to expand trade with Asia. The population of China exceeded one billion, a potentially vast market for American goods. In addition, the economies of Japan, South Korea, Taiwan, Hong Kong, Malaysia, and Singapore were booming, largely fueled by trade with the United States.

While the United States sought to develop new markets in China, the administration faced a serious challenge from aggressive Japanese manufacturers who flooded America with high-quality, low-priced products. The trade imbalance between Japan and United States, unfavorable to the United States, rose from $10 billion in 1980 to $35 billion in 1984. A large part of this deficit was due to imported Japanese cars. In the 1970s American auto manufacturers had lost 25 percent of their home market to Japanese automakers. Under pressure the Japanese agreed to a "voluntary" reduction in auto shipments to the United States.

DEALING WITH SOUTH AFRICA AND THE PHILIPPINES   The administration faced growing problems in South Africa, where the militant African National Congress (ANC) organized protests against an oppressive system of racial segregation and white supremacy known as *apartheid* (the Afrikaner word for "apartness"). In the mid-1980s government security forces began a serious crackdown against ANC demonstrators. When violence followed, American civil rights groups called for American corporations and institutions to withdraw investments in South Africa. Fourteen states and scores of cities refused to own stock in any corporation that did business in South Africa, and college students across the country demonstrated against their universities' investment policies.

The Reagan administration pursued what it called "constructive engagement." This policy applied diplomatic pressure through State Department channels while refraining from open criticism of apartheid. Under mounting public pressure, Congress in 1986 overrode a presidential veto and imposed an economic boycott on South Africa.

In 1986 Reagan's attention also turned to the Philippine Islands, where Corazon Aquino challenged military dictator Ferdinand Marcos for political power. Fearing a communist revolution in the islands, the United States had backed the Marcos government, until Aquino emerged to challenge what had become the Marcos "kleptocracy" (government by theft). America pressured Marcos to hold democratic elections in early 1986. Although Marcos claimed victory, the people believed the results had been rigged. Massive protests forced him to flee the country, and Mrs. Aquino assumed power. The new democratic government continued to face communist insurgency, a stagnant economy, and political pressure from the military.

MUDDLING THROUGH IN THE MIDDLE EAST   In the Middle East the Reagan administration sought to continue the peace process begun in the Carter years. Nevertheless, Secretary of State Alexander Haig appeared to encourage Israel's policy of gradually taking over the West Bank, which the Palestinians considered their homeland. In 1982 Israel invaded Lebanon to destroy refugee camps controlled by the Palestine Liberation Organization (PLO), a long-time foe of Israel. The Reagan administration sent Philip Habib, an envoy of Lebanese descent, to arrange for the safe withdrawal of PLO forces and refugees under attack by the Israelis. In September 1982, Christian Lebanese forces allied with Israel invaded two refugee camps and slaughtered hundreds of unarmed Palestinians.

The United States sent 1,500 troops to Beirut to help restore peace. Syrian forces backed by the Soviet Union occupied eastern Lebanon, while Israel controlled southern Lebanon. Militant Muslim factions despised the American troops, who remained isolated and in a poor defensive position. Early on the morning of October 23, 1983, a Muslim terrorist drove a truck filled with explosives directly into the U.S. marine compound. The explosion killed 241 sleeping marines, the worst military disaster since the Vietnam War. By early 1984 Reagan had quietly withdrawn the remaining marines from Lebanon, having achieved nothing.

INTERNATIONAL TERRORISM AND THE MIDDLE EAST   International terrorism haunted the government. The State Department estimated that in 1985 alone there were seven hundred terrorist assaults around the world. Most of these attacks came from Arab extremists committed to the destruction of Israel. In 1986, pro-Libyan terrorists, with cooperation from the communist government of East Germany, bombed American military installations in West Germany. In retaliation Reagan ordered an air strike on Libya. Public opinion supported this action, although some critics called the strike ineffective and counterproductive because it accomplished little militarily.

In 1987 the situation in the Middle East became extremely explosive when it looked like the United States might be drawn into the Iraq–Iran war. This grueling six-year war between Iraq and Iran had begun in 1981 and claimed an estimated 600,000 lives. When the Iranian navy began to attack Kuwaiti oil shipments destined for the United States, Western Europe, and Japan, Reagan ordered a U.S. naval fleet into the Persian Gulf. Tensions between the United States and Iran rose when the destroyer *USS Vincennes* mistakenly shot down an Iranian airliner, killing 290 passengers. A series of clashes between the Iranian navy and the American fleet ensued. The Iraq–Iran war finally ended in a negotiated stalemate in the summer of 1988, but tension between Iran and the United States remained.

THE CENTRALITY OF CENTRAL AMERICA   Two small nations, Nicaragua and El Salvador, became the focus of U.S. policy in Latin America during the 1980s. The administration remained intent on rolling back pro-Soviet socialism in Nicaragua, and on defeating an insurgent movement in El Salvador. United States policy in Latin America was designed to thwart Marxist revolutions in the Southern Hemisphere.

Evidence gathered by the CIA revealed that Marxist Sandinista supporters in Nicaragua were aiding communist rebels across the border in El Salvador. Following the murder of several American Catholic nuns by right-wing Salvadoran government forces, President Carter had cut off financial aid to El Salvador. In 1984 Jose Napoleon Duarte, a moderate democrat, was elected president. He initiated reforms curbing the right-wing "death squads" that had murdered thousands of civilians. Duarte's army, however, was unable to defeat the left-wing guerrillas or bring them to the negotiating table.

While civil war raged in El Salvador, Reagan authorized $19 million in late 1981 to arm five hundred rebel troops in Nicaragua. This counterrevolutionary army, called the Contras, became the focus of Reagan's foreign policy in Central America. Composed of anti-Sandinista Nicaraguans, including former supporters of the deposed dictator Anastasio Somoza Debayle, the Contras conducted raids and sabotage in Nicaragua. Congress remained skeptical of Reagan's support of the Contras and in December 1982 enacted the Boland Amendment, which barred the CIA and the Pentagon from directly funding these anticommunist insurgents.

Although the administration conducted a proxy war in Nicaragua and El Salvador without deploying U.S. troops, Reagan was not opposed to using direct force. In 1983 he sent U.S. marines to help overthrow a Marxist dictator on the tiny Caribbean island of Grenada. Deployed shortly after the debacle in Lebanon, the marines quickly overran the island and captured several hundred Cuban military advisers, who appeared to have been hurriedly constructing a Soviet air base. The United States installed a friendly government and granted $30 million in financial assistance. While both Congress and the Organization of American States condemned the invasion, public opinion polls in the United States and Grenada showed Reagan receiving wide support.

THE IRAN–CONTRA AFFAIR, 1986–1988   Relations with Iran proved enigmatic. In early November 1986, a Beirut magazine reported that in 1985 the United States had shipped more than five hundred antitank missiles to Iran. The article sparked accusations of illegal conduct. Reagan, however, claimed that the missiles were sold to Iran to persuade pro-Iranian radical groups to release the American hostages they were holding in Lebanon.

More bizarre details soon followed, including a report that Colonel Oliver North, a National Security Council aide, had used profits from the missile sales to help fund the Contras in Nicaragua, a subversion of the congressional directive embodied in the Boland Amendment. Congressional investigators also revealed that North had arranged a deal with the Saudi Arabians to sell them four hundred U.S. Stinger antiaircraft missiles if they would donate $10 million to the Contras. North also persuaded Israel, as well as private donors, to back the rebels. Just before the FBI arrived to seal the office for investigation, North and his secretary shredded documents that might have incriminated other high officials, including CIA director William J. Casey.

A joint House–Senate investigative committee convened in the summer of 1987 to investigate the Iran–Contra affair. More than 250 hours of testimony were taken in nationally televised hearings. The committee's final report roundly criticized the administration for its flagrant disregard of the law. An independent prosecutor continued the investigation through 1992 in an attempt to unravel the whole story of "who knew what, and when." In late 1992, shortly before leaving office, President George Bush pardoned key Reagan officials implicated in the affair, including former Secretary of Defense Caspar Weinberger.

THE COLD WAR ENDS   In his second term Reagan dramatically shifted his foreign policy toward negotiation with the Soviet Union. Shortly after the 1984 election, Reagan surprised leading advisers and critics as well by resuming negotiations with the Soviets. In late 1985 Reagan traveled to Geneva for a three-day summit meeting with the new Soviet leader, Mikhail Gorbachev. At the meeting Reagan insisted on America's right to develop the Strategic Defense Initiative (SDI). This position precluded reaching any major agreements, but Reagan and Gorbachev pledged to accelerate arms control negotiations in future meetings.

Finally, in 1987 Gorbachev flew to the United States to sign the historic Intermediate Nuclear Forces Treaty (INF), the first major arms control agreement that called for the destruction of deployed nuclear weapons systems. The treaty provided that inspectors from both nations would observe the destruction of intermediate-range missiles. Soviet and American leaders also announced that they would seek further arms reductions through the Strategic Arms Reduction Treaty (START) talks, which had been temporarily broken off in Reagan's first term. Gorbachev also began to withdraw Soviet troops from Afghanistan, to end support of the Sandinista government in Nicaragua, and to reduce commitments to Cuba and Vietnam. Moreover, Gorbachev urged Soviet-backed governments in Eastern Europe to undertake political and economic reform.

Reagan's success with the Soviet Union helped overcome setbacks related to the Iran–Contra scandal. Following that debacle, these successful negotiations with the Soviet Union restored public confidence in Reagan, the long-time cold warrior. As Reagan's administration drew to a close, the cold war appeared to have ended. These negotiations marked one of the greatest diplomatic feats since World War II.

BUSH FAILS TO FILL REAGAN'S SHOES, 1988–1993

Reagan passed the mantle of power to his vice president, George Bush, who easily won the 1988 presidential election. Domestically, Bush pursued a moderate program that called for less government intervention in the economy, modest social reform, and reduction of the deficit. His willingness to work with congressional Democrats led him to break a campaign pledge not to raise taxes. The Bush presidency coincided with the disintegration of the Soviet Union, whose rivalry with the United States had dominated international relations since World War II. The Soviet Union's demise transformed American foreign policy and defense strategy. The United States now exerted its strength in confronting dictators in Panama and Iraq.

An economic recession, however, marred the last two years of Bush's administration, weakening his popularity and enabling Bill Clinton to unseat him in the 1992 election.

BUSH STRUGGLES WITH THE DEFICIT   The Republicans picked Reagan's vice president, George Herbert Walker Bush, to head their ticket in 1988.

Bush appeared to have no clear ideological vision of his own and was seen as someone who would continue the Reagan agenda. He promised at the Republican Convention, "Read my lips: No new taxes." In a particularly nasty campaign, Bush defeated his Democratic opponent, Michael Dukakis, by assailing him for opposing legislation requiring school children to recite the Pledge of Allegiance, for failing to clean up pollution in Boston Harbor, and for allowing a convicted rapist and murderer to be furloughed from prison, during which time the rapist committed other heinous crimes. Bush won the election with 54 percent of the popular vote and 426 electoral votes to Dukakis's 46 percent and 112 electors.

Once in office, Bush promised to make America a "kinder, gentler nation." In a subtle reprimand of the Reagan administration, Bush expressed a willingness to be a "hands-on" president who would cooperate with Congress. Although he sought few domestic initiatives, he expressed a desire to balance the budget. The national debt stood at nearly $3 trillion when Bush took office.

Bush proposed sharp reductions in military spending by slashing $2.7 billion from Reagan's defense budget, including severe cutbacks in funding for the SDI ("Star Wars") program. Despite his campaign pledge to be an "education president," he requested $3 billion less for education than Reagan had in his last budget. Bush proposed, however, additional funding for child care, clean air, and AIDS research (AIDS is an acronym for *acquired immunodeficiency syndrome*, a disease that attacks the immune system). Declaring a new war on drugs, Bush called for increased funding for law enforcement.

Rising budget deficits dominated Bush's administration. By 1991 the budget deficit had risen to $268 billion, the largest in U.S. history. Finally, under pressure from Congress, in July 1990 Bush reneged on his campaign pledge not to raise taxes. The backlash from conservatives and working-class Reagan Democrats was immediate. Conservatives accused Bush of having broken his firm pledge on taxes. The break with conservatives within his party proved irreversible.

Bush sought to shore up conservative support by continuing the Reagan agenda of transforming the Supreme Court. Reagan's appointments had appeared to shift the Court in a decidedly more conservative direction. In *Webster v. Reproductive Health Care Services* (1989), the Court had upheld a Missouri law that limited a woman's right to an abortion. Yet the Court had also showed an independence that set it apart from any set conservative position when it ruled in *Texas v. Johnson* (1989) that First Amendment rights allowed flag burning.

In 1990, following the retirement of justices William Brennan and Thurgood Marshall, Bush appointed David Souter, a federal judge from New Hampshire, who easily won Senate approval. Bush's second appointee, Clarence Thomas, a conservative African American, ran into serious problems when Anita Hill, an African-American former employee of Thomas, accused him of having sexually harrassed her when she worked for him at two federal agencies in 1982 and 1983. Following televised hearings, the Senate narrowly confirmed Thomas's nomination.

In the midst of the Thomas fight, Bush signed the Civil Rights Act of 1991, which he had denounced earlier as a "quota bill." The civil rights bill only compounded a sense of betrayal among conservatives and Reagan Democrats.

THE SOVIET UNION COLLAPSES   The collapse of the Soviet Union, which began in 1989 with the crumbling of the communist government in Poland, soon spread throughout Eastern and Central Europe as regime after communist regime fell like dominoes. Republicans claimed that Reagan's aggressive anticommunist foreign policy had brought about the demise of the Soviet empire. Many Soviet leaders agreed that this was a contributing factor, although any full analysis of the collapse of communism must acknowledge the role played by the economic failure of Soviet-style communism.

During the Reagan administration, Mikhail Gorbachev became leader of the Soviet Union. Gorbachev called for economic restructuring *(perestroika)* and political openness *(glasnost)*. A deteriorating Soviet economy forced Gorbachev to accept political reform in Eastern Europe. Without Soviet support, communist regimes fell in Poland, Czechoslovakia, Hungary, Bulgaria, and Romania. The most dramatic event occurred on November 9, 1989, when East Germans were allowed to cross the border at the Berlin Wall, which separated East and West Germany. Later, West Germany absorbed East Germany, reuniting them as a single nation. The cold war had ended.

Events in the Soviet Union unleashed a pro-democratic movement in China, to which that government reacted with brutal suppression. Inspired by reform movements in Eastern Europe, thousands of Chinese students and their supporters occupied Tiananmen Square in the Chinese capital of Beijing in a massive demonstration for political reform. On the morning of June 4, 1989, Chinese leader Deng Xiaoping ordered the army to crush the dissident movement. A least a thousand demonstrators were killed when the army ruthlessly attacked the unarmed students. Bush condemned the attack but refused to sever diplomatic ties with China.

The crisis in the Soviet Union soon affected Latin America. Shortly after the Soviet Union announced that it would no longer continue to subsidize the Marxist Sandinista government in Nicaragua, the Sandinistas permitted the first democratic elections in Nicaragua in sixty years. To their surprise, a coalition of anti-Sandinista forces swept into office.

The Soviet decline left the United States the world's only superpower. Bush remained determined to assert America's military strength to shape what he described as the "new world order." To overthrow the drug-dealing dictator Manuel Noriega in Panama, Bush ordered military forces into Panama in December 1989. Most Panamanians welcomed the 25,000 invading American troops, who subsequently seized Noriega on charges of drug trafficking. Noriega was returned to the United States, where he was tried and convicted for his involvement in the international drug trade.

Most Americans cheered Bush's move against Noriega. This use of force in Panama set the stage for further U.S. action when Iraq invaded its oil-rich neighbor, Kuwait, in August 1990. Fearing an Iraqi invasion of Saudi Arabia and a subsequent threat to American oil interests, Bush forged an international coalition under United Nations' auspices to force Iraq to withdraw from Kuwait. When an economic boycott appeared to have little effect on the Iraqi leader, Saddam Hussein, Bush ordered massive air and ground assaults in which 700,000 Allied troops were eventually deployed against Iraqi-occupied Kuwait and southern Iraq.

Led by U.S. General Norman Schwarzkopf, the six-week campaign called Operation Desert Storm overwhelmed Saddam's army. An estimated 50,000 to 100,000 Iraqis were killed. Kuwait was liberated, although Saddam remained in power. Bush's popularity soared to 91 percent, the highest ever recorded for any president. In the fall of 1991, Bush's reelection for a second term seemed certain.

ECONOMIC DOWNTURN, RIOTS, AND THE ELECTION OF 1992   The record-long business expansion that began in 1983 halted in 1990 as the United States entered a recession that lasted until mid-1991. Even as signs of growth appeared, the economy continued to hover between recession and recovery. Unemployment rose to 7.5 percent in 1992. As the economy spiraled downward, so did George Bush's popularity. Convinced that he would easily win reelection, he accepted the advice of his advisers and refused to push new legislation to improve the economy.

Lingering economic recession and growing discontent among the electorate created a volatile political situation as the presidential race opened in 1992. Although Republicans under Reagan had made significant inroads among traditional Democratic blocs—white southerners, Catholics, and blue-collar workers—only 29 percent of the electorate expressed strong identification with either political party. A walloping 26 percent of the electorate considered themselves "independents." Surveys revealed deep cynicism among voters toward professional politicians.

In this situation the Democrats turned to Bill Clinton, governor of Arkansas, who campaigned as a moderate who would return the party to the middle class. In a departure from typical political wisdom, Clinton did not try for regional balance but selected another southerner as his running mate, Tennessee Senator Albert Gore, a strong environmentalist.

Confident of his own reelection, Bush nonetheless faced a sputtering economy and an array of social problems. The national debt had doubled in the Reagan–Bush years to $4 trillion. The banking

During his inaugural ball, President Bill Clinton played the saxophone. Earlier, he had campaigned by playing the sax on MTV in order to reach younger voters. (AP/Wide World Photos)

industry, especially savings and loan institutions, was in disarray caused by heavy debt. Unemployment hovered intractably at 7 percent. One American in ten was on food stamps, while one in eight lived in poverty.

The situation seemed ripe for an explosion. On April 29, 1992, that eruption came when a jury in Simi Valley, California, acquitted four white Los Angeles policemen accused of beating a young black man named Rodney King. The beating had been videotaped by a passing witness, providing what many considered obvious proof of the policemen's guilt.

For the next four days, Los Angeles experienced the worst riot in its history. Protesters targeted a section of south-central Los Angeles where 200,000 Koreans had settled and opened small businesses in a neighborhood called "Koreatown." At one point the smoke over Los Angeles caused by the upheaval forced Los Angeles International Airport to close all but one runway.

The national guard finally restored order, but estimates of property damage in Los Angeles varied from $750 million to $1 billion. Approximately fifty people died. More than fifteen thousand were arrested. Critics blamed the riot on the failure of the Reagan–Bush administrations to address the needs of the inner city.

The political situation became complicated when a Texas billionaire, Ross Perot, entered the presidential race as an independent. Polls showed him winning 30 percent of the vote in a three-way race, but then in July he abruptly withdrew. The Clinton–Gore ticket continued to hammer Bush on the economy, portraying Republicans as out of touch with the needs of the middle class. Republicans countered by raising issues of trust, charging that Clinton had dishonestly avoided the draft during the Vietnam War. Bush portrayed Clinton as a liberal who would raise taxes, increase social spending, and enact a radical cultural agenda. In mid-October Perot had a change of heart and reentered the race, conducting his campaign largely through controlled television advertising rather than direct contact with reporters or the public.

On election day Clinton swept the Electoral College, winning 370 electoral votes with 43 percent of the popular vote. Bush won 168 electoral votes with 38 percent of the vote. Perot failed to carry any state but won 19 percent of the popular vote, the largest vote received by any third-party candidate since Theodore Roosevelt had run as a Progressive in 1912.

For the first time in sixteen years, the Democrats had won the White House. The election of Bill Clinton promised historic change. The first president born after the Second World War, the forty-six-year-old Clinton promised a generational transfer of power. He received particularly strong support among blacks, the very poor, the elderly, and some groups of women.

The 1992 election proved to be a breakthrough for women and minorities. Of the eleven women running for the Senate, five won. Democrat Carol Moseley Braun became the first African-American woman to be elected to the Senate. California became the first state to be represented in the Senate only by women, Barbara Boxer and Dianne Feinstein. The first American Indian to sit in the Senate in sixty years was Democrat Ben Nighthorse Campbell of Colorado.

Table 30.1   The 1992 Presidential Election

Candidates	Popular Vote	Electoral Vote
Bill Clinton (Democrat)	43,726,375	370
George Bush (Republican)	38,167,416	168
Ross Perot (Independent)	19,237,247	0

CONCLUSION

The United States, a society founded on immigration, had become one of the most ethnically diverse nations in the world, home to people of European, African, Latin American, and Asian descent. American religions now included Protestants, Catholics, Jews, Muslims, Buddhists, Hindus, and secularists. Single-parent families were more common. In this social transformation, women increasingly entered professions formerly closed to them. Gender roles, too, changed as homosexuals, both gay and lesbian, sought recognition and acceptance.

The American political system reflected this diversity as more women, African Americans, Hispanics, and other minorities were elected to office. At the same time, confidence in democratic government and the two-party system appeared shaken as voter participation declined and the electorate expressed disillusionment with "politics as usual." The end of the cold war left the United States the preeminent military and economic power in the world, but many wondered if American civilization itself were not in decline. Americans remained an optimistic people but, as always, skeptical of the future and anxious about the noble experiment, American democracy.

Recommended Readings

(REAGAN/BUSH) Steve Bruce, *The Rise and Fall of the New Christian Right: Conservative Protestant Politics in America, 1978–1988* (1988); Lou Cannon, *Reagan* (1982) and *President Reagan: The Role of a Lifetime* (1991); Robert Dallek, *Ronald Reagan* (1984); Lawrence Freedman and Efraim Karsh, *The Gulf Conflict* (1993); Steven M. Gillon, *The Democrats' Dilemma: Walter F. Mondale and the Liberal Legacy* (1992); Patrick Glynn, *Closing Pandora's Box: Arms Races, Arms Control and the History of the Cold War* (1993); Jerome L. Himmelstein, *To the Right: The Transformation of American Conservatism* (1990); J. David Hoeveler, Jr., *Watch on the Right: Conservative Intellectuals in the Reagan Era* (1991); James Davison Hunter, *Culture Wars: The Struggle to Define America* (1991); Jonathan Lash, *A Season of Spoils: The Story of the Reagan Administration's Attack on the Environment* (1984); Jane Meyer and Doyle McManus, *Landslide: The Unmaking of the President* (1988); Peggy Noonan, *What I Saw at the Revolution: A Political Life in the Reagan Era* (1990); Robert Pastor, *Condemned to Repetition: The United States and Nicaragua* (1987); Nicol C. Rae, *The Decline and Fall of the Liberal Republican: From 1952 to the Present* (1989); Adolph Reed, *The Jesse Jackson Phenomenon* (1986) ; Kirkpatrick Sale, *Power Shift: The Rise of the Southern Rim and Its Challenge to the Eastern Establishment* (1975); Peter Steinfels, *The Neo-Conservatives* (1979); David Stockman, *The Triumph of Politics* (1987); Strobe Talbott, *Deadly Gambits* (1984) and *The Russians and Reagan* (1984); F. Clifton White, *Why Reagan Won* (1981); Garry Wills, *Reagan's America* (1986).

(SOCIETY) John Crewden, *The Tarnished Door: The New Immigrants and the Transformation of America* (1983); Reynolds Farley and Walter Allen, *The Color Line and the Quality of Life in America* (1987); Todd Gitlin, *Inside Prime Time* (1985); Kenneth Keniston, *All Our Children: The American Family Under Pressure* (1977); David Reimers, *Still the Golden Door: The Third World Comes to America* (1985); Alan Wolfe, *America's Impasse: The Rise and Fall of the Politics of Growth* (1981).

31

❧

America Enters the Twenty-first Century

OVERVIEW   As the United States entered the twenty-first century, rapid technological and scientific advances affected American society, culture, and politics. These advances also increased the world's destructive capacity: Missiles could now target pinpoint locations, and techniques of biological warfare could spread disease or toxic chemicals throughout civilian populations. At the same time, new communication and transportation technologies made the world seem smaller. The pace of globalization accelerated.

The United States became still more ethnically and culturally diverse. While the native birthrate declined from its 1950s high, the rate of population growth increased through the migration of people from Mexico, Central and Latin America, Asia, and (to a lesser extent) Europe, profoundly affecting American culture and politics. As the Hispanic population grew, becoming the largest ethnic minority group in America, Hispanics exerted more influence in politics, especially in the western states. Illegal immigration, especially from Mexico, Central America, and Asia, created political controversy that contributed to larger debates about cultural diversity, pluralism, and assimilation.

Even as ethnic and other minorities gained in political influence, many Americans appeared to lose confidence in established political leaders and government institutions. By the 1990s voter turnout for national and state elections had fallen to new lows. At the same time, American politics on the national level appeared increasingly polarized.

Internationally, the fall of the Soviet Union created new problems for the United States, causing ethnic and religious conflicts to erupt more often in Asia and Europe. The proliferation of weapons of mass destruction among smaller nations and the emergence of international terrorist groups presented new challenges.

SCIENCE AND TECHNOLOGY
PROMISE DRAMATIC CHANGE

Advances in biomedicine, computers, electronics, energy resources, and other scientific fields promised to make life better. In the last decade of the twentieth century, the use of computers grew in every aspect of Americans' lives: their homes, schools, workplaces, and stores. The personal computer allowed access to the Internet, a rich source of information and communication. At the same time, great advances in biogenetics and biotechnology promised to cure once-fatal and debilitating diseases and to extend and improve people's lives. Through genetic engineering, new foods, animals, and perhaps even humans could be created. Such advances would transform the way Americans lived, how long, and how well. Yet the same scientific and technological development also enlarged the capacity for destruction, as new weapons were developed. New technology also accelerated economic globalization.

THE COMPUTER BECOMES PERSONAL   The computer revolution in the last quarter of the twentieth century significantly changed research, commerce, defense, communication, and entertainment.

The computer had its roots in early calculating machines developed in the seventeenth century, but the electronics revolution after the Second World War marked the first real steps in developing the modern computer. In 1948 the electronic transistor was developed by William Shockley, and in 1957 the first integrated circuit or "chip" was designed, allowing the building of giant computers. In 1971 American engineer Marcian E. Hoff developed the microprocessor, which incorporated hundreds of components in a small silicon chip. In 1974 the first commercial personal computer was introduced by Micro Instrumentation Telemetry Systems. In 1976 Stephen Wozniak and Steven Jobs started Apple Computer, which became the fastest-growing company in U.S. history. In 1981 IBM introduced a personal computer that used a standard operating system designed by Bill Gates of Microsoft Corporation, making personal computers accessible to small businesses and average Americans. Fear that IBM

Founders Steven Jobs and Stephen Wozniak flank Apple Computer president John Sculley at the unveiling of a new model in 1984. The personal computer and the high-tech industry changed the way Americans learned, worked, and played. (AP/Wide World Photos)

would dominate the personal computer market proved groundless due to rapid technological innovation by competing companies.

During the 1980s computer chip technology improved a hundredfold; ten million circuits could be placed on a single chip the size of a fingernail. Software designers made sophisticated technology increasingly affordable for business and home. By 2000 computers came with rewritable CD and DVD players, full-color scanners, and digital cameras. By 2000 more than half the American households owned at least one computer.

Microsoft became one of the largest computer corporations in the United States and its founder, Bill Gates, one of the wealthiest people in the world. The company's Windows operating system gained 90 percent of market share, leading smaller companies to complain of unfair business practices. In May 1998, Microsoft was indicted by twenty state attorneys general and the U.S. Department of Justice for violations of the antitrust law. After Microsoft was declared a monopoly, in 2001 an agreement was worked out with the U.S. Department of Justice to avoid Microsoft's breakup.

Computer technology allowed engineers and designers to test and develop new products through computer-aided design (CAD), for companies to manufacture products through computer-aided manufacturing

(CAM), and for pilots to experience flight simulation through computer aided instruction (CAI).

The concept of the Internet grew out of the cold war, when huge computers needed to be networked for time-sharing and data transfer. In 1972 the first electronic messaging (E-mail) program was developed; in March 1989 the World Wide Web came online. By 2000 there were 56 million hosts on the Internet from 170 countries with more than 300 million Web sites, with the number of new sites increasing geometrially.

This new technology raised issues of personal privacy. Fears of unwanted access to personal information by computer led Congress to enact a number of privacy laws. Federal and state lawmakers also imposed a number of fair information practice regulations that required firms and agencies collecting information to disclose fully how such information was gathered and how it was to be used.

The development of the Internet also led to complicated questions regarding copyrights, intellectual property, and pornography. In 2000 a number of major record companies, distributors, and performers filed suit against Napster, an online site dedicated to downloading musical tracks. Although Napster was shut down, other sites and technologies were developed that made it difficult to control Internet distribution of commercial music and other entertainment. In 1996 Congress passed the Communications Decency Act (CDA) to prohibit under-age access to pornography, but in 1997 the Supreme Court struck down the Internet provision in *Reno v. ACLU*.

As Americans relied more and more on computers, society became increasingly vulnerable to computer attack. Fear of computer break-ins (hacking) and computer viruses (programs created to sabotage and disrupt operating systems) caused corporations and governmental agencies to develop security measures to protect their systems from pranksters, corporate rivals, criminals, political terrorists, and enemy states.

The computer revolution portends still further dramatic change as scientists work on faster processors and computers that combine biological processes with machines.

MEDICAL TECHNOLOGY IMPROVES HEALTH AND RAISES COSTS   Advancements in medicine and medical technology gave Americans longer and better lives. From 1960 to 2000, the death rate of Americans fell from 760 per hundred thousand to 470 per hundred thousand. Although this fall cannot be attributed solely to better health care or new medical technology—fewer deaths were caused by war, and working conditions became less hazardous—Americans were living longer. In 1960, 929,000 Americans were over eighty-five years old; by 2000 more than three million Americans were over eighty-five. During the twentieth century life expectancy increased nearly thirty years to an average of 76.5 years, leading to significant social changes in the treatment and care of the elderly. As the proportion of elderly Americans grew, their political influence increased. The American Association of Retired Persons (AARP) became one of the strongest lobbying organizations in Washington, D.C.

New technologies spurred the development of new medicines, vaccines, and drugs, especially in the treatment of heart disease. Although heart disease remains a major cause of death, especially in males, the disease is commonly treated with less invasive surgeries. Vaccines proved better alternatives to antibiotics, to which viruses have become increasingly resistant. By 2000 scientists had developed experimental vaccines for AIDS, malaria, hepatitis C, and tuberculosis. New psychotropic drugs, including antidepressants and antipsychotics, were also developed. In 1987 selective serotonin reuptake inhibitors (SSRI) were introduced by Eli Lilly Corporation under the name of Prozac and prescribed for both children and adults. Methylphenidate, a derivative of amphetamine marketed under the name of Ritalin, was commonly prescribed for attention deficit and hyperactivity disorder (ADHD). From 1990 to 2000, an estimated 10 percent of children aged six to fourteen had taken Ritalin.

Computer technology also benefited medicine. In 1984 magnetic resonance imaging (MRI) was invented by Raymond Damadian. MRI was especially useful for obtaining precise images of soft tissues in the brain and spinal cord. During the 1990s advances in laparoscopic surgery, which required very small incisions, transformed medical surgery. Robotic lasers allowed surgeons to perform operations on the arteries of newborn babies.

At the outset of the twenty-first century, the most significant development was the completion of the human genome map. This massive project, sponsored by the National Institutes of Health and the U.S. Department of Energy, identified thirty thousand genes in the human body. Congress appropriated $3 billion for this project. The map will aid in the discovery of ways to diagnose and treat diseases through customized drugs and effective drug therapy. Gene therapy promises ways to treat diseases that have plagued humankind since its inception: cancer, diabetes, sickle cell anemia, muscular dystrophy. The full implications of gene therapy and gene design are not known; their effects on society and culture will become apparent only in future generations.

TECHNOLOGY TRANSFORMS AMERICAN LIVES IN OTHER WAYS   Throughout the 1980s and 1990s, microprocessors brought new conveniences into the American home. Americans listened to music on compact disc (CD) and digital video disc (DVD) players. Americans filmed family events on their digital video recorders and took pictures with their digital cameras. Beamed into their home through satellite or cable were hundreds of television channels. Digital devices appeared everywhere.

Americans communicated through the Internet and on wireless telephones, faxes, and pagers. The Telecommunications Act deregulated local telephone service to increase competition among telephone companies. In 1995, 32 million Americans—more than a third of the world's users—had mobile phones; by 2001 more than 115 million Americans had them.

Computers transformed the automobiles Americans drove. Computer chips regulated fuel, suspension, air bags, and alarm systems. In its 1996 Cadillac, General Motors introduced the OnStar system, which provided emergency roadside assistance and computerized navigation through the Global Positioning System. By 2003 GPS could be found in most luxury cars. Minivan manufacturers included miniature televisions with VCR and DVD systems in family cars.

By 2000 more Americans were traveling by air than ever before. Deregulation of the airline industry introduced fierce competition among the airlines, leading to reduced prices and inducements for flying.

THE ECONOMY BOOMS AND AMERICAN SOCIETY DIVERSIFIES IN A GLOBAL ERA

In the early 1990s the United States entered a recession. The economy began to grow again in March 1991, too late to help George H. W. Bush win reelection. In the next nine years, 1992–2000, the nation enjoyed the longest economic expansion on record. Unemployment, inflation, and interest rates were low, and stock prices climbed. The boom was fed by technological innovation and an expanding global economy. At the same time, American society continued to become more socially and culturally diverse through immigration.

THE ECONOMY BOOMS IN THE 1990S AND THEN FIZZLES   In 1992, the U.S. economy began an expansion rivaling that of the 1980s. Much of this boom was fed by new technological innovations that raised productivity, reduced prices of consumer goods, and allowed new companies to emerge.

Federal economic policy encouraged this prospering economy. Tax cuts in the 1980s encouraged business expansion and consumer spending in the 1990s. Following the election of a Republican Congress in 1994, President William Clinton pursued a policy of deficit reduction and cutbacks in government spending. In 1998 the federal budget was balanced for the first time since 1973, and the government enjoyed surpluses for the remainder of Clinton's term.

Clinton also supported international free trade, the lifting of economic barriers that discouraged exchange of goods and services between countries. He persuaded Congress, especially members with ties to organized labor, to ratify the North American Free Trade Agreement (NAFTA), which took effect in 1994 and joined the United States, Mexico, and Canada into a single free-trade zone. In 1994 Clinton secured the adoption of the General Agreement on Tariffs and Trade (GATT), which advanced globalization by cutting tariffs and creating the World Trade Organization (WTO) to administer trade laws. Although Clinton's free trade policies won support in Congress and among the American public, concerns were raised about the potential pitfalls of globalization: the growing political power of multinational corporations unaccountable to electorates, the rising burden of debt in poorer countries, and the lack of enforceable regulations protecting the environment and the rights of workers in a global market. Some critics feared that globalization meant the export of American jobs to countries where cheap labor was available. Opponents of globalization—organized labor, environmentalists, and political radicals—expressed their sentiments by political protest.

In 2000 the economy began to slow down. The stock market, which had soared in the 1990s, began to decline. Especially hard hit were the technology stocks and the stocks of "dot-com" companies, which projected large profits through the Internet. After being unveiled with great fanfare, with the value of some stocks shooting upward astronomically, many of the dot-com companies failed. By March 2001 the nine-year expansion of the American economy ended, and a recession began.

The economy was further shocked by the terrorist attack on the World Trade Center on September 11, 2001. Fear of terrorism kept Americans at home, hurting the travel and tourism industries and their suppliers. Stocks plummeted, costing investors millions of dollars. Retirement plans and pension funds, invested in the stock market, declined. In December 2001 Enron Corporation, a large energy company, filed the largest bankruptcy claim in United States history. Later it was revealed that corporate officers in other companies had pursued insider and illegal accounting and stock trading practices. By June 2003 unemployment had reached a ten-year high of 6 percent. The Federal Reserve System under Alan Greenspan relied on interest rate cuts to stimulate the economy, which caused a decrease in the value of the American dollar relative to other international currencies, a move intended to benefit American exports abroad. The new president, George W. Bush, sought to encourage economic recovery through tax cuts enacted in 2002 and 2003.

THE AMERICAN POPULATION CONTINUES TO DIVERSIFY AND AGE   The population of the United States continued to grow steadily in the 1990s. During this decade the rate of population growth in the United States was the highest since 1970. As the United States entered the twenty-first century, its population stood at 281 million. The South had the largest population, more than 100 million people, over 35 million more than the next most populous region. The fastest-growing region was the West, which was expected to surpass the Midwest in the next decade. The Northeast was the least populous region and the one with the slowest growth rate.

The 2000 census showed other population trends. Females continued to outnumber males, a trend since 1940. By 2000 there were 142 million females and 138 million males, a difference attributed largely to women living longer than men. Suburbanization continued; by 2000 almost 80 percent of Americans lived in metropolitan areas.

The trend toward racial and ethnic diversity also continued, although the racial statistics collected in 2000 cannot easily be compared with previous census records. The 2000 census provided respondents with multiple racial categories from which to select. Many respondents refused to mark a racial category; of those who did, however, the largest category marked was "White" with 75.1 percent; 12.3 percent selected "African American"; 3.6 percent, Asian; 0.01 percent, "Hawaiian and Other Pacific Islander"; and 5.5 percent marked "some other race." Of those who marked "Asian," 23 percent indicated that they were from China, and 18.1 percent were from the Philippines. American Indians accounted for 0.9 percent of the respondents, and 12.5 percent of the respondents listed themselves as "Hispanic American."

Immigrants accounted for 10.4 percent of the American population, a figure comparable to the high numbers of immigrants at the turn of the nineteenth century. Only a small percentage of these new immigrants came from Europe; most came from Latin America and Asia. At least a third of immigrants were Spanish speaking, with Mexico accounting for one-fourth of all immigrants living in the United States. Mexican immigrants settled largely in California and the Southwest, but there were significant Spanish-speaking immigrant communities in Illinois, New York, and Florida. In the 1990s immigrants came from China, Southeast Asia, Korea, the Philippines, and India.

Yet even with this influx of younger immigrants, the American population continued to age. In 1970 the median age of the United States was 28 years; by 2000 it was 35.3 years. The 65-and-over age group grew to 35 million people, 12 percent of the population. The number of young adults 18 to 34 years of age declined by 4 percent, suggesting future social and economic problems as the Baby Boom generation begins to retire and collect Social Security and Medicare benefits. Although many people are living longer, the quality of life for many elderly remains a question. Changes in the American family have affected the care and support of elderly who cannot care for themselves. A large nursing home industry developed to care for these elderly people.

The 2000 census also revealed further changes in the American family. Sexual mores and practices changed, and the rate of divorce continued to increase. By 2000 52 percent of all marriages ended in divorce. The number of out-of-wedlock births also continued to increase. In 2000 some studies concluded that 60 percent of children were born into homes in which parents were either unmarried or divorced.

A public debate occurred in the 1990s over whether the legal definition of marriage should be changed to allow for same-sex, or gay, marriages. In 1993, the Hawaiian Supreme Court ruled that same-sex marriage licenses were constitutional, based on that state's equal rights amendment, enacted in 1972. In 1998 the voters of Hawaii amended the state constitution to forbid same-sex marriages. Similar legislation was enacted in thirty-one other states. In 1996 Congress passed the Defense of Marriage Act, which was signed into law by President Clinton. In 2001 Vermont was the first state to circumvent the Defense of Marriage Act by recognizing civil unions of same-sex couples.

PARTIES BATTLE AND GOVERNMENT DIVIDES

American politics reflected these technological, economic, social, and cultural changes. Elected in 1992, President Bill Clinton won reelection in 1996. In both cases he won less than a majority of the popular vote. At this same time, Republicans made steady gains in Congress and won the White House in 2000.

CLINTON'S FIRST TERM: A MIXED RECORD   Bill Clinton presided over a booming economy. Revelations of an extramarital affair and his subsequent attempt to deceive the public, however, tarnished his presidency by creating public controversy and leading to the first U.S. Senate impeachment trial since 1868.

Clinton was the first Democrat elected to the presidency since Jimmy Carter in 1976. Although many of his supporters and critics perceived him to be a liberal activist, Clinton ran for the presidency in both 1992 and

1996 as a "centrist." This strategy helped him win the White House and confront a liberal wing of his own party that wanted to expand federal social programs. Clinton also faced opposition from a Republican Party that had become increasingly conservative on economic and cultural issues. Further, he was handicapped by having failed to win a majority of votes in either the 1992 or 1996 elections.

When Clinton came into office, he reversed a number of Republican social policies, including the ban on fetal tissue research and the "gag rule" on abortion counseling at federally funded health clinics. He also appointed a record number of women and minorities to senior positions in his administration.

His first days in office were rocky. His proposal to end the ban of homosexuals from the military unleashed a furor, in response to which he accepted an alternative, "don't ask, don't tell" policy, allowing homosexuals into the military provided they did not openly reveal their sexual preferences.

Further difficulties came when Clinton sought to promote a national health care plan. Although his wife, Hillary Rodham Clinton, took charge of developing this program and promoting it to the public and Congress, it failed to draw support because of its complexity. The administration successfully enacted gun control legislation (the Brady law) and the Family and Medical Leave Act, which required employers to provide workers with unpaid leave for childbirth and family illnesses.

In foreign policy Clinton pursued a course he described as "assertive multilaterism." He believed that, with the collapse of the Soviet Union, the American military could be used to suppress "rogue" states and for peacekeeping missions in warring countries. He confronted a deteriorating situation in Somalia, to which President Bush had sent twenty-eight thousand troops as part of a United Nations effort to aid this famine-plagued, war-torn nation. In October 1993, Clinton changed the mission from a humanitarian one to a mission of "state-building." When American soldiers tried to arrest a local warlord, Muhammad Farah Aideed, on October 4, 1993, a pitched battle erupted in the Somalian capital of Mogadishu in which two American soldiers were killed and then dragged through the streets, cheered by the crowds. Following this highly televised incident, Clinton ordered the withdrawal of American troops in late March 1993.

After Somalia, Clinton hesitated to commit American troops as peacekeepers. In the spring of 1994 his failure to act against Slobodan Milošević's "ethnic cleansing" in Bosnia and against genocide in the African nation of Rwanda caused serious criticism of his foreign policy.

In 1996 Clinton successfully applied American pressure to oust the military government of Haiti. Aided by the diplomatic efforts of Jimmy Carter,

Clinton forced the resignation of General Raoul Cédras and restored Jean-Bertrand Aristide as Haiti's leader. In 1994, when Iraq continued to violate restrictions placed on it at the end of the Persian Gulf War, Clinton dispatched American troops to Kuwait, and ordered air strikes in 1996.

CLINTON FACES TERRORISM AT HOME AND ABROAD   While dealing with terrorist attacks abroad, the United States also experienced terrorism at home. In 1993 the Bureau of Alcohol, Tobacco, and Firearms (BATF) began to investigate a religious cult, the Branch Davidians, for possible arms violations and sexual and physical child abuse in the group's compound outside Waco, Texas. When the BATF tried to serve a warrant on David Koresh, the leader of the cult, on February 28, 1993, a gun battle ensued, in which six Branch Davidians and four BATF agents were killed. The Federal Bureau of Investigation (FBI) assumed control of the situation, and a fifty-one-day siege followed. Finally, Attorney General Janet Reno ordered an assault on the compound; a fire erupted, causing the deaths of eighty-six cult members. Later, a report by former senator John C. Danforth exonerated the FBI and the Justice Department of wrongdoing.

In 1998 terrorists, later identified as part of the al Qaeda network, bombed the U.S. embassy in Nairobi, Kenya. The bomb killed 247 people, including twelve Americans, and injured more than 5,400. Another bomb was set off at the embassy in Dar es Salaam, Tanzania, almost simultaneously. (AP/Wide World Photos/Khalil Senosi)

On April 19, 1995, a massive truck bomb destroyed the Alfred P. Murrah Federal Building in Oklahoma City. The tragedy was the largest attack yet on American soil. The bomb was set by two American anti-government radicals, Timothy McVeigh and Terry Nichols, who claimed it was in retaliation for the Branch Davidian disaster two years earlier. Timothy McVeigh was sentenced to death and executed on June 11, 2001. Terry Nichols was convicted on federal charges and sentenced to life in prison.

Fifteen months after the Oklahoma City bombing, a bomb exploded in Centennial Square at the Atlanta Olympic Games, killing one person and injuring 111 others. Shortly afterwards, in January 1997, bombs were exploded outside an abortion clinic in Atlanta.

Congress responded to these events by establishing the Domestic Counter-Terrorism Center in 1995 to monitor the sale and distribution of materials that might be used for mass destruction, and by passing the Anti-Terrorism and Effective Death Penalty Act of 1996, which allowed the federal government to seek the death penalty for terrorists.

More serious threats from terrorism came from abroad. In February 1993, a car bomb exploded in the parking garage of the World Trade Center, killing six people and wounding more than a thousand. Six Islamic militants were captured, tried, and convicted. Although the attack was ambitious, the Towers still stood, and the United States did not significantly alter its policies with regard to terrorism. Shortly after the Oklahoma City bombing, a car bomb exploded outside the U.S. military headquarters in Riyadh, Saudi Arabia, killing five American servicemen. This attack was followed by a truck bomb outside the Khobar Towers in Dhahran, Saudi Arabia, that killed nineteen Americans.

CLINTON IS INVESTIGATED AND THE REPUBLICANS WIN CONGRESS   In 1994 President Clinton found himself under attack for his investment in the Whitewater real estate development in Arkansas, which failed in 1978, before he became president. Clinton believed that political opponents were involved in petty rumor-mongering, but when White House counsel Vincent Foster committed suicide in July 1993, further speculation circulated about a "cover-up" in the White House. Under public pressure, Attorney General Janet Reno ordered the appointment of an independent counsel to investigate Bill and Hillary Rodham Clinton's involvement in the Whitewater development. On August 5, 1994, Kenneth Starr assumed the position of independent counsel. The Clinton White House drew further criticism when an Arkansas state employee, Paula Jones, filed a civil lawsuit against Clinton claiming that he had sexually propositioned her when he was governor of Arkansas.

In 1994 Republicans gained control of the Senate and the House. The Republican victory in the House was led by conservative Representative Newton (Newt) Gingrich (R-Georgia), who had persuaded Republican candidates to run on a unified platform called "The Contract with America." This campaign pledge promised that, in the first one hundred days, Republicans would work to pass bills related to crime, congressional term limits, welfare reform, budget reduction, social security, defense, illegal drugs, and taxation. Although Republicans in the House passed most of the items in this contract, the bills became bogged down in the Senate.

Under pressure from Republicans, Clinton distanced himself from liberals within the Democratic Party. Working with the new Republican majority, Clinton supported a compromise welfare reform act and persuaded Congress to raise the minimum wage

CLINTON WINS REELECTION ONLY TO FACE IMPEACHMENT   In November 1996 Clinton easily won reelection for a second term, defeating Senate Majority Leader Robert Dole (R-Kansas), a World War II hero. Clinton won less than 50 percent of the vote, while Dole received 41 percent. The third-party candidate, the Texas millionaire Ross Perot, gained about 8 percent of the vote, less than half of what he received in 1992.

As the economy boomed, tax revenues increased, enabling Clinton to announce a federal budget surplus. However, this remarkable success was marred by scandal. Republicans charged that the Clinton–Gore presidential campaign in 1996 had participated in illegal fund-raising activities. Under investigation, a former Democratic fund-raiser admitted having accepted illegal campaign contributions from a Chinese military official. Further troubles came when Paula Jones's attorneys began to take depositions in her previously filed sexual harassment lawsuit. In 1998 Linda Tripp, a former White House employee, released secretly recorded tapes that she had made of a White House intern, Monica Lewinsky, describing Lewinsky's intimate relations with the president. Clinton had denied the affair, but the existence and content of the tapes, as well as other evidence, finally forced Clinton to admit that he had had an "inappropriate" relationship with Lewinsky, although he denied having had sexual intercourse with her. Furthermore, although he admitted he had made a personal mistake, he maintained before a grand jury that what he had done was not illegal.

In December 1998 the House of Representatives, split along party lines, approved two articles of impeachment charging the president with perjury and obstruction of justice. The two-month Senate trial ended in a vote of acquittal, with not a single Democrat voting for a "guilty" verdict.

The scandal distracted Clinton for much of his second term. As a world recession swept Asia and spread to Latin America and Russia, Clinton moved to prevent this recession from becoming a worldwide depression.

TERRORISM IN CLINTON'S SECOND TERM   In his second term, Clinton confronted a series of foreign policy problems created by rogue governments and international terrorism.

Among these problems was North Korea, one of the last remaining communist countries in the world, which launched an extensive nuclear military buildup that included a missile delivery program. Initially, officials in the Clinton administration denied that North Korea had a ballistic missile program. In 1998, however, North Korea launched a missile over Japan. Through the diplomatic efforts of former president Jimmy Carter, who flew to Pyongyang to meet with North Korean dictator Kim Jong Il, an agreement was reached in which North Korea promised to stop its nuclear development program in exchange for millions of dollars worth of food and oil and a nuclear reactor.

On August 7, 1998, an Islamic terrorist group called al Qaeda, headed by Osama bin Laden, orchestrated the bombing of American embassies in Kenya and Tanzania. Clinton ordered missile air strikes on terrorist camps in Afghanistan and a missile attack on a pharmaceutical factory in the Sudan, but the attacks accomplished little. Clinton believed that the key to ending terrorism was to resolve the decades of hostility between the Palestinians and Israelis. In October 1998, in a settlement proposed in the Wye River Memorandum, a solution appeared possible; but the Palestinians rejected the settlement, saying it did not go far enough.

Clinton's efforts to bring peace to troubled parts in the world led him to become involved in Northern Ireland. Through the efforts of Clinton's personal envoy, the Good Friday Agreement was reached, which appeared to bring a permanent settlement to Northern Ireland.

In confronting ethnic conflict in the post–cold war world, the administration's greatest challenge was in Central Europe, where Yugoslavian president Slobodan Milošević initiated a harsh campaign against ethnic Albanians in the province of Kosovo. There, Islamic separatists had begun a struggle to split off Kosovo from Yugoslavia. Concerned that Milošević's campaign against the rebels was leading to a war against civilians, in March 1998 Clinton ordered U.S.–NATO coalition air strikes against Milošević. Milošević was driven from power in 2000 and placed on trial for genocide in 2001.

Clinton left a mixed record as president. He proved himself an able politician, having won election twice to the White House, a feat not accomplished since Ronald Reagan's election in 1984. He served the country during one of the longest economic booms in the nation's history. He balanced the budget and pushed through a major welfare bill. His foreign policy was less successful, and he left major problems in the Middle East, North Korea, and Iraq to his successor.

GEORGE W. BUSH LEADS THE NATION IN AN AGE OF TERROR

Republicans regained the White House in 2001 after George W. Bush's extremely narrow victory over Democratic Party nominee Albert Gore, Jr., vice president under Clinton. Because of contested votes in Florida, the election was decided by the Supreme Court. Entering the White House amid controversy, Bush promised to unite the nation through compassionate conservatism and political civility. Eight months later, the nation was rocked by Islamic terrorist attacks on the twin towers of the World Trade Center in New York and on the Pentagon in Washington, D.C. This event transformed the attitude of the nation and redirected President Bush's agenda. Under his leadership, American troops were sent to Afghanistan to remove a militant Islamic regime that supported terrorism. In 2003 Bush ordered an American invasion of Iraq to overthrow the regime of Saddam Hussein, who refused to allow international inspectors in his country as agreed to ten years earlier after the first Gulf War. The American invasion in 2003 was a continuation of the first Gulf War; it also marked a decided shift in American foreign policy toward active engagement against terrorists and regimes supporting terrorism. At home, Bush faced a weak economy as unemployment rose and stock prices fell, but by late 2002 the economy showed clear signs of recovery.

GEORGE W. BUSH WINS THE ELECTION OF 2000   The election of 2000 was the most hotly contested election in American history since 1876. In 1876 Congress reached a compromise that awarded the election to the Republican candidate. In 2000 the Supreme Court ruled in a 5-to-4 decision that time had run out for a recount of the disputed Florida ballots. The decision gave George W. Bush the twenty-five electoral votes he needed to win in the Electoral College. The Democratic Party candidates, Vice President Albert Gore and his running mate, Senator Joseph Lieberman (the first Jew to be nominated to the ticket of a major party) won 51,003,894 popular votes (48.41 percent) to 50,459,211 (47.89 percent) cast for George W. Bush and his running mate, Richard Cheney. But the Bush–Cheney ticket won the electoral vote by five votes: 271 to 266 for Gore–Lieberman. Consumer activist Ralph Nader, running on a third-party ticket for the Green Party, received only 2.69 percent of the popular vote, but he received 97,448 votes in Florida. Given that Bush won the disputed Florida vote by fewer than six hundred votes (2,912,790 to Gore's 2,912,253), Nader may have cost Gore the election.

Commentators noted Bush's narrow margin of victory. In the last three presidential elections, the victor had won without receiving the majority of the votes. The electorate appeared sharply divided along partisan lines, and Republicans and Democrats seemed to be ideologically polarized. Democrats were strong in the industrial Northeast, in New England, in the urban Midwest, and on the West Coast. Republicans found strong support in the majority of states and won the South, the Midwest, and most of the states in the Mountain West and the Far West.

Yet returns also revealed a disconcerting decline in voter participation. In the 2000 presidential election, only 51 percent of the eligible electorate voted. To put this in perspective, in the Kennedy–Nixon race in 1960, an equally close election, 63 percent of the electorate turned out. In 1996 more Americans did not vote than did: 96.3 million voted, but 100.2 million did not bother. Furthermore, Americans appeared uninterested in American politics in general. Since the 1970s fewer Americans were volunteering for political campaigns, and televised presidential debates had drawn smaller and smaller audiences. The four Kennedy–Nixon debates attracted 60 percent of households with television sets. The Clinton–Dole debates in 1996 drew 29 percent of households with television sets. The Gore–Bush race in 2000 drew no more than the previous presidential election had, even though the race was seen to be closer, and the third debate drew only 16 percent of households.

After studying this decline in voter interest, one scholar called this phenomenon the "incredible shrinking electorate." Some of this decline was attributed to the length of presidential campaigns, poor news coverage, and restrictive voter registration requirements, even though most states had relaxed their requirements. Although these factors are important, a decline of confidence in political institutions and political leaders among the American people is seen as having discouraged participation in the democratic process. Americans remain among the most patriotic people in the world; yet they have grown increasingly distrustful of the nation's political institutions, government, and political leaders.

In his victory speech on December 13, Bush sought to remove some of the partisan bitterness of the election by promising a bipartisan approach to politics, but after eight years of political rancor in Washington, most members of Congress and the national media dismissed the possibility of a new tone in Washington. Some Democrats claimed that Bush had been "selected," not elected. The Republicans maintained a majority in both houses of Congress after the 2000 election, but when Vermont Senator James Jeffords left the Republican Party and declared himself an independent in May 2001, control of the Senate switched to the Democratic Party. Nonetheless, Bush succeeded in pushing thorough a $1.35 trillion bill that reduced the top income tax rate to 35 percent and refunded money to middle-income taxpayers. In the 2002 midterm elections, Republicans gained control of both houses of Congress, controlling 51 Senate seats to the Democrats' 48, and 229 Congressional seats to the Democrats' 205.

SEPTEMBER 11, 2001, AND THE WAR ON TERRORISM   On September 11, 2001, nineteen terrorists hijacked four commercial jet planes and aimed them at American landmarks. Two of these planes struck the World Trade Center in New York City, while a third plane crashed into the Pentagon, outside of Washington, D.C. A fourth plane was prevented from

Three days after the terrorist attack on the World Trade Center, President George W. Bush visited Ground Zero, where the Fire Department of New York was digging through rubble. Including those killed aboard the four airplanes and on the ground in New York and at the Pentagon, almost three thousand Americans died on September 11, 2001. (AP/Wide World Photos/Doug Mills)

reaching its target in Washington, D.C., when passengers tried to retake the plane.

Thousands of lives were lost in this attack. The horror of the events, which many watched on their television sets, united the American people. On September 20 Present Bush gave a nationally televised address before a joint session of Congress. In the speech he outlined the nation's retaliatory response to terrorism. He declared war on terrorism and on those regimes that support terrorist groups. He blamed the attacks on an international terrorist organization, al Qaeda, headed by a Saudi Arabian billionaire, Osama bin Laden. Al Qaeda was also held responsible for a series of terrorist attacks during the Clinton administration: the World Trade Center bombing in 1993 and the bombings of U.S. personnel in Saudi Arabia in 1995, of U.S. embassies in Africa in 1998, and of the *USS Cole* in 2000.

In response to the attack, Congress passed a series of emergency measures, including the Combating Terrorism Act, which appointed a national director of homeland security. Tom Ridge, the former governor of Pennsylvania, was appointed to head the new Office of Homeland Security. In 2003 Congress made this office a cabinet position. In 2001 Congress passed the USA Patriot Act. This act provided substantial budget increases for the counterterrorism divisions of the FBI and Department of Defense and expanded the surveillance powers of the FBI, the CIA, and the Immigration and Naturalization Service. Civil libertarians worried that this legislation extended too much power to the federal government at a cost to personal liberties.

American fears of further terrorist attacks were heightened when a number of representatives of Congress received letters containing the lethal anthrax bacterium. A number of postal workers became ill; five died. To authorities, the anthrax scare revealed the vulnerability of the nation to biochemical, biological, and nuclear attack by terrorists.

As part of his declaration of "war on terrorism," Bush ordered the militant Islamic government in Afghanistan, under the control of a fanatical sect called the Taliban, to expel the head of the al Qaeda terrorist group, Osama bin Laden. When the Afghanistan government refused, President Bush called for "regime change" and ordered a military attack to replace the Taliban government. The president was joined in this effort by British Prime Minister Tony Blair. Launched in October 2001, the U.S.–British attack overthrew the Taliban government with the aid of anti-Taliban tribes in the north, the Northern Alliance. A new government was formed under President Hamid Karzai. To aid the establishment of this government and the rebuilding of the nation, the United States and other allies contributed over $900 million.

The United States also turned its attention to Iraq, which, under the brutal regime of Saddam Hussein, had refused to allow United Nations weapons inspectors into the country following their expulsion in 1998. The United States accused the Iraqi government of hiding weapons of mass destruction and not living up to terms of the treaty that ended the first Gulf War. In October Congress passed a joint resolution explicitly authorizing the United States to use armed force against Iraq. This resolution prompted the United Nations Security Council to vote unanimously for Resolution 1441 calling for the immediate and complete disarmament of Iraq. In December 2002 the chief UN inspector reported to the United Nations Security Council that Iraq had not proved that it had abandoned its programs to develop weapons of mass destruction.

On February 24, 2003, Secretary of Defense Colin Powell announced, "It is time to take action. The evidence is clear." The next day a resolution drafted by the United States, Britain, and Spain was introduced before the United Nations Security Council, stating that Iraq had "failed to take the final opportunity" to disarm. This resolution was opposed by France, Germany, and Russia. Finally, on March 17, 2003, in a televised address President Bush gave Saddam Hussein forty-eight hours to go into exile or face war. On March 20, 2003, ninety minutes after the lapse of the forty-eight-hour deadline, the United States, joined by the United Kingdom, Australia, and a small coalition of sixty smaller countries, attacked Iraq.

Antiwar protests occurred in the United States, Britain, Australia, France, Germany, and Denmark. In the United States, antiwar advocates organized "Not in Our Name" protests in opposition to the war. While huge antiwar marches were organized in major American cities, most Americans supported the war effort.

Under General Tommy Franks, the coalition army invaded Iraq. By April 2003 the coalition army had reached Baghdad, and within days the Hussein regime had fallen. By the end of the month, coalition partners declared the war effectively over. In the aftermath of the war, Iraq still remained unstable. Looting and unrest broke out in the major cities of Baghdad and Basra; in addition, tribal rivalries and conflict between the Shiite and Sunni sects presented major obstacles to forming a stable government. American occupying troops found themselves under sporadic guerrilla attack, even after Hussein's capture in December 2003.

The instability of the Iraqi regime led Democrats in Congress to criticize Bush's handling of the war, which some claimed had distracted from homeland security. Furthermore, critics pointed out that, during the presidential campaign, Bush had criticized Clinton for his policy of "nation-building," but in the aftermath of the wars in Afghanistan and Iraq, the United States had become involved in "nation-building" anyway. Critics also charged that evidence of weapons of mass destruction had not been found in Iraq, contrary to the administration's initial justification for the war.

BUSH LOOKS HOME   While confronting international terrorism abroad and guerrilla war in Iraq against American occupation troops, Bush faced a shaky economy at home. A sharply divided Congress restricted his ability to fulfill his domestic agenda. Still, there were some notable legislative successes. As a devout Christian, as one of his first acts President Bush established the Office of Faith-Based and Community Initiatives (2002), to strengthen and expand the role of church and religiously based community organizations in addressing the nation's social problems by providing government and privately funded services. His promise to address problems in American education led to the No Child Left Behind Act (2002), which required qualified teachers in every classroom by 2005–2006, the training of 2.2 million teachers, and increased federal grants to states for education. The Teachers' Protection Act (2002) protected teachers and school administrators from being sued for imposing order in schools. Bush also sought to spark economic growth through the Jobs and Growth Act (2003), which cut taxes an average of $1,126 for every American taxpayer. By November 2003 unemployment had dropped to 5.9 percent; the economy grew 8.2 percent in the third quarter, its largest growth in twenty years. Nonetheless, total job creation languished, and there was general anxiety that this boom might be short-lived.

In late 2003 Bush signed the Medicare Act (2003), which provided drug prescription benefits to the elderly. Although liberal critics denounced the program's cost and the lack of price caps on prescription drugs, conservatives supported the act because it established health savings accounts that would allow private citizens to set aside tax-exempt funds for medical costs. Nonetheless, this was the largest extension of a federal entitlement program since the early 1970s, and it led some conservative opponents to describe President Bush as a "big government Republican."

Other Bush proposals, presented to a highly partisan Congress, were less sucessful. His proposals for the modernization of the nation's electric power system and for the lowering of environmental regulations were blocked in Congress through 2003. More frustrating was the refusal of Democratic senators, led by Edward Kennedy (D-Massachusetts), to bring the federal court of appeals nominees to a Senate floor vote. Miguel Estrada, a Hispanic, finally withdrew from the nomination process in frustration in 2003. At the same time, Senator Kennedy refused to conduct hearings on other judicial nominees. The battle over appellate court judges portended exceptionally fierce battles over Supreme Court appointees in the future.

CONCLUSION

At the beginning of the twenty-first century, the United States was the most powerful nation in history. Its economy was the largest and the wealthiest. It was a leader in technological innovation. Its military was the most powerful the world. With this new power, however, came new global responsibilities. The international proliferation of nuclear and biological weapons, weapons with potential for mass destruction, brought new challenges. The two oceans separating the United States from Europe and Asia appeared smaller in this new world.

Most Americans were living longer and better, but this introduced economic and social problems as the population aged. A more ethnically and racially diverse population brought new social challenges. Although most Americans lived better than their ancestors and most other people in the world, poverty, social alienation, crime, and drug abuse persisted.

As the twentieth century came to a close, fewer and fewer Americans participated in the democratic process. In the 1996 presidential election, more eligible voters decided not to vote than to vote. In the 2000 presidential election, only 51 percent of the electorate voted. This raised questions about the health of the democracy.

Yet the American people take pride in the accomplishments of the nation and remain confident of the future. The history of the United States is one of challenges faced, problems resolved, and crises overcome. Throughout their history Americans have remained an optimistic people, carrying this optimism into the new century. The full promise of America has yet to be realized. This is the real promise of America: the ability to dream of a better world to come.

Recommended Readings

(GENERAL) Merle and Earl Black, *The Rise of Southern Republicans* (2002); Augustus Cochran, *Democracy Heading South: National Politics in the Shadow of Dixie* (2001); David Frum, *Dead Right* (1994); Jeffrey Isaac, *The Poverty of Progressivism: The Future of American Democracy in a Time of Liberal Decline* (2003); Ronald Radosh, *Divided They Fell: The Demise of the Democratic Party, 1964–1996* (1996); Clyde Wilcox, *Onward Christian Soldier? The Religious Right in American Politics* (1996). (CLINTON) Pete Baker, *The Breach: Inside the Impeachment and Trial of William Jefferson Clinton* (2000); Elizabeth Drew, *Showdown: The Struggle Between the Gingrich*

Congress and the Clinton White House (1996); Nina Easton, Gang of Five: Leaders at the Center of the Conservative Crusade (2002); David Maraniss, "Tell Newt to Shut Up" (1996); Herbert Weisberg and Samuel Patterson, Great Theater: The American Congress in the 1990s (1998); Donald R. Wolfensberger, Congress and the People: Deliberative Democracy on Trial (2000). (GEORGE H. W. BUSH) David Frum, The Right Man (2003); Michael Lind, Made in Texas (2002); Thomas E. Patterson, The Vanishing Voter (2003); Bill Sammon, Fighting Back: The War on Terrorism (2003); Jeffrey Toobin, Too Close to Call (2001). (SOCIETY) Peggy Noonan, A Heart, a Cross, and a Flag: America Today (2003); William Julius Wilson, When Work Disappears (1997); Alan Wolfe, One Nation, After All (2003). (ECONOMY) Hernando de Soto, The Mystery of Capital (2000); Joseph E. Stiglitz, Globalization and Its Discontents (2003).

Appendix I

❧

The Declaration of Independence

IN CONGRESS, JULY 4, 1776. *The unanimous Declaration of the thirteen United States of America.*

When in the Course of human Events, it becomes necessary for one People to dissolve the Political Bands which have connected them with another, and to assume among the Powers of the Earth, the separate and equal Station to which the Laws of Nature and of Nature's God entitle them, a decent Respect to the Opinions of Mankind requires that they should declare the causes which impel them to the Separation.

We hold these Truths to be self-evident, that all Men are created equal, that they are endowed by their Creator with certain unalienable Rights, that among these are Life, Liberty and the Pursuit of Happiness—That to secure these Rights, Governments are instituted among Men, deriving their just Powers from the Consent of the Governed, that whenever any Form of Government becomes destructive of these Ends, it is the Right of the People to alter or to abolish it, and to institute new Government, laying its Foundation on such Principles, and organizing its Powers in such Form, as to them shall seem most likely to effect their Safety and Happiness. Prudence, indeed, will dictate that Governments long established should not be changed for light and transient Causes; and accordingly all Experience hath shewn, that Mankind are more disposed to suffer, while Evils are sufferable, than to right themselves by abolishing the Forms to which they are accustomed. But when a long Train of Abuses and Usurpations, pursuing invariably the same Object, evinces a Design to reduce them under absolute Despotism, it is their Right, it is their Duty, to throw off such Government, and to provide new Guards for their future Security. Such has been the patient Sufferance of these Colonies; and such is now the Necessity which constrains them to alter their former Systems of Government. The History of the present King of Great Britain is a History of repeated Injuries and Usurpations, all having in direct Object the Establishment of an absolute Tyranny over these States. To prove this, let Facts be submitted to a candid World.

He has refused his Assent to Laws, the most wholesome and necessary for the public Good.

He has forbidden his Governors to pass Laws of immediate and pressing Importance, unless suspended in their Operation till his Assent should be obtained; and when so suspended, he has utterly neglected to attend to them.

He has refused to pass other Laws for the Accommodation of large Districts of People, unless those People would relinquish the Right of Representation in the Legislature, a Right inestimable to them, and formidable to Tyrants only.

He has called together Legislative Bodies at Places unusual, uncomfortable, and distant from the Depository of their public Records, for the sole Purpose of fatiguing them into Compliance with his Measures.

He has dissolved Representative Houses repeatedly, for opposing with manly Firmness his Invasions on the Rights of the People.

He has refused for a long Time, after such Dissolutions, to cause others to be elected; whereby the Legislative Powers, incapable of the Annihilation, have returned to the People at large for their exercise; the State remaining in the mean time exposed to all the Dangers of Invasion from without, and Convulsions within.

He has endeavoured to prevent the Population of these States; for that Purpose obstructing the Laws for Naturalization of Foreigners; refusing to pass others to encourage their Migrations hither, and raising the Conditions of new Appropriations of Lands.

He has obstructed the Administration of Justice, by refusing his Assent to Laws for establishing Judiciary Powers.

He has made Judges dependent on his Will alone, for the Tenure of their Offices, and the Amount and Payment of their Salaries.

He has erected a Multitude of new Offices, and sent hither Swarms of Officers to harrass our People, and eat out their Substance.

He has kept among us, in Times of Peace, Standing Armies, without the consent of our Legislatures.

He has affected to render the Military independent of and superior to the Civil Power.

He has combined with others to subject us to a Jurisdiction foreign to our Constitution, and unacknowledged by our Laws; giving his Assent to their Acts of pretended Legislation:

For quartering large Bodies of Armed Troops among us;

For protecting them, by a mock Trial, from Punishment for any Murders which they should commit on the Inhabitants of these States:

For cutting off our Trade with all Parts of the World:

For imposing Taxes on us without our Consent:

For depriving us, in many Cases, of the Benefits of Trial by Jury:

For transporting us beyond Seas to be tried for pretended Offences:

For abolishing the free System of English Laws in a neighbouring Province, establishing therein an arbitrary Government, and enlarging its Boundaries, so as to render it at once an Example and fit Instrument for introducing the same absolute Rules into these Colonies:

For taking away our Charters, abolishing our most valuable Laws, and altering fundamentally the Forms of our Governments:

For suspending our own Legislatures, and declaring themselves invested with Power to legislate for us in all Cases whatsoever.

He has abdicated Government here, by declaring us out of his Protection and waging War against us.

He has plundered our Seas, ravaged our Coasts, burnt our Towns, and destroyed the Lives of our People.

He is, at this Time, transporting large Armies of foreign Mercenaries to compleat the Works of Death, Desolation, and Tyranny, already begun with circumstances of Cruelty and

Perfidy, scarcely paralleled in the most barbarous Ages, and totally unworthy the Head of a civilized Nation.

He has constrained our fellow Citizens taken Captive on the high Seas to bear Arms against their Country, to become the Executioners of their Friends and Brethren, or to fall themselves by their Hands.

He has excited domestic Insurrections amongst us, and has endeavoured to bring on the Inhabitants of our Frontiers, the merciless Indian Savages, whose known Rule of Warfare, is an undistinguished Destruction, of all Ages, Sexes and Conditions.

In every stage of these Oppressions we have Petitioned for Redress in the most humble Terms: Our repeated Petitions have been answered only by repeated Injury. A Prince, whose Character is thus marked by every act which may define a Tyrant, is unfit to be the Ruler of a free People.

Nor have we been wanting in Attentions to our British Brethren. We have warned them from Time to Time of Attempts by their Legislature to extend an unwarrantable Jurisdiction over us. We have reminded them of the Circumstances of our Emigration and Settlement here. We have appealed to their native Justice and Magnanimity, and we have conjured them by the Ties of our common Kindred to disavow these Usurpations, which, would inevitably interrupt our Connections and Correspondence. They too have been deaf to the Voice of Justice and of Consanguinity. We must, therefore, acquiesce in the Necessity, which denounces our Separation, and hold them, as we hold the rest of Mankind, Enemies in War, in Peace, Friends.

We, therefore, the Representatives of the UNITED STATES OF AMERICA, in GENERAL CONGRESS, Assembled, appealing to the Supreme Judge of the World for the Rectitude of our Intentions, do, in the Name, and by Authority of the good People of these Colonies, solemnly Publish and Declare, That these United Colonies are, and of Right ought to be, FREE AND INDEPENDENT STATES; that they are absolved from all Allegiance to the British Crown, and that all political Connection between them and the State of Great Britain, is and ought to be totally dissolved; and that as FREE AND INDEPENDENT STATES, they have full Power to levy War, conclude Peace, contract Alliances, establish Commerce, and to do all other Acts and Things which INDEPENDENT STATES may of right do. And for the support of this Declaration, with a firm Reliance on the Protection of divine Providence, we mutually pledge to each other our Lives, our Fortunes, and our sacred Honor.

John Hancock
(MASSACHUSETTS)

NEW HAMPSHIRE	NORTH CAROLINA	PENNSYLVANIA
Josiah Bartlett	*William Hooper*	*Robert Morris*
William Whipple	*Joseph Hewes*	*Benjamin Rush*
Matthew Thornton	*John Penn*	*Benjamin Franklin*
		John Morton
MASSACHUSETTS	MARYLAND	*George Clymer*
Samuel Adams	*Samuel Chase*	*James Smith*
John Adams	*William Paca*	*George Taylor*
Robert Treat Paine	*Thomas Stone*	*James Wilson*
Elbridge Gerry	*Charles Carroll of Carrollton*	*George Ross*

DELAWARE
Caesar Rodney
George Read
Thomas McKean

NEW YORK
William Floyd
Philip Livingston
Frank Lewis
Lewis Morris

NEW JERSEY
Richard Stockton
John Witherspoon
Francis Hopkinson
John Hart
Abraham Clark

SOUTH CAROLINA
Edward Rutledge
Thomas Heyward, Jr.
Thomas Lynch, Jr.
Arthur Middleton

RHODE ISLAND
AND PROVIDENCE
Stephen Hopkins
William Ellery

CONNECTICUT
Roger Sherman
Samuel Huntington
William Williams
Oliver Wolcott

VIRGINIA
George Wythe
Richard Henry Lee
Thomas Jefferson
Benjamin Harrison
Thomas Nelson, Jr.
Francis Lightfoot Lee
Carter Braxton

GEORGIA
Button Gwinnett
Lyman Hall
George Walton

Appendix II

❧

The Constitution of the United States of America

Adopted September 17, 1787
Effective March 4, 1789

WE THE PEOPLE OF THE UNITED STATES, in order to form a more perfect union, establish justice, insure domestic tranquility, provide for the common defense, promote the general welfare, and secure the blessings of liberty to ourselves and our posterity, do ordain and establish this Constitution for the United States of America.

ARTICLE I

Section 1. All legislative powers herein granted shall be vested in a Congress of the United States, which shall consist of a Senate and House of Representatives.

Section 2. 1. The House of Representatives shall be composed of members chosen every second year by the people of the several states, and the electors in each state shall have the qualifications requisite for electors of the most numerous branch of the state legislature.

2. No person shall be a representative who shall not have attained to the age of twenty-five years, and been seven years a citizen of the United States, and who shall not, when elected, be an inhabitant of that state in which he shall be chosen.

3. Representatives and direct taxes shall be apportioned among the several states which may be included within this union, according to their respective numbers, [*which shall be determined by adding to the whole number of free persons, including those bound to service for a term of years, and excluding Indians not taxed, three-fifths of all other persons.*]* The actual enumeration shall be made within three years after the first meeting of the Congress of the United States, and within every subsequent term of ten years, in such manner as they shall by law direct. The number of representatives shall not exceed one for every thirty thousand, but each state shall have at least one representative; *and until such enumeration shall be made, the state of New Hampshire shall be entitled to choose three, Massachusetts eight, Rhode Island and Providence Plantations one, Connecticut five, New York six, New Jersey four, Pennsylvania eight, Delaware one, Maryland six, Virginia ten, North Carolina five, South Carolina five, and Georgia three.*

---

*Changed by section 2 of the Fourteenth Amendment.

4. When vacancies happen in the representation from any state, the executive authority thereof shall issue writs of election to fill such vacancies.

5. The House of Representatives shall choose their speaker and other officers; and shall have the sole power of impeachment.

Section 3. 1. The Senate of the United States shall be composed of two senators from each state, [*chosen by the legislature thereof*]* for six years; and each senator shall have one vote.

2. Immediately after they shall be assembled in consequence of the first election, they shall be divided as equally as may be into three classes. The seats of the senators of the first class shall be vacated at the expiration of the second year, of the second class at the expiration of the fourth year, and of the third class at the expiration of the sixth year, so that one third may be chosen every second year; [*and if vacancies happen by resignation, or otherwise, during the recess of the legislature of any state, the executive thereof may make temporary appointments until the next meeting of the legislature, which shall then fill such vacancies.*]**

3. No person shall be a senator who shall not have attained to the age of thirty years, and been nine years a citizen of the United States, and who shall not, when elected, be an inhabitant of that state for which he shall be chosen.

4. The vice president of the United States shall be president of the Senate, but shall have no vote, unless they be equally divided.

5. The Senate shall choose their other officers, and also a president pro tempore, in the absence of the vice-president, or when he shall exercise the office of the president of the United States.

6. The Senate shall have the sole power to try all impeachments. When sitting for that purpose, they shall be on oath or affirmation. When the president of the United States is tried, the chief justice shall preside: and no person shall be convicted without the concurrence of two thirds of the members present.

7. Judgment in cases of impeachment shall not extend further than to removal from office, and disqualification to hold and enjoy any office of honor, trust or profit under the United States: but the party convicted shall nevertheless be liable and subject to indictment, trial, judgment and punishment, according to law.

Section 4. 1. The times, places, and manner of holding elections for senators and representatives, shall be prescribed in each state by the legislature thereof; but the Congress may at any time by law make or alter such regulations, except as to the place of choosing senators.

2. The Congress shall assemble at least once in every year, and such meeting shall be [*on the first Monday in December*],*** unless they shall by law appoint a different day.

Section 5. 1. Each House shall be the judge of the elections, returns and qualifications of its own members, and a majority of each shall constitute a quorum to do business; but a smaller number may adjourn from day to day, and may be authorized to compel the attendance of absent members, in such manner, and under such penalties as each House may provide.

2. Each House may determine the rules of its proceedings, punish its members for disorderly behavior, and, with the concurrence of two thirds, expel a member.

3. Each House shall keep a journal of its proceedings, and from time to time publish the same, excepting such parts as may in their judgment require secrecy; and the yeas and nays of the members of either House on any question shall, at the desire of one fifth of those present, be entered on the journal.

---

*Changed by the Seventeenth Amendment.
**Changed by section 2 of the Twentieth Amendment.
***Changed by the Sixteenth amendment.

4. Neither House, during the session of Congress, shall, without the consent of the other, adjourn for more than three days, nor to any other place than that in which the two Houses shall be sitting.

Section 6. 1. The senators and representatives shall receive a compensation for their services, to be ascertained by law, and paid out of the treasury of the United States. They shall in all cases, except treason, felony, and breach of the peace, be privileged from arrest during their attendance at the session of their respective Houses, and in going to and returning from the same; and for any speech or debate in either House, they shall not be questioned in any other place.

2. No senator or representative shall, during the time for which he was elected, be appointed to any civil office under the authority of the United States, which shall have been created, or the emoluments whereof shall have been increased during such time; and no person holding any office under the United States shall be a member of either House during his continuance in office.

Section 7. 1. All bills for raising revenue shall originate in the House of Representatives; but the Senate may propose or concur with amendments as on other bills.

2. Every bill which shall have passed the House of Representatives and the Senate, shall, before it becomes a law, be presented to the president of the United States; if he approve he shall sign it, but if not he shall return it, with his objections to that House in which it shall have originated, who shall enter the objections at large on their journal, and proceed to reconsider it. If after such reconsideration two thirds of that House shall agree to pass the bill, it shall be sent, together with the objections, to the other House, by which it shall likewise be reconsidered, and if approved by two thirds of that House, it shall become a law. But in all such cases the votes of both Houses shall be determined by yeas and nays, and the names of the persons voting for and against the bill shall be entered on the journal of each House respectively. If any bill shall not be returned by the president within ten days (Sundays excepted) after it shall have been presented to him, the same shall be a law, in like manner as if he had signed it, unless the Congress by their adjournment prevent its return, in which case it shall not be a law.

3. Every order, resolution, or vote to which the concurrence of the Senate and the House of Representatives may be necessary (except on a question of adjournment) shall be presented to the president of the United States; and before the same shall take effect, shall be approved by him, or being disapproved by him, shall be repassed by two thirds of the Senate and House of Representatives, according to the rules and limitations prescribed in the case of a bill.

Section 8. The Congress shall have power:

1. To lay and collect taxes, duties, imposts, and excises, to pay the debts and provide for the common defense and general welfare of the United States; but all duties, imposts, and excises shall be uniform throughout the United States;

2. To borrow money on the credit of the United States;

3. To regulate commerce with foreign nations, and among the several States, and with the Indian tribes;

4. To establish a uniform rule of naturalization, and uniform laws on the subject of bankruptcies throughout the United States;

5. To coin money, regulate the value thereof, and of foreign coin, and fix the standard of weights and measures;

6. To provide for the punishment of counterfeiting the securities and current coin of the United States;

7. To establish post offices and post roads;

8. To promote the progress of science and useful arts, by securing for limited times to authors and inventors the exclusive right to their respective writings and discoveries;

9. To constitute tribunals inferior to the Supreme Court;

10. To define and punish piracies and felonies committed on the high seas, and offenses against the law of nations;

11. To declare war, grant letters of marque and reprisal, and make rules concerning captures on land and water;

12. To raise and support armies, but no appropriation of money to that use shall be for a longer term than two years;

13. To provide and maintain a navy;

14. To make rules for the government and regulation of the land and naval forces;

15. To provide for calling forth the militia to execute the laws of the Union, suppress insurrections and repel invasions;

16. To provide for organizing, arming, and disciplining the militia, and for governing such part of them as may be employed in the service of the United States, reserving to the States respectively, the appointment of the officers, and the authority of training the militia according to the discipline prescribed by Congress;

17. To exercise exclusive legislation in all cases whatsoever, over such district (not exceeding ten miles square) as may, by cession of particular states, and the acceptance of Congress, become the seat of the government of the United States, and to exercise like authority over all places purchased by the consent of the legislature of the state in which the same shall be, for the erection of forts, magazines, arsenals, dockyards, and other needful buildings; and

18. To make all laws which shall be necessary and proper for carrying into execution the foregoing powers, and all other powers vested by this Constitution in the government of the United States, or in any department or officer thereof.

Section 9. 1. The migration or importation of such persons as any of the states now existing shall think proper to admit, shall not be prohibited by the Congress prior to the year one thousand eight hundred and eight, but a tax or duty may be imposed on such importation, not exceeding ten dollars for each person.

2. The privilege of the writ of haheas corpus shall not be suspended, unless when in cases of rebellion or invasion the public safety may require it.

3. No bill of attainder or ex post facto law shall be passed.

4. [*No capitation, or other direct, tax shall be laid, unless in proportion to the census or enumeration hereinbefore directed to be taken.*]*

5. No tax or duty shall be laid on articles exported from any State.

6. No preference shall be given by any regulation of commerce or revenue to the ports of one state over those of another: nor shall vessels bound to, or from, one state be obliged to enter, clear, or pay duties in another.

7. No money shall be drawn from the treasury, but in consequence of appropriations made by law; and a regular statement and account of the receipts and expenditures of all public money shall be published from time to time.

8. No title of nobility shall be granted by the United States: and no person holding any office of profit or trust under them, shall, without the consent of the Congress, accept of any present, emolument, office, or title, of any kind whatever, from any king, prince, or foreign state.

Section 10. 1. No state shall enter into any treaty, alliance, or confederation; grant letters of marque and reprisal; coin money; emit bills of credit; make anything but gold and silver coin a tender in payment of debts; pass any bill of attainder, ex post facto law, or law impairing the obligation of contracts, or grant any title of nobility.

2. No state shall, without the consent of the Congress, lay any imposts or duties on imports or exports, except what may be absolutely necessary for executing its inspection laws;

------

*Changed by the Sixteenth Amendment.

and the net produce of all duties and imposts laid by any state on imports or exports, shall be for the use of the treasury of the United States; and all such laws shall be subject to the revision and control of the Congress.

3. No state shall, without the consent of Congress, lay any duty of tonnage, keep troops, or ships of war in time of peace, enter into any agreement or compact with another state, or with a foreign power, or engage in war, unless actually invaded, or in such imminent danger as will not admit of delay.

ARTICLE II

Section 1. 1. The executive power shall be vested in a president of the United States of America. He shall hold his office during the term of four years, and, together with the vice president, chosen for the same term, be elected as follows:

2. Each state shall appoint, in such manner as the legislature thereof may direct, a number of electors, equal to the whole number of senators and representatives to which the state may be entitled in the Congress: but no senator or representative, or person holding an office of trust or profit under the United States, shall be appointed an elector.

3. [*The electors shall meet in their respective states, and vote by ballot for two persons, of whom one at least shall not be an inhabitant of the same state with themselves. And they shall make a list of all the persons voted for, and of the number of votes for each; which list they shall sign and certify, and transmit sealed to the seat of the government of the United States, directed to the president of the Senate. The president of the Senate shall, in the presence of the Senate and House of Representatives, open all the certificates, and the votes shall then be counted. The person having the greatest number of votes shall be the president, if such number be a majority of the whole number of electors appointed; and if there be more than one who have such majority, and have an equal number of votes, then the House of Representatives shall immediately choose by ballot one of them for president; and if no person have a majority, then from the five highest on the list the said House shall in like manner choose the president. But in choosing the president, the votes shall be taken by states, the representation from each state having one vote; a quorum for this purpose shall consist of a member or members from two thirds of the states, and a majority of all the states shall be necessary to a choice. In every case, after the choice of the president, the person having the greatest number of votes of the electors shall be the vice president. But if there should remain two or more who have equal votes, the Senate shall choose from them by ballot the vice president.*]*

3. The Congress may determine the time of choosing the electors, and the day on which they shall give their votes; which day shall be the same throughout the United States.

4. No person except a natural born citizen, or a citizen of the United States, at the time of the adoption of this Constitution, shall be eligible to the office of president; neither shall any person be eligible to that office who shall not have attained to the age of thirty-five years, and been fourteen years a resident within the United States.

5. [*In case of the removal of the president from office, or of his death, resignation, or inability to discharge the powers and duties of the said office, the same shall devolve on the vice president, and the Congress may by law provide for the case of removal, death, resignation, or inability, both of the president and vice president, declaring what officer shall then act as president, and such officer shall act accordingly, until the disability be removed, or a president shall be elected.*]**

6. The president shall, at stated times, receive for his services a compensation, which shall neither be increased nor diminished during the period for which he shall have been

---

*Changed by the Twelfth Amendment.
**Changed by the Twenty-fifth Amendment.

elected, and he shall not receive within that period any other emolument from the United States, or any of them.

7. Before he enter on the execution of his office, he shall take the following oath or affirmation:—"I do solemnly swear (or affirm) that I will faithfully execute the office of president of the United States, and will to the best of my ability, preserve, protect and defend the Constitution of the United States."

Section 2. 1. The president shall be commander in chief of the army and navy of the United States, and of the militia of the several states, when called into the actual service of the United States; he may require the opinion, in writing, of the principal officer in each of the executive departments, upon any subject relating to the duties of their respective offices, and he shall have power to grant reprieves and pardons for offenses against the United States, except in cases of impeachment.

2. He shall have power, by and with the advice and consent of the Senate, to make treaties, provided two thirds of the senators present concur; and he shall nominate, and by and with the advice and consent of the Senate, shall appoint ambassadors, other public ministers and consuls, judges of the Supreme Court, and all other officers of the United States, whose appointments are not herein otherwise provided for, and which shall be established by law: but the Congress may by law vest the appointment of such inferior officers, as they think proper, in the president alone, in the courts of law, or in the heads of departments.

3. The president shall have power to fill up all vacancies that may happen during the recess of the Senate, by granting commissions which shall expire at the end of their next session.

Section 3. He shall from time to time give to the Congress information of the state of the Union, and recommend to their consideration such measures as he shall judge necessary and expedient; he may, on extraordinary occasions, convene both Houses, or either of them, and in case of disagreement between them with respect to the time of adjournment, he may adjourn them to such time as he shall think proper; he shall receive ambassadors and other public ministers; he shall take care that the laws be faithfully executed, and shall commission all the officers of the United States.

Section 4. The president, vice president, and all civil officers of the United States, shall be removed from office on impeachment for, and conviction of, treason, bribery, or other high crimes and misdemeanors.

ARTICLE III

Section 1. The judicial power of the United States shall be vested in one Supreme Court, and in such inferior courts as the Congress may from time to time ordain and establish. The judges, both of the Supreme and inferior courts, shall hold their offices during good behavior, and shall, at stated times, receive for their services, a compensation, which shall not be diminished during their continuance in office.

Section 2. 1. The judicial power shall extend to all cases, in law and equity, arising under this Constitution, the laws of the United States, and treaties made, or which shall be made, under their authority;—to all cases affecting ambassadors, other public ministers and consuls;—to all cases of admiralty and maritime jurisdiction;—to controversies to which the United States shall be a party;—to controversies between two or more states; [*between a state and citizens of another state;—*]* between citizens of different states;—between citizens of the same state claiming lands under grants of different states, and between a state, or the citizens thereof, and foreign states, citizens, or subjects.

---

*Changed by the Eleventh Amendment.

2. In all cases affecting ambassadors, other public ministers and consuls, and those in which a state shall be party, the Supreme Court shall have original jurisdiction. In all the other cases before mentioned, the Supreme Court shall have appellate jurisdiction, both as to law and to fact, with such exceptions, and under such regulations as the Congress shall make.

3. The trial of all crimes, except in cases of impeachment, shall be by jury; and such trial shall be held in the state where the said crimes shall have been committed; but when not committed within any state, the trial shall be at such place or places as the Congress may by law have directed.

Section 3. 1. Treason against the United States shall consist only in levying war against them, or in adhering to their enemies, giving them aid and comfort. No person shall be convicted of treason unless on the testimony of two witnesses to the same overt act, or on confession in open court.

2. The Congress shall have power to declare the punishment of treason, but no attainder of treason shall work corruption of blood, or forfeiture except during the life of the person attainted.

ARTICLE IV

Section 1. Full faith and credit shall be given in each state to the public acts, records, and judicial proceedings of every other state. And the Congress may by general laws prescribe the manner in which such acts, records and proceedings shall be proved, and the effect thereof.

Section 2. 1. The citizens of each state shall be entitled to all privileges and immunities of citizens in the several states.*

2. A person charged in any state with treason, felony, or other crime, who shall flee from justice, and be found in another state, shall on demand of the executive authority of the state from which he fled, be delivered up, to be removed to the state having jurisdiction of the crime.

3. [*No person held to service or labor in one state under the laws thereof, escaping into another, shall in consequence of any law or regulation therein, be discharged from such service or labor, but shall be delivered up on claim of the party to whom such service or labor may be due.*]**

Section 3. 1. New states may be admitted by the Congress into this Union; but no new state shall be formed or erected within the jurisdiction of any other state, nor any state be formed by the junction of two or more states, or parts of states, without the consent of the legislatures of the states concerned as well as of the Congress.

2. The Congress shall have power to dispose of and make all needful rules and regulations respecting the territory or other property belonging to the United States; and nothing in this Constitution shall be so construed as to prejudice any claims of the United States, or of any particular state.

Section 4. The United States shall guarantee to every state in this Union a republican form of government, and shall protect each of them against invasion; and on application of the legislature, or of the executive (when the legislature cannot be convened) against domestic violence.

ARTICLE V

The Congress, whenever two thirds of both Houses shall deem it necessary, shall propose amendments to this Constitution, or, on the application of the legislatures of two

---

*See the Fourteenth Amendment, section 1.
**Changed by the Thirteenth Amendment.

thirds of the several states, shall call a convention for proposing amendments, which in either case, shall be valid to all intents and purposes, as part of this Constitution when ratified by the legislatures of three fourths of the several states, or by conventions in three fourths thereof, as the one or the other mode of ratification may be proposed by the Congress: Provided that no amendment which may be made prior to the year one thousand eight hundred and eight shall in any manner affect the first and fourth clauses in the ninth section of the first article; and that no state, without its consent, shall be deprived of its equal suffrage in the Senate.

ARTICLE VI

1. All debts contracted and engagements entered into, before the adoption of this Constitution, shall be as valid against the United States under this Constitution, as under the Confederation.*

2. This Constitution, and the laws of the United States which shall be made in pursuance thereof; and all treaties made, or which shall be made, under the authority of the United States, shall be the supreme law of the land; and the Judges in every state shall be bound thereby, anything in the Constitution or laws of any state to the contrary notwithstanding.

3. The senators and representatives before mentioned, and the members of the several state legislatures, and all executive and judicial officers, both of the United States and of the several states, shall be bound by oath or affirmation to support this Constitution; but no religious test shall ever be required as a qualification to any office or public trust under the United States.

ARTICLE VII

The ratification of the conventions of nine states shall be sufficient for the establishment of this Constitution between the states so ratifying the same.

Done in Convention by the unanimous consent of the States present the seventeenth day of September in the year of our Lord one thousand seven hundred and eighty-seven, and of the independence of the United States of America the twelfth. In witness whereof we have hereunto subscribed our names.

George Washington
President and deputy from
VIRGINIA

Attest: *William Jackson*, Secretary

---

*See the Fourteenth Amendment, section 4.

DELAWARE
Geo. Read
Gunning Bedford, jun
John Dickinson
Richard Bassett
Jaco: Broom

MARYLAND
James McHenry
Dan: of St Thos Jenifer
Danl Carroll

VIRGINIA
John Blair
James Madison Jr.

NORTH CAROLINA
Wm Blount
Richd Dobbs Spaight
Hu Williamson

SOUTH CAROLINA
J. Rutledge
Charles Cotesworth Pinckney
Charles Pinckney
Pierce Butler

GEORGIA
William Few
Abr Baldwin

NEW HAMSPHIRE
John Langdon
Nicholas Gilman

MASSACHUSETTS
Nathaniel Gorham
Rufus King

CONNECTICUT
Wm Saml Johnson
Roger Sherman

NEW YORK
Alexander Hamilton

NEW JERSEY
Wil. Livingston
David Brearley
Wm Paterson
Jona: Dayton

PENNSYLVANIA
B Franklin
Thomas Mifflin
Robt. Morris
Geo. Clymer
Thos. FitzSimons
Jared Ingersoll
James Wilson
Gouv Morris

AMENDMENTS

First Ten Amendments proposed by Congress September 25, 1789.
Ratified by three-fourths of the States December 15, 1791.

AMENDMENT I

Congress shall make no law respecting an establishment of religion, or prohibiting the free exercise thereof; or abridging the freedom of speech, or of the press; or the right of the people peaceably to assemble, and to petition the government for a redress of grievances.

AMENDMENT II

A well regulated militia, being necessary to the security of a free state, the right of the people to keep and bear arms, shall not be infringed.

AMENDMENT III

No soldier shall, in time of peace, be quartered in any house, without the consent of the owner, nor in time of war, but in a manner to be prescribed by law.

AMENDMENT IV

The right of the people to be secure in their persons, houses, papers, and effects, against unreasonable searches and seizures, shall not be violated, and no warrants shall issue, but upon probable cause, supported by oath or affirmation, and particularly describing the place to be searched, and the persons or things to be seized.

AMENDMENT V

No person shall be held to answer for a capital, or otherwise infamous crime, unless on a presentment or indictment of a grand jury, except in cases arising in the land or naval forces, or in the militia, when in actual service in time of war or public danger; nor shall any person be subject for the same offense to be twice put in jeopardy of life or limb; nor shall be compelled in any criminal case to be a witness against himself, nor be deprived of life, liberty, or property, without due process of law, nor shall private property be taken for public use without just compensation.

AMENDMENT VI

In all criminal prosecutions, the accused shall enjoy the right to a speedy and public trial, by an impartial jury of the state and district wherein the crime shall have been committed, which district shall have been previously ascertained by law, and to be informed of the nature and cause of the accusation; to be confronted with the witnesses against him; to have compulsory process for obtaining witnesses in his favor, and to have the assistance of counsel for his defense.

AMENDMENT VII

In suits at common law, where the value in controversy shall exceed twenty dollars, the right of trail by jury shall be preserved, and no fact tried by a jury shall be otherwise reexamined in any court of the United States, than according to the rules of the common law.

AMENDMENT VIII

Excessive bail shall not be required, nor excessive fines imposed, nor cruel and unusual punishments inflicted.

AMENDMENT IX

The enumeration in the Constitution of certain rights shall not be construed to deny or disparage others retained by the people.

AMENDMENT X

The powers not delegated to the United States by the Constitution, nor prohibited by it to the states, are reserved to the states respectively, or to the people.

AMENDMENT XI

Proposed by Congress March 5, 1794. Ratified January 8, 1798.

The judicial power of the United States shall not be construed to extend to any suit in law or equity, commenced or prosecuted against one of the United States by citizens of another state, or by citizens or subjects of any foreign state.

ARTICLE XII

Proposed by Congress December 12, 1803. Ratified September 25, 1804.

The electors shall meet in their respective states, and vote by ballot for president and vice president, one of whom, at least, shall not be an inhabitant of the same state with themselves; they shall name in their ballots the person voted for as president, and in distinct ballots, the person voted for as vice president, and they shall make distinct lists of all persons voted for as president and of all persons voted for as vice president, and of the number of votes for each, which lists they shall sign and certify, and transmit sealed to the seat of the government of the United States, directed to the president of the Senate;—The president of the Senate shall, in presence of the Senate and House of Representatives, open all the certificates and the votes shall then be counted;—The person having the greatest number of votes for president, shall be the president, if such number be a majority of the whole number of electors appointed; and if no person have such majority, then from the persons having the highest numbers not exceeding three on the list of those voted for as president, the House of Representatives shall choose immediately, by ballot, the president. But in choosing the president, the votes shall be taken by states, the representation from each state having one vote; a quorum for this purpose shall consist of a member or members from two-thirds of the states, and a majority of all the states shall be necessary to a choice. [*And if the House of Representatives shall not choose a president whenever the right of choice shall devolve upon them, before the fourth day of March next following, then the vice president shall act as president, as in the case of the death or other constitutional disability of the president.*]* The person having the greatest number of votes as vice president shall be the vice president, if such number be a majority of the whole number of electors appointed, and if no person have a majority, then from the two highest numbers on the list, the Senate shall choose the vice president; a quorum for the purpose shall consist of two-thirds of the whole number of Senators, and a majority of the whole number shall be necessary to a choice. But no person constitutionally ineligible to the office of president shall be eligible to that of vice president of the United States.

AMENDMENT XIII

Proposed by Congress February 1, 1865. Ratified December 18, 1865.

Section 1. Neither slavery nor involuntary servitude, except as punishment for crime whereof the party shall have been duly convicted, shall exist within the United States, or any place subject to their jurisdiction.

Section 2. Congress shall have power to enforce this article by appropriate legislation.

AMENDMENT XIV

Proposed by Congress June 16, 1866. Ratified July 23, 1868.

Section 1. All persons born or naturalized in the United States, and subject to the jurisdiction thereof, are citizens of the United States and of the state wherein they reside. No state shall make or enforce any law which shall abridge the privileges or immunities of citizens of the United States; nor shall any state deprive any person of life, liberty, or property, without due process of law; nor deny to any person within its jurisdiction the equal protection of the laws.

Section 2. Representatives shall be apportioned among the several States according to their respective numbers, counting the whole number of persons in each state, excluding Indians not taxed. But when the right to vote at any election for the choice of electors for president and vice president of the United States, representatives in Congress, the executive and judicial officers of a state, or the members of the legislature thereof, is denied to any of the male inhabitants of such state, being twenty-one years of age, and citizens of the United States, or in any way abridged, except for participation in rebellion, or other crime, the basis of representation therein shall be reduced in the proportion which the number of such male citizens shall bear to the whole number of male citizens twenty-one years of age in such state.

Section 3. No person shall be a senator or representative in Congress, or elector of president and vice president, or hold any office, civil or military, under the United States, or under any state, who, having previously taken an oath, as a member of Congress, or as an officer of the United States, or as a member of any state legislature, or as an executive or

---

*Superseded by section 3 of the Twentieth Amendment.

judicial officer of any state, to support the Constitution of the United States, shall have engaged in insurrection or rebellion against the same, or given aid or comfort to the enemies thereof. But Congress may by a vote of two-thirds of each House, remove such disability.

Section 4. The validity of the public debt of the United States, authorized by law, including debts incurred for payment of pensions and bounties for services in suppressing insurrection or rebellion, shall not be questioned. But neither the United States nor any state shall assume or pay any debt or obligation incurred in aid of insurrection or rebellion against the United States, or any claim for the loss or emancipation of any slave; but all such debts, obligations, and claims shall be held illegal and void.

Section 5. The Congress shall have power to enforce, by appropriate legislation, the provisions of this article.

AMENDMENT XV

Proposed by Congress February 27, 1869. Ratified March 30, 1870.

Section 1. The right of citizens of the United States to vote shall not be denied or abridged by the United States or by any state on account of race, color, or previous condition of servitude.

Section 2. The Congress shall have power to enforce this article by appropriate legislation.

AMENDMENT XVI

Proposed by Congress July 12, 1909. Ratified February 25, 1913.

The Congress shall have power to lay and collect taxes on incomes, from whatever source derived, without apportionment among the several states, and without regard to any census or enumeration.

AMENDMENT XVII

Proposed by Congress May 16, 1912. Ratified May 31, 1913.

The Senate of the United States shall be composed of two senators from each state, elected by the people thereof, for six years; and each senator shall have one vote. The electors in each state shall have the qualifications requisite for electors of the most numerous branch of the state legislature.

When vacancies happen in the representation of any state in the Senate, the executive authority of such state shall issue writs of election to fill such vacancies: Provided, That the legislature of any state may empower the executive thereof to make temporary appointments until the people fill the vacancies by election as the legislature may direct.

This amendment shall not be so construed as to affect the election or term of any senator chosen before it becomes valid as part of the Constitution.

AMENDMENT XVIII

Proposed by Congress December 17, 1917. Ratified January 29, 1919.

Section 1. [*After one year from the ratification of this article, the manufacture, sale, or transportation of intoxicating liquors within, the importation thereof into, or the exportation thereof from the United States and all territory subject to the jurisdiction thereof for beverage purposes is hereby prohibited.*]

Section 2. [*The Congress and the several states shall have concurrent power to enforce this article by appropriate legislation.*]

Section 3. [*This article shall be inoperative unless it shall have been ratified as an amendment to the Constitution by the legislatures of the several states, as provided in the Constitution, within seven years from the date of the submission hereof to the states by Congress.*]*

AMENDMENT XIX

Proposed by Congress June 5, 1919. Ratified August 26, 1920.

The right of citizens of the United States to vote shall not be denied or abridged by the United States or by any state on account of sex.

The Congress shall have power to enforce the provisions of this article by appropriate legislation.

AMENDMENT XX

Proposed by Congress March 3, 1932. Ratified January 23, 1933.

Section 1. The terms of the president and vice president shall end at noon on the 20th day of January, and the terms of Senators and Representatives at noon on the 3d day of January, of the years in which such terms would have ended if this article had not been ratified; and the terms of their successors shall then begin.

Section 2. The Congress shall assemble at least once in every year, and such meeting shall begin at noon on the 3d day of January, unless they shall by law appoint a different day.

Section 3. If, at the time fixed for the beginning of the term of the president, the president-elect shall have died, the vice president-elect shall become president. If a president shall not have been chosen before the time fixed for the beginning of his term, or if the president-elect shall have failed to qualify, then the vice president-elect shall act as president until a president shall have qualified; and the Congress may by law provide for the case wherein neither a president-elect nor a vice president-elect shall have qualified, declaring who shall then act as president, or the manner in which one who is to act shall be selected, and such person shall act accordingly until a president or vice president shall have qualified.

Section 4. The Congress may by law provide for the case of the death of any of the persons from whom the House of Representatives may choose a president whenever the right of choice shall have devolved upon them, and for the case of the death of any of the persons from whom the Senate may choose a vice president whenever the right of choice shall have devolved upon them.

Section 5. Sections 1 and 2 shall take effect on the 15th day of October following the ratification of this article.

Section 6. This article shall be inoperative unless it shall have been ratified as an amendment to the Constitution by the legislatures of three-fourths of the several states within seven years from the date of its submission.

AMENDMENT XXI

Proposed by Congress February 20, 1933. Ratified December 5, 1933.

Section 1. The Eighteenth Article of amendment to the Constitution of the United States is hereby repealed.

Section 2. The transportation or importation into any state, territory, or possession of the United States for delivery or use therein of intoxicating liquors in violation of the laws thereof, is hereby prohibited.

---

*Repealed by the Twenty-first Amendment.

Section 3. This article shall be inoperative unless it shall have been ratified as an amendment to the Constitution by conventions in the several states, as provided in the Constitution, within seven years from the date of the submission thereof to the states by the Congress.

AMENDMENT XXII

Proposed by Congress March 24, 1947. Ratified February 26, 1951.

Section 1. No person shall be elected to the office of the president more than twice, and no person who has held the office of president, or acted as president, for more than two years of a term to which some other person was elected president shall be elected to the office of the president more than once. But this article shall not apply to any person holding the office of president when this article was proposed by the Congress, and shall not prevent any person who may be holding the office of president, or acting as president, during the term within which this article becomes operative from holding the office of president or acting as president during the remainder of such term.

Section 2. This article shall be inoperative unless it shall have been ratified as an amendment to the Constitution by the legislatures of three-fourths of the several states within seven years from the date of its submission to the states by the Congress.

AMENDMENT XXIII

Proposed by Congress June 16, 1960. Ratified March 29, 1961.

Section 1. The district constituting the seat of government of the United States shall appoint in such manner as the Congress may direct:

A number of electors of president and vice president equal to the whole number of Senators and Representatives in Congress to which the district would be entitled if it were a state, but in no event more than the least populous state; they shall be in addition to those appointed by the states, but they shall be considered, for the purposes of election of president and vice president, to be electors appointed by a state; and they shall meet in the district and perform such duties as provided by the twelfth article of amendment.

Section 2. The Congress shall have the power to enforce this article by appropriate legislation.

AMENDMENT XXIV

Proposed by Congress August 27, 1962. Ratified January 23, 1964.

Section 1. The right of citizens of the United States to vote in any primary or other election for president or vice president, for electors for president or vice president, or for Senator or Representative in Congress, shall not be denied or abridged by the United States or any state by failure to pay any poll tax or other tax.

Section 2. The Congress shall have the power to enforce this article by appropriate legislation.

AMENDMENT XXV

Proposed by Congress July 6, 1965. Ratified Febuary 10, 1967.

Section 1. In case of the removal of the president from office or of his death or resignation, the vice president shall become president.

Section 2. Whenever there is a vacancy in the office of the vice president, the president shall nominate a vice president who shall take office upon confirmation by a majority vote of both Houses of Congress.

Section 3. Whenever the president transmits to the president pro tempore of the Senate and the Speaker of the House of Representatives his written declaration that he is unable to discharge the powers and duties of his office, and until he transmits to them a written declaration to the contrary, such powers and duties shall be discharged by the vice president as acting president.

Section 4. Whenever the vice president and a majority of either the principal officers of the executive departments or of such other body as Congress may by law provide, transmit to the president pro tempore of the Senate and the Speaker of the House of Representatives their written declaration that the president is unable to discharge the powers and duties of his office, the vice president shall immediately assume the powers and duties of the office as acting president.

Thereafter, when the president transmits to the president pro tempore of the Senate and the Speaker of the House of Representatives his written declaration that no inability exists, he shall resume the powers and duties of his office unless the vice president and a majority of either the principal officers of the executive department or of such other body as Congress may by law provide, transmit within four days to the president pro tempore of the Senate and the Speaker of the House of Representatives their written declaration that the president is unable to discharge the powers and duties of his office. Thereupon Congress shall decide the issue, assembling within forty-eight hours for that purpose if not in session. If the Congress, within twenty-one days after receipt of the latter written declaration, or, if Congress is not in session, within twenty-one days after Congress is required to assemble, determines by two-thirds vote of both Houses that the president is unable to discharge the powers and duties of his office, the vice president shall continue to discharge the same as acting president; otherwise, the president shall resume the powers and duties of his office.

AMENDMENT XXVI

Proposed by Congress March 23, 1971. Ratified June 30, 1971.

Section 1. The right of citizens of the United States, who are eighteen years of age or older, to vote shall not be denied or abridged by the United States or by any state on account of age.

Section 2. The Congress shall have power to enforce this article by appropriate legislation.

AMENDMENT XXVII

Proposed by Congress September 25, 1789. Ratified May 8, 1992.

No law, varying the compensation for the services of the Senators and Representatives, shall take effect, until an election of Representatives shall have intervened.

Appendix III

❧

U.S. Population Characteristics

U.S. Population Characteristics for Selected Years (in Thousands)

	1790	1840	1890	1940	2000
White	3,172	14,196	55,101	118,215	211,461
Black	757	2,874	7,489	12,866	34,658
(slave)	(698)	(2,487)			
Asian	NA	NA	NA	204	10,243
Amerindian	NA	NA	NA	334	2,476
Other Minorities*	—	—	358	589	22,584
(Hispanic)**	—	—	NA	NA	(35,306)
Urban***	202	1,845	22,106	74,424	NA
Women	NA	8,381	30,711	65,608	143,368
Median Age	NA	17.8	22.0	29.0	35.3
Total	3,929	17,069	62,980	132,165	281,422

*Definitions varied in different census years; in 2000 includes persons who were of more than one race.
**Hispanics may be of any race.
***Defined as living in a place with 2,500 inhabitants.

Appendix IV

❧

Population for Selected Large Cities

Population for Selected Large Cities for Selected Years (in Thousands)

	1800	1850	1900	1950*	2000*
New York	60	696	3,437	12,912	21,200
Los Angeles	—	2	102	4,152	16,374
Chicago	—	30	1,699	5,586	9,158
San Francisco	—	35	343	2,136	7,039
Philadelphia	70	409	1,294	3,671	6,188
Boston	25	137	561	2,411	5,819
Detroit	—	21	286	3,016	5,456
**Dallas	—	—	43	744	5,222
**Washington	3	40	279	1,464	4,923
**Houston	—	2	45	807	4,670
**St. Louis	NA	78	575	1,755	2,604
**Baltimore	27	169	509	1,405	2,553
Cincinnati	1	115	326	1,023	1,979
**New Orleans	NA	116	287	712	1,338

*Metropolitan area population.
**City with slavery before the Civil War.

Appendix V

❧

Presidential Elections

Year	Candidates	Party	Electoral Vote	Popular Vote (in Thousands)
1788	**George Washington**	Federalist	69	—
1792	**George Washington**	Federalist	132	—
1796	**John Adams**	Federalist	71	—
	Thomas Jefferson	Democrat	68	—
1800	**Thomas Jefferson**	Democrat	73*	—
	Aaron Burr	Democrat	73	—
	John Adams	Federalist	65	—
	Charles Pinckney	Federalist	64	—
	John Jay	Federalist	1	—
1804	**Thomas Jefferson**	Democrat	162	—
	Charles Pinckney	Federalist	14	—
1808	**James Madison**	Democrat	122	—
	Charles Pinckney	Federalist	47	—
	George Clinton	Democrat	6	—
1812	**James Madison**	Democrat	128	—
	DeWitt Clinton	Federalist	89	—
1816	**James Monroe**	Democrat	183	—
	Rufus King	Federalist	34	—
1820	**James Monroe**	Democrat	231	—
	John Quincy Adams	Democrat	1	—
1824	**John Quincy Adams**	Democrat	84**	114
	Andrew Jackson	Democrat	99	153
	William H. Crawford	Democrat	41	47
	Henry Clay	Democrat	37	47
1828	**Andrew Jackson**	Democrat	178	647
	John Quincy Adams	Natl. Repub.	83	508

Year	Candidates	Party	Electoral Vote	Popular Vote (in Thousands)
1832	**Andrew Jackson**	Democrat	219	702
	Henry Clay	Natl. Repub.	49	484
	William Wirt	Antimason	7	101
	John Floyd	Democrat	11	
1836	**Martin Van Buren**	Democrat	170	764
	William H. Harrison	Whig	73	
	Hugh L. White	Whig	26	738
	Daniel Webster	Whig	14	
	Willie P. Mangum	Whig	11	
1840	**William H. Harrison**	Whig	234	1,275
	Martin Van Buren	Democrat	60	1,129
1841	**John Tyler***	Ind. Democrat	—	—
1844	**James K. Polk**	Democrat	170	1,339
	Henry Clay	Whig	105	1,300
	James G. Birney	Liberty	—	62
1848	**Zachary Taylor**	Whig	163	1,361
	Lewis Cass	Democrat	127	1,223
	Martin Van Buren	Free Soil	—	292
1850	**Millard Fillmore***	Whig	—	—
1852	**Franklin Pierce**	Democrat	254	1,608
	Winfield Scott	Whig	42	1,387
	John P. Hale	Free Soil	—	155
1856	**James Buchanan**	Democrat	174	1,836
	John Frémont	Republican	114	1,342
	Millard Fillmore	American	8	873
1860	**Abraham Lincoln**	Republican	180	1,866
	Stephen A. Douglas	N. Democrat	12	1,380
	John Breckinridge	S. Democrat	72	848
	John Bell	Const. Union	39	591
1864	**Abraham Lincoln**	Republican	212	2,218
	George McClellan	Democrat	21	1,813
1865	**Andrew Johnson***	Union Democrat	—	—
1868	**U. S. Grant**	Republican	214	3,014
	Horatio Seymour	Democrat	80	2,709
1872	**U. S. Grant**	Republican	286	3,598
	Horace Greeley	Democrat	66	2,835
1876	**Rutherford B. Hayes**	Republican	185	4,034
	Samuel J. Tilden	Democrat	184	4,289
1880	**James A. Garfield**	Republican	214	4,454
	Winfield Hancock	Democrat	155	4,445
1881	Chester A. Arthur***	Republican	—	
1884	**Grover Cleveland**	Democrat	219	4,875
	James Blaine	Republican	182	4,852

Year	Candidates	Party	Electoral Vote	Popular Vote (in Thousands)
1888	**Benjamin Harrison**	Republican	233	5,440
	Grover Cleveland	Democrat	168	5,540
1892	**Grover Cleveland**	Democrat	277	5,557
	Benjamin Harrison	Republican	145	5,176
	James B. Weaver	Populist	22	1,041
1896	**William McKinley**	Republican	271	7,112
	William J. Bryan	Democrat	176	6,509
1900	**William McKinley**	Republican	292	7,220
	William J. Bryan	Democrat	155	6,358
1901	**Theodore Roosevelt*****	Republican	—	—
1904	**Theodore Roosevelt**	Republican	336	7,629
	Alton Parker	Democrat	140	5,084
1908	**William H. Taft**	Republican	321	7,679
	William J. Bryan	Democrat	162	6,409
1912	**Woodrow Wilson**	Democrat	435	6,293
	Theodore Roosevelt	Progressive	88	4,119
	William H. Taft	Republican	8	3,486
	Eugene V. Debs	Socialist	—	900
1916	**Woodrow Wilson**	Democrat	277	9,130
	Charles E. Hughes	Republican	254	8,538
1920	**Warren G. Harding**	Republican	404	16,153
	James M. Cox	Democrat	127	9,133
1923	**Calvin Coolidge*****	Republican	—	—
1924	**Calvin Coolidge**	Republican	382	15,720
	John W. Davis	Democrat	136	8,387
	Robert La Follette	Progressive	13	4,833
1928	**Herbert Hoover**	Republican	444	21,437
	Alfred E. Smith	Democrat	87	15,007
1932	**Franklin Roosevelt**	Democrat	472	22,830
	Herbert Hoover	Republican	59	15,761
1936	**Franklin Roosevelt**	Democrat	523	27,757
	Alfred Landon	Republican	8	16,680
1940	**Franklin Roosevelt**	Democrat	449	27,313
	Wendell Willkie	Republican	82	22,348
1944	**Franklin Roosevelt**	Democrat	432	25,613
	Thomas E. Dewey	Republican	99	22,018
1945	**Harry Truman*****	Democrat	—	—
1948	**Harry Truman**	Democrat	303	24,179
	Thomas E. Dewey	Republican	189	21,991
	Strom Thurmond	States Rights	39	1,176
	Henry Wallace	Progressive	—	1,157
1952	**Dwight Eisenhower**	Republican	442	33,936
	Adlai Stevenson	Democrat	89	27,315
1956	**Dwight Eisenhower**	Republican	457	35,590
	Adlai Stevenson	Democrat	73****	26,023

Year	Candidates	Party	Electoral Vote	Popular Vote (in Thousands)
1960	**John F. Kennedy**	Democrat	303	34,227
	Richard Nixon	Republican	219	34,108
	Richard Byrd	Independent	15	286
1963	**Lyndon B. Johnson***	Democrat	—	—
1964	**Lyndon B. Johnson**	Democrat	486	43,130
	Barry Goldwater	Republican	52	27,178
1968	**Richard Nixon**	Republican	301	31,785
	Hubert Humphrey	Democrat	191	31,275
	George Wallace	American Ind.	46	9,906
1972	**Richard Nixon**	Republican	520	47,170
	George McGovern	Democrat	17	29,170
1974	**Gerald Ford***	Republican	—	—
1976	**Jimmy Carter**	Democrat	297	40,831
	Gerald Ford	Republican	40****	39,148
1980	**Ronald Reagan**	Republican	489	43,904
	Jimmy Carter	Democrat	49	35,484
	John Anderson	Independent	—	5,720
1984	**Ronald Reagan**	Republican	525	54,455
	Walter Mondale	Democrat	13	37,527
1988	**George H. W. Bush**	Republican	426	48,881
	Michael Dukakis	Democrat	112	41,805
1992	**William J. Clinton**	Democrat	370	44,908
	George H. W. Bush	Republican	168	39,102
	Ross Perot	Independent	—	19,217
1996	**William J. Clinton**	Democrat	379	47,401
	Robert Dole	Republican	159	39,197
	Ross Perot	Reform	—	8,085
2000	**George W. Bush**	Republican	271	50,459
	Albert Gore	Democrat	266****	51,004
	Ralph Nader	Green	—	2,834

Winners in bold.
*Jefferson and Burr tied in electoral votes, and the House of Representatives elected Jefferson.
**No candidate had an electoral majority, and the House of Representatives elected Adams.
***Vice presidents who succeeded to the presidency.
****In these elections one elector strayed from a pledged vote.

Appendix VI

❧❦

Chronology

B.C.	38,000	Ice Age land bridge migration from Asia
	6000	Central Americans raise corn and beans
A.D.	300–900	Mayan civilization
	700–1600	Southeastern mound builders
ca.	1000–1010	Vikings in Vinland
	1300–1500	Aztec civilization
	1492	Columbus sails to America
	1534–1542	Cartier in Canada
	1539–1542	DeSoto in Southeast
	1585–1590	Roanoke colony
	1607	Virginia founded
	1618	Virginia headright system
	1619	First slaves in Virginia
		Virginia House of Burgesses
	1620	Pilgrims go to Plymouth
	1624	Dutch found New Netherland
	1629	Dutch patroon plan
	1630–1642	Puritan migration to Massachusetts
	1632	Maryland chartered to Lord Baltimore
	1636	Roger Williams flees to Rhode Island
		Thomas Hooker founds Connecticut
	1638	Massachusetts banishes Anne Hutchinson
	1649	Maryland Toleration Act
	1651–1696	English Navigation Acts
	1663	Carolina chartered to eight lord proprietors
	1664	English capture New Netherland (renamed New York)
		New Jersey split from New York
	1675–1676	Bacon's Rebellion in Virginia
		King Philip's War in New England
	1676	New Jersey split into East and West Jersey (reunited in 1702)
	1682	William Penn founds Pennsylvania

1686–1689	Dominion of New England
1689	Leisler's Rebellion in New York
1692	Salem Village witchcraft trials
1704	Delaware split from Pennsylvania
1729	North Carolina split from South Carolina
1732	Gen. James Oglethorpe founds Georgia
1733	John Peter Zenger wins libel trial
1741–1742	Jonathan Edwards leads Great Awakening
1754–1763	French and Indian War
1764	Sugar Act
1765	Stamp Act
1767	Townshend Acts
	Tryon's Palace built
1771	North Carolina Regulators
1773	Tea Act
1774	Coercive Acts
	Shakers arrive
1775	Battles of Lexington, Concord, and Bunker Hill
1776	Declaration of Independence
1777	Battle of Saratoga
1780–1846	North abolishes slavery
1781	Cornwallis surrenders at Yorktown
1781–1789	Articles of Confederation
1783	Peace treaty grants independence
1785	Land ordinance
1786	Shay's Rebellion in Massachusetts
1787	Northwest Ordinance
	Constitutional Convention (ratified 1788)

1789–1797	George Washington's presidency
1789	Bill of Rights
1790s	Second Great Awakening begins
1790	Assumption of war debts
	Slater's spinning mill founded
1791	Bank of the United States chartered
1793	Citizen Genêt
	Whitney's cotton gin invented
1794	Whiskey Rebellion in Pennsylvania
1795	Treaties with Britain, Indians, and Spain
1796	Washington's Farewell Address

1797–1801	John Adams's presidency
1797	XYZ Affair
1798	Alien and Sedition Acts
	Kentucky and Virginia Resolutions
1798–1800	Quasi-War with France

1801–1809	Thomas Jefferson's presidency
1803	*Marbury v. Madison*
	Louisiana Purchase

1804–1806	Lewis and Clark expedition
1807	Fulton's steamboat invented
1808	Embargo of foreign trade
	Congress abolishes slave trade
1809–1817	James Madison's presidency
1810	Macon's Bill No. 2
1811	Bank of the United States expires
1812–1815	War of 1812
1813	Waltham weaving mill founded
1816	Second Bank of the United States chartered
	African Methodist Episcopal Church founded
1817–1825	James Monroe's presidency
1817	American Colonization Society founded
1819	*Dartmouth College Case*
	McCulloch v. Maryland
1820s	Americans settle Texas
1820	Missouri Compromise
1822	Liberia founded
1823	Monroe Doctrine
	Lowell weaving mills founded
1825–1829	John Quincy Adams's presidency
1825	Erie Canal opens
1828	Tariff of Abominations
1829–1837	Andrew Jackson's presidency
1829–1832	Nullification
1830–1840	Indian removal
1830	Peggy O'Neal Eaton affair
	First railroads open in Baltimore and Charleston, S.C.
	Church of Jesus Christ of Latter-day Saints founded
1831	*Cherokee Nation v. Georgia*
	Nat Turner's Rebellion
	Garrison's *The Liberator* begins
1832	Second Bank of the United States recharter veto
	Worchester v. Georgia
1833	American Antislavery Society founded
1836	Specie Circular
	Texas independence
1837–1841	Martin Van Buren's presidency
1837–1845	Depression
1837	*Charles River Bridge Case*
1838	Frederick Douglass escapes from slavery
1839–1841	*Amistad Case*
1840–1860	Record Irish and German immigration
1840	Independent Treasury

1841	William Henry Harrison's presidency
	Brook Farm founded
1841–1845	John Tyler's presidency
1844	Millerites
	Morse's telegraph invented
1845	Texas annexed
	Thoreau retreats to Walden Pond
1845–1849	James K. Polk's presidency
1846	U.S.–Canada boundary settled
1846–1848	Mexican War
1846–1847	Wilmot Proviso
1848	California and New Mexico acquired
	Seneca Falls Declaration of Female Independence
	Oneida Community founded
1849–1850	Zachary Taylor's presidency
1849–1852	California Gold Rush
1849–1860	Filibusterers
1850–1853	Millard Fillmore's presidency
1850	Compromise of 1850
1851	Maine Prohibition begins
1852	Harriet Beecher Stowe's *Uncle Tom's Cabin* published
1853–1857	Franklin Pierce's presidency
1854	Gadsden Purchase
	Kansas-Nebraska Act
	Ostend Manifesto
1854–1856	Bleeding Kansas
1856	Charles Sumner caned
1857–1861	James Buchanan's presidency
1857	*Dred Scott v. Sandford*
1857–1858	Kansas's Lecompton Constitution
1859	John Brown's Harper's Ferry raid
1860	South Carolina secedes
1861	Confederate States of America founded
1861–1865	Abraham Lincoln's presidency
1861	Fort Sumter falls
	Upper South secedes
	Battle of Bull Run
1862	Battles of Shiloh, Antietam
1862–1863	Drafting of soldiers
1863	Emancipation Proclamation
	Battles of Vicksburg, Gettysburg
	Port Royal experiment
1864	Battles of Petersburg, Atlanta

1864	Wade-Davis Bill veto
1865	Lee surrenders
	Lincoln assassinated

1865–1869	Andrew Johnson's presidency
1865	Thirteenth Amendment
	Black Codes
1865–1866	Freedmen's Bureau
1866	Civil Rights Act
	Fourteenth Amendment
	Ku Klux Klan founded
1867	Reconstruction Act
	Alaska bought
1868	Johnson impeached (but not convicted)

1869–1877	Ulysses S. Grant's presidency
1869	Fifteenth Amendment
1872	Crédit Mobilier scandal
1873	Depression
1876–1877	Disputed election
1877	Last Reconstruction government falls

1877–1881	Rutherford Hayes's presidency
1877	National railway strike
	Thomas Edison invents phonograph
1879	Bland-Allison Act requires silver purchase
	Terence Powderly elected head of Knights of Labor
	Edison invents electric light
	F. W. Woolworth opens five-and-ten-cents store

1881	James Garfield's presidency
	Garfield shot by disturbed office-seeker and dies

1881–1885	Chester Arthur's presidency
1882	Chinese Exclusion Act
1883	Pendleton Act passed

1885–1889	Grover Cleveland's first presidency
1886	Haymarket riot and bombing
	Geronimo surrenders
	American Federation of Labor (AFL) founded
1887	Interstate Commerce Commission created

1889–1893	Benjamin Harrison's presidency
1890	Battle of Wounded Knee
	Sherman Antitrust Act passed
	Sherman Silver Purchase Act passed
1892	Populists organize
	Homestead strike

1893–1897	Grover Cleveland's second presidency
1893	Financial panic begins depression
1894	Coxey's Army
	Pullman strike
1895	United States intervenes in Venezuela boundary issue
1896	*Plessy v. Ferguson* establishes "separate but equal" doctrine

1897–1901	William McKinley's presidency
1898	Spanish-American War
1899	Hay's "Open Door" policy
	Philippine guerrilla war begins
1900	Boxer Rebellion in China
1901	McKinley shot by anarchist

1901–1909	Theodore Roosevelt's presidency
1901–1917	Progressive years
1901	U.S. Steel formed
1903	Panama declares independence; signs Canal Treaty
	Wright Brothers' first flight
1906	Pure Food and Drug Act and Meat Inspection Act passed
1907	Financial panic
1908	Henry Ford introduces Model T

1909–1913	William Taft's presidency
1909	Payne-Aldrich Tariff passed
1910	Pinchot controversy
1911	Triangle Shirtwaist Factory fire
1912	Progressive Party (Bull Moose) formed

1913–1921	Woodrow Wilson's presidency
1913	Sixteenth Amendment (income tax) and Seventeenth Amendment (direct election of senators) ratified
	Federal Reserve System founded
1914	First World War begins in Europe; Wilson declares neutrality
	Clayton Antitrust Act
	Federal Trade Commission created
	"Ludlow Massacre" in Colorado
1916	Wilson sends General John Pershing to Mexico
1917	Bolsheviks take power in Russia
1917–1918	United States fights in World War I
1918	Wilson's Fourteen Points
	Sedition Act
	War Industries Board created
1919	Race riots
1920	Red Scare
	Defeat of Versailles Treaty by Senate
	Eighteenth Amendment (Prohibition) and Nineteenth Amendment (woman suffrage) go into effect

1921–1923	Warren G. Harding's presidency
1921	Immigration restriction through national quotas
	Limitation of Armaments Conference in Washington
	Ku Klux Klan begins revival
1923	Teapot Dome scandal
	Harding dies

1923–1929	Calvin Coolidge's presidency
1924	National Origins Immigration Act
	Nellie Taylor Ross elected governor of Wyoming, first woman governor
1925	Scopes trial
1926	National Broadcasting Corporation, first radio network, formed
1927	Charles A. Lindbergh's solo Atlantic flight
	First "talkie" motion picture, *The Jazz Singer*
1928	Kellogg-Briand Pact outlaws war

1929–1933	Herbert Hoover's presidency
1929–1941	Great Depression
1930	Smoot-Hawley Tariff raises protective barriers
1931	Japan invades Manchuria; Stimson Doctrine issued
1932	Bonus Army
	Reconstruction Finance Corporation founded

1933–1945	Franklin Roosevelt's presidency
1933	Frances Perkins, U.S. Secretary of Labor; first woman in cabinet
	"100 Days" special session, March 9–June 16
	Twenty-first Amendment (repealing prohibition) ratified
	Emergency Banking Act halts banking crisis
	National Industrial Recovery Act (NRA) provides wage-price codes
	Agricultural Adjustment Act (AAA) provides farm supports
	Glass-Steagall Act establishes Federal Deposit Insurance Corporation (FDIC)
1934	Father Charles Coughlin starts National Union for Social Justice
	Francis Townsend proposes old-age pensions
1935	Works Progress Administration (WPA) established
	Supreme Court strikes down NRA
	Wagner Act sets up National Labor Relations Board (NLRB)
	Social Security Act passed
	Huey Long assassinated
	Congress of Industrial Organizations (CIO) founded
1936	Supreme Court strikes down AAA
1937	Roosevelt proposes packing Supreme Court
	CIO expelled from AFL
	Japan invades China
1938	Munich Conference

1939	Germany and Soviet Union sign pact
	Germany invades Poland; World War II begins
	Neutrality Act
1940	Germany captures Belgium, Holland, and France
	Roosevelt wins third term
1941	Lend-Lease Act
	Germany invades Soviet Union
	Japan attacks U.S. naval forces at Pearl Harbor; United States enters the war
1942	United States evacuates Japanese from West Coast
	Battle of Midway; North African invasion
1943	Race riot in Detroit
	Allied invasion of Italy
1944	GI Bill enacted
	Allied invasion of France (D-Day)
1945	Yalta Conference
	Roosevelt dies

1945–1953	Harry Truman's presidency
1945	Germany surrenders
	Atomic bombs dropped on Hiroshima and Nagasaki; Japan surrenders
1946	Military demobilization
1947	Taft-Hartley Act
	Truman Doctrine announced
	Marshall Plan launches economic recovery in Europe
1948–1949	Berlin airlift
1948	Truman integrates armed forces
1949	North Atlantic Treaty Organization (NATO) established
1950	Alger Hiss convicted of perjury
	United States sends troops to Korea
1951	Julius and Ethel Rosenberg sentenced to death
	MacArthur removed from Korean command
	Twenty-second Amendment (presidential term limits) ratified
1952	H-bomb developed

1953–1961	Dwight Eisenhower's presidency
1953	Korean War ends
1954	*Brown v. Board of Education of Topeka* decision ordering integration of schools
	Senate censures Senator Joseph McCarthy
1955–1956	Montgomery, Alabama, bus boycott
1956	Interstate highway system begins
	Suez crisis
1957	First civil rights law since Reconstruction passed
	National Guardsmen sent to Little Rock, Arkansas
	Soviet Union launches *Sputnik*
1960	Black students stage sit-in in Greensboro
	First birth control pill introduced in United States

1961–1963	John Kennedy's presidency
1961	Peace Corps established
	Bay of Pigs invasion of Cuba fails
	Freedom rides in South begin
1962	Cuban missile crisis
1963	Nuclear Test Ban Treaty ratified
	Betty Friedan's *The Feminine Mystique* published
	Kennedy assassinated
1963–1969	Lyndon Johnson's presidency
1964	Gulf of Tonkin Resolution authorizes war in Vietnam
	Civil Rights Act passed
1965	Race riot in Watts
	Great Society begins, including Medicare, federal aid to education, and urban renewal
	U.S. combat troops sent to Vietnam
	Voting Rights Act passed
1967	Thurgood Marshall becomes first black appointed to Supreme Court
	Black riots in Newark, New Jersey, and Detroit, Michigan
1968	Tet offensive in Vietnam
	Johnson withdraws from presidential race
	Martin Luther King, Jr., assassinated
	Robert Kennedy assassinated
1969–1974	Richard Nixon's presidency
1969	Nuclear Nonproliferation Treaty signed
1970	Environmental Protection Agency founded
	U.S. troops invade Cambodia; student strikes
1971	United States goes off international gold standard
	Twenty-sixth Amendment lowers voting age to eighteen
	Pentagon Papers reveal U.S. involvement in Vietnam
1972	Nixon travels to China
	United States enters into Strategic Arms Limitation Treaty with the Soviet Union
	Equal Rights Amendment sent to states for ratification
1973	U.S. role in Vietnam War ends
	Senate begins Watergate break-in hearings
	Supreme Court upholds abortion in *Roe v. Wade*
	Arab oil boycott creates stagflation in U.S. economy
1974	Nixon resigns from the presidency
1974–1977	Gerald Ford's presidency
1974	Ford pardons Nixon
	Economic recession
1975	South Vietnam and Cambodia fall to communists
1976	United States celebrates bicentennial of independence
1977–1980	Jimmy Carter's presidency
1977	Energy Department created

1978	Panama Canal turned over to Panama
1979	Chrysler Corporation federal bailout
1979–1981	Iranian hostage crisis
1980	Soviet invasion of Afghanistan

1981–1989	Ronald Reagan's presidency
1981	Iranian hostages released
	Tax cut
	Federal air traffic controllers' strike broken
	Sandra Day O'Connor first woman appointed to Supreme Court
1982	Equal Rights Amendment defeated
	Economic recession
	U.S. marines sent to Lebanon
1983	United States invades Grenada
1984	CIA acknowledges mining of Nicaraguan harbors
	Reagan visits China
1985	Reagan and Soviet leader Mikhail Gorbachev meet
1986	William Rehnquist appointed as chief justice and Antonin Scalia appointed as associate justice of the Supreme Court
	Tax Reform Act enacted
1987	First trillion-dollar budget
	Iran-Contra hearings
	Arms limitation treaty with the Soviet Union
1988	Amnesty offered to 1.4 million illegal immigrants

1989–1993	George Bush's presidency
1989	Savings and loan bailout
	Supreme Court allows state laws restraining abortion
	United States invades Panama
1990	Physical and Mental Disabilities Act passed
	Iraq invades Kuwait; United States sends troops to Saudi Arabia
	Clean Air Act passed
	Taxes increased
1991	United States and allies defeat Iraq in Gulf War
	Economic recession
	Clarence Thomas appointed to Supreme Court

1993–2001	William Clinton's presidency
1993	Branch Davidian complex assaulted at Waco
1994	North American Free Trade Association Agreement (NAFTA) ratified
	Whitewater investigation
	Republicans gain control of Congress for first time since 1954
1995	Oklahoma City bombing
	Khobar Towers, Saudi Arabia, bombing
1996	Welfare Reform Act passed
	Defense of Marriage Act passed
1998	U.S. embassies in Nairobi and Dar es Salaam bombed
	U.S. attacks Serbia after Serbia invades Kosovo

1998–1999	Monica Lewinsky affair; Clinton impeachment fails
2000	Disputed Bush–Gore presidential election

2001–	George W. Bush's presidency
2001	Al Qaeda attacks World Trade Center and Pentagon
	Department of Homeland Security established
2002	U.S. topples Taliban in Afghanistan; bin Laden sought
2003	U.S. invades Iraq; Saddam caught
	Massachusetts court rules for same-sex marriage

Glossary

abolition/abolitionist the policy of the government to end slavery; abolitionists were people who urged government action to end slavery

adventurist a term often used in foreign policy to connote a hazardous or dangerous undertaking or policy

Allies those nations that fought against the **Axis powers** (Germany, Italy, Japan) during World War II

amnesty an act of government pardoning a large number of individuals

Anaconda a copper-mining city in southwestern Montana; site of the world's largest copper **smelter**

Anglophobia hatred of England or English customs, people, manners, or institutions; used by certain American politicians to inflame voters, especially Irish voters

annex/annexation the process by which a government takes in a new territory

antebellum literally, "before the war," usually before the Civil War

anti-Semitism intolerance of Jews or Jewish culture

antitrust federal and state statutes that limit the ability of businesses and unions to exercise monopolistic control or restrain trade, such as the Sherman Antitrust Act of 1890 (see also **trust**)

apartheid a policy of **segregation** and political and economic discrimination against non-European groups in the Republic of South Africa

appeasement/appease to bring peace by making concessions; a policy of appeasement was pursued by Neville Chamberlain, prime minister of Great Britain (1937–1940) in negotiating with the Nazis

apprenticeship a system for training youths for careers in skilled crafts

appropriations funds set aside by a legislature to pay for something authorized by law

aristocracy a hereditary ruling class; commonly found in Europe

Articles of Confederation the document that in the 1780s created the government of the United States before the U.S. Constitution; like Canada today, the United States under the Articles was a weak alliance of loosely associated states

artillery very heavy guns used for long-range firing in war

artisans skilled workers such as butchers, bakers, and candlestick makers

assimilation the process by which one group of people gradually becomes like another group of people by adopting the other group's language, religion, and culture

asylum a refuge, retreat, or shelter

Axis powers a **coalition** that developed from the Rome-Berlin Axis of 1936 and eventually included Germany, Italy, Japan, and others; opposed by the **Allies** in World War II

belligerent a person or nation engaged in warfare or fighting

Bible Belt those portions of the rural South and Midwest dominated from the early 1800s to the present by **evangelical Protestant** Christians

Big Three Franklin Roosevelt (United States), Winston Churchill (Great Britain), and Josef Stalin (Soviet Union)

bill draft of a proposed law not yet passed by Congress or signed by the president

bimetallic standard the concurrent use of both gold and silver as the standard of currency and value; advocated by the Populist Party in 1896

black nationalism the belief that African Americans should form their own nation or society separate from white society

bohemian a person, usually of artistic or literary tastes, who lives in an unconventional manner; a term that became popular among intellectuals at the turn of the twentieth century

boll weevils a long-used term for southern Democrats in Congress, including those who supported Ronald Reagan during his presidency

Bolsheviks a political faction of **communists** who gained control of Russia in 1917 following the overthrow of the czar

bond in finance, an interest-bearing certificate of debt, usually issued by a government, municipality, or corporation; the federal government issues bonds to finance its debt

bootlegging/bootlegger the sale and distribution of illegal alcohol during **Prohibition** in the 1920s

breastworks hastily built low barriers from behind which gunners fire

burgess a legislator, specifically a member of Virginia's House of Burgesses during colonial times

busing a method of transporting students from one school district to another to ensure racial balance

Calvinism the religion of John Calvin and his followers, including Presbyterians, **Puritans,** and **Pilgrims,** which stressed that only certain people could be saved and go to heaven (compare with **universal salvation**)

capital wealth (money and property); an accumulated source of wealth used to produce more wealth; also, used to define **capitalists** collectively as distinguished from labor

capitalists/capitalism people who invest money in business enterprises in the hope of making profits; an economic system in which all or most of the means of production and distribution are privately owned and operated for profit

capitalization the total capital funds of a corporation, represented by stocks, bonds, undivided profit, and surplus

carpetbaggers northerners who moved south to assist Radical Republicans during Reconstruction (compare with **scalawags**)

cash and carry a system imposed by the Neutrality Act (1937) in which goods were to be paid in cash

charter an important government document; under English law, charters were more important than laws or court rulings; they could be granted either by the king or by **Parliament**; persons often gained great power through the land or privileges granted in a charter; colonies such as Virginia and Massachusetts were started under the authority of charters

checks and balances the principle in the U.S. Constitution, derived from colonial and English experience, that power should be divided rather than concentrated; the U.S. Constitution divides power among three branches of government: legislative, executive, and judicial

Church of England the official **Protestant** church in England founded when Henry VIII broke with the Catholic church; in America, it became the Episcopal church after the American Revolution

coalition an alliance of interests or groups; the New Deal coalition brought together urban ethnic groups with southern whites and blacks

coattails a political expression meaning to help win an election for a follower or supporter; a congressional candidate will sometimes win election on the coattails of a strong presidential candidate from the same party

coinage the act to make coins; free coinage meant unlimited use of certain metal, often used in the silver controversy in 1872–1900

cold warrior a person who supported the cold war against the Soviet Union

cold war war by other than military means; the hostile but nonlethal relations between the United States and the Soviet Union, 1945–1989

collective a body of people brought together in a common enterprise; the Soviet Union formed agricultural collectives under Stalin; in the 1970s, New Left students formed revolutionary collectives to challenge **capitalist** society

collectivism a general term often suggesting **socialism** or **communism**, as opposed to individualism

colonizationists/colonization people who favored abolishing slavery and resettling the ex-slaves from the United States to Africa; this movement was strongest from 1817 to 1830 (not to be confused with colonialism)

combine an agricultural machine that reaps, threshes, and cleans grain while harvesting it; invented and manufactured by Cyrus McCormick

communes groups in which members live together on an equal basis, sharing work and leisure; there were many communes in the 1800s; the most successful had religious roots

communion a Christian ceremony commemorating Christ's resurrection through the partaking of wine and bread; Christians often disagree on the ceremony's conduct and meaning

communist/communism a member of the Communist Party; or one who supports communism, a theory and social system conceived by German philosopher Karl Marx (see also **Bolsheviks, socialism, Marxism**)

compensated emancipation a system by which the government freed **slaves** by paying slaveholders for the value of their slaves

congregational churches churches governed by their congregations rather than by bishops or other outside groups; in New England both **Puritans** and **Pilgrims** governed their churches this way, and they became known by this name

conscientious objector a person who is opposed to war on religious or moral grounds

contraband in warfare, any items valuable to an enemy that might therefore be seized; during the Civil War, the North for a time considered **slaves** to be contraband

conversion experience for some Christians, the process by which a person becomes a Christian; Puritans believed that a person had to undergo a rebirth of the spirit that could be described convincingly to others; later **evangelicals** found a statement of having had such an experience sufficient

cotton gin Eli Whitney's 1793 invention, no bigger than a breadbox, for easily separating cotton fibers from the seeds

covert not openly shown, as in "covert CIA operations"

cubism a movement in modern art about 1907–1925, concerned with abstract and geometric interpretation of form

customs duties see **tariff**

daguerreotype an early photographic process that did not use negatives; the pictures were remarkably clear and detailed, but the cost was high and no copies could be made

dark horse an obscure presidential candidate picked by a political party as a compromise to break a deadlock; James Polk and Warren Harding are examples of dark horses who won

deferment the act of delaying or postponing, especially used with the draft, such as a student deferment, which allowed students to postpone entering the draft during the Vietnam War

deficit the amount by which expenditures exceed revenues

defoliant a chemical spray or dust applied to plants to make leaves fall off prematurely

depression a period marked by slackening business activity, widespread unemployment, falling prices, and falling wages (compare with **recession**)

desegregate to end segregation, which is often practiced in schools, businesses, and public places against racial minorities (primarily African-American)

détente a relaxation of strained relations between two nations (pronounced *day-TAHNT*)

discount rate the interest rate paid by a commercial bank when it borrows from the Federal Reserve System

disfranchisement removal of a person's right to vote; many southern states disfranchised African Americans in the late 1800s

divisions military units usually composed of three **regiments;** in the American Civil War, about five thousand soldiers

dole that which is distributed through charity in the form of a small gift of food or money; often used for those receiving public aid during the Great Depression in the 1930s

domino effect the theory that if a critically situated country falls to **communism,** its neighbors will soon follow; a rationale for American involvement in the Vietnam War

dove an advocate of peace; a term often used for those opposed to the war in Vietnam (compare with **hawk**)

draft compulsory military service; the practice of drafting people into military service is called *conscription*

due process the constitutional requirement that "no person shall be deprived of life, liberty, or property without due process of law," a right guaranteed by the Fifth, Sixth, and Fourteenth Amendments to the U.S. Constitution

duties see **tariff**

egalitarian favoring absolute equality

Electoral College the U.S. Constitution's method for electing presidents; the members of the Electoral College, called *electors*, elect the president; the states determine how the members of the Electoral College are picked (see also **electoral vote**)

electoral vote the votes cast for president and vice president by the **Electoral College** as established in Article II, Section 1, and the Twelfth and Twenty-third Amendments of the U.S. Constitution

elitism rule by an elite or dominant group

emancipate/emancipation the voluntary freeing of a slave by a slaveholder

Emancipation Proclamation the executive order by President Abraham Lincoln in 1863 that freed the slaves inside the Confederacy on the grounds that slavery aided the Confederate military cause

embargo a federal law barring merchant ships from leaving or entering port and thus totally ending all foreign trade; imposed by Thomas Jefferson in 1807, the embargo prevented war with Britain but ruined the American economy (compare with **blockade**)

eminent domain the right of the government to take private property forcibly but with compensation, for public purposes such as to build a road or railroad

enfranchise to give the right to vote

Enlightenment a movement occurring in the 1700s based on the idea that reason and logic determined all; highly favorable to science and suspicious of religion (see also **romanticism**)

envoy a diplomatic representative

evangelical a **Protestant** Christian who stresses the authority of the Bible, exhortation to faith, and usually the availability of universal salvation

expansionism the act of expanding the state

expressionist a movement in the arts, originating about 1914, that had as its object the free expression of the artist's inner experience

factionalism the practice of dividing an organization or other body into contentious or self-seeking groups

fascism a political philosophy that advocates governance by a dictator to maintain a totalitarian, regimented society; fascism appeared in Italy and Germany in the 1920s and 1930s (pronounced *FASH-izm*)

Federal Reserve System the central bank of the United States created by the Federal Reserve Act (1913)

feudalism the political, economic, and social system emphasizing graded classes by which Europe was organized in the Middle Ages, circa 1000–1500

filibuster the use of a delaying tactic to prevent action in a legislative assembly, especially the U.S. Senate; the taking of foreign territory in a private war in the 1850s

filibusterers leaders of private armies who tried to seize territory in the 1850s for the purpose of adding it to the United States (not to be confused with **filibuster**)

flapper an informal name given to women in the 1920s who tried to appear sophisticated in dress and behavior

flotilla a fleet of boats or ships

foreclosure to take away the right to redeem a mortgage when regular payments have not been made on a home, farm, or other property

49th parallel in the West, the boundary between the United States and Canada, which runs along this straight line of latitude

franchise the right to vote

free coinage the issuing of currency based on a silver or bimetallic standard

free love a celebration of sex and a rejection of traditional restrictions, including marriage; advocated by Frances Wright in New York in the 1830s

free silver the free and unlimited coinage of silver, particularly at a fixed ratio to gold

free soil the policy of keeping **slavery** out of the western territories without interfering with slavery in the South; Van Buren's position in 1848; the Republican Party position in 1856 and 1860

free trade the right to buy or sell anything to anyone across national borders without regulation or taxes; free trade exists among states within the United States (see also **tariff**)

freedmen the name given to the former **slaves** during Reconstruction

frieze a three-dimensional sculpture placed in a band around the top of a building

fundamentalism a movement organized in the early twentieth century to defend orthodox **Protestant** Christianity against the challenges of theological liberalism, evolution, and liberal interpretations of the Bible

Gatling guns machine guns invented and first used in the Civil War

Gentlemen's Agreement an agreement reached with Japan in 1908 by which the Japanese government promised to issue no more passports to peasants or workers coming directly to the continental United States

gentry in England, the landowning farmers who enjoyed some wealth, some prestige, and some political power; in Virginia and the South, the owners of **plantations**

GI Bill Servicemen's Readjustment Act (1944) under which $13 billion was spent for veterans on education, medical treatment, unemployment insurance, and loans for homes and businesses

gold standard a monetary system in which gold is used as the standard of value for the money of a country; inflationists in the 1800s wanted a bimetallic standard of gold and silver; the United States remained on a domestic gold standard until 1933

GOP Grand Old Party, the Republican Party

Grange laws state laws passed in the 1870s with the support of farmers, represented by the **Grange**, that strove to regulate railway rates and storage fees charged by railroads and by operators of warehouses and grain elevators; these laws were overturned when the Supreme Court decreed in the *Wabash* case (1886) that individual states had no power to regulate interstate commerce

Grange formally called the Order of Patrons of Husbandry, an association of U.S farmers founded in 1867 to promote agricultural interests

Great Awakening a series of religious **revivals** that swept the colonies in the 1740s

greenbacks United States paper money, first issued during the Civil War, so called because the back side was printed in green ink (compare with **specie** and **hard money**)

gross domestic product the value of all the nation's goods and services in a given year

guerrilla/guerrilla war a combatant who fights secretly and with terrorism; a type of warfare carried on behind enemy lines through surprise raids, sabotage, and disruptive attacks; used in the Philippines against American troops following the Spanish-American War and later during the Vietnam War (1965–1973)

habeas corpus a court order requiring authorities to free a person held in custody

Halls of Montezuma Mexico City, captured by the U.S. marines in the Mexican War in 1847

hard money money issued in gold coins; the opposite of paper (or **soft**) money (see also **specie**)

hawk a person who supports a military action or war, as opposed to a **dove**

headright system the method in some colonies by which a person could gain free land in return for bringing laborers from England to America

hierarchy persons arranged by rank or status, often for political purposes; a king, for example, would be at the top of the hierarchy

holding company a company that invests in the stocks of one or more other corporations, which it may thus control

holocaust a thorough destruction, often used to describe Hitler's destruction of Jews in World War II or the result of using nuclear weapons

Holy Spirit God's presence in the third person of the Trinity; also called the Holy Ghost

homestead/homesteading a tract of land occupied under the Homestead Act (1862) that provided a person with 160 acres of free public land in return for settling and farming it

Huguenots French Protestant Christians who left France to avoid persecution after 1685

impeach/impeachment the U.S. Constitution's method for removing the president, vice president, or judges from office before their terms have expired; used against Federalist judges in 1801, against Andrew Johnson in 1868, against Richard Nixon in 1974, and against Bill Clinton in 1998–1999; charges are brought by the House, and conviction requires a two-thirds vote in the Senate; Johnson and Clinton were not convicted; Nixon resigned

imperialism the creation or extension of an empire comprising many nations and areas; advocated in the late 1800s by certain social thinkers and policy makers

import duties see **tariff**

impound the withholding by the executive branch of funds authorized and appropriated by law

impressment the British policy, especially in the early 1800s, of stopping American ships at sea and seizing sailors by claiming that they were British subjects whether they were or not; a main method used to staff the British navy; impressment led to poor relations between Britain and the United States and helped cause the War of 1812

indemnity that which is given as compensation for a loss or for damage

indentured servants persons whose passage from England to America was paid in return for signing a written contract (called an *indenture*) agreeing to serve as laborers for a term of years, usually seven; a large number of whites used this method to migrate to the South and to the Middle Colonies in the 1700s; used in Texas in the 1830s as a disguised form of slavery

inflation the rise in prices resulting from an increase in circulating currency and a mounting demand for available commodities and services

initiative a procedure that allows citizens, as opposed to legislators, to propose the enactment of state and local laws; promoted by progressive reformers in the early twentieth century

internationalism the belief that mutual understanding and cooperation among nations will advance the common welfare

isolationism the policy of curtailing a nation's international relations; isolationism was dominant in U.S. foreign policy during much of the 1800s and the two decades between the world wars

Jesuit a member of the Catholic religious order called the Society of Jesus; Jesuits were very active in missions and education throughout the world after 1600

Jim Crow a name given to racial **segregation;** the name comes from a popular dance tune in the 1830s performed by a black-faced white actor

jingoism an aggressive, highly nationalistic foreign policy

journeymen skilled workers who had completed apprenticeships but lacked the means to go into business for themselves *journeyed* around working for other craftsmen; they used part of their wages to set up their own businesses

junta a Latin American legislative council, or a political body gathered together for some secret purpose; exiled Cuban rebels opposed to Spanish rule (pronounced *HOON-tah*)

kaiser title of German emperors, 1871–1918

kamikaze a suicidal Japanese tactic of ramming with a piloted airplane or boat carrying explosives in World War II; from Japanese *kami* (god) and *kaze* (wind) (pronounced *kahm-i-KAHZ-ee*)

kleptocracy government by theft

Kremlin the governing center of Russia

Ku Klux Klan a white supremacist group established in the South following the Civil War and revived in the early twentieth century

laissez-faire literally, "to let do"; a hands-off style of governance that emphasizes economic freedom; the concept is associated with Adam Smith and his book *The Wealth of Nations* (1776) (pronounced *lay-say FAIR)*

lame duck an officeholder who has not been reelected and who waits for his or her successor to assume office

land grants land given to a person, usually by government, often for political reasons

legal tender items defined by law as money, which must be accepted in payment of debts; governments have frequently made paper money legal tender; such paper money could be produced by the government in large quantities cheaply

lend-lease terms of the Lend Lease Act (1941) which furnished goods to Allied powers

lien a legal right to claim or dispose of property in payment for a debt (pronounced *lean*)

lobbyist a person, group, or organization that seeks to influence legislation or administrative action

lode a deposit of ore located in rock; also called a *vein*

lyceum a series of well-organized public lectures stressing self-improvement, held each year in most northern towns and cities in the 1840s and 1850s (pronounced *lie-SEE-um)*

machine an informal political organization, often centered on a single politician, that controls the formal process of government through corruption, **patronage,** and service to its constituents

magnate an important or influential person, often in business, e.g., John Pierpont Morgan

Manifest Destiny the belief that Americans had a God-given right to own all of North America and perhaps South America too; common from 1844 to 1861

manors large tracts of land owned by wealthy, politically powerful New Yorkers during the colonial period; most manors were along the Hudson River

martial law law administered by military force, invoked by a government in an emergency

Marxist a follower of German philosopher Karl Marx; a **communist** or socialist

masonic pertaining to Freemasons, whose lodges stress charity and sociability

McCarthyism extreme and irresponsible anticommunism; the use of unproven association with any individual, organization, or policy that the accuser perceives as un-American (see also **communism, Marxism**)

mechanic a skilled manual worker; an artisan

mercantilism an economic theory and practice popular from 1500 to 1800 that used government regulation and **monopolies** to control business, and especially to maintain colonies as part of a global system; the British empire is one example

midterm election a congressional election held midway between presidential elections

militia ordinary citizens called to temporary duty as soldiers, especially from the colonial period to about 1850; the equivalent of the National Guard

mobilization to prepare for war by organizing industry, personnel, and national resources

monopoly the exclusive control of a commodity, service, or means of production in a particular market that allows the fixing of prices and the elimination of competition (see also **trust**)

moratorium a waiting period set by an authority

mores folkways considered conducive to the welfare of society (pronounced *MOHR-ayz*)

mugwump a Republican who bolted the party when James G. Blaine was nominated as the presidential candidate in 1884; a term used for any political independent

munitions guns, bullets, and other necessary war materiel

nationalism strong, sometimes chauvinistic, devotion to one's own nation (see also **jingoism;** not to be confused with **nationalization**)

nationalization to transfer ownership of land, resources, or industries to the federal government; advocated by various parties such as the Populists and the Socialist Party (not to be confused with **nationalism**)

nativism/nativist a belief in the superiority of Americans born in the United States and a rejection of the foreign born

natural law the idea prevalent in the 1700s that nature operates according to rules laid down by God; discovering the rules was a major undertaking

naval blockade use of warships to close off trade to or from a seaport or coastline (see also **embargo**)

Nazi a member or supporter of Adolf Hitler's National Socialist German Workers' Party

New World North and South America; the term used by Europeans after Columbus's voyage in 1492

nullification the idea, promoted by John C. Calhoun, that a state could act to overrule a federal law inside its own borders; thus, laws would be declared unconstitutional by the states rather than by the Supreme Court; opponents pointed to the chaos caused by different states acting differently

Open Door policy the policy or practice of giving to all nations the same commercial privileges in a region or area open to trade; the United States advocated an Open Door policy toward China in the late 1800s

out work in certain industrial processes, especially shoemaking, the practice of sending some work out of the main shop or factory, often to be performed in the home by women or children at low wages

papal edict a Catholic pope's proclamation, which has great authority among Catholics both spiritually and politically

parity a level for farm prices that gives to the farmer the same purchasing power averaged during each year of a chosen period; also used during the cold war to refer to the rough equivalence of missiles between the United States and the Soviet Union

Parliament the legislative body that governs England

party ticket a political term used to pair presidential and vice-presidential candidates

patronage the system by which political winners fill all government jobs with their supporters (see also **spoils system**)

patroons wealthy, powerful landowners in Dutch New Netherland who received much land in the 1600s in return for bringing settlers to the colony

pay dirt soil containing enough metal, especially gold, to be profitable to a mine

peace protocol the preliminary draft of an official peace treaty

Pentagon headquarters of the Defense Department; the U.S. military establishment

pig iron crude iron as it comes from the blast furnaces

Pilgrim one of a group of **Protestant** Christians who found the **Church of England** so corrupt that a new church must be formed; they migrated to Holland, then to Plymouth, Massachusetts (compare with **Puritan**)

pink a derogatory term often associated with a position or person accused of being sympathetic to a socialist or **communist** (**red**) position

Pinkerton a name given to employees of the Pinkerton Detective Agency, who were often used to infiltrate labor organizations and break strikes in the late 1800s

plantations large-scale farm units in the South usually devoted to one crop for sale in the world market and worked with **slave** or, less commonly, **indentured servant** labor; plantations began in the 1600s and lasted until the end of slavery in 1865

pluralism cultural diversity in a society stratified along racial lines; also, any political system in which there are multiple centers of legitimate power and authority

plurality the greatest number of votes cast for a candidate, but not more than half of the votes cast

pocket veto an indirect **veto** in which the president declines to sign a **bill** after Congress has adjourned; after adjournment, a bill passed by Congress does not become law without the president's signature

polarized broken up into opposing groups

political machine an informal organization, often centered on a single politician, that controls the formal process of government through corruption, **patronage**, and service to its constituents

polity an organized society, such as a state; governing structures of a political community

pool the combined investment of a group of persons or corporations, and the sharing of responsibility for a joint enterprise; employed by John D. Rockefeller in the oil industry in the late 1800s

populism a political movement that grew out of a farmers' protest movement in the 1890s

pork barrel favoritism by a government in the distribution of benefits or resources; legislation that favors the district of a particular legislator, often through public works

preemptive strike a military attack aimed to prevent aggressive military action by an opponent or enemy

primary election a state or local election held before a general election to nominate a political party's candidates for office

privateer/privateering a private ship commissioned by a government in time of war to act as a warship against an enemy country's merchant ships

profiteer/profiteering a person who obtains excessive profits during times of shortages, frequently during wartime

progressivism a designation applied to reform in the decades between 1890 and 1920, a period of rapid urbanization and industrialization

Prohibition law forbidding the manufacture, transportation, or sale of alcoholic beverages; adopted by some cities and counties in the 1840s and by some states beginning with Maine in 1851; enacted nationally in the Eighteenth Amendment (1919), repealed with the Twenty-first Amendment (1933) (compare with **temperance movement**)

proprietary colony a colony owned by one person, called a proprietor, such as Lord Baltimore's Maryland or William Penn's Pennsylvania; a few proprietary colonies, such as North and South Carolina, had multiple owners

protectionist one who favors high **tariffs** to protect a domestic market from foreign trade competition

protectorate a country or region under the protection or political domination of another

Protestant a Christian belonging to any number of groups that rejected the Catholic Church

Puritan a **Protestant** Christian who wished to purify the **Church of England** but did not wish to form a separate church; some stayed in England, others went to Massachusetts (compare with **Pilgrim**)

quagmire literally, soft mucky ground which, once stepped in, is difficult to get out of; a difficult or dangerous situation; the war in Vietnam was often described as a quagmire

Quaker a member of a militantly pacifist Protestant group, more formally called the Society of Friends, that settled Pennsylvania in 1682

rapprochement establishment or state of peaceful relations (pronounced *ra-prosh-MAHN*)

ratify/ratification approval by a legislature of a treaty, a constitutional amendment, or a new constitution

rationing during times of scarcity and war, the allotment of fixed allowances or portions of food, fuel, or goods

reactionary one who favors political and social reaction and is hostile to radicalism or rapid political change

receivership a legal term in which a business enterprise is placed in the hands of a court-appointed administrator

recession a period of reduced economic activity, less serious than a **depression** (compare with a **depression**)

Redcoats British soldiers in the American Revolution; this nickname came from the color of the soldiers' uniforms

reds a name given to **communists**; the Red Scare in 1919 expressed anxiety among the public and politicians concerning communist influence in America (see also **pink**)

referendum a procedure for submitting proposed laws or state constitutional amendments to voters for their direct approval or rejection; favored by **Progressive** reformers at the turn of the twentieth century (compare with **initiative**)

regiments military units of one thousand to two thousand soldiers; the most common Civil War units (see also **divisions**)

reparations compensation paid by defeated countries for acts of war; following World War I, the Allied Powers, especially France and Great Britain, insisted that Germany pay war reparations

republic a democratic, constitutional form of government, such as that established by the U.S. Constitution; not to be confused with the Republican Party

reservations land set apart by the government for a particular use; for example, Indian reservations

revival a large, popular gathering for religious purposes, especially among **Protestants**; revivals have been common in America at periodic intervals since the 1740s

romanticism/romantic movement in the early 1800s, the rejection of the rational **Enlightenment** in favor of seeing emotion and the need for its expression as the central element in life; many romantics were poets and artists (see also **transcendentalism**)

run (on a bank) a panic in which all of the bank's customers try to withdraw all of their deposits at the same time, thereby causing the bank to fail; bank runs often occurred during a **depression** or a panic

salt pork pork stored and preserved without refrigeration by packing it in barrels filled with salt

salvation the Christian idea that people could be saved spiritually and go to heaven (see also **Calvinism** and **universal salvation**)

sanctions coercive measures, usually economic and usually adopted by several nations at the same time, to force a nation to stop violating international law

Sandinista a member of a revolutionary group that came to power in Nicaragua in the late 1970s; named after Cesar Augusto Sandino, a Nicaraguan rebel who resisted U.S. marines sent into the country in the 1920s

scalawags white southerners who supported Radical Republican rule during Reconstruction (compare with **carpetbaggers**)

secession formal declaration by a state that it is no longer part of the United States

securities any evidence of debt or ownership, especially stocks and bonds

segregate/segregation to separate by race, often imposed by law (see also **apartheid**)

separatism the belief that white and black races should be separated physically, culturally, and socially (see also **apartheid** and **segregation**)

settlement house a welfare institution established in a congested part of a city, having a resident staff to conduct educational and recreational activities for the community

sharecropper/sharecropping a **tenant farmer**, usually heavily in debt to a local merchant or bank, who rented land and paid the rent by splitting the money from the sale of the crop with the landowner; common in the South after the Civil War

Sino Chinese (pronounced *SIGH-no*)

sit-in a demonstration of protest, as by African Americans in the southern United States in the 1960s, in which participants entered and remained seated in a public place

skid row a district of a city inhabited by vagrants and derelicts (slang); originally, a road used to skid logs to a mill in Seattle

Slave Power Republican Party phrase in the 1850s to describe slaveholders' political influence

slave/slavery a person totally owned and controlled by another person under the law; slavery became an important institution in colonial America, especially in the South

smelter a furnace used to reduce ores to obtain a metal

Social Security the popular name for the Old Age, Survivors, and Disability Insurance system established by the Social Security Act (1935)

socialism a system of government in which the government owns many of the means of production and trade and in which many welfare needs are provided directly by the government; an early advocate was Eugene Debs, leader of the Socialist Party (see also **communism**, **Marxism**, and **Bolsheviks**)

soft money paper money, as opposed to hard money and coins (see also **specie** and **greenbacks**)

sortie one mission or attack by a single plane

sovereignty complete independence and self-government

specie gold or silver money, as opposed to paper money (see also **hard money** and **soft money**)

speculators/speculation persons who engage in risky business, often with borrowed money, in the hope of large profits; Americans have often speculated with land

spiritualism a movement founded in the 1840s whose followers believed the living could communicate with the dead, especially through séances with crystal balls

spoils system the widespread practice of awarding government jobs to political supporters without consideration of their qualifications for the jobs (see **patronage**)

squatters frontier farmers who used land they did not own without anyone's permission; they moved frequently

Stalinist a follower of the Soviet dictator Josef Stalin, chief of state in the Soviet Union, 1924–1953

states' rights a political view that power more properly belongs to the states than to the federal government; most often found in the South

steerage a section in a passenger ship for passengers paying the lowest fare and given inferior accommodations

strict construction an interpretation of the U.S. Constitution that stresses the limited powers of government rather than broad provisions; Thomas Jefferson first argued this view in the 1790s

subsistence farmers farmers who produced food and clothing for their own use and only rarely sold their produce in the market

suffrage the right to vote; by the 1830s most states had universal white male suffrage; the Fifteenth Amendment (1870) held that suffrage shall not be denied "on account of race"; the Nineteenth Amendment (1920) extended the right to vote to women in all states

supply-side economics the belief that lower tax rates encourage capital to flow into the economy; an economic theory adopted by President Reagan and his advisers

tariff taxes placed on goods brought into the United States; in the late 1800s Republicans favored high tariffs, and Democrats favored low tariffs or no tariffs (**free trade**)

tax base the value on which taxes are levied, including individual income, real property, corporate income, and wealth

tax shelter an investment in which any profits are fully or partially tax free

teetotaler one who abstains totally from alcoholic beverages

temperance movement in the 1790s, a movement urging people to use alcohol only in moderation; by the 1830s, a movement asking people to give up all alcohol voluntarily; strongly connected to **evangelical** religion; many female reformers were involved in this movement; especially well-known was the Woman's Christian Temperance Union (WCTU) (compare with **Prohibition**)

tenant farmers farmers who lacked the means to buy land and therefore rented it; already common in colonial America, the practice grew in the late 1800s, especially in the South (see also **sharecropper**)

tenement an urban apartment building that is poorly constructed and maintained, typically overcrowded, and often part of a slum

theocracy government controlled by a church or church leaders

ticket a political term referring to the presidential and vice-presidential candidates of a particular party for a particular election; for example, the Bush–Cheney ticket of the Republican Party for the 2000 presidential election

titled nobility the highest rank in British society, except for the royal family; examples are dukes and lords

Tories in the 1700s in England, the conservative political faction emphasizing the king and hierarchy; in 1776, Americans who opposed the American Revolution and sided with the British

transcendentalism associated with Ralph Waldo Emerson in the 1840s and 1850s, the belief that doing good deeds, **romanticism**, and contemplating nature enabled people to transcend ordinary life and get close to God intuitively

transcontinental railroad railroad begun during the Civil War under acts of 1862 and 1864, completed in 1869 by the Union Pacific Railroad and Central Pacific Railroad, and linking Omaha, Nebraska, and Sacramento, California

Trotskyist a follower of the radical **communist** Leon Trotsky, an exiled rival of Soviet dictator Josef Stalin

trust a group of companies that work together to maintain an effective monopoly that inhibits competition, such as the Standard Oil Trust developed by John D. Rockefeller in the late 1800s to control the oil industry

U-boat a German submarine or *Unterseeboot* (undersea boat); a popular term during World War I and World War II

unilateral undertaken by a single nation, party, or society without reference to other nations, parties, or societies

universal salvation the belief of some Christians that everybody can be saved as a Christian and go to heaven (compare with **Calvinism**)

vagrancy shiftless or idle wandering

veto the U.S. Constitution's method by which a president may stop a **bill** passed by Congress from becoming law; the House and the Senate, each by a two-thirds vote, can overturn a veto

war hawks in 1812, supporters of war against Britain on the grounds that Britain had snubbed American rights

weir a fence or obstruction placed in a stream to catch fish; this technology was known and used by American Indians before white contact (pronounced *weer*)

wet a political term used to designate a person opposed to **Prohibition**, especially in the 1920s; Al Smith ran for president in 1928 as a "wet" opposed to Prohibition

Whig in the 1700s in England, the liberal and political faction emphasizing rural interests and liberty; in 1776, a supporter of the American Revolution; in the 1830s to 1840s, an American political party led by Henry Clay and favorable to a national bank

Wilmot Proviso in 1846, Wilmot's amendment to a **bill** that sought to keep slavery out of any Mexican territory acquired by the United States in the Mexican War

Wobbly a slang term for a member of the Industrial Workers of the World (IWW), a radical labor group, circa 1900

write-off a tax deduction

Yankee in a narrow sense, a resident of New England; in the broad sense, any American; during the Civil War, any northerner

yellow press a type of journalism that features cheap, sensational news to attract readers, from the use of yellow ink in a cartoon strip, "The Yellow Kid" in the *New York Journal* (1896)

yeoman a farmer who owned and operated a small farm

Zionism originally a movement to resettle Jews in Palestine; support for the state of Israel

Index

Abbott, Grace, 549
Abdul, Sufi, 550
Abernathy, Ralph, 597
Abolitionism: and American Revolution, 215; and Civil War, 286–88; and colonization, 220–22, 223, 226, 229; and *Dred Scott v. Sanford*, 266–67; and evangelical Protestantism, 224–28, 257, 270; and Fugitive Slave Law, 257; Harper's Ferry raid, 265, 269–70; militant, 228–32; and Port Royal experiment, 303; and sectional conflicts, 223–24, 270; and *Uncle Tom's Cabin*, 226, 257; Underground Railroad, 230; Virginia debate (1831–1832), 222–23. *See also* Sectional conflicts
Abortion: and Clinton presidency, 679; and Great Depression, 549; 1950s, 595; 1960s, 612; 1970s, 633, 642; Reagan-Bush era, 663
Abraham Lincoln Brigade, 556
Acoma, New Mexico, 8
Adams, Abigail, 125*ill*, 126, 134
Adams, Charles Francis, 249, 289
Adams, Henry, 315
Adams, John: and American Revolution, 99; and Constitutional Convention, 115; and election of 1800, 129; and Enlightenment, 88; and Federalists, 125; and Jefferson presidency, 134; New England Puritan background, 50; presidency, 124–30, 136, 200; and religion, 176–77; and War of 1812, 143; and Washington presidency, 119

Adams, John Quincy: and *Amistad* case, 223; and election of 1824, 146–47; and Monroe presidency, 144, 200–201; New England Puritan background, 50; presidency, 147–50
Adams, Samuel, 97, 99, 117
Adamson Act (1914), 487
Adams-Onís Treaty (1819), 144
Addams, Jane, 416–18, 418*ill*, 474, 475–76; and anti-Semitism, 506; and election of 1912, 485; and World War I, 496
Adler, Dankmar, 412
Advertising, 1920s, 511, 512
Affirmative action, 653
Afghanistan: Soviet invasion, 643, 656, 657, 662; U.S. invasion, 687–88
AFL. *See* American Federation of Labor
African Americans: and American Revolution, 96, 106, 214; and baseball, 420; and Civil War draft riots, 295; Colored Farmers' Alliance, 427, 438; and election of 1960, 601; and election of 1992, 667; and emancipation, 305–6; and Gilded Age labor, 359; and Gilded Age politics, 374; and labor unions, 361, 363, 367; life expectancy, 593; military service, 288, 451, 454, 499, 565; and music, 218–19, 512, 549, 598; and New

I-1

About the Authors

W. J. Rorabaugh is professor of history at the University of Washington, Seattle. In addition to this book, he is author of *The Alcoholic Republic: An American Tradition* (1979), *The Craft Apprentice: From Franklin to the Machine Age* (1986), and *Berkeley at War: The 1960s* (1989).

Donald T. Critchlow is professor of history and chair of the Department of History at Saint Louis University. He is the founding editor of the *Journal of Policy History*, the author of *The Brookings Institution, 1916–1952: Expertise and the Public Interest in a Democratic Society* (1985), and the editor of four books on history and public policy in the United States.

Paula Baker is an associate professor of history at Ohio State University. She is the author of *The Moral Frameworks of Public Life* (1991), and edited volumes on recent American history and the history of campaign finance in the United States.